Management Accounting for the
Hospitality, Tourism and Retail Sectors

About the Authors

Donncha O'Donoghue B.Comm, FCCA

Donncha O'Donoghue is a lecturer in accounting at the Dublin Institute of Technology, based in the Faculty of Tourism and Food. He was educated at University College Galway and Athlone Institute of Technology and has over seventeen years' experience lecturing at undergraduate, postgraduate and professional levels. He is the co-author of *Financial Accounting for the Hospitality, Tourism and Retail Sectors* (Blackhall Publishing: 2005) and acts as external examiner to a number of tourism programmes in Ireland.

Alice Luby MAAT, ACMA, MSc

Alice Luby is a lecturer in accounting at Dublin Institute of Technology, based in the Faculty of Business. She has fourteen years' lecturing experience at undergraduate and professional levels in addition to twelve years' industrial experience. Educated at Dublin Institute of Technology and Dublin City University she is the author of *Cost and Management Accounting: Learning through Practice* (Gill & Macmillan: 1999) and co-author of *Financial Accounting for the Hospitality, Tourism and Retail Sectors* (Blackhall Publishing: 2005). She is to the forefront in utilising web technology for distance education.

Management Accounting for the Hospitality, Tourism and Retail Sectors

Donncha O'Donoghue
with
Alice Luby

BLACKHALL
Publishing

This book was typeset by Folio Publishing Services for

Blackhall Publishing
33 Carysfort Avenue
Blackrock
Co. Dublin
Ireland

e-mail: info@blackhallpublishing.com
www.blackhallpublishing.com

ISBN 10: 1 84218 114 9
ISBN 13: 978 1 84218 114 0

A catalogue record for this book is available from the British Library.

Printed in Ireland by
SPRINT-print Ltd

To Terri, Jack, Cian and Josh.
Donncha

To Peter, Emily and Lindsey.
Alice

Acknowledgements

We are indebted to many individuals for their ideas and assistance in preparing this book.

- ❑ Elizabeth Brennan and Gerard O'Connor of Blackhall Publishing and Peter O'Brien whose patience, perseverance and advice was invaluable in producing this text.
- ❑ Dr Sheila Flanagan (Head of the School) and the management team in the School of Hospitality Management and Tourism, Faculty of Tourism and Food, for their continued support and goodwill, and in particular for the granting of a sabbatical for the completion of this book.
- ❑ Our colleagues for their counsel throughout this project, especially Marc Mc Donald, Noel O'Connor, and Frances O'Brien.
- ❑ Our colleagues who have made contributions towards the text, in particular Gerry Dunne and Eamonn Moane.
- ❑ Our colleagues in the hospitality, tourism and retail sectors especially Fáilte Ireland, Jurys Doyle plc., Gresham Hotels plc., Arnotts plc., Next plc., Aerlingus and Ryanair Plc. for the vast amount of information provided.
- ❑ The accounting associations and in particular the Association of Certified Accountants (ACCA) and the Chartered Institute of Management Accountants (CIMA) for providing materials and other information for this book.
- ❑ The academics who reviewed the earlier drafts of this book, in particular Eamonn Moane. Your advice and comments were invaluable in developing the final version.
- ❑ The students we have both lectured over the years for their inspiration and feedback.
- ❑ Terri, Jack, Cian and Josh for all your support and patience.
- ❑ Peter, Emily and Lindsey for all your encouragement.

Contents

While lecturing on applied management courses it was apparent that the generic accounting texts available did not provide sufficient examples geared towards the relevant sectors. They also focused on many complex issues appropriate only for students of professional accounting. We decided to tackle these limitations with this management accounting text. In essence, this text is geared to non-accountants and relates specifically to the hospitality, tourism and retail sectors.

Aims and objectives

The aim of this text is to provide a comprehensive guide to management accounting for undergraduate students participating in applied management programmes in hospitality, tourism and retail. The text assumes no previous knowledge of management accounting and seeks to provide a good understanding of the subject area, avoiding complicated technical detail more suited to courses in professional accountancy. A balanced approach to studying accounting is promoted by providing both a conceptual background that is appropriate for managers and a practical application of the subject to the targeted sectors.

Target audience

This text is primarily targeted at undergraduate students studying accounting within applied management programmes relating to the hospitality, tourism and retail sectors. It is also suitable for services management (including transport management), marketing and business studies programmes. The examples and illustrations used throughout provide students with material that they can relate to, either from their studies or from their day-to-day experience as consumers of tourism and retail services. This facilitates student learning by presenting the theory in a practical and easy-to-understand context.

Structure

The structure adopted suits both the traditional and modular approach to learning. The text begins with an overview of the structure and characteristics of the hospitality, tourism and retail sectors.

❏ Chapter 1 introduces the reader to the whole area of management accounting, providing a backround from which the principles of management accounting can be applied.

❏ Chapters 2 and 3 focus on cost analysis and classification systems for both planning and control purposes. They also focus on the process of allocating overhead costs to cost centres and cost units as well as introducing the reader to activity based costing.

❏ Chapters 4, 5, 6, and 7 are dedicated to accounting for management planning and decision-making focusing on areas such as marginal costing, CVP analysis, relevent costs and revenues for decision-making, profit sensitivity analysis, pricing and customer profitability analysis.

❏ Chapters 8, 9, 10 and 11 focus on the budgetary process from budgetary planning and the development of strategic and short-term budgets to budgetary control and variance analysis.

❏ Chapters 12 and 13 are dedicated to performance appraisal for both centralised and decentralised organisation structures. They focus on key financial performance measures used to appraise performance as well as performance measurement frameworks that integrate the use of financial and non-financial measures and that translate the aims and objectives of a business into a series of performance targets that can be measured.

❏ Finally, Chapter 14 focuses on capital investment appraisal techniques which inform management decision-making in relation to capital expenditure and investment.

Pedagogical features

This text adopts a structured approach to learning, with each chapter commencing with clear learning outcomes. There are numerous illustrations and examples explaining each learning outcome clearly. The use of diagrams, tables, charts and accounts provides a visual addition to the text commentary. Real-life examples and accounting news stories provide additional material relevant to the target sectors. A number of additional pedagogical features are employed such as 'Did You Know?' and 'Consider this', which help to relate and illuminate learning points. Up-to-date research on the use and influence of the various management accounting tools and techniques within the hospitality, tourism and retail sectors is also provided. Chapters conclude with a comprehensive executive summary and review questions. The review questions include conceptual and computational tasks that test the learning outcomes of the chapter. Solutions to the review questions are available to both students and lecturers on the accompanying website (www.blackhallpublishing. com/managementaccounting). References and recommended readings are provided for students who want to explore certain topics in more detail.

Each chapter contains:

❑   Clear learning outcomes.
❑   Illustrations and worked examples relevant to the sectors.
❑   Real-life examples and accounting news stories relevant to the sectors.
❑   A comprehensive executive summary.
❑   End-of-chapter review questions.

Resources

An accompanying website (www.blackhallpublishing.com/managementaccounting) contains resources for both students and lecturers. Student resources include solutions to all review questions. Lecturer resources (password required) include downloadable colour slide presentations for each chapter as well as suggested solutions and additional questions and answers.

Sector Overview: Tourism and Hospitality in Ireland

Tourism (incorporating hospitality, travel and leisure) is increasingly being referred to as 'the world's biggest industry', representing 10.7 per cent of the global economy (Youell, 1998). In recent years, many countries have been showing increased interest in the potential of global travel and tourism as an important contributor to economic development, particularly in terms of investment, revenue, employment and balance of payments. In Ireland, the tourism sector has proved to be a key engine for economic growth. Throughout the 1990s, Irish tourism registered year-on-year growth, consistently outperforming other European countries. The economic benefits accruing from such growth are felt in many areas. Revenue from visitors to Ireland (including receipts paid to Irish carriers by foreign visitors) was estimated to be worth €4.1 billion in 2003. This accounts for almost 4 per cent of national exports (Fáilte Ireland, 2003). Because tourism activity is particularly concentrated in areas which lack an intensive industry base, the sector is credited with having a significant regional distributive effect, i.e. the poorer or less developed regions of the country, such as the western seaboard, tend to benefit particularly well from tourism. Employment is another area where tourism has made a significant impact, with the industry supporting over 230,000 jobs (Fáilte Ireland, 2003). Tourism is commonly regarded as having a high 'people requirement' compared to other industries.

Characteristics of tourism and hospitality businesses

Tourism businesses are commonly regarded as having a number of distinctive characteristics. These include the following:

Sensitivity of demand: Many tourism goods are viewed as being luxury items (for example package holidays) and therefore tend to be quite sensitive to price. This means that economic conditions such as recession, inflation and taxation can play a significant role in the demand for tourism and hospitality products and services. The industry is also sensitive to occurrences and events in the external environment such as terrorism, natural disasters, political instability and other factors. These are usually events which are outside the control of individual businesses but can nonetheless have a dramatic effect on their profits or indeed survival.

Seasonality of demand: Many tourism businesses have seasonal demand patterns, for example holiday centres and city sightseeing buses. This results in establishments experiencing uneven cash flow patterns and, in some cases, the reduction or closure of their businesses in off-peak periods.

Fixity of costs: High fixed costs (costs that remain constant and are not affected by volume of business) are a feature commonly associated with the tourism industry. Businesses such as hotels, airlines and tourist attractions employ various yield management systems to try to ensure that they generate sufficient turnover to cover their fixed costs.

Perishability of product: In common with other service industries, tourism consists of products which are perishable by nature, i.e. they have a limited 'shelf life'. If a hotel room or an airplane seat is not sold it cannot be stored or saved and sold at a later date and this results in the loss of potential revenue. Many tourism firms try to counteract this by using tactical pricing techniques to encourage the buying of their products/services.

Scale of operation: Although many large tourism companies exist around the world, the industry is, to a large extent, comprised of quite modest sized enterprises. The majority of tourism businesses in Ireland consist of firms employing less than ten people.

Structure of the tourism and hospitality industry

Tourism is a multi-faceted industry, made up of organisations from the private, public and voluntary sectors. The tourism product itself is made up of an amalgam of businesses which can be loosely divided into three main sectors, each of which is quite distinct but at the same time interdependent.

Transport: This includes air, sea, road and rail carriers. In addition transport providers are often subdivided into those who provide access transport and those who provide internal transport.

Attractions: Tourist attractions can be divided into natural and man-made features and facilities. These include historical sites, museums, theme parks, events, cinemas and a wide range of other attractions and leisure facilities which help to entice visitors to a destination.

Hospitality: This sector usually represents the bulk of businesses that make up the tourism industry. It consists of two main components:

1. Accommodation: This consists of hotels, guesthouses, B&Bs, self-catering, hostels and other forms of accommodation.

2. Restaurants and bars: This component includes full service and self-service restaurants, fast-food establishments, cafés, bars and pubs.

These businesses represent the main recipients of tourist expenditure at a destination. In Ireland, the accommodation, food and drink sectors receive the majority of overseas tourist spend. The full breakdown can be seen in the table below (note this does not include spend on access transport):

Breakdown of overseas tourists spend in Ireland (%) 2003

Bed and board	27
Other food and drink	36
Sightseeing/entertainment	4
Internal transport	10
Shopping	17
Miscellaneous	6

Source: Fáilte Ireland Tourism Fact 2003

A number of intermediaries exist in the tourism industry through which the tourism product can be sold. These include travel agents (the traditional retailers of the tourism industry), tour operators (who can be seen as wholesalers) and a variety of specialist intermediaries such as professional conference organisers.

Today, an increasing number of internet websites are being used by customers to purchase travel and tourism products direct from the suppliers. The global tourism industry has been one of the most dynamic sectors in this regard. This trend towards dis-intermediation is having a significant impact on the traditional practices and workings of the industry. The years ahead should prove very interesting in relation to how the industry is structured and how the tourism product is distributed.

Sector Overview: Retail in Ireland

It has been forecast that the services sector will be the largest contributor to Irish employment by 2010. Retail represents the largest element within this sector, generating 11 per cent of the total employment in the Irish economy. According to Forfás, 'retailing is defined as the means by which goods and services are provided to consumers in exchange for payment.' Retailing can be categorised as follows:

The definition above relates retailing to 'consumers' and therefore wholesaling and business-to-business selling are excluded. There has been a significant change in the make-up of the retailing sector in Ireland over the last 30 years. In the 1970s, it consisted of a large number of small shops offering specialised services such as general stores, bakers, butchers and drapery. Large department stores existed but there were few which matched the size of the stores in existence today. The type and style of products on offer were often dictated by the manufacturers who wielded considerable power.

The retail sector responded to the changes created by the prospering economy in the later half of the twentieth century. The make-up of the sector shifted from the small independent stores, to larger retail outlets, particularly in the food sector. This movement has led to the development of a range of retailers who are larger than many of the manufacturers (suppliers). Within the supply chain, the power has shifted from manufacturing to retailing. Diversification (getting involved in different activities) and improved customer services are other trends that have developed in the retail sector today.

In a more consumer-driven society, the retail sector has a significant role to play in the economy. Currently one in five new Irish jobs is in the retail sector.

Introduction to Management Accounting

Learning Outcomes

By the end of this chapter you will be able to:

❑ Describe the nature and purpose of accounting.
❑ Outline and explain the distinctions between financial and management accounting.
❑ Outline the role of management in commercial organisations.
❑ Outline the functions of management accounting.

Introduction

Developments in the global economy have provided significant challenges for business managers. The accounting profession has had to develop and broaden its scope to provide relevant, timely, accurate and understandable financial information required in the modern economy of today. Managers use this information to develop efficiencies within their business, grow their business and ultimately gain competitive advantage over business rivals.

The tourism, hospitality and retail sectors in Ireland have seen rapid growth and development and are operating in a highly competitive environment. Management accounting provides managers operating in these sectors with management information systems that can assist in both day to day business decision situations and in long term strategy issues.

This chapter provides a background from which the principles of management accounting can be applied. The nature and purpose of accounting and the elements of accounting are outlined, before focusing on the role and information needs of managers and how management accounting supports that role. The chapter concludes by outlining the characteristics of good accounting information to support managers in their role.

Nature and Purpose of Accounting

'...The process of identifying, measuring and communicating economic information about an organisation or other entity, to permit informed judgements and decisions by the users of the information'

American Accounting Association

The definition above outlines the process of providing economic information to assist in making informed decisions. Identifying, measuring and communicating are used to explain the nature of accounting.

The definition of accounting put forward by the American Institute of Certified and Public Accountants, provides more detail on the purpose of accounting by including control in the definition. They define accounting as:

'...the collection, measurement, recording, classification and communication of economic data relating to an enterprise for the purposes of reporting, decision making and control'

To summarise

Nature of accounting involves:		Purpose of accounting:
1. Identifying		To report financial information
2. Classifying	financial	
3. Measuring	information	To provide information to make informed judgements and decisions
4. Recording		
5. Communicating		To provide information for control purposes

Elements of Accounting

Accounting can be broken into the key areas of financial accounting and management accounting. The diagram below draws a distinction between the two areas.

Diagram 1.1: *Financial accounting and management accounting*

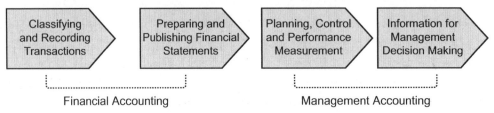

Financial accounting

Financial accounting involves the recording and summarising of business transactions, and communicating this data through the uniform financial statements. It is important to remember that businesses are required by law to keep 'proper records' and that these records are made available to auditors and the revenue commissioners so they can verify the figures given to them in the financial statements. Businesses produce three main financial statements to satisfy the needs of the various users of accounting information. These are:

❑ **The income statement (profit and loss account):** This shows the revenue the company has earned (income), less the amounts incurred (expenses) in earning it. The difference between the income and the expenses is the profit or loss that has occurred.

❑ **The balance sheet:** This is a statement showing what the business owns (assets) and what it owes (liabilities) on the very last day of the financial year. It is like a snapshot of a business at one point in time and helps to answer the question 'is the business financially stable?'

❑ **The cash flow statement:** This statement identifies the main sources of cash and the main uses of cash in a financial period. It shows the flow of cash through the business and summarises the cash performance of a business.

These financial statements are multi-purpose documents as they provide financial information to the different users of accounting data such as shareholders, loan providers, potential investors, creditors, the revenue commissioners and management. Each user will have to extract the information they need from these documents. These statements are produced by every business (although small businesses are exempt from producing cash flow statements). Ultimately, financial accounting is a backward looking process that helps answer questions on how well the business has performed. The role of financial accounting focuses on the recording, summarising and reporting of business transactions to the various users both internal (management) and external (creditors, loan providers, shareholders) to an organisation.

Management accounting

In addition to the financial statements outlined above, businesses will produce other statements for their own internal use and these will be tailored to their specific requirements. These internal reports are intended to help management manage more effectively and ultimately provide timely, relevant, accurate and understandable management information to enhance the decision making process.

A good management accounting system should provide the following:

❑ Information for planning, control and performance measurement. Planning is concerned with the means by which an organisation achieves its objectives. For management accounting purposes this is achieved through the preparation of budgets (financial plans) both long-term (2-7 years) and short-term (1 year). The control process involves the measurement and comparison of actual performance to budget on a periodic basis. The management accounting system must provide management with periodic performance reports to enable them to assess if targets are being achieved and to take corrective action where this is not the case. These reports are used also to evaluate managerial performance and thus the whole process of target setting, measurement and evaluation has significant motivational aspects.

❑ Relevant information to enhance management decision-making. For example, managers require up-to-date information on profitable and unprofitable product lines and departments. This type of information is required for resource allocation as well as discontinuation decisions. Pricing decisions require relevant up-to-date cost information. Decisions on the introduction of new products, services or the purchase of new assets require relevant information, which must be provided by the management accounting system.

The role of management accounting involves the analysis and presentation of information to assist in the internal running of an organisation, and the preparation of budgets and standards so that control can be achieved.

Management accounting in business

Management accounting involves providing information for planning, controlling, decision making and the formulation of business policy and strategy. Across all business sectors, management accounting helps provide answers to the following questions:

❑ What are future costs likely to be?
❑ How do actual costs compare with budget?
❑ Is the organisation achieving the objectives set by management?

Regarding the hospitality, tourism and retail sectors, management accounting helps provide management with answers to the following typical questions that empower managers to plan, control and make decisions.

❑ Is the hotel operating at an optimum level – is occupancy level acceptable?
❑ How many customers does the restaurant require to break even?
❑ What strategy will maximise profits?

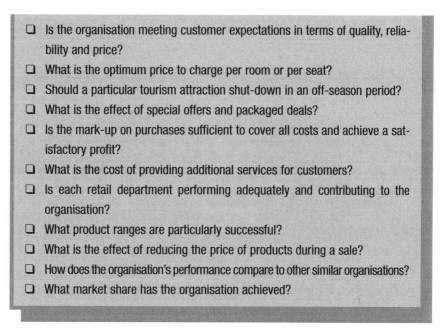

❏ Is the organisation meeting customer expectations in terms of quality, reliability and price?
❏ What is the optimum price to charge per room or per seat?
❏ Should a particular tourism attraction shut-down in an off-season period?
❏ What is the effect of special offers and packaged deals?
❏ Is the mark-up on purchases sufficient to cover all costs and achieve a satisfactory profit?
❏ What is the cost of providing additional services for customers?
❏ Is each retail department performing adequately and contributing to the organisation?
❏ What product ranges are particularly successful?
❏ What is the effect of reducing the price of products during a sale?
❏ How does the organisation's performance compare to other similar organisations?
❏ What market share has the organisation achieved?

Financial and management accounting fulfil different roles within an organisation and provide different information. Unlike financial accounting, management accounting provides detailed and focused information that relates to past, current and future projected performance. The frequency is much greater for management accounting reports. As they are only used internally, there is no requirement to follow the recommendations of the accounting profession or legislation which protects third parties relying on accounting information. The table below summarises the distinction between financial and management accounting.

Table 1.1: *Financial versus management accounting*

Source	Financial accounting	Management accounting
Primary users	External (shareholders)	Internal (management)
Type of information	Summarised balance sheet, profit and loss, and cash flow	A range of very detailed and specifically focused reports
Frequency	Once / twice a year	As required by management Usually weekly / monthly
Time focus	Historic	Both historic and future focused
Format of accounting governed by	Company's Acts and standards issued by the accounting profession	Not governed by legislation or standards

Adapted from Peter Clarke (2002), *Accounting Information for Managers*

Role of Management

'To manage is to forecast and plan, to organise, to command, to coordinate and to control'
H. Fayol (1916)

Similar to Fayol, Koontz and O'Donnell (1984) focus on the functions of management in their definition; *'managing is an operational process initially best dissected by analysing the managerial functions…The five essential managerial functions are: planning, organising, staffing, directing and leading, and controlling.'*

Cole (2004) summed it up by stating that *'management is a process that enables organisations to set and achieve their objectives by planning, organising, and controlling their resources, including gaining the commitment of their employees (motivation).'*

From an accounting perspective, the role of management can also be described as making decisions that are likely to ensure the viability of an organisation and to plan and control the implementation of these decisions. Ultimately, management is concerned with planning, decision-making and control. This process can be summarised as follows:

Diagram 1.2: *Framework for managerial planning, decision-making and control*

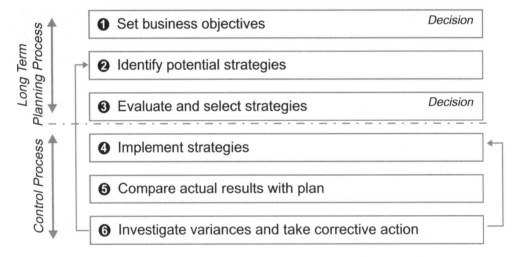

Set business objectives

The aims of a business are often couched in broad terms and may be set out in the form of a mission statement. This statement is usually brief and will generally articulate high standards or ideals for the business. This is essentially the guiding aim of the business and will help management choose one course of action over another.

The objectives of a business are usually quantifiable and more specific and should be consistent with the aims of the business. Examples could include:

❑ The kind of market it wishes to serve.
❑ The market share it wishes to achieve.
❑ The range of products and services to be offered.
❑ The desired levels of profit and return on capital and cash flow.
❑ Levels of growth as measured in sales, employees, physical assets etc.

There is controversy over what the objectives of a firm are or should be. For example, is the primary objective profit maximisation or is it to increase the wealth of the owners of the business? Some writers on management and financial theory believe in the satisfactory profits theory which states that businesses are content to find a plan that provides satisfactory profits rather than maximising profits. Social objectives that in the short run at least, conflict with profit maximisation also cause controversy. Ultimately a business will define a number of objectives to achieve its aims. Many of these objectives can in the short run have conflicting qualities.

Identify potential strategies

This second stage involves the search for a range of strategies for the business to achieve its objectives. This task is undertaken by management and involves much data collection and analysis of both the external market and an internal analysis of the resources and expertise available to the business to pursue each option. Much of the external analysis focuses on the future, for example new markets, future demand, and the changing business environment.

External Analysis	Internal Analysis
Market size and growth prospects	Organisation culture
Competition within the market place	Human resources and capability
Period of likely competitive advantage	Physical capacity
Threat of substitute products	Financial resources
Exchange rates	Research and development
Tax rates and incentives	Information systems
Government policy	
Socio-cultural values	

These decisions are referred to as long-run or strategic decisions and generally have a profound effect on a business' future position. Thus it is essential that there is sufficient research, data collection and analysis, not just about new and future markets, but also about the internal constraints and limitations affecting the business. By comparing the environmental influences (opportunities and threats) and the resource limitations (strengths and weaknesses), a strategic plan can be put together setting the organisation on a course to follow in the hope of achieving specific goals.

Adapting to environmental change

Wigoders, the home decorating group has downsized from 17 stores to 5 as the arrival of DIY superstores increased the competitiveness in this sector. Efforts made to adapt to the changing environment failed and restructuring was felt the only option for survival.

Shrinking market share and the effect of the large discount stores resulted in the ESB deciding to exit the retail sector. The final stores closed in December 2005.

The role of management accounting at this stage involves the collection and analysis of data for alternative strategies. The analysis should provide detailed cost estimates and projected profit levels for each strategy. The effect each strategy has on overall profit and return on capital for the business should also be projected.

Evaluate and select strategies

Decision-making involves choosing between alternative, competing courses of action and selecting the alternative(s) that best meets the objectives of the organisation. When deciding on the most appropriate option(s) to choose, management must examine information relating to each option to see if that option fits with the objectives that have been set and assess whether or not it is feasible to provide the resources required. Management must consider the effects of pursuing each option on the future financial performance and position of the business. Projected financial statements play an invaluable role in the evaluation of the various options open to management.

Diagram 1.3: *A framework for decision-making*

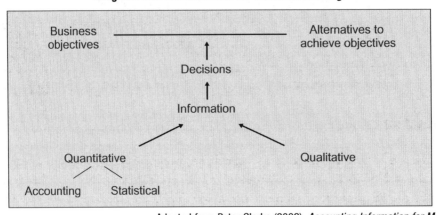

Adapted from Peter Clarke (2002), *Accounting Information for Managers*

The key element in the whole decision process is information. Information is generally classified as either:

1. Quantitative/numerical – this is generally made up of accounting information such as net profit or return on investment, and statistical information such as market share.
2. Qualitative – this is mainly information that is non-quantifiable such as the business is in a prime location or it has an excellent management team.

Ultimately, decisions require accurate and timely information and the likelihood of making a good decision is enhanced by judiciously using the information at hand. Good decision-making will help ensure in the long run, a profitable and successful business. Accounting for decision-making is a common thread in all the chapters of this book, with Chapters 4, 5, 6, 7 and 14 showing how various specific accounting tools and models are used to provide information that enhances management decision-making.

Expansion and diversification strategy

Jurys Doyle plc. agreed on a strategy for expansion and diversification through the development of low cost quality accommodation based on the North American motel model. In the late 1980s the group identified market demand for economy accommodation in Ireland. Thus the company developed their Jurys Inns brand initially in Dublin and Galway before expanding to Cork and Limerick. The company financed each of the Inns through leveraged lease agreements whereby the lessor (property developers) availed of capital allowances and the lessee (Jurys) obtained double rent and rates relief for the 10 years of the lease agreement. After 10 years Jurys had the option to purchase outright the properties at original cost. The Inns brand has been a great success for the company, not just in Ireland but also in the UK, where the company has achieved expansion since the late 1990s through concentrating on the development of the Inns.

Implement the strategies

Once decisions have been made at stage three, they should be implemented as part of the normal budget process. A budget is a financial plan outlining the projected effects of the decisions management has made. They are prepared based on the differential costs and revenues associated with the particular course of action chosen and although these costs and revenues are estimates, generally management will apply probabilities to calculate a likely basis for the costs and revenues estimated. The planning process leads with an overall or strategic plan, which is divided into annual plans, which show in detail how the strategic plan is to be achieved.

Management accounting provides the framework for budget preparation and presentation. The master budget is a formal document bringing together all the subbudgets and presenting them in the traditional format of a trading, profit and loss account and balance sheet for the year. These annual plans are quite detailed and show exactly how the business is to achieve each annual plan and, ultimately, the strategic plan. This area, known as budgetary planning, is covered in greater detail in Chapters 8 and 9.

Compare actual results with plan

This is where progress on achieving the plan is monitored. This involves daily, weekly or monthly comparison of actual performance against budget. In particular, budgeted costs and revenues are compared to actual performance and any variances are identified.

Ultimately this control or monitoring process is provided by the management accounting function. Performance reports and regular feedback on key variances (differences between budget and actual performance) are provided to help decide if corrective action is required. This area, known as budgetary control, is covered in greater detail in Chapters 10 and 11.

Investigate variances and take corrective action

The control process should provide management with relevant, reliable and timely information to help them decide on possible corrective action when variances between budgeted and actual costs and revenues occur. All significant variances must be investigated and this must be done quickly to ensure management have timely information to take corrective action. This process involves focusing on possible reasons for the variances and then deciding on the corrective type of action required. This corrective action can involve changing the plan slightly as it may have been too ambitious and unachievable or too easily achieved. Management must also be aware of the external factors that can influence actual performance and create variances.

Management accounting provides the analysis of performance and highlights significant variances that warrant further investigation. This area is covered in detail in Chapter 11.

Characteristics of Good Information

Accounting information needs to be timely, relevant, accurate and understandable to support management in its role. Information providers should always consider the following:

❏ Is the information communicated early enough to be effective?
❏ Is the information up-to-date?
❏ Is the information produced at appropriate intervals?
❏ Is the information presented relevant to the purpose for which it is intended?
❏ Is the information addressed to the correct person?
❏ Is the information accurate?
❏ Is the information complete?
❏ Is the information clear and unambiguous so the user can understand it?
❏ Is the information detailed enough?
❏ Is the information concise enough?

Characteristics of useful information

In order to be useful for decision-making, accounting information must possess the following characteristics as outlined by the ASB (Accounting Standards Board) in its Statement of Principles published in December 1999.
1. Relevance: It must relate to the decision being taken.
2. Understandability: Accounting information must be presented in such a way that it is comprehensible to the less informed user of accounts.
3. Timeliness: The earlier the information the earlier a decision can be made and put into effect.
4. Accuracy: If the information is not accurate it could be misleading.

Summary

This chapter was concerned with giving a brief overview of the role of management within commercial organisations and how accounting and in particular management accounting, supports that role. The accounting information needs of managers are quite varied. The published financial statements alone do not provide the necessary information to effectively manage and control a business. Accounting has developed to meet the needs of managers by providing an internal management information system through the function of 'Management Accounting'.

The main information points covered in this chapter are as follows:

❑ Accounting is concerned with identifying, classifying, measuring, recording and communicating financial information.
❑ Financial accounting involves recording, summarising and communicating the financial performance of the business through the financial statements or final accounts. It is primarily a backward looking process.
❑ Management accounting focuses on the accounting information needs of managers by providing a wide variety of accounts and reports.
❑ The role of management can be described as making decisions that are likely to ensure the viability of an organisation and to plan and control the implementation of these decisions. Ultimately, management is concerned with planning, decision-making and control.
❑ Accounting information is only a part of the total information available to management through its management information systems. Accounting information on its own is seldom enough to permit an informed decision. Non-financial factors will always play a significant role in the planning, decision-making and control issues facing management.
❑ Accounting information needs to be timely, relevant, accurate and understandable to support management in its role.

Review Questions

Question 1.1

Distinguish between financial and management accounting and discuss the role both have in an organisation.

Question 1.2

Briefly outline the role of management within an organisation.

Question 1.3

Outline the role of accounting as a support tool for management.

CHAPTER 2

Cost Analysis and Classification Systems

Learning Outcomes

By the end of this chapter you will be able to:

❑ Appreciate the importance of cost analysis and cost classification systems as management information tools.
❑ Understand the main cost classification systems and their uses as part of an overall management accounting information system.
❑ Distinguish between direct and indirect costs.
❑ Distinguish between fixed and variable costs.
❑ Outline the various approaches to estimating cost behaviour and thus predicting future costs.

Introduction

The term 'cost' can be defined as *'the resources consumed or used up to achieve a certain objective'*. This objective may be the running of a business or a department within a business. Thus cost represents the expenditure occurred in running a business on a day to day basis.

The analysis of costs and how they behave is an essential element of management accounting and provides a wealth of information for management decision-making. Management must minimise costs at the same time as maximising product or service quality and sales. An effective manager should be aware of costs, what creates and drives these costs, and how costs behave in relation to various events or stimuli.

This chapter focuses on how costs are analysed and how this analysis provides management with relevant information to enhance planning, decision-making and control. Cost information can enhance management decision-making in the following areas:

❏ **Control:** This is where cost analysis is focused on the past and helps management identify any costs that are out of line with budget.
❏ **Planning:** This is where the focus is on the future and how to predict cost levels based on cost behaviour theory.

Cost analysis involves classifying costs according to their common characteristics. There are a number of different classification systems, each differing according to the purpose to which the cost data is to be used. In other words each classification system helps provide different information to support different aspects of management. The following are the main cost classification systems used in management accounting:

❏ Cost classification by element.
❏ Cost classification for control (direct and indirect).
❏ Cost classification by cost centre.
❏ Cost classification by behaviour. Ch 4, 5, 7

Classifying Cost by Element

This system classifies costs according to what they are. It normally classifies cost into three categories namely materials, labour and expenses that are incurred in making a product or offering a service. Thus in the case of a restaurant, materials represent food and beverages; subsequently, labour (chefs and waiters) and production facilities (kitchen equipment) are used to convert the materials into a finished product to be sold. Expenses include the light and heat, insurance, advertising, depreciation, repairs, maintenance and rent used to ensure the product is sold. This classification system is generally used for profit and loss presentations in financial reporting and is the classification system most people are familiar with. It is sometimes called *'the elements of cost'*.

Diagram 2.1: *Elements of cost*

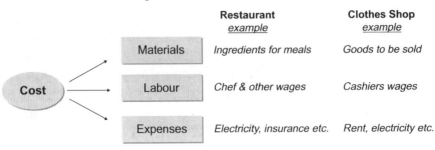

		Restaurant *example*	Clothes Shop *example*
	Materials	*Ingredients for meals*	*Goods to be sold*
Cost	Labour	*Chef & other wages*	*Cashiers wages*
	Expenses	*Electricity, insurance etc.*	*Rent, electricity etc.*

Cost Classification for Control

One of the responsibilities of management is to ensure costs are minimised without a loss of quality to the product or service provided. To control costs, one must be able to trace costs to either a product line or a department. This can help management identify where cost over-runs have occurred, identify the problems and decide on appropriate solutions. The process of tracing costs to departments or product lines involves classifying costs according to whether they are direct costs or indirect costs.

Direct costs

CIMA Official Terminology describes direct cost as *'expenditure that can be attributed to a specific cost unit'*. A direct cost is a cost that can be traceable and thus attributable to a particular product or service. These direct costs can be further broken into direct materials, direct labour and direct expenses.

❑ **Direct materials:** The cost of materials which form part of the product on sale. Examples of direct materials would be the ingredients used when preparing a meal in a restaurant or timber in the manufacture of furniture.

❑ **Direct labour:** The cost associated with the work performed by an employee on the product itself. Examples include a chef's wages earned while catering for a Christmas party or a carpenter's wages for work done in producing a piece of furniture.

❑ **Direct expenses:** Costs, other than material or labour, involved in producing a specific product or service. Examples of a direct expense would be a royalty due for the use of a patented recipe not owned by the organisation, or a television or cable licence for a room in a hotel.

The total of all direct costs is termed *'Prime Cost'*.

Indirect costs (overheads)

Indirect costs are costs that cannot be traced to an individual product or service. This would include all costs that are not direct costs. Indirect costs can be further broken down into indirect material, indirect labour and indirect expenses. The total of all indirect costs is known as overhead. CIMA Official Terminology describes overhead as *'expenditure on labour, materials or services that cannot be economically identified with a specific saleable cost unit.'* Overheads include costs such as supervision and management (unless only one product or service is involved), electricity, depreciation, insurance and advertising.

Total Cost	=	Prime Cost	+	Overhead
=		=		=
Total material cost	=	Direct material	+	Indirect material
+		+		+
Total labour Cost	=	Direct labour Cost	+	Indirect labour Cost
+		+		+
Total expense Cost	=	Direct expenses	+	Indirect expenses

Classifying direct and indirect costs

Confusion can occur when deciding whether a cost item is direct or indirect. For example a production manager's salary would be classified as a direct expense in terms of costing an overall department. However it would be termed an indirect cost or overhead if the costing system was a unit/product based one as it would be very difficult to trace the cost to individual product lines. Ultimately, traceability is the essence of this cost classification system.

Illustration 2.1 below shows a cost classification system for a hotel, based on departments rather than products. The direct costs are the costs associated with each department and the indirect costs are those associated with general administration, accounting and head–office costs not directly associated with any one department.

Illustration 2.1: Cost classification system for hotels

Product / department	Direct materials	Direct labour	Direct expenses
Accommodation	Laundry & toiletries	Cleaning staff	TV & cable licence
Restaurant	Food	Kitchen staff	Plates & cutlery
Bar	Beverages	Bar staff	Glasses
	Indirect costs		
	Insurance		
	Administration		
	Accounting		
	Advertising		

Adapted from Peter Clarke (2002), *Accounting Information for Managers*

Classification of costs into direct and indirect categories helps management to control and question costs. The most efficient way to do this is to ensure costs are classified according to departments or better still, products and product lines. Then, management can easily identify where cost over-runs have occurred and take timely, corrective action. By associating costs with products, management can evaluate if the cost is really necessary and assess what value has been created by this cost. This helps ensure that costs are controlled. Also the classification of costs into direct and indirect groups provides a basis for assigning cost responsibility and accountability to departments or segments of a business. This again can help in ensuring costs are controlled.

Calculating the Direct Cost of a Product or Service

Direct and indirect costs can be explained by using the Newtown Castle Hotel as an example. In addition to providing top class accommodation, the hotel caters for weddings. The hotel needs to calculate the direct cost per unit, in this case a meal, served. This can be established by examining the direct materials, direct labour and direct expense cost of the meal.

Direct materials

The main steps in calculating the direct materials cost of a product are:

1. Identify the component parts that constitute the finished product or service.
2. Ascertain the quantities required of each component to produce a final finished product or batch of products.
3. Calculate the cost of each component. As many components are purchased in bulk, to calculate the cost per component one must divide the total cost of the batch by the number of components in the batch.
4. Multiply the cost of the component by the quantities of each component used to get the total direct materials cost of the product.

To illustrate this process let us use the example of a standard meal provided by the Newtown Castle Hotel for a wedding function.

Example 2.1: *Calculation of direct material cost*

The clients for the wedding function have chosen a steak meal for the main course. The ingredients, quantities required, quantities purchased and costs are given below.

Ingredients	Quantities required per meal	Quantities ordered / purchased	Cost per purchase order
Steak	0.25 kg ← *Divide* *50 g*	20 kg box of assorted cuts	€300 per 20 kg box
Mixed salad	1 bag	50 bags	€20 per 50 bags
French fries	0.25 kg	30 kg box	€50 per 30 kg box
Onion rings	5	1 bag of 60	€5 per bag

Calculate the direct materials cost per meal.

Approach

The quantities required are multiplied by the relevant price.

Ingredients	Quantity required		Total cost €
Steak	0.25 kg	€300 ÷ 80 portions =	3.75
Mixed salad	1 bag	€20 ÷ 50 bags =	0.40
French fries	0.25 kg	€50 ÷ 120 portions =	0.42
Onion rings	5	5 rings x (€5 ÷ 60) =	0.42
Total cost per meal			4.99

If, for example, the steak cuts were frozen, then the weight attributable to the frozen water would have to be considered. If this was estimated at 10 per cent then the weight of the frozen cuts would amount to 18 kgs and with each portion approximating to 0.25 kgs, then the number of portions per box would equal 72 and thus the cost of the steak component would equal €300 ÷ 72 = €4.17. The direct materials cost per meal would increase to €5.41.

Direct labour

The direct labour costs are the costs associated with the labour performed on the product itself. In the example of a hotel wedding function it is important to realise that a hotel sells more than just a product (the meal) but also a service or as some would say, 'an experience'. Thus it is necessary to take into account not just the kitchen staff that are directly involved in the production process but also the waiting staff that provide the service.

The process for calculating the direct labour costs of a product or service is as follows:

1. Identify the work processes, jobs and staff that are directly involved in the production of the product or service.
2. Ascertain the rates of pay that apply to the jobs or staff involved.
3. Ascertain the hours required by each staff category to complete a batch of products. For some sectors, staff are required to be on duty for a time period (i.e. shifts of seven hours) and thus the average or standard output for that time period must be ascertained.
4. Calculate the total direct labour cost per batch or time period.

5. Calculate the direct labour cost per product by dividing the total cost calculated above by the average number of products produced for the batch or time period.

Example 2.2: *Calculation of direct labour cost*

Returning to the example of the steak dinner chosen for the wedding function at the Newtown Castle Hotel, the following information is provided regarding relevant staff, wage rates and standard hours worked per category of employee.

Staff	Number of persons	Wage rates per hour €	Standard hours worked per person
Chef	1	25	3
Commi chef	3	10	4
Waiting staff	5	10	2

The wedding function is to cater for 50 guests.

Calculate the direct labour cost per meal.

Approach

The total cost is established by multiplying the hours worked by the rate of pay.

Staff	Hours worked	Rate per hour €	Total cost €
Chef (1 person)	3	25	75
Commi chefs (3 persons)	12	10	120
Waiting staff (5 persons)	10	10	100
Total direct labour cost			295

The €295 represents the total direct labour cost per meal. As the wedding function will cater for 50 guests, the direct labour cost per meal is €5.90 (€295 divided by 50 meals).

Direct expenses

The direct expenses are simply calculated by identifying those expenses that are directly related to the production process and relating them to the activity level to calculate the direct expenses per product.

Example 2.3: *Calculation of direct expenses*

In catering for the meal at the wedding function, it is anticipated that direct expenses including fresh table arrangements, serviettes, place cards and sundry items will amount to €150 for a wedding party of 50.

Calculate the direct expense cost per meal.

Approach

The total direct expenses of €150 divided by 50 meals will amount to €3.00 per meal. Based on the above examples, the total direct cost (prime cost) per steak meal will amount to:

Overall direct cost per meal

	€
Direct materials	4.99
Direct labour	5.90
Direct expenses	3.00
Prime cost per meal	13.89

Indirect cost

Indirect cost or overhead will be incurred during the wedding function. For example, electricity costs will be incurred by the hotel. Other overhead costs could include the salaries of the duty manager and the hotel receptionist who are spending a portion of their time serving the wedding function. A portion of costs such as insurance, rent and depreciation should also be charged to the wedding function. The process for sharing overhead to cost units is outlined and explained in detail in Chapter 3.

Cost Classification by Cost Centre

This is an extension of cost classification for control purposes. A cost centre is a location or person or item of equipment for which costs may be ascertained, and for which an individual is responsible. Examples of cost centres based on a location are a maintenance workshop, the personnel department, or the administration office. A cost centre based on a person could be the health and safety officer, while one based on an item of equipment could be a specialist printing machine.

In many educational institutes the various schools are treated as cost centres. The classification by cost centre allows the grouping of costs by means of a location or action. It is another classification method, which ensures traceability and promotes accountability.

Diagram 2.2: *Cost classification by cost centre*

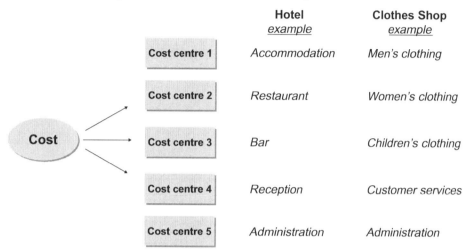

	Hotel *example*	Clothes Shop *example*
Cost centre 1	Accommodation	Men's clothing
Cost centre 2	Restaurant	Women's clothing
Cost centre 3	Bar	Children's clothing
Cost centre 4	Reception	Customer services
Cost centre 5	Administration	Administration

Cost Classification by Behaviour

↳ planning decisions - predict cost

Whereas the previous classification systems are primarily used for control (traceability and accountability) purposes, cost classification by behaviour is primarily used for management planning decisions. It is a crucial classification in that it allows an insight into how costs react to different circumstances. In trying to predict and plan for the future, it is essential to understand costs and what drives and creates costs. In particular, this classification looks at the relationship between costs and sales volume/pro- *→ amount of product sold* duction output. When planning to increase output (sales volume), it is important to understand and appreciate how costs will react to this.

What is meant by sales volume/production output is for example, a restaurant selling more covers, or a hotel selling more bedrooms, or a furniture shop selling more furniture as distinct from increasing sales by simply increasing the selling price.

Example 2.4: *Cost behaviour*

Joseph Ryan has undertaken to hire a stall at a village market to sell home produced luxury jams. The weekly market attracts many visitors to the village. The cost of the stall amounts to €100 per day. Joseph has estimated that the cost of providing each jam product approximates to €1.50.

Calculate the cost per jar if Joseph sells:

a) *100 jars per day.*
b) *200 jars per day.*

Approach

In this simplistic setting there are only two costs involved.

1. The €100 per day fixed charge to hire the stall. This expense will not be affected by the level of sales.
2. The cost of making each jam product. This is a cost that fluctuates with sales and as sales increase, this cost will also increase.

Cost per 100		Cost per 200	
Jam cost (100 x €1.50)	€150	Jam cost (200 x €1.50)	€300
Stall hire	€100	Stall hire	€100
Total cost	€250	Total cost	€400
Cost per jam = €250 ÷ 100 =	€2.50	Cost per jam = €400 ÷ 200 =	€2.00

From the above example it can be seen that costs can be classified into two main categories, variable costs and fixed costs.

Variable costs

Variable costs are costs that increase as sales or production volume increases. For example if sales volume fluctuates by 10 per cent then variable costs will fluctuate also by 10 per cent or close to it. Thus a variable cost is a cost that is sensitive to changes in sales activity. Examples would include direct materials as identified above. The cost of food or beverages for a restaurant would be considered a variable cost. The cost of toys in a toyshop would be a variable cost.

Diagram 2.3 illustrates the variable cost of producing a meal in a restaurant is €2 and, as

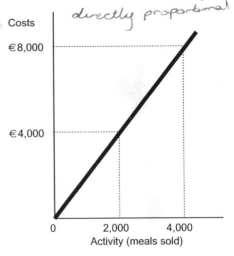

Diagram 2.3: *Variable costs*

sales volume increases, the variable costs increase. The variable cost graph shows that the variable cost of producing 2,000 meals is €4,000 and the variable cost of producing 4,000 meals is €8,000.

Note, as sales volume doubles, variable cost also doubles. A general rule of thumb is that variable costs should increase in proportion to increases in activity.

It should be noted that variable costs in total change in response to changes in sales activity levels. However, variable cost per unit will remain constant in relation to changes in sales activity. Taking the above example, the variable cost per unit is €2.00 and will remain at that level irrespective of the activity level. However total variable costs will change from €4,000 at a sales activity level of 2,000 meals to €8,000 at a sales activity level of 4,000 meals. Thus as activity levels increase, variable cost per unit will remain constant, but total variable costs will increase.

Fixed costs

Fixed costs are costs that are a function of time rather than sales activity and thus are not sensitive to changes in sales volume. As sales volume increases, these costs would be expected to remain the same or maybe increase due to other reasons such as inflation. Examples of fixed costs would include rent, rates, insurance and management salaries. Any of these costs would not be expected to increase as sales volume increases. It does not matter if there are 100 people or one person in a restaurant, the same rent must still be paid.

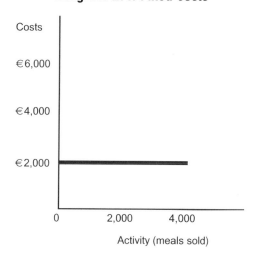

Diagram 2.4: *Fixed costs*

Diagram 2.4 shows that fixed costs are €2,000 per week. Irrespective of sales volume, fixed costs should remain the same or maybe change in relation to inflation or an agreed wage increase. The point is, fixed costs are not sensitive to increases in sales activity.

It should be noted that fixed costs in total do not change in response to changes in sales activity levels. However fixed cost per unit will change in relation to changes in sales activity. Taking the above example, fixed costs will remain at €2,000 within the activity level of up to 4,000 meals. However fixed costs per unit at the 2,000 and 4,000 activity levels are €1.00 and €0.50. Thus as activity levels increase, fixed cost per unit will decrease.

The relevant range of activity

An important point to make at this stage is that in some situations, increases in sales activity can lead to increases in fixed costs. Take for example a situation where sales volume increases to a level that a new manager or supervisor is required to support this extra volume of activity. In this case fixed costs will be affected and will increase. Thus we have the concept of *'the relevant range of activity'* which states that fixed costs will be unaffected by sales volume fluctuations as long as these fluctuations ensure sales activity remains within a certain range. In the example above, fixed costs remain at €2,000 per week as long as sales activity remains between 0 and 4,000 covers or meals sold. Should sales increase beyond 4,000 covers then maybe an extra supervisor is required, or if opening times are extended additional staff may be required. The relevant range concept is critical when management is considering significant increases or reductions in activity levels.

Some costs are called step costs due to the fact that they are fixed for a given level of activity but they eventually increase by a significant amount at some critical point. Examples include renting an additional warehouse unit or hiring an additional supervisor when activity reaches a critical point.

Diagram 2.5 shows that fixed costs are €2,000 up to an activity level of 2,000 meals. At this point the fixed costs increase significantly. Again at 4,000 meals another critical point is reached and fixed costs increase again.

Diagram 2.5: *Step cost*

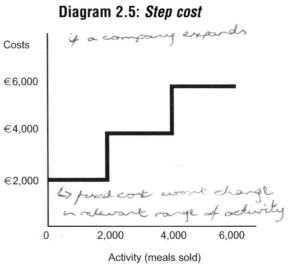

if a company expands

↳ fixed cost won't change in relevant range of activity

Semi-variable cost patterns   *eg phonebill – calls = variable / price = fixed*

We have identified typical costs that fall into the fixed and variable category. However when considering cost behaviour, many costs fall into an additional category called semi-variable or semi-fixed costs. These are costs that have both a fixed and variable component. For example telephone charges include a rental cost, which would be considered fixed and the cost of the number of phone calls which could be considered variable. When one analyses these costs further, part of the 'phone call costs' could be considered fixed as the phone would be used even if sales were non-existent. Thus a phone bill would be considered predominantly fixed, with a variable element. Another example would be light and heat. In a restaurant light and heat is required even if there are no customers in the restaurant. However as the restaurant gets busier more cookers will be needed and this would be classified as the variable element. Thus light and heat could be considered a predominantly fixed cost with a variable element. Diagram 2.6 graphically presents two typical semi-variable cost patterns.

Diagram 2.6: *Semi-variable cost patterns*

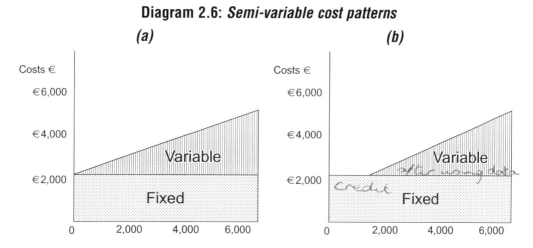

Diagram 2.6 (a) shows the fixed and variable elements of a typical landline telephone charge as described above.

Diagram 2.6 (b) shows the fixed and variable elements of a mobile phone charge where the user pays a fixed charge for a required level of usage (number of minutes) after which the user pays for each phone call.

Surveys of reasons for businesses distinguishing between fixed and variable costs

A survey conducted by Blayney and Yokuyama in 1991 of companies in Australia, Japan and the UK reported the following purposes for distinguishing between fixed and variable costs with 1 representing the most important purpose. The survey shows the many areas of management decision-making where an understanding of cost behaviour is important.

Purpose	Ranking by Australian companies	Ranking by Japanese companies	Ranking by UK companies
Pricing decisions	1	5	1
Budgeting	2	2	3
Profit planning	3	1	2
Cost reduction	6	3	5
CVP analysis	4	4	4
Cost benefit analysis	4	6	5

Determining How Costs Behave

The models and decision-making tools used by management based on cost behaviour theory require all costs to be classified into a fixed or variable category. Knowing how costs vary by identifying the drivers of costs and distinguishing between fixed and variable costs is frequently the key to making considered management decisions. Many managerial functions within the planning, decision-making and control realm, rely on cost behaviour information. This requires a knowledge of how to determine cost behaviour and measure cost relationships. There are a number of basic accounting and statistical techniques that can be used to scientifically establish cost relationships and break down a semi-variable cost into its fixed and variable components. These are:

❑ Accounts analysis method.
❑ High-low method.
❑ Scatter-graph method.
❑ Linear regression.

All these methods focus on analysing past or historic data to establish a cost function which describes cost behaviour patterns within the relevant range of activity. A cost function is generally expressed as follows:

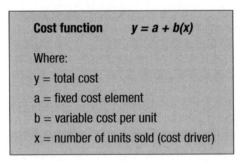

Cost function   **y = a + b(x)**

Where:
y = total cost
a = fixed cost element
b = variable cost per unit
x = number of units sold (cost driver)

Each cost item has a cost function, which describes the fixed and variable elements within the cost item and the relationship the variable element has to the cost driver. The cost driver is generally expressed in terms of sales volume/activity.

Two simplifying assumptions are made when estimating cost functions.

1. There is one single cost driver. This is assumed to be sales volume or some measure of sales activity. For example rooms sold in a hotel or covers in a restaurant.
2. The cost relationship to the cost driver is assumed to follow a linear cost function within the relevant range. Thus if the cost driver increases by 10 per cent the variable element of the cost increases by 10 per cent.

The following methods seek to provide an approximation to the cost function for each individual cost item that a business has.

Accounts analysis method

Under this method each cost is examined and, using judgement and experience, classified into fixed, variable and semi-variable categories. The semi-variable category is further apportioned individually into its fixed and variable components, normally on a percentage basis. This method is based mainly on experience and personal judgement and thus can be quite subjective. Management can reduce this level of subjectivity as follows.

1. Asking a person associated with the cost item who knows its behavioural pattern and can give a best estimate of the variable and fixed components to the cost.
2. Analysing how the cost item has responded to sales volume levels in past periods before categorising the cost.

The main advantages of the accounts analysis method is that it is quick and inexpensive, however the subjectivity involved can lead to inaccuracies. Where the cost item is immaterial and is largely fixed or variable, then the accounts analysis method is acceptable. However if this is not so, other more scientific methods should be used with the accounts analysis method providing the first stage of a more analytical approach to cost behaviour analysis.

High-low method

The high-low method is a statistical method that establishes a cost to sales volume relationship based on past observations of how the cost reacted to changes in sales volume. Ultimately all the statistical methods mentioned below seek to measure this relationship by analysing the average change in one variable (the cost item or dependent variable) that is associated with a change in another item (the independent variable or activity level). This relationship is expressed in terms of the cost function $y = a + b(x)$. The high-low method focuses on the highest and lowest levels of activity (sales volume) within the relevant range over a period of time. The total cost at these two extreme levels of activity is recorded and the difference is attributed to the behaviour of the variable cost element, which changes as activity levels change. The process seeks to calculate this variable element. The fixed element can then be calculated to complete the cost function.

Example 2.5 shows the workings of the high-low method.

Example 2.5: *High-low method*

This example is based on establishing the relationship between the overhead cost of repairs and maintenance in a hotel, to the occupancy levels of the hotel.

Month	Rooms sold	Repairs and maintenance €
January	600	5,000
March	800	5,800
May	900	6,000
July	300	4,200
September	560	4,900
November	350	4,000

Establish the cost function for repairs and maintenance using the high-low method.

Approach

The process involves the following steps:

1. Identify the high and low activity levels and record the cost at each level.
2. Calculate the difference in activity levels and the difference in costs.
3. Divide the cost difference by the difference in activity levels. This gives us the variable cost per room sold (b).
4. Take either the high or the low activity level and input the data including (b) as calculated in step 3 and solve the equation by finding the fixed cost element.

		Activity	Cost
Step 1			
	High	900	€6,000
	Low	300	€4,200
Step 2	Difference	600	€1,800

Step 3   €1,800 ÷ 600 = €3.00 (the variable cost per unit)

Step 4   Total cost = fixed costs + (variable cost per unit x number of units sold)

$$y = a + b(x)$$
$$6,000 = a + 3.00 \ (900)$$
$$6,000 = a + 2,700$$
$$3,300 = a \ (\text{the fixed cost amounts to €3,300})$$

Thus the cost function for repairs and maintenance in this hotel is summarised as:

$$y = 3,300 + 3 \ (x)$$

Management can use this cost function to predict what repairs and maintenance would be, based on any level of activity within the relevant range.

If the above four steps are examined, you will see that steps 1, 2 and 3 calculate the variable cost per unit. Logically, the difference in cost between two different volume activities can only be caused by variable costs. Fixed costs don't change with sales activity changes. The variable cost per unit was found by dividing the extra variable cost by the extra number of units involved; €1,800 ÷ 600 = €3.00. As total cost is made up of both variable and fixed costs, it is possible to find the fixed cost by choosing an activity level and inputting the data into its cost function. For example, the total cost of repairs and maintenance at an activity level of 300 rooms sold was €4,200. At this activity level the variable cost is €900. Fixed cost of €3,300 is found by taking the variable cost of €900 away from the total cost of €4,200.

Issues to consider when using the incremental cost method of separating semi-variable costs include:

❑ The two sets of data selected may not be representative of the real behaviour patterns of the costs. For example, the highest and lowest activities may have occurred during exceptional circumstances.
❑ The method assumes that costs behave in a linear fashion, i.e. costs vary by the same constant amount per unit as activity changes. In reality this may not be the case, as economies of scale can be achieved if activity increases significantly, for example bulk discounts may be received. Also, as activity increases, additional costs may be incurred, such as overtime premium.
❑ It assumes that fixed costs are truly fixed, ignoring step fixed costs.
❑ It ignores inflation.

The main advantage of the high-low method is its simplicity. However, should the high and low activity levels chosen not represent normal conditions then the cost volume relationship expressed in the cost function could be misleading.

Scatter-graph method

As with the high-low method, the scatter-graph approach is a statistical method that uses historical data to determine cost behaviour. The scatter-graph approach plots on a graph all the historic observations of the cost items in relation to the activity levels of the business, within the relevant range. A line of best fit is then drawn visually through the data on the graph. As with the high-low method, the form of the line is assumed linear. The angle or gradient of the line represents the variable cost per unit and the fixed cost is the point where the fitted line intersects the vertical axis.

Example 2.6: *Scatter-graph method*

The data from example 2.5 can be used to illustrate the scatter-graph approach.

Month	Rooms sold	Repairs and maintenance €
January	600	5,000
March	800	5,800
May	900	6,000
July	300	4,200
September	560	4,900
November	350	4,000

Establish the cost function using the scatter-graph method.

Approach

The data is plotted on the graph and a line of best visual fit is drawn and extends down to the Y (total cost) axis. The point of intersection with the Y axis represents the estimated fixed costs in this cost equation, which amounts to €2,900. The variable costs can be calculated by inputting the fixed cost and the total cost figures into a cost function based on any activity point on the line of best fit.

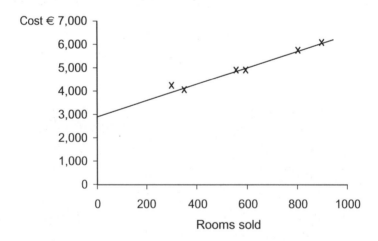

Taking an activity level of 650 rooms sold, the total cost is €5,100. Thus the cost function is as follows:

$$y = a + b(x)$$
$$€5,100 = €2,900 + b(650)$$
$$€2,200 = 650b$$
$$€3.38 = b$$

The cost function using the scatter-graph approach is Y = 2,900 + 3.38 (x).
The cost function using the high-low method is Y = 3,300 + 3.00 (x).

The main difference between the scatter-graph and high-low method lies with the sample data used to ascertain the cost function. The scatter-graph approach uses all the data in the sample to estimate the line of best fit and hence the cost function. The high-low method uses only two extreme points within the sample to estimate the cost function. The main weakness of the scatter-graph approach is that once all the data is plotted on a graph, deciding on a line of best fit is still a subjective judgement.

Linear regression – least squares method

This method is a statistical approach to determine the line of best fit for a given set of data. It is an extension of the scatter-graph approach and is based on the principle that the sum of the squares of the vertical distances from the regression line to the plots of the data points is less than the sum of the squares of the vertical distances from any other line that may be determined. In other words a truly objective line of best fit is calculated which minimises the squared deviations between the regression line and the observed data.

The linear regression equation, which meets the above requirement, is obtained by solving two equations simultaneously. This gives us values for both (a) (fixed costs) and (b) (variable cost per unit) in the total cost function. The equations are as follows:

$$1. \ \sum y = na + b \sum x$$
$$2. \ \sum xy = a(\sum x) + b \sum x^2$$

Where:
a = fixed cost
b = variable cost per unit
n = number of observations
$\sum x$ = Sum of the observations of the independent variable
$\sum y$ = Sum of the observations of the dependent variable
$\sum xy$ = Sum of the product of each pair of observations
$\sum x^2$ = Sum of the squares of the x observations.

Example 2.7: Linear regression

Using the data from example 2.5

Month	Rooms sold	Repairs and maintenance €
January	600	5,000
March	800	5,800
May	900	6,000
July	300	4,200
September	560	4,900
November	350	4,000

determine the total cost function for repairs and maintenance using linear regression.

Approach

The calculations required to determine the total cost function for repairs and maintenance using linear regression are as follows:

Month	Activity x	Cost € y	xy	x2	y2
1	600	5,000	3,000,000	360,000	25,000,000
2	800	5,800	4,640,000	640,000	33,640,000
3	900	6,000	5,400,000	810,000	36,000,000
4	300	4,200	1,260,000	90,000	17,640,000
5	560	4,900	2,744,000	313,600	24,010,000
6	350	4,000	1,400,000	122,500	16,000,000
	3,510	29,900	18,444,000	2,336,100	152,290,000

Equation 1 $29,900 = 6a + b3510$
Equation 2 $18,444,000 = a3,510 + b2,336,100$

By multiplying equation 1 by 585 we bring the number of (a)s to the same number in each equation and thus cancel the (a) variable.

Equation 1   17,491,500 = a3,510 + b2,053,350
Equation 2   18,444,000 = a3,510 + b2,336,100

Subtract equation 1 from equation 2

952,500 = b282,750
3.369 = b

Substituting 3.369 for (b) in equation 1 should give us a value for (a)

29,900 = 6a + 3.369(3,510)
29,900 = 6a + 11,824
18,075 = 6a
3,013 = a

Thus the repairs and maintenance costs for the hotel show a fixed element of €3,013 and a variable element of €3.369 per room sold.

As can be seen below, each method will give a different cost function.

1. High-low   y = €3,300 + €3.00 (x)
2. Scatter-graph   y = €2,900 + €3.38 (x)
3. Linear regression   y = €3,013 + €3.369 (x)

Of the three methods, the linear regression model is considered to have the least number of limitations. The cost function can be used in the intelligent prediction of future costs based on forecast sales activity.

Measures of reliability

There are a number of other statistical methods that can be used to assess the goodness or quality of the cost equation once calculated. Correlation analysis and the calculation of the coefficient of correlation (r) tests the quality or 'goodness of fit' of the cost function. Another statistic called the coefficient of determination (r2) indicates the percentage variation in the total cost item that is accounted for by changes in the activity levels. (r2) ranges from −1 to +1 where a 0 rating indicates zero correlation (no linear relationship) between the two variables and a + 1 rating indicates a perfect positive correlation. A rating of −1 indicates a perfect negative correlation. For example, let's say the (r2) for the above cost function of repairs and maintenance is + 59 per cent. This tells us that 59 per cent of the variation in repairs and maintenance can be explained by the variation in room sales. The higher the (r2), the higher the linear relationship.

Summary

This chapter focused on cost classification systems used to provide management with information to make decisions relating to planning and controlling the activities of a business. Classifying costs according to how they are related to a product, department or cost centre, helps ensure traceability and accountability and is primarily used for control purposes. Classifying cost according to behaviour is primarily used for planning and forecasting purposes. Horngren points out that *'a knowledge of how costs behave under a variety of influences is essential to intelligent prediction, decision-making and performance evaluation.'*

The main information points covered in this chapter are as follows:

❑ The analysis of costs and how they behave is an essential element of management accounting, and provides a wealth of information to management in informing their decision-making.

❑ Cost analysis involves classifying costs according to their common characteristics. There are a number of different classification systems, each differing according to the purpose for which the cost data is to be used.

❑ Classifying costs by element simply classifies costs according to what they are. Costs are normally classified into three categories, materials, labour and expenses that are used to make a product or offer a service. This classification system is generally used for profit and loss presentations in financial reporting.

❑ To control costs one must be able to trace costs to either a product line or a department. By having the ability to trace costs one can identify where cost over-runs have occurred and thus identify the problem and decide on a solution. Costs can be classified or traced according to the following:

    Departments.

    Specific products or product lines.

❑ The process of tracing costs to departments or product lines involves classifying costs according to whether they are direct costs or indirect costs.

❑ Direct costs are costs that can be traceable and thus attributable to a particular product, service or department. These direct costs can be further broken into direct materials, direct labour and direct expenses.

❑ Indirect costs are costs that cannot be traced to individual product lines or departments and thus would generally include all costs that are not direct costs. These would include administration costs, accounting and audit costs, insurance, marketing and the running costs of departments not directly involved in producing the product.

❑   A cost centre is a location or person or item of equipment for which costs may be ascertained and for which an individual is responsible. Examples of cost centres might be departments such as maintenance, production, personnel, sales or administration.

❑   Cost classification by behaviour is primarily used for management planning decisions and focuses on how costs react to different circumstances. In particular this classification looks at the relationship between costs and sales volume/production output. Costs are classified into two main categories; fixed costs and variable costs.

❑   Many costs fall into a third category called semi-variable or semi-fixed costs. These are costs that have both a fixed and variable component.

❑   The *'relevant range of activity'* concept states that fixed costs will be unaffected by sales volume fluctuations as long as these fluctuations ensure sales activity remains within a certain range of activity.

❑   There are a number of basic accounting and statistical techniques that can be used to scientifically establish cost relationships and break down a semi-variable cost into its fixed and variable components.

Review Questions

Question 2.1

a) Explain what you understand by the term 'cost'.
b) Explain what you understand by the 'elements of costs'.
c) Distinguish between the following, giving examples of each.
    i.   Direct and indirect costs.
    ii. Fixed and variable costs.

Question 2.2

You are required to classify each of the following costs according to whether they are direct or indirect, based on tracing the cost to:

a) A department.
b) A product line.

Cost	Direct or indirect Department	Direct or indirect Product line
Salary of restaurant supervisor	Direct	Indirect
Rent of shop unit	Indirect	Indirect
Depreciation of computer reservation system		Indirect
Sales commission	Direct	Direct
Purchase of goods for resale in a shop	Direct	Direct
Paint for each product	Indirect	indirect
Oil for central heating system	Indirect	Indirect
Home delivery service costs for supermarket	Indirect	Indirect
Cashiers' wages	Indirect	Indirect
Facilities managers' salary		

Question 2.3

The following details relate to the direct materials and labour costs relating to a wedding function serving 70 people.

Direct materials information:

Ingredients	Quantities required per meal	Quantities ordered / purchased	Cost per purchase order
Steak	0.33 kg	20 kg box of assorted cuts	€400 per 20 kg box
Mixed salad	1 bag	100 bags	€30 per 100 bags
French fries	0.20 kg	30 kg box	€60 per 30 kg box
Onion rings	5	1 bag of 100	€5 per bag

Direct labour information:

Staff	Number of persons	Wage rates per hour €	Standard hours worked per person
Chef	1	40.00	3
Commi chef	2	15.00	3
Waiting staff	4	10.00	3

Required:
a) Calculate the direct materials cost per meal.
b) Calculate the direct labour cost per meal.
c) If the direct expenses relating to the wedding function amount to €300, calculate the prime cost per meal.

Question 2.4

a) Explain what you understand by 'cost behaviour' using an example to illustrate.
b) Explain the concept of the relevant range.

Question 2.5

a) Explain the term 'semi-variable costs' giving at least two examples.
b) Why is it necessary to distinguish between fixed and variable costs?

c) Classify the following expense items according to whether they are a fixed or variable cost.

Cost	Fixed or variable
Salary of restaurant supervisor	
Rent of shop unit	
Depreciation of computer reservation system	
Sales commission	
Purchase of goods for resale in a shop	
Paint for each product	
Oil for central heating system	
Home delivery service costs for supermarket	
Cashiers' wages	
Facilities managers' salary	

Question 2.6

A hotel offers the following quotations from its banqueting menu to companies enquiring about their annual Christmas dinner.

Menu	Number of covers	Selling price per cover €
A	100	25.00
A	150	20.00
A	200	15.00

Menu A is a single menu and the quality and portion size are the same irrespective of the selling price per cover.

Required
Explain in your own words how the hotel can reduce its selling price based on the number of covers and still maintain or even increase its net profit percentage.

Question 2.7

The data presented below relates to the monthly security costs incurred by the Eden Shopping complex.

	Hours	Total cost €
January	280	20,400
February	224	18,720
March	240	19,200
April	216	18,480

Required

a) Use the high-low method to separate the fixed and variable cost elements of the security costs presented above.

b) As the complex manager plans on increasing opening hours by 10 per cent, re-calculate the costs for the four months presented above, based on the cost function calculated in (a).

Question 2.8

The following data relates to the Emerald Towers Leisure Centre who operate a 'pay as you use' total leisure experience.

Month	No. of persons	Maintenance costs €
January	500	2,000
February	600	2,200
March	900	2,500
April	400	1,900
May	300	1,800
June	450	2,000

Required

a) Compute the maintenance cost function based on the high-low method.

b) Draw a scatter diagram of the above data and draw a line of best fit through the data. From the graph, calculate the maintenance cost function.

c) Compute the maintenance cost function based on least squares regression analysis.

d) Outline the main reasons for the differences in the maintenance cost function calculated by each of the methods.

e) What is the advantage in calculating a cost function for a cost item?

[handwritten annotation:]

(Prime)
Direct → Materials   1.50
         Labour   2.50
         Expense   0.50
                      4.50
(overhead)
Indirect → Rent
           Insurance 2.50
           Salaries   6.50

Cost

Accounting for Overhead Cost

[handwritten:] indirect costs

Learning Outcomes

By the end of this chapter you will be able to:

❑ Define and explain the terms, overhead, cost centre and cost unit.
❑ Appreciate the importance of overhead cost.
❑ Apportion overhead cost to cost centres.
❑ Re-apportion the costs of service centres.
❑ Calculate and explain overhead absorption rates.
❑ Outline the key approaches in accounting for overheads, namely:
  – Absorption costing.
  – Activity based costing.
❑ Calculate the overhead unit cost of a product or service.

Introduction

Chapter 2 described alternative approaches to classifying costs. One approach is to identify if costs are either direct or indirect. The emphasis in this chapter moves to indirect costs and appropriate approaches to accounting for such costs. Overhead represents the total of the indirect costs incurred by a business and includes such items as light and heat, rent, administration and selling and distribution expenses. The amount spent on overhead or indirect costs can be significant for an organisation and hence this expenditure needs to be monitored and controlled.

The full cost of a product or service includes both the direct costs and indirect (overhead) costs incurred in providing the product or service. While it is simple to calculate the prime or direct cost of a product, the process of finding the overhead cost per unit is more complex and subjective. *[handwritten:] matter of opinion*

This chapter begins by describing what is termed overheads and explains the process of apportioning overhead cost. Two approaches to establishing the overhead cost per unit are presented, the traditional approach of absorption costing and a modern approach, known as activity based costing.

Overhead Cost

'expenditure on labour, materials or services that cannot be economically identified with a specific saleable cost unit'
Overhead cost as defined by CIMA Official Terminology

Overhead is the term applied to the total of all indirect costs. Indirect costs are made up of indirect materials, indirect labour and indirect expenses. Overhead represents all the costs incurred that cannot be traced directly to a specific cost unit but is shared amongst a number of products or services. Examples include costs such as supervision (unless only one product or service is involved), electricity, insurance, advertising, depreciation, rent and rates.

Overhead cost examples

	Hospitality area	Retail area
Indirect materials	Serviettes	Bags
+		
Indirect labour	Restaurant manager	Floor supervisor
+		
Indirect expenses	Electricity	Rent

In some cases, a cost may be identifiable with a particular product or customer but it may not be of significant value. The administration effort of treating this cost as a direct cost would be high, therefore this cost is treated as an indirect cost. For example the cost of providing a serviette in a restaurant or a bag to a customer at a point of sale terminal in a shop could be treated as overhead.

Overhead as a per cent of total cost

According to the '2003 Survey of Management Accounting' carried out by Ernst and Young, overheads on average amount to 34 per cent of total cost for retail organisations operating in the United States. Research by Luby (2006) in relation to retail organisations in Ireland indicated that overheads as a percentage of total costs was well below the US average of 34 per cent. However the majority of respondents were not willing to disclose exact details of overhead cost levels.

According to the Restaurants Association of Ireland (RAI), overheads amount to over 25 per cent of sales. In hotels this figure can rise to 35 per cent of sales.

Why is overhead cost important?

Management need to be aware of the level of expenditure on overheads. If left uncontrolled, the amount spent can increase year on year, eroding significant proportions of gross profit and reducing competitiveness. Managers need to know:

❑ Overhead expenditure per cost centre or department. ⎤ to monitor/
❑ Overhead costs per unit. ⎦ control

Analysing overhead costs per cost centre or department helps in the overall control of overhead within an organisation. If responsibility accounting (where individual managers are accountable for expenditure under their control) is in operation, analysing overhead ensures that the manager is aware of the entire cost of running the department or cost centre.

Diagram 3.1: *Dealing with overhead cost*

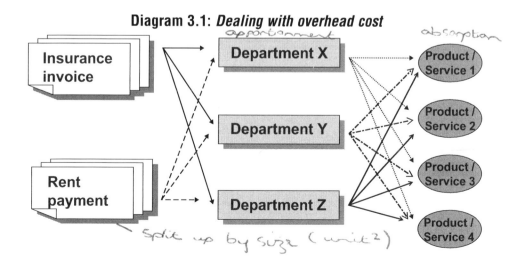

The diagram above illustrates a process of sharing overhead firstly to departments or cost centres and secondly to each individual product or service provided by the department or cost centre. Establishing the overhead cost per unit assists in insuring that all overhead cost is covered when setting individual selling prices.

There are a number of stages or steps involved in establishing the overhead cost per unit. Before discussing these it is important to understand the concepts of cost centres and cost units.

Cost Centres	*Cost Units*
A cost centre can be explained as a location, a person, or an item of equipment for which costs can be ascertained.	A cost unit is a quantitative unit of product or service in relation to which costs are ascertained.

Hotel example

Restaurant	→	*Meal served*
Accommodation	→	*Occupied bed night*
Bar	→	*Drink served*

When developing a management accounting system that accounts for overhead cost, it is first necessary to identify cost centres or departments to which overheads can be apportioned. Once all overheads have been apportioned to cost centres or departments they can then be charged to products or services produced by the cost centre or department.

Apportioning Overhead Cost

In diagram 3.1 above, overhead costs are divided or shared among a number of departments or cost centres. When an overhead cost can be identified with a particular cost centre, the whole cost is allotted to that cost centre. The process by which overheads are divided between several cost centres in a 'fair' proportion is referred to as cost apportionment. Each overhead type is examined and a suitable base for sharing out the cost is established. For example, the best way of sharing out property rental cost can be justified as 'floor space' or square metres occupied, because each cost centre occupies floor space within the property. Cost is apportioned by dividing the total overhead cost of rent by the total floor space and multiplying by the space used by the cost centre.

Illustration 3.1: *Apportioning cost to a cost centre*

The overhead cost in relation to rent is €1,000 and floor space was chosen as the most suitable basis for sharing or apportioning this cost. The total floor space available is 500 square metres (300 for department A and 200 for department B). The overhead in relation to rent would be shared or apportioned as follows:

	Department A	Department B	Total
Square metres	300 sq m	200 sq m	500 sq m
	Total cost of €1,000 divided by 500 square metres = €2 per metre		
	As dept A has 300 square metres, €600 overhead is apportioned to it (300 x €2).	*As dept B has 200 square metres, €400 overhead is apportioned to it (200 x €2).*	
Summary	€1,000 ÷ 500 = €2 x 300 = €600	€1,000 ÷ 500 = €2 x 200 = €400	€1,000

Different bases may be chosen for each overhead category. The base chosen should be the fairest for the given situation. The following examples present an idea of what base can be used for items of overhead.

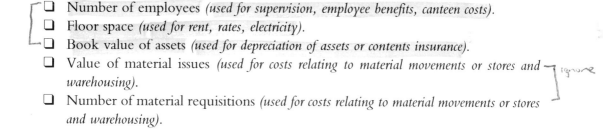

- ❑ Number of employees *(used for supervision, employee benefits, canteen costs).*
- ❑ Floor space *(used for rent, rates, electricity).*
- ❑ Book value of assets *(used for depreciation of assets or contents insurance).*
- ❑ Value of material issues *(used for costs relating to material movements or stores and warehousing).*
- ❑ Number of material requisitions *(used for costs relating to material movements or stores and warehousing).*

The basis of apportioning costs to various departments is a matter of opinion and there is no single best objective method to use. There may be a number of options available for a particular overhead cost. Supervision, for example, could be apportioned based on the number of employees or labour hours or even floor space. The nature of super-vision within the organisation should be examined and, depending on what drives the cost, the most appropriate base would be chosen. Floor space, for example, could be chosen for a supervisor in a retail outlet whose role is to ensure that the shop floor was operating adequately, with shelves stocked, staff working efficiently, and customer needs being served. If the supervisor role solely involved staff issues, then the number of employees or the total labour hours would be more appropriate.

Example 3.1: *Apportioning overhead cost*

Fashion Retailing Ltd sells clothing from a city centre location. Management have identified four departments.

The following cost information is available:

	Men's Clothing	Women's Clothing	Children's Clothing	Footwear	Total
	€	€	€	€	€
Direct materials	390,000	295,000	270,000	135,000	600,000
Direct labour	120,000	96,000	195,000	69,000	480,000
Indirect labour	16,750	12,250	12,050	7,450	48,500
Electricity	10,000	25,000	10,000	5,000	50,000
Rent and rates					70,000
Personnel costs					35,000
Depreciation of assets					18,000
Insurance of assets					45,000

(handwritten margin notes: F.A., F.A., N.O.S, F.A.V)

Other information:

	Men's Clothing	Women's Clothing	Children's Clothing	Footwear	Total
Floor area (square metres)	600	1,500	600	300	3,000
Number of staff members	11	9	7	8	35
Fixed asset value	€1.5m	€3.5m	€0.9m	€.1m	€6m

Prepare an overhead statement apportioning the overhead costs to each department.

Approach

It is important to realise that only overhead items (indirect costs) appear in an overhead statement, therefore direct material and direct labour costs are excluded. As the choice of base for apportioning is subjective, it is important to state the base used in apportioning the overhead item.

Overhead Statement

	Basis	Men's Clothing	Women's Clothing	Children's Clothing	Footwear	Total
		€	€	€	€	€
Indirect labour	Provided	16,750	12,250	12,050	7,450	48,500
Electricity	Area	10,000	25,000	10,000	5,000	50,000
Rates	Area	14,000	35,000	14,000	7,000	70,000
Personnel costs	Staff	11,000	9,000	7,000	8,000	35,000
Depreciation	Value	4,500	10,500	2,700	300	18,000
Plant insurance	Value	11,250	26,250	6,750	750	45,000
Total overhead		67,500	118,000	52,500	28,500	266,500

Workings

	Basis	Men's Clothing	Women's Clothing	Children's Clothing	Footwear	Total
		€	€	€	€	€
Electricity (€16.67 per sq m)	Area	50,000÷3,000 x 600 = 10,000	50,000÷3,000 x 1,500 = 25,000	50,000÷3,000 x 600 = 10,000	50,000÷3,000 x 300 = 5,000	50,000
Rates (€23.33 sq m)	Area	70,000÷3,000 x 600 = 14,000	70,000÷3,000 x 1,500 = 35,000	70,000÷3,000 x 600 = 14,000	70,000÷3,000 x 300 = 7,000	70,000
Personnel costs (€1,000 per person)	Staff	35,000÷35 x 11= 11,000	35,000÷35 x 9= 9,000	35,000÷35 x 7= 7,000	35,000÷35 x 8= 8,000	35,000
Depreciation (€0.003 per €)	Value	18,000÷6 x 1.5= 4,500	18,000÷6 x 3.5= 10,500	18,000÷6 x 0.9= 2,700	18,000÷6 x 0.1= 300	18,000
Plant insurance (€0.0075 per €)	Value	45,000÷6 x 1.5= 11,250	45,000÷6 x 3.5= 26,250	45,000÷6 x 0.9= 6,750	45,000÷6 x 0.1= 750	45,000

Absorption Costing

Cost unit = Unit which we sell

Absorption costing (overhead recovery) can be explained as the process whereby the overheads of the various cost centres are added to cost units or jobs. Absorption costing is the traditional approach to charging overhead costs to cost units. It is particularly relevant in manufacturing organisations as they must include a relevant proportion of production overhead in stock valuation. Absorption costing can be explained as a process for sharing out the overhead costs of each cost centre to each product or service that is provided by that cost centre. The following steps can be used in applying absorption costing:

Steps in absorption costing

1. Apportion all overheads to cost centres.

2. Identify the support or service cost centres, and re-apportion the costs of these to the cost centres involved in producing the products or services.

3. Calculate the overhead absorption rate (OAR) for each cost centre involved in producing products or services, using the most appropriate base.

4. Use the OAR to establish the overhead cost per unit.

Step 1 – Apportion overhead to each cost centre

An absorption costing approach requires the identification of cost centres. These cost centres can be directly involved in providing the product or service, or they can be support or service cost centres like warehousing or maintenance. The first step involves the allocation and apportionment of overhead costs to each cost centre that has been identified. This was demonstrated in example 3.1 above.

Step 2 – Re-apportion support or service centre costs

Some businesses may have service departments such as canteen, sports facilities, maintenance, and administration, which do not produce any products and are not related to any income-producing activity. In keeping with the whole concept of responsibility accounting, these departments are allowed to accumulate and account for their costs separately. This ensures the department manager is responsible for the costs that have occurred in his department. However for the purposes of calculating a full cost of a product, these service department costs must also be absorbed into the unit cost of a product. Thus they must be apportioned to the various departments producing the products or services. Failure to do this will result in overheads not being absorbed into the cost of a product resulting in overhead absorption rates that are too low. The apportionment of service departments should be on an appropriate basis, usually on the principle of the 'greatest benefit'. In other words the department that gets the greatest benefit from the service or support centre would be assigned most of the actual cost. Once the service department costs have been assigned to the revenue producing departments (added to the indirect costs already assigned to these departments), the focus is moved to calculating an overhead absorption rate.

Example 3.2: *Re-apportioning service centre costs*

FunZone Limited operates a busy complex providing ten pin bowling, snooker and an outdoor adventure maze. Cost centres have been established for each of the key activities provided. In addition to the three cost centres there are two support centres for administration and maintenance. Overhead cost has been apportioned to each of the cost centres as follows:

	Bowling	Snooker	Maze	Admin.	Maintenance	Total
Total overhead	€362,000	€187,000	€245,000	€96,000	€78,000	€968,000

It is policy to re-apportion the cost of maintenance using maintenance hours, and administration using revenue earned. The following information is available for the period:

	Bowling	Snooker	Maze	Total
Maintenance time	2,600 hours	1,000 hours	1,400 hours	5,000 hours
Revenue earned	€450,000	€230,000	€320,000	€1,000,000

You are required to re-apportion the costs of the two service centres.

Approach

Overhead Re-apportionment

	Bowling	Snooker	Maze	Admin.	Maintenance	Total
Total overhead	€362,000	€187,000	€245,000	€96,000	€78,000	€968,000
Administration	€43,200	€22,080	€30,720	(€96,000)		€0
Maintenance	€40,560	€15,600	€21,840		(€78,000)	€0
Total overhead	€445,760	€224,680	€297,560	€0	€0	€968,000

Workings for re-apportionment of administration:

	Bowling	Snooker	Maze
Administration is re-apportioned using revenue earned	€43,200	€22,080	€30,720
	€96,000 ÷ €1,000,000 x €450,000	*€96,000 ÷ €1,000,000 x €230,000*	*€96,000 ÷ €1,000,000 x €320,000*

Workings for re-apportionment of maintenance:

	Bowling	Snooker	Maze
Maintenance is re-apportioned using maintenance hours	€40,560	€15,600	€21,840
	€78,000 ÷ 5,000 hrs x 2,600 hrs	*€78,000 ÷ 5,000 hrs x 1,000 hrs*	*€78,000 ÷ 5,000 hrs x 1,400 hours*

When service centre costs are being re-apportioned, it is important to investigate and establish if any of the service centres provide a service to the other service centres. A service centre that provides a service to another service centre should be re-apportioned first. A typical example would be where the human resource centre provides a support service for customer services and warehousing by providing employees and supporting the employees. Example 3.4 illustrates this point.

The apportionment of overhead and the subsequent re-apportionment of service centre costs provides useful management information which can be used for monitoring, control and performance appraisal at cost centre or department level. If an organisation wishes to establish the total cost of a product or service (including overhead), one further step is required. This is the establishment of an overhead absorption rate.

Step 3 – Establishing an overhead absorption rate

This step involves the establishment of an overhead absorption rate that allows the overhead cost of a product or service to be calculated. The calculation of an overhead absorption rate requires two variables:

❑ The total overhead attributable to a cost centre.
❑ The absorption base.

Formula for overhead absorption rate

$$\frac{\text{Cost centre overhead}}{\text{Absorption base}} = \text{Overhead absorption rate (OAR)}$$	

[handwritten notes at top:] O/H Dept = 100,000
No. of units = 10,000
O. A.R = €10
O/H cost/unit = €10.
overhead absorption rate.

The absorption base is used to share overhead to the cost unit. There are six possible bases to choose from.

1. Number of units *some product*	Should only be used if all products are similar or if the level of service is similar to all customers.
2. Direct machine (operating) hours *no. of machine staff hours machinery*	May be more suitable than the number of units if there is a significant difference in the time taken to produce the various products or services.
3. Direct labour hours *labour*	Can be used in labour intensive situations.
4. Percentage direct labour cost	Can be used in labour intensive situations if all direct workers are paid similar wage rates.
5. Percentage direct material cost *not on exam*	Can be used when direct material is a significant proportion of total cost and appears to drive the overhead cost.
6. Percentage prime cost	Can be used when both direct material and direct labour are significant.

The absorption base chosen should best reflect how overhead is incurred. For example, in labour intensive areas, overhead may consist of a significant proportion of costs that relate to people, while in a machine intensive area, overhead is likely to include a high proportion of costs related to the use of the machinery such as, machine depreciation, power and insurance.

Example 3.3: *Overhead absorption rates*

Protective Gear Limited is a small retail organisation selling protective clothing to builders. The company is currently making a loss and is reviewing accounting procedures. The following information relates to the three products sold by the company:

	Selling price	Purchase cost	Numbers sold
Hard hats	€16	€10	12,000
Shoes	€60	€35	10,000
Luminous vests	€5	€2	18,000
			40,000

Total overhead for the period in question amounted to €200,000. The owner considers that both the number of units, and a rate based on the percentage of material cost, are equally suitable as a basis to absorb overheads to the three products and is not sure which is the best to adopt.

a) *Calculate an overhead absorption rate based on number of units.*
b) *Calculate an overhead absorption rate based on the percentage of material cost.*

Approach

a) Overhead absorption rate based on the number of units.

$$\frac{\text{Overhead €200,000}}{\text{40,000 units}} = \text{€5 per unit}$$

This approach is very simple as total overhead is divided by the total number of units sold.

b) Overhead absorption rate based on a percentage of material cost.

	Purchase cost	Numbers sold	
Hard hats	€10	12,000	€120,000
Shoes	€35	10,000	€350,000
Luminous vests	€2	18,000	€36,000
			€506,000

$$\frac{\text{Overhead €200,000}}{\text{Materials €506,000}} = \ 39.5\% \text{ of material cost}$$

This approach requires the calculation of the total cost of purchases. The total overhead is divided by the total purchase cost and multiplied by 100 to establish the percentage. Overhead is charged to each product by taking the purchase cost of the item and multiplying by 39.5%.

Step 4 – Establishing the overhead cost per unit

Once the overhead absorption rate is established then the total cost of a product or service can be calculated. This can be demonstrated by using the data from example 3.3 above.

Total cost and profit using OAR based on the number of units

	Hats	Shoes	Vests
Material cost	€10.00	€35.00	€2.00
Overhead cost	€5.00	€5.00	€5.00
Total cost	€15.00	€40.00	€7.00
Selling price	€16.00	€60.00	€5.00
Profit	€1.00	€20.00	(€2.00)

When the number of units is used as a base, the overhead cost per unit will be identical for each product. It is therefore important to use this approach only when all units are similar in relation to how overhead is consumed. Hats and shoes for example will require more storage space compared to vests. Shoes and hard hats may require complex measuring and fitting before the sale, unlike vests. Vests are incurring the same amount of overhead cost as hats and shoes when the number of units is used as a base. This would seem an inappropriate overhead burden for vests and thus at the present selling price, vests are incurring a loss of €2 each.

Total cost and profit using OAR based on a percentage of material cost

	Hats	Shoes	Vests
Material cost	€10.00	€35.00	€2.00
Overhead cost 39.5%	€3.95	€13.83	€0.79
Total cost	€13.95	€48.83	€2.79
Selling price	€16.00	€60.00	€5.00
Profit	€2.05	€11.17	€2.21

If the percentage of material cost is used, the overhead cost is shared based on the purchase cost of the goods sold. In a retail setting this may be considered appropriate because many overheads, such as storage costs, insurance and security of products, are related to the materials cost. It is therefore appropriate to use percentage of direct material cost if costs such as storage, insurance and security of products are a high proportion of overhead cost. In a manufacturing setting, it is unlikely to be appropriate and direct labour hours or direct machine hours would be more suitable.

The two examples above show that the total cost and resulting profit per unit may vary significantly depending on the base chosen. Management should be aware that the apportionment and absorption of overhead is a subjective process and does not provide a 'true' cost. Costing information based on absorption costing principles should not be solely relied upon in decision-making.

It is important to clearly see the process of establishing the overhead cost of a unit of product using absorption costing. The diagram below illustrates the process.

Diagram 3.2: *The absorption process*

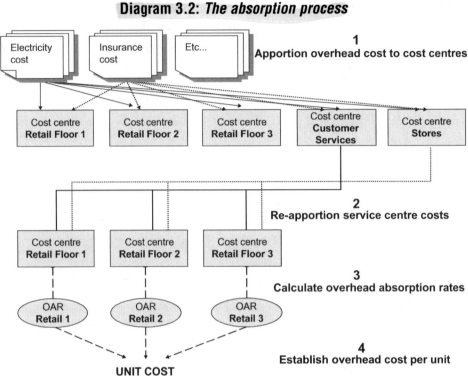

The steps explained above will now be applied to one example to show the full approach.

Example 3.4: Absorption Costing

The Manor Country Lodge provides four star hotel accommodation with full amenities including a modern leisure complex. Six cost centres have been identified for accounting purposes comprising accommodation, restaurant, bar, leisure complex, administration and facilities management. Administration and facilities management are both treated as support service centres. Facilities management also provides a support to the administration department.

	Accommodation	Restaurant	Bar	Leisure complex	Admin.	Facilities management
Indirect labour	€220,000	€99,000	€44,000	€110,000	€28,000	€49,000

Overheads yet to be apportioned:

Electricity and gas	€10,000
Building insurance	€55,000
Employee benefits	€50,000
Asset depreciation	€400,000

Other information available for use in apportioning overhead cost:

	Floor space (square metres)	Number of employees	Value of assets	Administration split
Accommodation	3,000	5	€4.4 m	50%
Restaurant	600	12	€0.8m	20%
Bar	300	6	€0.4m	5%
Leisure complex	900	7	€1.6m	25%
Administration	200	5	€0.6m	-
Facilities management	-	15	€0.2m	-
Total	5,000	50	€8.0m	100%

Cost unit

Occupied bed nights	23,445 bed nights
Meals served	45,348 meals
Drinks purchased	136,280 drinks
Client hours	29,895 leisure hours

a) Calculate overhead absorption rates for the four main cost centres.
b) Establish the overhead cost to be included in a quotation to a travel agent for a mid-week special that includes:
❏ Three bed nights.
❏ Two evening meals.
❏ One glass of champagne in the bar.
❏ Five hours in the leisure centre.

Approach

Part a) The steps explained above should be used to establish the overhead rates. As the choice for apportioning overhead is subjective, you should always indicate clearly the base used.

Manor Country Lodge Overhead Statement

Step 1: Apportion overhead to each cost centre

	Basis	Accom. €	Restaurant €	Bar €	Leisure complex €	Admin. €	Facilities management €	Total €
Overhead already apportioned	Given	220,000	99,000	44,000	110,000	28,000	49,000	550,000
Electricity and gas	Floor	6,000	1,200	600	1,800	400	0	10,000
Building insurance	Floor	33,000	6,600	3,300	9,900	2,200	0	55,000
Employee benefits	Employees	5,000	12,000	6,000	7,000	5,000	15,000	50,000
Asset depreciation	Value	220,000	40,000	20,000	80,000	30,000	10,000	400,000
Total overhead		484,000	158,800	73,900	208,700	65,600	74,000	1,065,000

Step 2: Re-apportion support service centre costs

	Basis	Accom. €	Restaurant €	Bar €	Leisure complex €	Admin. €	Facilities management €	Total €
Facilities management	Floor	44,400	8,880	4,440	13,320	2,960	(74,000)	0
						68,560		
Administration	Percentage	34,280	13,712	3,428	17,140	(68,560)	0	0
Total overhead		562,680	181,392	81,768	239,160	0	0	1,065,000

Note: As the administration department provides services to facilities management, the overhead for facilities management is apportioned between the various departments including administration before the administration overheads are apportioned.

Step 3: Establish an overhead absorption rate

Calculating an overhead absorption rate requires the total overhead for each cost centre and an appropriate base for each cost centre. The total overhead for each cost centre was calculated in step 2 above. The details provided in the Manor Country Lodge example itemised the number of cost units produced by each cost centre. This can be used to calculate the overhead absorption rates for each area.

	Accommodation	Restaurant	Bar	Leisure complex
Cost centre overhead	€562,680	€181,392	€81,786	€239,160
Number of units	23,445 nights	45,348 meals	136,280 drinks	29,895 leisure hours
	= €24 per night	= €4 per meal	= €0.60 per drink	= €8 per leisure hour

Part b) (example 3.4) Overhead cost for travel agents quotation.

		€
Three bed nights	3 x €24	72.00
Two evening meals	2 x €4	8.00
One glass of champagne in the bar	1 x €0.60	0.60
Five hours in the leisure centre	5 x €8	40.00
Total overhead		120.60

Note: The €120.60 established above only covers overhead cost. Direct costs must be included in the quotation. Direct costs would include those associated with the room (cleaning and laundry), meals and the champagne.

Further Aspects to Absorption Costing

Price thought of in beginning of the year.

An overhead absorption rate is calculated by dividing total overheads by an appropriate activity level (units or machine hours or direct labour hours). If actual rates are to be calculated, then it is not possible to calculate the rates until the end of the accounting period when the total figures have been established. However for pricing purposes, management may need to know the full cost of a product or service } *Important* during the accounting period, before actual overheads and the actual activity level can be established. To overcome this problem, a predetermined overhead absorption rate can be calculated at the start of a period (based on budgeted figures) to estimate the full cost of a product or service. A predetermined overhead absorption rate can help management estimate the full cost of a product or service during the year to help ensure pricing is accurate.

Estimate / Plannic Figure

Using predetermined overhead absorption rates

Predetermined overhead absorption rates are based on budgeted figures. If a predetermined rate is used, the overhead cost per unit is calculated prior to the accounting period, using budgeted figures for overheads and units of activity.

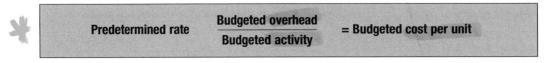

Predetermined rate $\dfrac{\text{Budgeted overhead}}{\text{Budgeted activity}}$ = Budgeted cost per unit

In the Manor Country Lodge (example 3.4 above), the budgeted cost of accommodation and the budgeted number of occupied bed nights would be established. The budgeted overhead cost per occupied bed night would be found by dividing the budgeted overhead cost by the budgeted number of occupied bed nights.

Example 3.5: *Predetermined overhead absorption rates*

City Guides Limited is a successful business which provides professional tour guides to the tourist industry. Budgets for the coming year indicate that overhead will amount to €100,000. As the service is labour intensive, direct labour hours is considered to be the most appropriate absorption base and it is forecast that direct labour hours will total 20,000 in the year.

Calculate the predetermined overhead absorption rate.

Approach

The predetermined overhead absorption rate would be calculated as follows:

$$\frac{\text{Budgeted overhead}}{\text{Budgeted labour hours}} \quad \frac{€100,000}{20,000} \quad = €5 \text{ per labour hour}$$

This means that in addition to direct costs, €5 per labour hour will be charged to each client.

Under- or over-recovery of overhead

Because the overhead cost per unit is based on estimates, it is almost inevitable that at the end of the accounting year there will have been an under-recovery or over-recovery of the overhead actually incurred. The estimates for both overhead and activity level are unlikely to be the same as what actually occurred. In an absorption costing system where the predetermined cost per unit is charged in the accounting records, it is necessary to check the amount under- or over-recovered (charged) and make an adjustment in the accounts.

To check under- or over-absorption

	€
Actual overhead cost for the period compared to	XXX
Overhead charged for the period (actual hours or units x predetermined rate)	XXX
Difference is the under- or over-recovery	XXX

Example 3.6: Under- or over-recovery of overhead

Actual overhead for City Guides Limited amounted to €106,500 and the actual direct labour hours amounted to 21,000 hours. The company were absorbing overhead at a predetermined overhead rate of €5 per direct labour hour (see example 3.5 above).

Calculate the amount of under- or over-recovery of overhead that occurred.

Approach

The amount under- or over-absorbed is found by taking the absorbed overhead (the actual labour hours worked by the predetermined overhead rate) from the actual overhead cost.

Actual overhead cost	€106,500
Absorbed overhead (21,000 hours x €5)	€105,000
Under-absorbed (recovered)	€1,500

Both the actual overhead and actual activity level were higher than the estimates resulting in a lower charge against profit for overhead than what was required. An adjustment for the under-recovered amount of €1,500 should be charged in the profit statement, reducing the profit figure. The opposite would apply with over-absorbed overhead.

Arguments in favour of absorption costing: *advantages*

Important!

❏ Absorption costing recognises that selling price must cover all costs incurred. If absorption costing is used, then organisations should ensure that all costs are included when setting selling prices.

AB costing requires the absorptionment of overhead to dept. thus, insuring each department manager is aware of the level of overhead associated with his department, which helps in the control of OH.

❑   Production cannot be achieved without incurring overheads. Therefore all such costs should be included in stock valuations. This is in accordance with the requirements of the accounting standard (SSAP 9) which requires that production cost should include all costs incurred (including fixed overhead) in bringing the product to its current condition and location.

❑   Absorption costing recognises the importance of working at full capacity. The under- and over-absorption (recovery) explained above can focus attention on the cost effect of actual activity being different to the budget or capacity levels established prior to the period. If an organisation fails to work to full capacity, then the overhead cost per unit may be higher than necessary. This is because overhead cost is charged out to fewer units.

Arguments against the use of absorption costing:

❑   Absorption costing involves the apportionment of overhead, which can be subjective. The resulting information can be misleading for management decision-making.

❑   Profits can be manipulated in a manufacturing organisation by simply increasing production without actually selling the additional items. Because fixed overhead is included in stock valuation, increasing production without increasing sales will result in a higher closing stock figure and hence a lower cost of sales and a higher profit figure. Fixed overhead is transferred from the current period's cost (reducing costs in the profit statements) to a future period. Although this approach complies with accounting concepts, it may encourage management to build excessive stock levels to achieve a short-term profit increase.

Blanket or Single Rate Approach

A company can take the simplistic view of choosing a single overhead absorption base for the entire organisation, one which is most reflective of the organisation's activity. This is known as using a blanket overhead absorption rate or a single factory-wide rate. This is a simplistic approach and not very accurate. If the organisation invests the time in developing a more sophisticated approach by identifying all the cost centres involved and calculating an overhead absorption rate for each cost centre, a more accurate share of overhead may be charged to each product or service, as shown in example 3.4. The cost of the more sophisticated approach needs to be evaluated against the benefits it can bring.

Advantages of a single rate approach

❑   A single rate is quicker to calculate than separate departmental (cost centre) rates.

❑   It avoids the need for any arbitrary apportionment of overheads to departments or cost centres.

❑ It can be quicker and easier to monitor and control as one person can be made responsible for monitoring any under- or over-recovery of overheads.

Disadvantages of a single rate approach

❑ A single rate takes no account of the different nature of operations in different departments. For example, some departments may be machine intensive and others may be labour intensive. This is the main drawback to using the single rate approach. Thus the overhead recovery rate will not be accurate and for pricing purposes, products can be under- or over-priced.

❑ The incidence of overheads may be different in each department and this is not reflected in a single rate. For example, a department may contain expensive machines and therefore incur more depreciation cost than another department without machines. The cost of products produced using the more expensive machinery will be understated while products produced using less expensive machinery will be overstated. Thus the cost figures produced will not be accurate.

❑ Some products or services may not require effort from every department or cost centre. Alternatively, some products may require more effort in some departments than in others. A single rate fails to reflect these differing burdens which products place on facilities. If a single rate is used, the cost of products may not be accurate. The cost of products that involve a smaller number of cost centres or less department effort will be overstated.

❑ Separate departmental costing rates facilitate the division of responsibility for the control of overhead costs. This division of responsibility becomes more difficult with a single rate.

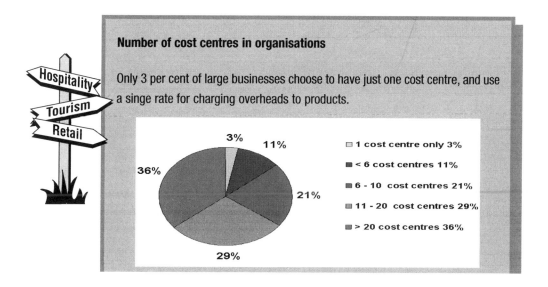

Number of cost centres in organisations

Only 3 per cent of large businesses choose to have just one cost centre, and use a singe rate for charging overheads to products.

3% 11%
36%
21%
29%

▫ 1 cost centre only 3%
▪ < 6 cost centres 11%
▪ 6 - 10 cost centres 21%
▪ 11 - 20 cost centres 29%
▪ > 20 cost centres 36%

Hospitality
Tourism
Retail

> For organisations that develop the cost centre approach, the number of cost centres established varies quite significantly.
>
> Source: Drury C. and Tayles M. (2000)
>
> Research by Luby (2006) found that retail outlets responded differently to the businesses surveyed by Drury and Tayles. In Irish retail outlets, between 11 and 20 cost centres is the most common occurrence with over 44 per cent of respondents indicating this range. 33 per cent of respondents reported more than 20 cost centres. No respondents reported only one cost centre.

Activity Based Costing

In the late 1980s Professors Cooper and Kaplan of Harvard University criticised the traditional approaches to dealing with overheads and in particular the absorption costing approach. The main focus of the criticisms was that the most popular bases for recovering overheads, namely direct labour hours and direct machine hours, had little relevance to overhead and the complexity of the modern business environment. The concept of Activity Based Costing (ABC) was presented as a superior alternative to dealing with overhead cost. ABC is based on the concept that it is the activities involved in providing a product or service that incur cost. It is therefore more accurate to charge overhead cost based on the amount of activity consumed when the product or service is provided. It was argued that the ABC approach is more reflective and accurate, as it identifies each activity that occurs in an organisation and charges overhead to each product on the basis of its consumption, or use, of each activity. The objective of activity based costing is to arrive at a more accurate product cost. This is achieved by assigning overhead cost to the activities carried out within the organisation and then relating how often these activities occur for each product or service produced.

Implementing ABC

Since an ABC system is generally more complex and sophisticated than traditional approaches, the decision to implement an ABC system is significant. A detailed cost benefit analysis should be carried out before a commitment to the introduction of ABC is given. It is important that senior management buy into the system from the onset and encourage its implementation throughout the organisation. It is essential that the resources necessary for implementation of the new system are made available. This includes the finance to purchase software, consultancy, training and if necessary, the hire of additional accounting staff for the implementation period.

Diagram 3.3: *Implementing ABC*

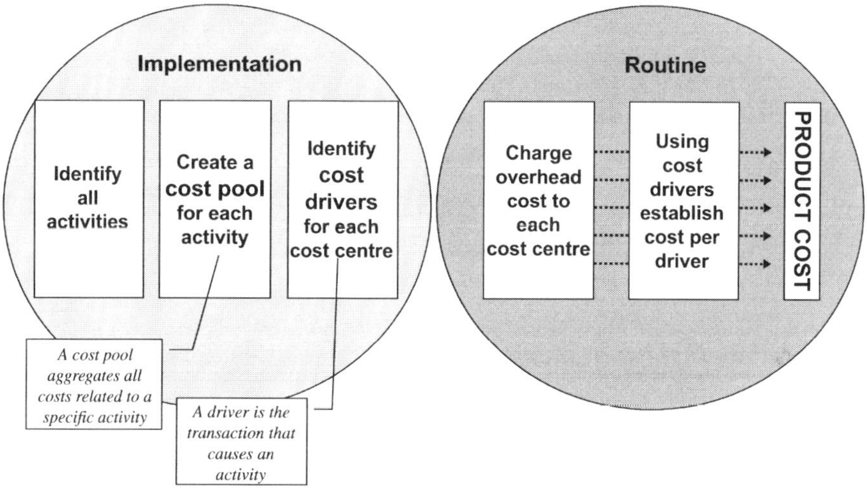

The implementation of an ABC approach requires a thorough examination of the organisation to identify every activity that occurs. A cost pool is created for each activity and the most suitable cost driver is established. The terms 'cost pools' and 'cost drivers' are central in explaining the concept.

The costs associated with each activity are gathered together in cost pools for each activity. Cost pools are similar in principle to cost centres in traditional systems. However, cost pools relate to activities regardless of conventional departmental boundaries. A cost pool should be created for each activity identified. All costs relating to the activity will be pooled together accumulating the total cost of the activity. Examples of three separate cost pools in a hotel setting could include room reservations, check-ins and luggage handling. It is evident that there will be many more cost pools than traditional cost centres. Each traditional cost centre may have a number of different activities, each requiring a separate cost pool.

The key idea behind ABC is to focus attention on those factors that cause or drive costs. These factors are known as cost drivers. A cost driver is the event and factors that cause an activity to occur and to consume resources. Examples of cost drivers could be, in a hotel, the number of reservations made that drives reservation costs, or the number of customers checked in that drives check-in costs.

Once the design of an ABC system is complete, the steps in relating overhead costs to cost units are as follows:

ABC steps in calculating overhead cost per unit

1. Apportion all overheads to cost pools.
2. Calculate cost driver rates for each cost pool.
3. Establish the overhead cost per unit.

Step 1 – Apportion all overheads to cost pools

In the same way as overheads are apportioned to cost centres under absorption costing, overheads must be apportioned to cost pools under activity based costing. The
process of apportionment is the same as under absorption costing. Each cost pool
accumulates the total cost of the related activity.

Step 2 – Calculate cost driver rates for each cost pool

The ABC approach requires a cost driver rate to be established for each cost pool.
The total cost of each cost pool should be divided by the cost driver assigned to that
pool to establish the rate. For example, in a health club setting, a fitness examination
could be identified as an activity cost pool and the cost driver could be the minutes
spent checking clients. The total cost assigned to the fitness examination cost pool is
divided by the total number of minutes spent checking clients to establish a rate per
minute for fitness examinations.

Example 3.7: *ABC cost pools and cost drivers*

The management team of Mathews Stores Limited are investigating the feasibility of
implementing ABC. The customer services area has been selected to pilot the
approach. The overhead costs have already been apportioned to the cost pools identified. The following cost pools, costs and drivers have been established:

Activity cost pool	Cost	Driver
Phone enquiries	€2,800	Number of calls received = 3,240
Examining returned stock	€4,400	Number of items examined = 4,450
Returning stock to shelves	€3,900	Number of items returned to shelves = 4,000
Processing refunds	€2,400	Number of refunds generated = 2,300
Handling exchanges	€1,000	Number of exchanges = 2,150
Investigating other complaints	€6,800	Number of other complaints = 1,200
Total overhead	**€21,300**	

You are required to calculate cost driver rates for each cost pool using the drivers identified.

Approach

The cost of each cost pool is divided by the relevant driver to establish each rate.

Activity cost pool	Cost		Driver		Rate per cost driver
Phone enquiries	€2,800	÷	3,240	=	€0.86
Examining returned stock	€4,400	÷	4,450	=	€0.99
Returning stock to shelves	€3,900	÷	4,000	=	€0.98
Processing refunds	€2,400	÷	2,300	=	€1.04
Handling exchanges	€1,000	÷	2,150	=	€0.47
Investigating other complaints	€6,800	÷	1,200	=	€5.67

Step 3 – Establish the overhead cost per unit

Once the rate per cost driver is established, each product or service can then be charged with overhead using the level of activity required by the product or service. For example, in the health club setting discussed above, the overhead charged for a fitness examination will be based on the number of minutes taken to check an individual client multiplied by the cost per minute (cost driver rate).

Example 3.8: *ABC to establish unit cost*

Ultimate Experience Limited operates a chain of five star health farms offering a complete range of alternative health and relaxation experiences. The management accountant has used the massage room as a pilot for the development of a new ABC system. Each activity carried out in the area has been identified and a cost pool has been created for each. Suitable cost drivers have been identified. Overhead has been apportioned and the following rates established:

Processing bookings	35 cent per booking
Taking client details and consent	75 cent per form
Preparing room	€1.20 per session
Applying detox material	€2.30 per session
Massage	30 cent per minute
Remove detox material	€1.80 per session

Demonstrate how the system can be used to calculate the total overhead cost associated with offering a client three massage sessions. The actual massage time chosen by the client is 30 minutes for each session. The client details and consent are taken once during the stay and kept on file. Assume three separate bookings are made.

Approach

The client requires three sessions, so each activity is multiplied by three, except for taking client details. The cost of the massage is driven by the minutes of massage time.

Massage cost

Processing bookings	3 x €0.35	€1.05
Taking client details and consent	1 x €0.75	€0.75
Prepare room	3 x €1.20	€3.60
Apply detox material	3 x €2.30	€6.90
Massage	3 x 30 minutes x €0.30	€27.00
Remove detox material	3 x €1.80	€5.40
Total		€44.70

It is important to clearly see the process of establishing the overhead cost of a unit of product or service using ABC. The diagram below illustrates the process in a retail setting.

Diagram 3.4: *The ABC process*

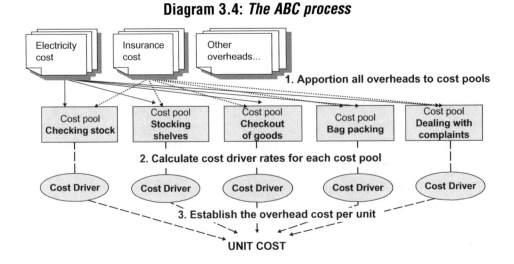

The steps explained above will now be applied to an example to show more clearly how the approach works.

Example 3.9: *The ABC approach*

Quality Pictures Limited operates a successful retail outlet providing framed, high quality reproductions of original paintings by leading artists. The customer chooses from a range of pictures and has a choice of three frame sizes. An activity based costing system is in operation.

The apportionment of overhead costs to each cost pool has already been carried out producing the following costs:

Activity cost pools	€
Order processing	22,500
Material movement	34,200
Set-up time	33,000
Printing	28,512
Framing	60,000
Quality checks	10,325
	188,537

The following cost driver details have been accumulated for the period under review:

	Total
Number of pictures ordered	2,500
Direct material cost	€57,000
Number of set-ups	6,000
Printing time (minutes)	35,640
Number of frames	2,500
Quality checking time (minutes)	7,375

The following details have been established for each frame size:

	Size 1	Size 2	Size 3
Sales price	€80.00	€130.00	€130.00
Number of orders per picture	1	1	1
Direct material cost per picture	€15	€24	€30
Number of set-ups per picture	1	3	3
Printing time (minutes)	10	15	18
Number of frames	1	1	1
Minutes spent checking quality	2	3	4

Using activity based costing, calculate the overhead cost for each frame size.

Approach

Step 1: Apportion overhead cost to cost pools.
This has been completed and given in the example, so it is necessary to start at the second step.

Step 2: Calculate the cost driver rates for each cost pool.
The total cost of each cost pool is divided by the total for each driver.

Order processing	€22,500	÷	2,500	=	€9 per order
Material movement	€34,200	÷	€57,000	=	€0.60 per €
Set-up time	€33,000	÷	6,000	=	€5.50 per set-up
Printing	€28,512	÷	35,640	=	€0.80 per minute
Framing	€60,000	÷	2,500	=	€24 per frame
Quality testing	€10,325	÷	7,375	=	€1.40 per minute

Step 3: Establish the overhead cost per unit.
This is achieved by multiplying the unit data for each frame by the cost driver rates established in step 2 above.

Overhead cost details

		€	€	€
Order processing	(€9 per order)	9.00	9.00	9.00
Material movement	(€0.60 per € material cost)	9.00	14.40	18.00
Set-up time	(€5.50 per set-up)	5.50	16.50	16.50
Printing	(€0.80 per minute)	8.00	12.00	14.40
Framing	(€24 per frame)	24.00	24.00	24.00
Quality testing	(€1.40 per minute)	2.80	4.20	5.60
Total overhead cost		58.30	80.10	87.50

As stated above, ABC can help in pricing decisions. The profitability of each frame size can be examined. The figures presented below assume that direct material cost is the only direct cost incurred in the operation.

	Size 1	Size 2	Size 3
	€	€	€
Sales price	80.00	130.00	180.00
Direct material cost	15.00	24.00	30.00
Overhead cost	58.30	80.10	87.50
Profit	6.70	25.90	62.50
Profit margin	8.4%	19.9%	34.7%

More than a product costing system

ABC was developed to overcome the limitations in traditional methods of dealing with overheads. But ABC is more than a product costing system. It provides a revolutionary approach to cost control by analysing costs based on activities rather than traditional departmental boundaries. Management attention focuses now on the activities required and their cost. Unnecessary activities can be eliminated and costly activities examined with a view to significantly reducing costs. While ABC was initially popular in manufacturing due to its provision of superior product costs and stock valuations, the cost control aspect has resulted in many service organisations also implementing ABC systems.

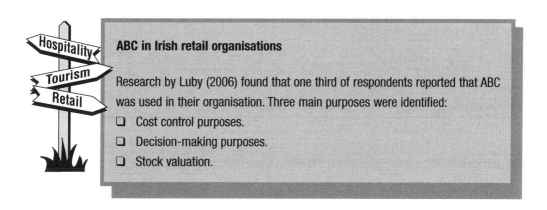

ABC in Irish retail organisations

Research by Luby (2006) found that one third of respondents reported that ABC was used in their organisation. Three main purposes were identified:
- ❏ Cost control purposes.
- ❏ Decision-making purposes.
- ❏ Stock valuation.

Advantages of ABC

ABC, if implemented correctly, can provide more accurate information on overhead and product costs than absorption costing. Accurate cost information can help an organisation gain competitive advantage and compete successfully in a competitive environment. The main benefits associated with ABC are:

❑ Product costs produced by an ABC system should be more accurate than those produced by an absorption costing system.

❑ ABC is approved as a method of valuing stock in accordance with accounting standards.

❑ ABC systems produce useful information for decision-making. As detailed costs of products or services are available, managers are provided with more information which informs and improves decision-making.

❑ As ABC systems focus on identifying activities in an organisation, unnecessary activities or activities that do not add value can be identified, adjusted, or eliminated, thus increasing efficiencies.

❑ The ABC approach provides a new emphasis on cost control by focusing attention on the cost of each activity.

❑ The ABC approach is useful in cost reduction programmes. A cost reduction programme involves a conscious decision to actively reduce the cost of specific activities or areas. As ABC provides information on activities and their related costs, costly activities can be highlighted and targeted.

Criticisms of ABC

While there are many prominent advocates for the ABC approach, there are notable criticisms that need to be considered.

❑ ABC systems are generally complex, difficult and expensive to implement.

❑ ABC systems can be time consuming and expensive to administer.

❑ An ABC system should not be introduced unless it can provide additional information which management can use to make better decisions. The information produced must be clear and unambiguous so that managers are willing to use it in decision-making.

❑ Where an organisation deals in similar products or provides a similar service level to all clients, ABC will provide little benefit as a costing system, because it produces similar costs to other simpler approaches. There may be some benefits from a cost control perspective.

❑ Some argue the merits of implementing ABC, questioning if it actually contributes to company profit or merely moves overhead costs from one product to another. They argue that total overhead is unlikely to change in the short-term. Advocates of the ABC approach would argue that enhanced information can improve decision-making and long-term profitability.

❑ It does not solve the problem of allocating all overhead. Overhead costs like electricity, insurance and rent still need to be apportioned. The process of sharing overhead costs to cost pools can be subjective.

❑ Complex situations may have multiple cost drivers. When establishing what drives the cost of an activity there may be more than one cost driver. Decisions have to be made and judgement is involved. This level of subjectivity can result in inaccurate information.

❑ If the approach is not applied properly it can result in a costly exercise with no significant benefits achieved.

❑ Developing appropriate cost pools and cost drivers can be difficult. If the design is flawed or the gathering of necessary data inaccurate, the outputs (product costs) will be misleading.

While ABC provides a more accurate and reflective product cost, it should be remembered that it does not provide the 'true' cost of a product or service. This is because overheads are shared costs that require apportionment. For example the rental cost of premises benefits all products or services produced in the building. Apportioning this overhead is always a subjective process no matter how sophisticated the system.

Summary

This chapter outlined the importance of dealing with overhead costs. It focused on two alternative approaches to dealing with overheads, namely absorption costing and the modern approach of activity based costing.

The main information points covered in this chapter are as follows:

❑ Overhead is the term applied to the total of all indirect costs (indirect material, indirect labour and indirect expenses). It represents the total cost incurred that cannot be traced directly to a specific cost unit as there is an element of sharing involved.

❑ A cost centre can be explained as a location, a person or an item of equipment for which costs can be ascertained. A cost unit is a quantitative unit of product or service in relation to which costs are ascertained.

❑ The process by which cost items are divided between several cost centres in a 'fair' proportion is referred to as 'apportioning overhead cost' or 'cost apportionment'.

❑ The costs of service centres not dealing in saleable units must first be re-apportioned before calculating overhead absorption rates.

❑ Absorption costing (overhead recovery) can be explained as the process whereby the overheads of the various cost centres are added to cost units or jobs.

❏ As the calculation of the overhead absorption rate requires figures for total overheads and the total of the activity level to be used as the base, an actual rate cannot be calculated until the end of a period. Often organisations choose to calculate a pre-determined rate based on budgeted figures at the start of a period. If a predetermined rate is used, the overhead cost per unit is calculated prior to the accounting period, using budgeted figures for both overheads and units of activity.

❏ Because the overhead cost per unit is based on estimates, it is almost inevitable that at the end of the accounting year there will have been an under-recovery or over-recovery of the overhead actually incurred.

❏ Activity based costing (ABC) is a modern costing approach which has the objective of establishing more accurate product costs. It assigns the costs of indirect and support resources to the specific products or services that benefit from these resources, based on the activities that incur the costs.

❏ The costs associated with each activity are gathered together in cost pools. Cost pools are similar in principle to cost centres in traditional systems. Costs are pooled, or collected, on the basis of the activity that drives the costs, regardless of conventional departmental boundaries. The key idea behind ABC is to focus attention on what factors cause or drive costs. These factors are known as 'cost drivers'.

❏ A cost driver is the event and factors which cause an activity to occur and to consume resources. The ABC approach requires the total cost of each cost pool to be divided by the cost driver assigned to that pool. Each product or service is then charged with overhead by its consumption/use of the activity driver.

Review Questions

Question 3.1

a) Explain the following terms:
  i. Overhead.
  ii. Cost centre.
  iii. Cost unit.
b) Explain why overheads may need to be apportioned and outline how this might be achieved.

Question 3.2

The following information relates to Heather's Department Stores Ltd for the year ended 30 June 2006.

Overhead cost not directly associated with any department	€'000
Rent	800
Electricity	150
Insurance	200
Administration	200
Personnel	80
Marketing costs	120
General expenses	50
Depreciation	10
Canteen costs	20

Floor [handwritten annotation beside Rent/Electricity/Insurance]

turnover [handwritten annotation beside Marketing costs/General expenses/Depreciation]

It is company policy to apportion overhead costs that cannot be attributed to any particular department as follows:

☐ Floor area should be used for rent, electricity and insurance.
☐ Turnover should be used for general expenses, marketing costs and depreciation.
☐ The number of employees should be used for administration, personnel and canteen costs.

The following details are available:

	Retail department 1	Retail department 2	Retail department 3	Total
Floor area (square metres)	5,000	6,000	4,000	15,000
Number of employees	20	15	5	40
Turnover	€2,100,000	€3,000,000	€1,200,000	€6,200,000

2,105,020

Required

Apportion the overhead cost to each of the three retail departments in Heather's Department Stores Ltd.

Question 3.3

You are employed as an accounts clerk at a local sports and leisure centre. The centre has been divided into five cost centres for accounting purposes.

Overheads already apportioned to:

Outdoor sports	€51,650
Indoor sports	€31,925
Swimming pool	€27,955
Administration services	€12,395
Computer services	€20,325

Overheads yet to be apportioned:

Light and heat	€10,000
Rent and rates	€2,500
Equipment depreciation	€6,000
Employee benefits	€4,500

Other information:

	Outdoor Sports	Indoor Sports	Swimming Pool	Admin. Services	Computer Services	Total
Floor space	5,000	1,500	2,500	500	500	10,000
Value equipment	€17,500	€17,500	€42,000	€63,000	€210,000	€350,000
Employees	20	10	5	10	5	50
% computer usage	25%	25%	25%	25%	-	100%
% admin. service usage	40%	25%	35%	-	-	100%

Required

Prepare an overhead statement, clearly showing the overhead apportioned to each cost centre and the re-apportionment of the two service centre costs (administration and computer services).

Question 3.4

a) What do you understand by the term 'overhead absorption rate'? Explain using a numerical illustration.
b) What are the main bases used when calculating overhead absorption rates?
c) Choose appropriate bases for the calculating of overhead absorption rates for the following business types:
  i.   Accounting services.
  ii. Hairdressers.
  iii. Automated manufacturing business.
  iv. Hotels.
  v.   Leisure centres.

Question 3.5

In addition to traditional requirements, the Garrymore Country Club provides access to a private health and fitness centre and a golf course. The golf course also accepts public bookings. The following overhead costs have already been apportioned to the cost centres below:

Accommodation	€1,276,550
Catering	€31,780
Health & fitness centre	€24,810
Golf course	€191,610
Administration	€145,100

Costs yet to be apportioned:

Power	€48,000
Insurance (assets)	€90,000
Asset depreciation	€225,000
Employee benefits	€135,000

Other information:

	Accommodation	Catering	Fitness centre	Golf course	Administration	Total
Number of employees	40	20	15	5	10	90
Floor area (buildings only)	1,400	500	800	200	300	3,200
Value of assets (€'000)	1,850	550	960	920	220	4,500
Administration split	50%	30%	10%	10%		
Expected customer usage	25,500 bed nights	21,500 meals	6,500 hourly sessions	9,000 rounds of golf		

(handwritten margin notes: "Not likely" beside Number of employees; "→" beside Floor area; "Not likely" beside Administration split)

Required

a) Prepare an overhead statement, clearly showing the overhead apportioned to each cost centre and the re-apportionment of the administration services centre costs.

b) Calculate overhead absorption rates based on expected customer usage.

c) Calculate the selling price to be quoted for a stag party booking requiring two nights accommodation, two evening meals, two rounds of golf and three hours at the fitness centre for each of eight guests. It is policy to have a profit margin of 40 per cent on group bookings.

Question 3.6

a) What is a pre-determined overhead absorption rate?

b) Why might overhead be under- or over-absorbed? Explain with a simple illustration.

Question 3.7

The Empire Hotel has been experiencing poor financial performance. Management wish to ascertain the full cost of the different services it provides. The hotel has three main cost centres dealing in saleable units; functions, accommodation and the restaurant. There are two service areas; maintenance and administration.

The following budgeted information is available for 2006:

Departments	Functions	Accommodation	Restaurant	Maintenance	Admin.	Total
Overheads *Floor*						€
Insurance of property *Floor*						21,000
Insurance (employer liability) *employees*						20,000
Heat and light *electricity*						40,000
Depreciation *value*						60,000
Advertising and prom. *sales*						40,000
Indirect labour	0	0	0	40,000	50,000	90,000
Indirect materials	0	0	0	30,000	20,000	50,000
Total overheads	0	66%	25%	8%		321,000

Additional Information:

	Functions	Accommodation	Restaurant	Maintenance	Admin.	Total
Electricity usage, kw hrs	6,000	7,000	3,000	1,000	3,000	20,000
Value of fixed assets, €	270,000	80,000	50,000	50,000	150,000	600,000
Floor area in square metres	1,000	400	200	500	900	3,000
Maintenance hours	4,000	1,500	500			6,000
Number of employees	6	4	5	2	3	20
Sales revenue, €	200,000	500,000	300,000	0	0	1,000,000
Customer usage	1,200	15,000	20,000			
	function hrs	nights	covers			

Required

a) Apportion the budgeted total overheads to each cost centre.

b) Re-apportion the two service centre costs.

c) Calculate appropriate overhead absorption rates for each main cost centre dealing with saleable units.

d) Using the actual data presented below, establish the under- or over-absorption of overhead for each department.

	Functions	Accommodation	Restaurant
Total actual overhead	€159,100	€95,500	€66,650
Actual usage	1,220 conference hours	14,900 nights	20,250 covers

Question 3.8

Bob Collins has been appointed as general manager of the Comfort First chain of hotels. Bob is concerned that at 38 per cent of total cost, overheads are out of control in the organisation and he is concerned about the lack of information available on overhead costs.

Sally Russell has been a senior manager with EHS Electrical. EHS own 12 retail outlets selling hi-tech home entertainment equipment. The organisation has recently expanded to include computer equipment. Sally is concerned that the activities are becoming more complex and costly. Overhead cost has increased by 4 per cent in the past year.

Both managers attended a seminar that briefly touched on the topic of activity based costing and wondered if it would be beneficial to introduce the concept.

Draft a report to either manager, outlining how activity based costing works and the benefits of introducing such a system in the organisation concerned.

Question 3.9

'Activity based approaches have been implemented in many manufacturing organisations in an attempt to provide the "true" cost of products. The approach has little relevance in the service industry as product cost is not needed for stock valuation'

Comment on the validity of the above statement.

Question 3.10

Horizon Hotels are investigating the feasibility of implementing ABC. The front office has been selected to pilot the approach. The overhead costs have already been apportioned to the cost pools identified. The following cost pools, costs and drivers have been established:

Activity cost pool	Cost	Driver
Phone enquiries	€ 3,300	Number of calls received = 2,200
Making a reservation	€ 4,500	Number of reservations = 3,000
Allocating rooms	€ 3,500	Number of rooms allocated = 2,800
Processing accounts	€ 5,500	Number of accounts processed = 2,750
Handling baggage	€ 1,300	Number of customers with baggage = 650
Investigating other complaints	€ 3,600	Number of other complaints = 600

Required
a) Explain the terms cost pool and cost driver.
b) Calculate cost driver rates for each cost pool using the drivers identified.

Question 3.11

Personalise Limited operates a successful retail outlet providing good quality personalised story books, calendars and t-shirts for children. On placing an order, the customer provides names and other personal information for a story book or pictures for a calendar or t-shirt. An activity based costing system is in operation.
The apportionment of overhead costs to each cost pool has producing the following costs:

Activity cost pool	
Order processing	€1,500
Material movement	€19,875
Set-up time	€18,000
Printing	€19,800
Binding	€3,750
Packing	€2,700
Quality checks	€2,100

The following cost driver details have been accumulated for the period under review:

Number of items ordered	10,000
Direct material cost	€26,500
Set-up time (hours)	1,500
Printing time (hours)	1,100
Binding time (hours)	250
Packing time (hours)	300
Quality checking time (hours)	350

The following details have been established for each product:

	Book	Calendar	T-shirt
Items ordered	4,500	1,500	4,000
Sales price	€15	€9	€10
Direct material cost per item	€3	€2	€3
Set-up time (minutes)	10	14	6
Printing time (minutes)	10	6	3
Binding time (minutes)	3	1	–
Packing (minutes)	2	2	1.5
Quality checks (minutes)	2	4	1.5

Required

Using an ABC approach establish the unit profit or loss for each of the three products.

CHAPTER 4

Marginal Costing and Cost–Volume–Profit Analysis

Learning Outcomes

By the end of this chapter you will be able to:

☐ Distinguish between marginal and absorption costing.
☐ Outline the advantages and disadvantages of marginal costing.
☐ Outline the uses of CVP analysis for managers.
☐ Use the CVP model within various decision-making scenarios.
☐ Use the CVP model in a multi-product business.
☐ Interpret information from the CVP model.
☐ Present information from the CVP model graphically.
☐ Outline the limitations of the CVP model.
☐ Outline the conflict between the accountant's and economist's theories on the CVP model.
☐ Be aware of the methods used to deal with uncertainty regarding the estimates of the various inputs in the CVP model.

Introduction

Chapters 2 and 3 were primarily concerned with cost classification systems used for control purposes with a focus on tracing costs to cost units and the calculation of a full cost per unit. This chapter focuses on cost classification by behaviour, which is primarily used in management planning decisions. In Chapter 2, cost behaviour and the distinction between fixed and variable costs were introduced. This chapter briefly summarises the main points of cost behaviour theory before describing the marginal costing approach to dealing with fixed cost. It focuses on the cost–volume–profit (CVP) model which is based on cost behaviour theory and is a very useful management information tool. CVP analysis shows how costs, revenues and therefore profits, behave or react in response to changes in the volume of business activity.

Cost Behaviour

To use marginal costing and the CVP model, all costs must be classified according to how they will react to changes in volume of activity. Costs need to be classified into either a fixed cost or a variable cost category. In reality, many costs are part fixed and part variable (semi-fixed costs). These costs must be broken down into their variable and fixed components. Before discussing marginal costing and the CVP model, relevant material based on cost behaviour is briefly summarised.

Revision of cost behaviour concepts

❑   Costs are classified into two main categories:

Variable costs are costs that fluctuate with changes in sales volume. For example if sales volume fluctuates by 10 per cent then variable costs will fluctuate also by 10 per cent or close to it. Thus a variable cost is a cost that is sensitive to changes in sales activity. An example would include the cost of food or beverages for a restaurant.

Fixed costs are costs which are not sensitive to changes in sales volume or activity. Thus as sales volumes increase, these costs would be expected to remain the same or maybe increase due to other reasons such as inflation. Examples of fixed costs would include rent, rates, insurance, management salaries and fixed wages. Any of these expenses would not be expected to increase as sales volumes increase.

❑   The relevant range of activity concept states that fixed costs will be unaffected by sales volume fluctuations as long as these fluctuations ensure sales activity remains within a certain range. However, increases in sales activity beyond this range can lead to increases in fixed costs. Take for example a situation where sales volume increases so much that a new manager or supervisor is required to support this extra volume of activity. In this case fixed costs will be affected and will increase. The relevant range concept is critical when management is considering significant increases or reductions in activity levels.

❑   Semi-variable cost patterns occur when costs have both a fixed and variable component. Examples would include a telephone bill, as part of the bill includes a rental cost which would be considered fixed, and the number of phone calls, which could be considered variable.

Marginal Costing

Chapter 3 showed how both absorption costing and ABC apportioned fixed costs/ overheads to cost units, establishing the full cost of a product or service. However apportioning fixed costs to units can be quite subjective and can result in inaccurate and misleading calculations of unit costs. This cost information can lead to poor decision-making. An alternative basis that avoids the arbitrary apportionment of fixed costs is called marginal costing.

Marginal costing is an approach where variable costs are charged to cost units, but the fixed cost for the relevant period is written off in full against the total contribution for that period. Contribution is a key term in marginal costing. It is simply the difference between total sales and total variable cost. While marginal costing can be used as part of a routine cost accounting system, its main use is in providing relevant information for planning and decision-making. The following illustration distinguishes between profit statements based on marginal costing and absorption costing.

Illustration 4.1: *Marginal versus absorption costing*

Marginal Approach			Absorption Approach		
Sales		X	Sales		X
Less Variable costs			Less Production costs		
Production	X		Variable	X	
Non production	X	X	Fixed	X	X
Contribution		X	*Gross profit*		X
Less Fixed costs			Less Non production costs		
Production	X		Variable	X	
Non production	X	X	Fixed	X	X
Net profit		X	Net profit		X

The principle of marginal costing is that since fixed costs are constant within the relevant range of volume sales, it follows that by selling one extra unit or creating one extra sale:

❑ Revenue will increase by the sales value of one item.
❑ Costs will only increase by the variable cost per unit.
❑ The increase in profit will equal sales value less variable costs, i.e. the contribution.

If the volume of sales falls by one unit, then profit will fall by the contribution of that unit. If the volume of sales increases by one unit, profit will increase by the contribution of that unit. Fixed costs relate to time and do not change with increases or decreases in sales volume. Profit measurement should therefore be based on an analysis of total contribution.

Illustration 4.2: *Marginal costing profit statement*

	Restaurant	Bar	Function rooms	Total
	€	€	€	€
Sales	450,000	386,000	275,000	1,111,000
Less Variable costs	290,000	270,000	165,000	725,000
Contribution	160,000	116,000	110,000	386,000
Less Fixed Costs				365,000
Profit				21,000

In illustration 4.2, contribution for each department is shown. Fixed cost is not apportioned to the different areas or departments, therefore only the total profit figure is shown. This approach avoids the often arbitrary apportionment of fixed cost and highlights contribution, which is considered more appropriate for decision-making purposes.   cost per unit

Example 4.1: *Marginal v absorption costing*

The following profit statement was prepared by Gaelic Home Stores Limited using absorption costing principles. Gaelic Home Stores consists of one large retail outlet with three main departments; Electrical, Furniture and Soft Furnishings.

Profit Statement – Absorption Approach

	Electrical	Furniture	Soft Furnishings	Total
	€'000	€'000	€'000	€'000
Sales	2,100	3,000	1,200	6,300
Cost of sales	1,110	1,105	745	2,960
Gross profit	990	1,895	455	3,340
Less				
Wages & salaries	383	460	307	1,150
Employee benefits	40	30	10	80
Sales commission	210	300	120	630
Administration	110	83	27	220
Depreciation	20	29	11	60
Rent & insurance	40	57	23	120
Net profit (loss)	187	936	(43)	1,080

variable

Cost of sales represents the purchase cost of goods sold. Wages and salaries are fixed while sales commission varies directly with sales volume. All other costs are fixed in nature.   *variable*

You are required to prepare a profit statement based on marginal costing principles.

Approach

The key difference in absorption costing is that overhead costs are apportioned to each department while in marginal costing, fixed costs are deducted from the total contribution for the period.

better for decision making

Profit Statement – Marginal Approach

	Electrical	Furniture	Soft Furnishings	Total
	€'000	€'000	€'000	€'000
Sales	2,100	3,000	1,200	6,300
Cost of sales	1,110	1,105	745	2,960
Sales commission	210	300	120	630
Contribution	780	1,595	335	2,710
Wages & salaries				1,150
Employee benefits				80
Administration				220
Depreciation				60
Rent & insurance				120
Net profit				1,080

Less VC →
Less FC →

if closed, would be 335 000 worse off, no change to fixed costs

Looking at the profit statement produced by the absorption approach, the soft furnishings department is making a loss of €43,000. This could prompt management to consider closing the department. However it would be unwise to close the department as it is unlikely that fixed costs would change if the department were to close. The marginal approach shows that the department is making a positive contribution of €335,000 to cover fixed costs, and so it is viable. From this example, it can be seen how marginal costing can provide more relevant data to inform management decision-making.

Advantages of marginal costing

❑ The marginal costing approach is preferable for decision–making, as contribution is the most reliable criteria upon which to base a decision.
❑ It avoids arbitrary apportionment of fixed costs and the under- or over-absorption of overheads.
❑ Separating fixed and variable costs can help in short-term pricing decisions. As fixed costs will remain unaffected by fluctuations in activity within a relevant range, management can focus on variable costs and contribution.
❑ Fixed costs, by their nature, relate to periods of time rather than volume of production and thus should be treated as such in the preparation of profit statements.
❑ It gives a more accurate picture of how an organisation's cash flows and profits are affected by sales and volume.
❑ In manufacturing organisations, it avoids the manipulation of profits through increased production volumes. In the absorption or ABC approaches, profits will increase by simply producing more units without generating any additional sales, because manufacturing fixed overhead cost is included in stock valuation. This has the effect of transferring cost from the current period, to a future period when the stock will be sold. While this approach adheres to accounting concepts, it can encourage an increase in production volume (and closing stock levels) at the year–end in an attempt to increase the profit for the current year.

Disadvantages of marginal costing

❑ A marginal costing system identifies the contribution each item earns. It does not establish the fixed cost per item, so there is a danger that items will be sold on an ongoing basis at a price which fails to cover fixed costs.
❑ Marginal costing does not conform to the principles required by the accounting standards for stock valuation, which requires that stock is valued based on the total cost incurred in bringing the product to its present condition and location. This is because no element of fixed cost is included in the stock valuation provided by marginal costing. Therefore, year-end adjustments are necessary before the preparation of the financial statements for reporting purposes.

Cost-Volume-Profit Analysis

CVP analysis considers the interaction between sales revenue, total costs and the volume of activity, which between them make up profit. Using the CVP model, profit can be predicted for given situations. The model can be used for example, to evaluate a number of proposed solutions to a problem. Management then choose the solution that maximises the benefit to the business.

CVP analysis can be used by management to evaluate various proposals and strategies and answer questions such as the following:

- How many products do we need to sell to break even? Break-even is the point where neither a profit or loss occurs. It occurs when sales revenue equals total cost.
- How many products must be sold to achieve a required or target profit level?
- What level of revenue (euro sales) will ensure the business achieves break-even or a target profit?
- How far can we afford sales to fall to before making a loss? This is known as the margin of safety. *falling into a net off a tightrope - bigger net = lower risk*
- What selling price should be charged per product to achieve a required profit, at a given level of business activity?
- What level of sales volume increases would justify increased expenditure on advertising?
- If we reduce selling prices by a specific amount, what extra level of sales is required to maintain existing profit levels?

The objective of CVP analysis is to establish what would happen to profit if sales volume fluctuates in the short term. Thus the focus is on volume of activity for a business, because this is one of the most important variables affecting sales, costs and profit. Once a cost-volume relationship has been established, it can be combined with a volume-revenue relationship to evaluate alternatives in terms of profit impact in the short term. CVP analysis provides profit estimates at various levels of volume/activity, given information on selling prices, fixed costs and variable costs, thus the CVP model is a method of profit planning. The CVP model is based on the following equation:

CVP equation

Profit = total sales – total costs

Expands to

Profit = total sales – [total fixed costs + total variable costs]

Expands to

Profit = selling price per unit x no of units sold – {fixed costs + (variable cost per unit x number of units sold)}

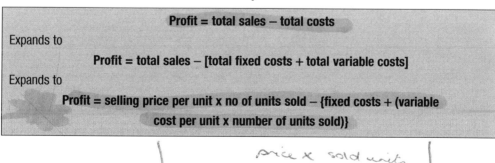

The equation can be presented in mathematical form as follows:

CVP formula – mathematical form

$$\pi = p\,(x) - \{a + b(x)\}$$

Where

  π = Net profit for the period

  p = Selling price per product

  x = No. of products sold

  a = Fixed costs

  b = Variable cost per unit

The CVP formula can also be presented in an accounting profit statement format as follows:

Profit Statement

Sales Revenue (price x volume sold)	X
Less Variable costs (cost x volume sold)	X
Total Contribution	X
Less Fixed costs	X
Net profit	X

important

The statement above refers to contribution. Contribution is the difference between sales and variable costs. It is quite similar to gross profit. It is called contribution as it represents the contribution each sale makes to cover fixed costs. For example if the selling price of a meal is €12 and the variable costs associated with the meal amount to €4, then each meal contributes €8 to cover fixed costs and hopefully help make a profit.

example of contribution

Sales, variable costs and thus contribution can be broken down into price/cost per unit multiplied by the number of units sold. However, fixed costs are not broken down into unit costs, as fixed costs are not a product of units sold but more a product of time. For example, the expense of rent will not change if a business sells more products.

Let us now focus on the key information the CVP model can provide to inform management in planning and decision-making.

Break-even point

The break-even point is the point at which neither a profit or a loss is incurred. Break-even occurs where total contribution is exactly equal to fixed cost and hence sales revenue is exactly equal to variable cost plus fixed cost.

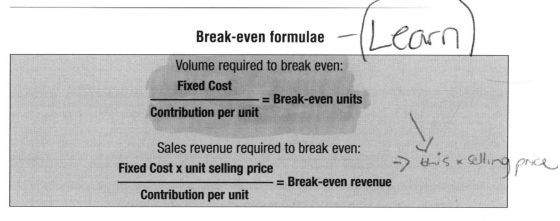

Break-even formulae — (Learn)

Volume required to break even:

$$\frac{\text{Fixed Cost}}{\text{Contribution per unit}} = \text{Break-even units}$$

Sales revenue required to break even:

$$\frac{\text{Fixed Cost} \times \text{unit selling price}}{\text{Contribution per unit}} = \text{Break-even revenue}$$

→ this × selling price

Knowledge of the break-even point is vital in business planning and decision-making, as it represents a crucial point in determining the success or failure of a business.

Example 4.2: *Break-even*

The following forecast information relates to the Blue Dolphin restaurant for the month of March. The restaurant is located in a busy shopping 'mecca' in Dundrum and its main customer base is shoppers. Forecast sales are based on an average spend of €12 per customer and a sales volume of 20,000 covers.

	Unit information	Total
	€	€
Sales	12.00	240,000
Variable costs	4.00	80,000
Contribution	8.00	160,000
Fixed costs		120,000
Forecast profit		40,000

a) Calculate the break-even point in covers.
b) Calculate the break-even point in sales revenue.

Approach

a) Calculate the break-even point in covers.
To calculate the break-even point, the fixed costs and the contribution per unit should be identified. The fixed costs amount to €120,000 while the contribution per unit is €8.00 (sales of €12 less variable costs of €4).

$$\frac{\text{Fixed cost}}{\text{Contribution per unit}} = \frac{€120,000}{€8} = 15,000 \text{ covers must be sold to break even.}$$

b) Calculate the break-even point in sales revenue.

The sales revenue required to break even can be found by multiplying the answer from part (a) by the selling price as follows:

15,000 covers x €12 = €180,000 revenue required to break even.

The answer to the above can be checked by preparing a profit statement based on the break-even requirement of 15,000 covers.

Profit Statement

		€
Sales	(€12 x 15,000)	180,000
Variable cost	(€4 x 15,000)	60,000
Contribution	(€8 x 15,000)	120,000
Fixed cost		120,000
Profit / loss		0

Target profit

In profit planning, management set profit targets and need information such as the sales levels in units or revenue required to achieve this target profit. The break–even formula can be expanded to establish the volume required to achieve a desired profit level.

Target profit formula

$$\frac{\text{Fixed Cost} + \text{Target Profit}}{\text{Contribution per unit}} = \text{Volume sales to achieve target profit}$$

This can be illustrated by returning to the Blue Dolphin restaurant. If the owner requires a profit of €20,000 then the formula presented above could be used to establish the number of covers required.

$$\frac{\text{Fixed cost} + \text{profit}}{\text{Contribution per unit}} = \frac{€120,000 + €20,000}{€8} = 17,500 \text{ covers must be sold}$$

The revenue required for a €20,000 profit is 17,500 covers at an average spend of €12, which amounts to €210,000.

This figure can be proved by simply calculating the total contribution and deducting fixed costs as follows:

		€
Contribution	(€8 x 17,500)	140,000
Fixed cost		120,000
Profit / loss		20,000

Note: The business is making a profit of €20,000 for an extra 2,500 (17,500 − 15,000) covers. Once the business reaches the break-even point of 15,000 covers, fixed costs are covered and hence the business makes a clear profit equal to the contribution made per cover which is €8. Thus €8 x 2,500 covers equals €20,000.

The margin of safety

The margin of safety is the amount of sales the business can afford to lose and still not make a loss. It is the difference between the budgeted sales volume (or revenue) and the budgeted break-even volume (or revenue). It can be expressed in units / products or € sales or as a percentage.

Margin of safety formulae

Margin of safety (units):

Budgeted sales volume
less   **= Margin of safety volume**
Break-even volume

Margin of safety (revenue):

Budgeted sales revenue
less   **= Margin of safety revenue**
Break-even revenue

Margin of safety (percentage):

$$\frac{\text{Forecast sales} - \text{Break-even sales} \times 100}{\text{Forecast sales}} = \text{Margin of safety revenue}$$

The margin of safety is vital in assessing the level of risk associated with a project. It can be illustrated by returning to the Blue Dolphin restaurant example. Budgeted sales were forecast at 20,000 covers with the break-even point calculated at 15,000 covers. The margin of safety is thus calculated at 5,000 covers (20,000 less 15,000).

In sales revenue, this is €60,000 (5,000 x €12) and in percentage terms it is calculated at 25 per cent (20,000 - 15,000 ÷ 20,000). Thus actual sales could be 25 per cent less than budgeted and the business would still not make a loss.

Using the contribution to sales ratio

In some instances, key information may be unavailable. For example, total revenue may be presented without unit price or volume data. In these situations the contribution to sales ratio (C/S ratio) can be used to calculate the break-even point in revenue. The C/S ratio is simply the contribution divided by sales, multiplied by 100. The break-even point in revenue, as well as the revenue required to achieve a target profit can be calculated using the following formulae based on the C/S ratio:

Formulae using C/S ratio

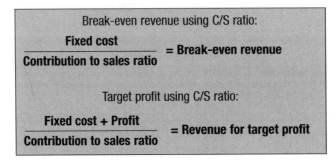

Break-even revenue using C/S ratio:

$$\frac{\text{Fixed cost}}{\text{Contribution to sales ratio}} = \text{Break-even revenue}$$

Target profit using C/S ratio:

$$\frac{\text{Fixed cost + Profit}}{\text{Contribution to sales ratio}} = \text{Revenue for target profit}$$

Example 4.3: *Using the C/S ratio*

Sales revenue for Electrical Retailing has been forecast at €2,000,000 for the coming year with a contribution of €800,000 expected. Fixed costs have been estimated at €700,000.

a) What is the break-even revenue?
b) What is the margin of safety?
c) What revenue is required if a profit of €500,000 is required?

Approach

a) What is the break-even revenue?
It is first necessary to calculate the C/S ratio:

$$\frac{\text{Contribution x 100}}{\text{Sales}} = \frac{\text{€800,000 x 100}}{\text{€2,000,000}} = 40\% \text{ or €0.40 of every € sales}$$

Then use the C/S ratio in calculating the break–even point:

$$\frac{\text{Fixed costs}}{\text{C/S ratio}} = \frac{\text{€700,000}}{0.40} = \text{€1,750,000 revenue}$$

b) *What is the margin of safety?*

The margin of safety is the difference between forecast sales revenue and break–even sales revenue:

$$\text{€2,000,000} - \text{€1,750,000} = \text{€250,000.}$$

c) *What revenue is required if a profit of €500,000 is required?*

If the company requires a target profit of €500,000, then the contribution required must cover fixed costs of €700,000 and the profit of €500,000.

$$\frac{\text{Fixed costs} + \text{profit}}{\text{C/S ratio}} = \frac{\text{€700,000} + \text{€500,000}}{0.40} = \text{€3,000,000 revenue}$$

CVP in decision-making

The CVP model is an important tool in profit planning. The break–even point and margin of safety are figures management should be aware of in assessing the likely performance of a business and the level of risk involved. A high break–even point and a low margin of safety indicates high business risk. CVP analysis informs management decision-making. It provides financial information for key decisions facing management including:

❑ What level of sales volume increases would justify increased expenditure on advertising?
❑ If we reduce selling prices by a specific amount, what extra level of sales is required to maintain existing profit levels?

Example 4.4: *Decision evaluation using CVP*

The management of the Blue Dolphin Restaurant are considering launching an advertising campaign at a cost of €5,000 per month. It is expected that sales output will increase by 5 per cent as a result of the campaign.

Current level of sales (before campaign) is estimated at 20,000 covers.
Average selling price per meal = €12
Variable costs per meal = €4
Fixed costs for one month = €120,000 (before campaign)

Would this be a worthwhile policy to pursue?

Approach

In this decision, increasing advertising (a fixed cost) will have the effect of increasing fixed costs to €125,000 per month. Sales will increase from their forecast level of 20,000 to 21,000 covers (20,000 x 105%). As variable costs and sales price remain unchanged, contribution per unit is €8. A simple profit statement can decide whether this proposal should go ahead. The following forecast profit is based on a decision to increase advertising.

Contribution	(€8 x 21,000)	€168,000
Less Fixed costs		€125,000
Net profit		€43,000

This needs to be compared with forecast profit based on fixed costs remaining at €120,000 and sales levels at 20,000.

Contribution	(€8 x 20,000)	€160,000
Less Fixed costs		€120,000
Net profit		€40,000

Thus profit is forecast to increase by €3,000 should they advertise.

This could also be calculated based on extra contribution generated by selling 1,000 extra meals multiplied by the contribution per meal of €8 which amounts to €8,000. After deducting the extra costs of €5,000, profits increase by €3,000.

Obviously, increasing fixed costs with no change to contribution per unit will ensure the break-even point and margin of safety increase. These two measures can give management a feel for or sense of the risk inherent in the business. The new break-even point based on fixed costs increasing to €125,000 amounts to 15,625 covers, an increase of 625 covers or 4 per cent. However, the margin of safety increases to 5,375 covers (21,000 – 15,625), an increase of 375 covers. In these decision points, management must be aware of the increased risk associated with increasing fixed costs.

CVP Analysis – A Mathematical Approach

Most of the information supplied by the CVP model can be calculated using the mathematical format of the CVP equation.

$$\pi = p\,(x) - \{a + b(x)\}$$

Where

π = Net profit for the period

p = Selling price per product

x = No. of products sold

a = Fixed costs

b = Variable cost per unit

Using the information from the Blue Dolphin Restaurant, this is demonstrated as follows:

Example 4.5: *The mathematical approach*

The following forecast information relates to the Blue Dolphin Restaurant.

> Sales per month are estimated at 20,000 covers.
> Average selling price per meal = €12
> Variable costs per meal = €4
> Fixed costs for one month = €120,000

Fixed costs are not expected to change in relation to sales as long as sales remain within a forecast range of between 12,000 and 25,000 covers per month.

The management of the restaurant needs to know the following information to plan for next month.
a) *How many meals must be sold to break even?*
b) *How many meals must be sold to achieve a profit of €10,000 per month?*
c) *What level of revenue is required to achieve the break-even point in (a) and profit level in (b)?*
d) *What is the margin of safety based on the forecast level of sales and also based on the profit level in (b)?*
e) *If an advertising campaign was launched at a cost of €5,000 per month and, as a result sales output could be increased by 5 per cent, would this be a worthwhile policy to pursue?*

Approach

a) *How many meals must be sold to break even?*

$$\pi = p\,(x) - \{a + b(x)\}$$
$$0 = 12\,(x) - \{120{,}000 + 4(x)\}$$
$$120{,}000 = 8\,x$$
$$15{,}000 = x$$

b) *How many meals must be sold to achieve a profit of €10,000 per month?*

$$\pi = p\,(x) - \{a + b(x)\}$$
$$10,000 = 12\,(x) - \{120,000 + 4(x)\}$$
$$130,000 = 8\,x$$
$$16,250 = x$$

c) *What level of sales in € is required to achieve the break-even point in (a) and profit level in (b)?*
This is simply calculated by multiplying the answers to (a) and (b) by the selling price of €12.

$$(a)\ 15,000 \times €12 = €180,000$$
$$(b)\ 16,250 \times €12 = €195,000$$

d) *What is the margin of safety based on the forecast level of sales and also based on the profit level in (b)?*
The margin of safety based on the forecast level of sales is calculated by comparing the sales level of 20,000 covers to the break-even point in covers calculated in part (a) 15,000. The margin of safety is 5,000 covers.

The margin of safety based on the profit level in (b) is calculated by comparing the sales levels answers in (b) 16,250 covers, to the break–even point in covers calculated in (a) 15,000. The margin of safety is 1,250 covers.

e) *If an advertising campaign was launched at a cost of €5,000 per month, and as a result sales output could be increased by 5 per cent, would this be a worthwhile policy to pursue?*
Based on sales volume of 20,000 covers, profit is estimated as follows:

$$\pi = p\,(x) - \{a + b(x)\}$$
$$\pi = 12\,(20,000) - \{120,000 + 4(20,000)\}$$
$$\pi = 40,000$$

Based on this new scenario profit is estimated as follows:

$$\pi = p\,(x) - \{a + b(x)\}$$
$$\pi = 12\,(21,000) - \{125,000 + 4(21,000)\}$$
$$\pi = 43,000$$

Thus it is worthwhile to launch the advertising campaign.

CVP Analysis – A Graphic Approach

CVP information can also be presented in graphical format. This can be quite useful for management as they get a visual insight into the overall cost-volume-profit relationship for the business. The graphic approach is normally presented in two ways.

❑ Break-even chart.
❑ Profit-volume chart.

Break-even chart

Break-even charts give a graphical view of CVP analysis. The chart is simple to understand and is particularly useful when communicating to non-accountants. It gives a visual display of how much output needs to be sold to make a profit and the likelihood of making a loss, if actual sales fall short of targets.

The following is a step-by-step procedure for drawing up a break-even chart.

1. Determine the parameters for the chart. This is done by finding out the minimum and maximum sales activity (units) and € sales the business can achieve in the period. In the previous example, maximum sales in covers is 25,000 and in euro it amounts to €300,000 (25,000 x €12). Minimum sales activity is obviously zero.
2. Draw an L-shaped chart with the X axis (horizontal line) representing activity in units/covers/hours, and the Y axis (vertical line) representing € sales/costs.
3. Map out the € sales on the Y axis and unit sales on the X axis, starting with 0 (the point where the X and Y axis meet).
4. Draw the fixed cost line. To draw a line, one needs two points. The first point should always be based on the situation if the business has zero sales. If the business sells nothing, what would fixed costs be? In the above example this would be €120,000. Take another activity level; the forecast level of 20,000 covers. Fixed costs would still amount to €120,000. Join up these two points and continue the line. This is the fixed cost line and should run parallel to the X axis.
5. Draw the sales revenue line. Again two points are needed. Firstly, if there are zero sales then € sales will amount to 0. Thus one point is where the X and Y axis meet. The second point is found by taking sales at the forecast level of 20,000 covers and calculating the € sales on it which would amount to 20,000 x €12 = €240,000. Thus the second point is where the 20,000 covers line meets with the €240,000 line. Join the two points and continue the line. This is the sales revenue line.
6. Draw the total cost line. Total costs are fixed costs + variable costs represented by one side of the CVP equation a + b(x). Again, two points are needed here. The first point is taken at zero sales; what will be the total costs? Total costs will equal fixed costs of €120,000. For the second point, take the forecast activity level of 20,000

covers sold and predict the total costs which would equal €120,000 + (€4 x 20,000) = €200,000. Again join the two points and this is the total cost line.

To summarise

Activity level (units sold)	Zero	20,000
Sales revenue @ €12	0	€240,000
Variable costs @ €4	0	€80,000
Fixed cost	€120,000	€120,000
Total cost	€120,000	€200,000
Profit / loss	(€120,000)	€40,000

Break-even point = 15,000 units (€180,000)
Margin of safety = 5,000 units (€60,000)

Diagram 4.1: *Break-even Chart*

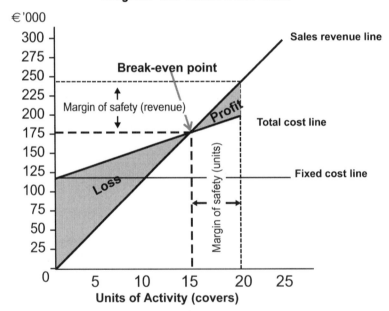

The following can be read from the chart:

1. The break-even point is 15,000 covers sold, or €180,000 in sales revenue.
2. If the business sells less than 15,000 covers, it makes a loss. One can read the loss from the chart. For example if sales in covers amount to 10,000, then the total cost line is greater than the sales revenue line at 10,000 covers. The loss amounts to €40,000.
3. Beyond the break-even point, the sales revenue line is greater than the total cost line and the business is in profit. The level of profit can be read from the chart. At forecast sales of 20,000 covers, profit equals €40,000.

Profit-volume chart

While the break-even chart is quite useful in determining the break-even point and giving a visual overview of revenue and cost relationship for a business, the profit volume chart is very useful in showing the impact on profit of different activity levels.

A step-by-step procedure for drawing a profit-volume chart is as follows:

1. Calculate the parameters. What are the maximum profit levels and sales volume levels? Calculate the maximum possible losses. In our example, the maximum sales volume levels are 25,000 covers, the maximum profit level is based on sales of 25,000 covers and amounts to €80,000. The maximum possible loss occurs if the business has zero sales, thus the losses would equal fixed costs.
2. Draw the chart (like a T turned sideways to the left). The vertical line represents profits and losses and the horizontal line represents sales volume or € sales.
3. Only one line needs to be drawn, called the contribution or profit line. Again, two points are needed for this line. The first point should be based on what losses would be if no products were sold. This maximum loss would equal the fixed costs of €120,000. The second point would involve taking any activity level and calculating the profit or loss at that level of activity. Take an activity level of 10,000 covers. At this level the business would make a loss of €40,000. Connect the two points and continue the line.

Diagram 4.2: *Profit-volume chart*

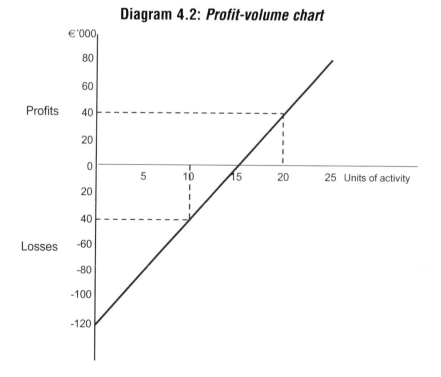

The contribution/profit line can point out, for any level of activity, what the profit or loss is estimated to be. For example, if sales are estimated at 10,000 covers for the period, then the graph will show the business making a loss of €40,000. If sales are estimated at 20,000 covers for the period, then the graph will show the business making a profit of €40,000.

limitations

Assumptions Underlying CVP Analysis

As with any model, there are necessary, simplifying assumptions on which the whole model is based. These assumptions also represent the limitations of the CVP model. It is essential that managers, when interpreting CVP information, keep in mind these limitations and try to assess their influence in practical terms.

The assumptions are as follows:

— most are realistically curved linear

1. Revenue and cost behaviour are linear over the relevant range, i.e. they take the form of a straight-line on a chart.
2. Variable costs per unit remain constant, thus ignoring the impact of quantity discounts.   *→ won't change when buying with discounts*
3. Variable costs are directly proportional to sales.   *may get quantity discounts*
4. Fixed costs remain constant within the relevant range.
5. All costs can be classified into their fixed and variable components.   *difficult to do - some have fixed + variable*
6. Volume/activity levels are the only factors that influence costs. Clearly there are many other factors that influence revenues and costs such as quality of management and staff, industrial relations, economic conditions, working methods and conditions etc.   *other factors eg quality of mgmt, and staff*
7. Selling price per unit remains constant although economists point out that in order to sell additional units, selling price is normally reduced.   *to sell more you may drop but is ignored*
8. The sales mix remains constant.

Chelsea plan to break even by 2009/2010

Chelsea F.C. are reigning premiership champions and, with 15 games left to play, are romping away with this seasons (2005/06) title. However they collected a new accolade by reporting a £140 million net loss for the season 2004/05. The club made a loss of £87.8 million in 2003/04. This is the largest loss in English football history and is mainly funded by Roman Abramovich who invested £166.6 million in the club in 2004/05. The club CEO Peter Kenyon has announced a five year plan to break even. This they hope, will be achieved through the following strategies.

❏ To stabilise wages which currently amount to 75 per cent of revenue. For this to happen, wages would need to fall to 50 per cent of revenue. This they hope, will be achieved partly through the development of their football academy to develop home-grown talent.

❏ To generate extra revenues through planned tours to the USA and China and generating a more global brand to increase merchandising income. Up to one third of Manchester United's revenue is generated through merchandising.

❏ The club management have also made no secret of the fact that the capacity of Stamford Bridge is inadequate and there is speculation about a move to a bigger stadium.

Source: *Irish Times* Sports Supplement 28 January 2006.

CVP Analysis and the Sales Mix

Many businesses in the hospitality, tourism and retail sectors sell a variety of different products/services that generate different contribution margins for example, an airline selling different priced tickets or a hotel that offers accommodation, food and beverages, all at different selling prices and contribution margins. Retail businesses can sell a wide range of product lines all at different profit margins. In these multi-product firms, one can still use CVP analysis, however an extra assumption (assumption 8 above) must be made. This assumption is that the proportion each product represents of total sales (sales mix) remains constant. There are two ways of calculating the break-even point and thus applying CVP analysis.

1. The first is to calculate the break-even point for all products separately and aggregate the answers to give an overall break-even point for the business.
2. The second approach is to calculate an average C/S ratio assuming that the product sales mix remains constant.

Example 4.6: *CVP and the sales mix*

A tour operator offers 3 different tour packages priced and costed as follows:

	Tour 1	Tour 2	Tour 3
	€	€	€
Selling price per package	400	800	1,200
Variable costs per package	280	500	600
Contribution per package	120	300	600
C/S ratio	30%	37.5%	50%
Each tours sales as a % of total sales (sales mix)	30%	30%	40%
Fixed costs for the business are €210,000. These are apportioned to the 3 product lines as follows:	50,000	70,000	90,000

Calculate the break-even point using:
a) The aggregation of separate break-even points.
b) The total average C/S ratio.

Approach

Part a) This approach requires the calculation of the break-even point for all three tours separately. Then aggregate the answers to give an overall break-even point for the business.

	Tour 1	Tour 2	Tour 3
Fixed costs	€50,000	€70,000	€90,000
C/S ratio	30%	37.5%	50%
Break-even point € (sales value)	€166,667	€186,666	€180,000

The BEP for the business as a whole is €533,333 (the sum of all three). This approach assumes that fixed costs can be accurately apportioned to each product line.

Part b) This approach requires the calculation of a total average C/S ratio assuming that the product sales mix remains constant. The total average C/S ratio is calculated by multiplying the C/S ratio for each tour by its related sales mix percentage and then aggregating the answers as follows:

Average C/S (30% x 30%) + (37.5% x 30%) +(50% x 40%) = 40.25%

The break-even point is calculated by dividing fixed costs by the total average C/S ratio.

$$\frac{\text{Total fixed costs } (50{,}000 + 70{,}000 + 90{,}000)}{\text{Average C/S}} = \frac{€210{,}00}{.4025} = €521{,}740 \text{ revenue}$$

The difference in the BEP, although not significant, is due to the different assumptions that underlie both calculations. In the first calculation it is assumed that fixed costs can be apportioned accurately to each product line. In reality, this assumption is unreasonable. In the second, it is assumed that the projected sales mix will remain constant and thus will not change. Again this is quite unreasonable, however, the second method (at least in an exam situation) is the preferred option.

Example 4.7: *CVP and the sales mix*

Celtic Souvenirs Ltd, a chain of retail stores, is at present considering opening a new store in Athlone. The following information relates to the budgeted figures for the first years trading. The company deals in three main distinct product lines as follows:

	Celtic clothing	Celtic cds/ videos/tapes	Traditional souvenirs
Projected sales	€200,000	€150,000	€50,000
Projected C/S ratio	30%	40%	50%

The estimated fixed costs for the first year of operation are expected to amount to €150,000.

What is the projected annual break-even point for the business?

Approach

The first step is to calculate the total sales and total contribution so that an average contribution to sales ratio can be calculated.

	Celtic clothing	Celtic cds/ videos/tapes	Traditional souvenirs	Total sales
Sales	€200,000	€150,000	€50,000	€400,000
C/S ratio	30%	40%	50%	
Contribution	€60,000	€60,000	€25,000	€145,000
Sales mix	50%	37.5%	12.5%	

The average C/S ratio is calculated as follows:

$$\frac{\text{Forecast total contribution x 100}}{\text{Forecast sales}} = \frac{145,000 \times 100}{400,000} = 36.25\%$$

Note: The average C/S can also be calculated as (30% x 50%) + (40% x 37.5%) + (50% x 12.5%) = 36.25% or .3625.

The break-even point in sales revenue can now be calculated as follows:

$$\frac{\text{Fixed costs}}{\text{C/S ratio}} = \frac{€150,000}{0.3625} = €413,793$$

Based on the projected sales figures, the business just fails to generate sufficient revenue to break even in the first year. Before making a decision on whether to invest, management must assess the reasonableness of the projected figures as well as assessing whether the sales mix used in the projections is appropriate. The projected sales mix in this scenario is 50 per cent clothing, 37.5 per cent music with 12.5 per cent souvenirs. However, if the actual sales mix was 40 per cent clothing, 35 per cent music and 25 per cent souvenirs then the break-even point would be as follows:

	Celtic clothing	Celtic cds/ videos/tapes	Traditional souvenirs	Total sales
Sales	€160,000	€140,000	€100,000	€400,000
C/S ratio	30%	40%	50%	
Contribution	€48,000	€56,000	€50,000	€154,000

The average C/S ratio is calculated as follows:

$$\frac{\text{Forecast total contribution x 100}}{\text{Forecast sales}} = \frac{154,000 \times 100}{400,000} = 38.5\% \text{ or } .385$$

The break-even point in sales revenue is:

$$\frac{\text{Fixed costs}}{\text{C/S ratio}} = \frac{€150,000}{0.385} = €389,610$$

The point at which the company breaks even has decreased, and hence is more achievable and less risky. This is due to the increased sales of the most profitable product range, souvenirs. Thus, based on a change to the projected sales mix, sales of €400,000 are sufficient to achieve a small profit for the company in its first year.

Break-even in the Irish retail sector

Research by Luby (2006) on the use of break-even (CVP) analysis in the retail sector found that 56 per cent of those surveyed indicated that it was used. Respondents who used break-even analysis indicated it was used for the following purposes:

Decision support tool	100%
Capital investment decisions	100%
Planning purposes	60%

The Economist's Approach to CVP Analysis

Some of the above assumptions that underlie CVP analysis come into conflict with economic theory, especially the assumption of linearity and the constancy of selling price and variable cost per unit. Economists argue that lowering selling price acts as a catalyst to increasing demand and thus as sales volumes increase, so will variable costs. However, on account of economies of scale and quantity discounts, the variable cost per unit should fall. This is reflected in the total revenue and total cost curves that economists use, rather than the straight lines simplifications in the accountant's CVP model.

1. The total revenue curve begins to slope upwards but less steeply, as price reductions become necessary and then slope downward as the effect of price reductions outweigh the beneficial effect of volume increases, as the business approaches capacity.
2. The total cost curve increases at a slower rate as the effects of economies of scale and quantity discounts show up. However the curve begins a steeper upward trend as the business rises towards full capacity, because the variable cost per unit will normally increase as a result of diminishing returns.

Economists assume revenues and costs are curvilinear and this can result in two break-even points as per the break-even chart below.

Diagram 4.3: *Economist's CVP chart*

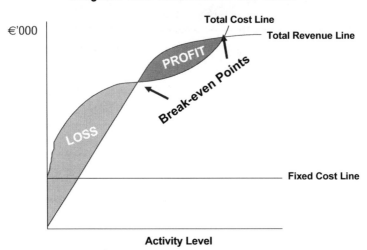

Proponents of the accounting model argue that it is not intended to provide a precise representation of total revenue and cost functions throughout all levels of activity. The objective of the accountant's CVP model is to represent an approximation of revenue and cost behaviour over the relevant range in the short term. As the relevant range of activity can be narrow and the short term time period less than 12 months, the linearity assumption is reasonable. Also, the cost of obtaining more accurate cost and revenue functions may outweigh the benefits to be gained from such information.

CVP Analysis and Uncertainty

The output and information provided by the CVP model is only as good as its inputs. The model requires inputs such as likely sales mix, selling price levels, total fixed costs and variable cost per unit. These inputs are all estimated and thus will be subject to varying degrees of uncertainty.

Risk can simply be defined as the likelihood that what is expected to occur will not actually occur. Thus there is a strong possibility that the financial estimates and inputs for the CVP model will not turn out as expected. How do managers deal with this? In practice there are several methods available to managers to deal with uncertainty concerning estimates and predictions. These are:

❑   Sensitivity analysis.
❑   Use of probabilities.
❑   Simulations.

Sensitivity analysis

With regard to projected financial statements, each element of sales and costs are uncertain to some extent. Some elements may be subject to more uncertainty than others, while some uncertainties will have greater consequences than others. Sensitivity analysis helps by showing how sensitive profit and the break-even point are to changes in assumptions about volume, price and costs.

Sensitivity analysis involves taking a single variable (e.g. volume of sales) and examining the effect of changes in that variable on the projected profit and break-even levels. By examining the shifts that occur in projected profit and break-even levels, it is possible to arrive at some assessment of how sensitive profit and the break-even point is to changes in these variables.

Example 4.8: *Sensitivity analysis*

The following information relates to the Blue Dolphin Restaurant.

Forecast sales per month are estimated at 20,000 covers.
Average selling price per meal = €12
Variable costs per meal = €4

The total fixed costs for one month amount to €120,000 and are not expected to change in relation to sales so long as sales remain within a forecast range of between 12,000 and 25,000 covers per month. The break-even point is calculated at 15,000 covers and the company must generate sales of 16,250 covers to achieve a profit of €10,000.

Calculate the sensitivity of the break-even point to changes in selling price.

Approach

If the average spend per customer was €11, what effect would this have on profitability and the break-even point.

In this situation, average spend has fallen to €11 and this has the effect of reducing contribution to €7. Thus the break-even point is recalculated as follows:

$$\frac{\text{Fixed costs}}{\text{Contribution per unit}} = \frac{€120,000}{€7} = 17,143 \text{ covers}$$

The break-even point has increased from 15,000 to 17,143 covers, an increase of 14.3 per cent (2,143 ÷ 15,000) due to a fall in the average spend of €1 or 8.3 per cent (1/12). A sensitivity rating can be calculated by dividing the percentage change in the break-even point by the percentage change in the average spend variable. This sensitivity rating is 1.72 (14.3 ÷ 8.3) times. Thus, if selling price decreases by 1%, the break–even point is expected to increase by 1.72 per cent.

Profit sensitivity analysis will be discussed in greater detail in Chapter 6.

Use of probabilities

Another approach to helping managers develop a sense of the effects of inaccurate fore-casting is to prepare projected profit statements according to different possible scenarios. For example, management may wish to examine a profit statement prepared on an optimistic, pessimistic and most likely outlook on future events This approach involves changing a number of variables simultaneously in order to portray the effects of each possible economic scenario. Management can then apply probabilities to each stated scenario to estimate a most likely effect. At the end of this process, management have an idea of effects on the business of worst and best case scenarios and hence a better feel for a most likely scenario. The use of probabilities is covered in more detail in Chapter 14.

Simulations

This approach is really a development of sensitivity analysis. It involves the use of specific simulation computer software. In essence, the approach applies a range of possible values to the various key variables (sales volume, sales price, variable costs, fixed costs) in the projected profit statement. The computer software then selects, at random, a value for each variable from the range given and proceeds to generate the projected profit or loss based on the values chosen. This process is repeated using other values for each variable until many (usually thousands of) combinations of values for each key variable have been selected, all producing different profit outcomes. From this huge amount of information, a range of likely outcomes can be predicted with probabilities attached.

Example 4.9: *Simulation*

Breen Retailers Ltd carried out 6,000 trials on key variables in a projected profit and loss account. The trials indicate that the expected profit for the following year will fall within a range of €150,000 to €550,000. Further analysis shows that of the 6,000 trials,

22 per cent produced expected profits of €150,000 − €250,000
31 per cent produced expected profits of €250,001 − €350,000
35 per cent produced expected profits of €350,001 − €450,000
12 per cent produced expected profits of €450,001 − €550,000

This information gives management more confidence in their projections and thus helps ensure proper planning for future events. It forces management to critically evaluate the underlying assumptions and issues that may affect the business in the future.

The use of computerised spreadsheet packages ensures that management can study various combinations of selling price, variable cost per unit, sales mix, and fixed costs within the CVP model and react to this information in a timely fashion. Chapter 7 will focus in more detail on sensitivity analysis as a management information tool in dealing with uncertainty.

CVP in the Hospitality Sector

The CVP model as a management information tool in hotels

Research conducted by Smullen and O'Donoghue (2005) in relation to the use and influence of certain financial decision support models within the hospitality sector showed the following in relation to the use of CVP analysis as part of an overall management information system in hotels.

❏ Of the hotels surveyed, 58 per cent use CVP and break even analysis as a decision support tool.

❏ The main decision areas the CVP model influenced were:
   − Investment.
   − Capital expenditure on new cost saving equipment.
   − Conference and bedroom pricing.

The research was conducted in early 2005 and was based on hotels with a 3 star standard or higher and with 30 or more bedrooms.

Only 58 per cent of hotels surveyed above use CVP analysis as a decision support tool. This is quite low compared to other sectors. The reason put forward is that using CVP analysis in a hotel operation can be complicated, as a hotel operation involves a complicated sales structure. Revenue for hotels includes room, catering, telephone, club and other sales. Catering sales can involve the same food items sold at different prices if served in the bar compared to the restaurant, therefore margins vary throughout the hotel. Senior managers need and want to know at what level of occupancy the hotel will break even. Although many will give estimates such as 'around 45 per cent', the truth is that, owing to the complicated sales and cost structure, it is difficult to arrive at an accurate break–even occupancy. However according to B.S. Wijeysinghe in his article 'Break–even Occupancy for a Hotel Operation' (*Management Accounting,* Feb 1993), catering, telephone, club and other sales are largely dependent on room sales and have a fairly consistent sales to room sales ratio. Thus a reasonably accurate calculation of break-even occupancy can be measured.

The following example shows how CVP analysis can be useful in enhancing management decision-making within a hotel environment.

Example 4.10: *CVP analysis in a hotel operation*

The following profit statement and additional information relates to Joshua Hotels, currently making a loss of €1.5 million with an occupancy level of 50 per cent.

Profit Statement		Additional information:	
	€'000		
Sales: Rooms	10,950	Rooms available per day	300
Catering	7,720	Rooms available for 365 days	109,500
Telephone	2,000	Average room rate	€200
Other	1,330	Rooms let (for 365 days)	54,750
Total sales	22,000	Occupancy achieved	50%
Total direct costs	7,700		
Contribution	14,300		
Fixed costs	15,800		
Operating profit	(1,500)		

Senior management have put forward three separate strategies to achieve break-even. These are:

1. Increase room rates by 10 per cent. Market research has indicated that a 10 per cent increase in prices will not adversely affect occupancy rates.
2. Reduce room rates by 10 per cent. According to market research, occupancy will increase to 60 per cent, with revenue streams from telephone, catering and other categories all increasing their yield by an estimated 10 per cent. It also estimates that variable costs will increase by 11.35 per cent.
3. Focus on analysing and reducing fixed costs.

Evaluate each of the strategies put forward by management and calculate the break-even point for the hotel under the current situation and for each of the strategies suggested.

Approach

In evaluating each of the strategies, management will want to calculate:

❑ The required break-even point for each strategy.
❑ The forecast profit or loss for each strategy.

The following table outlines the calculation of profit and the break-even point for the existing situation as well as for each of the strategies. The calculation of the break-even point is achieved through the following steps.

1. Calculating the total income/sales per room let.
2. Calculating the contribution to sales ratio and using this to get the contribution per room let.
3. Dividing fixed costs by the contribution per room let to get the break-even point in room sales.

	Existing	Strategy 1	Strategy 2	Strategy 3
	€'000	€'000	€'000	€'000
Sales: Rooms	10,950	12,045	11,826	10,950
Catering	7,720	7,720	8,492	7,720
Telephone	2,000	2,000	2,200	2,000
Other	1,330	1,330	1,463	1,330
Total sales	22,000	23,095	23,981	22,000
Total variable costs	7,700	7,700	8,574	7,700
Contribution	14,300	15,395	15,407	14,300
Fixed costs	15,800	15,800	15,800	14,300
Profit before interest	**(1,500)**	**(405)**	**(393)**	**0**
Rooms available per day	300	300	300	300
Rooms available for 365 days *(365 x 300 rooms)*	109,500	109,500	109,500	109,500
Average room rate	€200	€220	€180	€200
Rooms let (for 365 days)	54,750	54,750	65,700	54,750
Occupancy achieved *(54,750 rooms ÷ 109,500 rooms)*	50%	50%	60%	50%
Income per room let *(€22,000,000 ÷ 54,750 rooms)*	€402	€422	€365	€402
Contribution to sales % *(€14,300 ÷ €22,000)*	65%	66.66%	64.24%	65%
Contribution per room let *(€14,300,000 ÷ 54,750 rooms) or (402 x 65%)*	€261.3	€281	€234.5	€261.3
Rooms let required to break even *(€15,800,000 ÷ 261.3)*	60,466	56,228	67,377	54,726
Break-even occupancy *(60,466 rooms ÷ 109,500 rooms)*	55%	51.35%	61.53%	50%

Strategy 1 focuses on how to eliminate the loss through increasing the price per room. The current room rate is €200 and, if a selling price increase of 10 per cent can be achieved without affecting occupancy then room sales increase to €12,045 (10,950 x 1.1). Other income, variable costs and fixed costs remain the same and thus the loss falls to €405,000. Under this scenario, sales volume (rooms sold) remains the same as do variable and fixed costs. This strategy can have the effect of reducing the required break-even occupancy levels from 55 per cent to 51 per cent. Management need to assess what effect further increases in room rates will have on occupancy and how this effects the net loss situation.

Strategy 2 focuses on boosting volume changes by reducing price. In this scenario, occupancy will increase by 20 per cent (going from 50 per cent to 60 per cent) but price will fall by 10 per cent. Thus, room sales is calculated as €11,826 (€10,950 x 90% x 1.2). As occupancy has increased, catering, telephone and other services offered by the hotel will increase by 10 per cent. Variable costs will increase by 11.35 per cent. Fixed costs remain unchanged. Under this strategy the company's break-even occupancy will increase to 61 per cent, however this is more achievable due to the room rate reduction.

Strategy 3 focuses on reducing fixed costs. This strategy is the only one that is forecast to achieve the required goal to break even. By reducing fixed costs by 9.5 per cent, the hotel will break even. The process of reducing fixed costs requires firstly an analysis of the component elements of fixed costs and then secondly, management need to actively question the make-up and value achieved by each cost item. Management need to be aware of how each cost requires a number of rooms to be sold to cover that cost. For example, if a component of fixed costs such as property maintenance costs amount to €3.3 million or €9,041 per day, then the hotel must sell 35 rooms (9,041 ÷ 261.3) per day to cover this fixed cost alone. Thus attention would focus on how to reduce these costs through, for example, more efficient utilisation of power (reducing waste) etc. Ultimately, if fixed costs are reduced by €1,500,000 or 9.5 per cent (1,500 ÷ 15,800), then the hotel breaks even. This analysis is valuable not just in terms of focusing on questioning each cost item, but also in educating line-management in understanding the 'magic number of rooms' required to be sold on a daily basis to break even. Exhibit 4.1 shows how the fixed costs in the above example can be broken into their component parts and how each component contributes to the break-even occupancy level calculated on a daily basis.

Exhibit 4.1: *Fixed costs and break-even*

	€'000	Cost per day €	Daily room sales required to cover costs Fixed costs ÷ cpu	
Service wages	5,000	13,699	52	(13,699 ÷ 261.3)
Service expenses				
Sales and promotion	1,800	4,931	19	(4,931 ÷ 261.3)
Administration	2,300	6,301	24	(6,301 ÷ 261.3)
Property costs	3,300	9,041	35	(9,041 ÷ 261.3)
Maintenance	1,000	2,740	10	(2,740 ÷ 261.3)
Depreciation	350	959	4	(959 ÷ 261.3)
Rent	550	1,507	6	(1,507 ÷ 261.3)
	14,300	39,178	150	

Other strategies the hotel should investigate would be reducing variable costs or increasing advertising, to boost occupancy. These strategies would be evaluated on the same basis.

Overall the above example shows how a hotel operation can use and benefit from the CVP model as part of its management information system. Ultimately, line managers need to understand the daily or weekly room sales figures required to break even.

Summary

For both marginal costing and CVP analysis, it is necessary to classify costs according to whether they are variable or fixed. The concept behind marginal costing is the charging of total fixed cost without arbitrary apportionment and concentrating on presenting contribution earned. CVP analysis is an excellent management information tool that empowers managers to predict costs and assess the profit volume relationship. As with any decision support model, its limitations are in its assumptions and thus, when using CVP analysis, management must be aware of these.

The main information points covered in this chapter are as follows:

❏ Marginal costing is an approach where variable costs are charged to cost units whereas fixed costs are charged in full against the contribution for that period. Contribution is a key term in marginal costing. It is simply the difference between total sales and total variable costs.

❑ CVP analysis shows how costs, revenues and therefore profits behave or react in response to volume of business changes. It considers the interaction between sales revenue, total costs and volume of activity, which between them make up profit.

❑ To use the CVP model, all costs must be classified in relation to their behaviour to changes in volume of activity. This is known as the cost volume relationship. Costs need to be classified into either a fixed cost category or a variable cost category.

❑ Once a cost-volume relationship has been established, it can be combined with a volume-revenue relationship to evaluate alternatives in terms of profit impact in the short term. CVP analysis provides profit estimates at various levels of volume/activity given information on selling prices, fixed costs and variable costs, thus the CVP model is a method of profit planning.

❑ CVP analysis information can also be presented in graphical format. This can be quite useful for management as they get a visual insight into the overall cost-volume-profit relationship for their business. The more popular graphic presentations are:
  − Break-even chart.
  − Profit-volume chart.

❑ Many businesses in the tourism and hospitality industry sell a variety of different products and services that generate different contribution percentages. In these multi-product firms, one can still use CVP analysis, however, one must assume that the proportion each product represents of total sales (sales mix) remains constant.

❑ As with any model, there are necessary, simplifying assumptions on which the whole model is based. These simplifying assumptions are the limitations of the CVP model. It is essential that managers, when interpreting CVP information, keep in mind these limitations and try to assess their influence in practical terms.

❑ The output and information provided by a CVP model is only as good as its inputs. These inputs are all estimated and thus will be subject to varying degrees of uncertainty. In practice, there are several methods available, the most popular being sensitivity analysis.

❑ Some of the accounting CVP assumptions come into conflict with economic theory, especially the assumption of linearity and the constancy of selling price and variable cost per unit inputs in the CVP model. Economists argue that total revenue and total costs functions are curvilinear rather than pure linear as in the accountant's CVP model.

❑ Proponents of the accounting model argue that the objective of the accountant's CVP model is to represent an approximation of revenue and cost behaviour over the relevant range in the short term.

Review Questions

Question 4.1

a) Explain the following terms:
  i.   Marginal cost.
  ii. Contribution.
  iii. Fixed cost.
b) Restate the following statement in a marginal format.

Sales	€4,300,000
Direct material	€1,250,000
Direct labour	€760,000
Variable overhead	€95,000
Fixed overhead	€1,165,000
Variable sales expenses	€75,000
Fixed sales expenses	€450,000
Fixed administration	€550,000
Total costs	€4,345,000
Net loss	€45,000

Question 4.2

D & H Department Stores Limited sell goods from one major outlet in Dublin. Currently the store has three main departments with the following break-down in sales and costs.

	Dept. 1	Dept. 2	Dept. 3	Total
Volume sold	100,000	160,000	40,000	300,000
Revenue	€4,000,000	€1,920,000	€4,080,000	€10,000,000
Purchase cost of sales	€2,600,000	€1,152,000	€2,244,000	€5,996,000
Specific departmental costs	€460,000	€520,000	€770,000	€1,750,000
Overhead costs:				
Centralised ordering & warehousing				€750,000
Centralised administration				€500,000

Centralised ordering and warehousing overhead is apportioned using volume sales as a basis. Centralised administration is apportioned using departmental revenue as a basis.

Required
a) Prepare a profit statement showing the profit/loss for each department after the apportionment of overheads.
b) Prepare a profit statement using marginal costing principles.
c) Management are concerned about the performance of department 2 and are considering the viability of it. It is anticipated that €150,000 in centralised ordering and warehousing can be saved if the department is closed. Centralised administration will be unaffected by the closure. Advise management on the viability of department 2, showing calculations to support your view.

Question 4.3

Explain the following terms:
a) Break-even point.
b) Margin of safety.
c) Contribution margin.

Question 4.4

a) Explain the relationship between cost structure and profit stability.
b) Compare and contrast the break–even chart and profit volume chart as providers of useful information to management.
c) Outline the arguments in favour of both the economist's approach and the accountant's approach to CVP analysis.

Question 4.5

The manager of a clothes shop is considering expanding the nature of the outlet to provide a clothing alteration service for customers. It has been estimated that 75,000 items will be altered in the period. The customer will be charged a fee of €5.00 per item altered. The following costs have been estimated:

Variable labour is estimated at €2.50 per item.

Variable overhead is estimated at 50 cent per item.

Fixed costs for the period have been budgeted at €140,000.

Required

a) Calculate the profit or loss if the above estimates prove to be correct.
b) What is the break-even point in units and revenue.
c) What is the margin of safety in units and revenue.
d) How many alterations need to be sold to achieve a profit of €30,000.
e) How much should be charged for each alteration if a profit of 20 per cent of selling price is required based on existing forecast sales volume.
f) Prepare a break-even chart summarising the above CVP relationship showing clearly the break-even point and the margin of safety.

Question 4.6

A computer retailer is considering providing a modem installation service aimed at home computer users. Each service will provide a modem fully installed and a half hour's training in modem use and care. It is estimated that 2,000 modems will be installed in the first year. Each installation will be charged to clients at €300. Variable costs have been estimated at €110 per installation (including cost of modem). Fixed costs are estimated at €342,000 per annum.

Required

a) Calculate the break-even point in units and revenue.
b) Calculate the margin of safety in units and revenue.
c) Calculate the number of installations needed to earn €50,000 profit.
d) Calculate the installation price to be charged to ensure that the venture breaks even, if the number of installations falls to 1,600.
e) Explain the term 'contribution sales ratio' (C/S ratio) and show how it is calculated.

Question 4.7

Charlie Brown owns a farm in West Cork and has decided to diversify from his farming activities into agri-tourism. He hopes to provide farm tours to tourists as a means of increasing his income and in the future to invest in providing farm accommodation to tourists. He estimates that the price per tour should be set no higher than €5.00 including VAT at 13.5 per cent. His daughter has decided to take on the role of managing the whole operation for a fixed salary of €15,000 per annum and a commission of 10 per cent of turnover net of VAT. He estimates the annual costs associated with the venture as follows:

	€
Advertising	8,000
Insurance	6,000
Repairs and maintenance	3,500
Administration and accounting expenses	3,000
Depreciation	2,000
Commissions to coach operators as a percentage of turnover	5%
General expenses	2,000

The capital required to set up the operation is estimated at €75,000 which will be financed through an agri-tourism grant of €15,000 and loan capital of €60,000 at 8 per cent per annum.

Required
a) Calculate the break-even point in both sales volume and revenue.
b) If Charlie requires a profit of €10,000, what turnover must he achieve?
c) If fixed costs increase by 10 per cent, calculate the level of sales Charlie will have to achieve to maintain his profit requirement.
d) Prepare a profit volume graph showing clearly the break-even point and the margin of safety, if he achieves his required profit.
e) Comment on the viability of the venture.

Question 4.8

The launch of a heritage centre in East Galway is being considered by Galway County Council. After initial market research, four possible levels of demand are being considered. The variable costs associated with these levels are shown below.

Consumer reaction	Adverse	Average	Good	Excellent
Variable costs €	30,000	45,000	60,000	85,000

Based on similar heritage centres around the country, the average contribution to sales ratio (C/S ratio) is expected to be 60 per cent. Fixed costs are estimated at €46,000. The initial capital investment for the project to get it up and running is estimated at €500,000.

Required

a) The profit or loss at each of the four levels of projected demand.
b) The break-even point in sales value.
c) The level of sales required for the business to make a return on an initial investment of 20 per cent.
d) Briefly comment on the viability of the venture.

Question 4.9

Hausen Airlines is a small family run charter airline company that operates a passenger service from Kerry airport to Dublin. They operate two aircraft and provide four return journeys per day. Information on their pricing and costing structure is as follows:

Maximum number of passengers per flight	120
Average selling price per return flight	€120
Variable cost per passenger per return flight	€20
Staff cost per return flight	€1,000
Airport charges per one way flight	€250
Aircraft insurance per annum	€1,152,000
Fuel cost per return flight	€4,500
Administration cost for the year	€100,000

Required

a) Calculate the break-even point per return flight and the overall break-even point per annum, assuming flights run 360 days per year.
b) Calculate the annual profit given a load factor of 75 per cent. — 90 People
c) Prepare a break-even chart showing the break-even point and margin of safety based on a load factor of 75 per cent.
d) Calculate the number of customers per flight required to achieve a profit of €4,000,000 per annum.

Question 4.10

The Ballycumber Heritage Centre is considering opening a restaurant adjacent to the centre. The estimated investment required is as follows:

Expenditure on fixed assets	€300,000
Working capital requirement	€10,000
	€310,000

An initial study of costs and numbers indicate that variable costs will vary between 35 per cent and 45 per cent of selling price. The average spend per customer is estimated at €9 including VAT at 12.5 per cent. Labour costs are estimated at €70,000 per annum, with overheads, including depreciation, estimated at €65,000 per annum.

Required
a) Calculate the following, based on variable cost levels of 35 per cent, 40 per cent and 45 per cent respectively:
  i.   The annual break-even point for the heritage centre.
  ii. The number of customers required to give the heritage centre a return on investment of 20 per cent.
  iii. The margin of safety at this level of profit.
b) Based on variable cost levels of 40 per cent, prepare a profit volume chart estimating profit at demand levels of 25,000, 30,000 and 35,000 customers.
c) If the initial study forecasts a demand of between 25,000 and 35,000 customers, comment on the viability of the venture.

Question 4.11

Gary Dunne, owner and manager of Naas Leisure Holidays Ltd, offers a package deal to customers which, during the current year, has sold for €250, with variable costs amounting to €125. The company's accountant Mr Donnelly has estimated the profit for the year at €150,000, allowing for fixed costs of €120,000.

During discussions on the 2005/2006 budget, Mr Donnelly recommended a unit variable cost rise of €10 following a recent wage award. He also expected fixed costs to rise 20 per cent, mainly due to impending rent reviews on its leasehold property. Mr Alex Gibson, the marketing manager, thought the market was buoyant and he expressed the view that:

1. If the price is maintained at €250, the number of packages sold next year would increase by 10 per cent.
2. If the price was reduced by €20, increases in sales of as much as 25 per cent could be achieved.

Required

a) Present a statement showing which of the marketing manager's proposals provide the greater amount of profit.

b) Calculate, in respect of each alternative, the break-even point in terms of sales volume and sales value.

c) Prepare a profit volume chart based on the marketing manager's first proposal. From the chart, estimate the profit or loss based on demand levels of 800, 1,000 and 1,500 packages sold.

d) Briefly outline four limitations of CVP analysis as a management information tool.

Question 4.12

Stanley Wise has established a small door-to-door sales business selling stationery sets. The following budgeted information is available:

	Set 1	Set 2	Set 3	Set 4
Volume	15,000	5,000	10,000	7,500
Total sales revenue	€37,500	€16,250	€43,000	€13,125
Unit costs & profit:				
Variable costs	€0.95	€1.25	€2.00	€0.65
Fixed overhead	€0.50	€0.50	€0.50	€0.50
Profit	€1.05	€1.50	€1.80	€0.60

Required

a) Calculate the total revenue required to break even based on the current sales mix.

b) Calculate the number of units of each product required to break even based on the current sales mix.

c) Calculate the margin of safety in revenue.

d) Calculate the break-even point and margin of safety if the business follows a strategy of increasing advertising by €15,000 which is forecast to increase sales by 10 per cent.

e) Should the increase in advertising be implemented?

Question 4.13

Water Pleasure Ltd is a company located in Westport, Co. Mayo. They specialise in the sale of water sports equipment of which their two main products are water-skis and surfboards. The projected financial information for the new season is as follows:

	Water-skis	Surfboards
	€	€
Selling price including VAT at 20 per cent	168	240
Purchase costs including VAT at 20 per cent	84	144
Estimated sales	300	400

Other annual costs are as follows:	
Sales commissions to staff as a percentage of sales	20%
Wages & salaries	45,000
Overheads (excluding loan interest)	14,400
Depreciation of fixed assets	10,000

The company is financed by shareholders' funds of €160,000 and a long-term loan of €50,000, with a fixed rate of interest of 8 per cent.

Required

a) How much sales revenue must be generated per week from the shop in order to break even. (You may assume the trading year is 50 weeks).

b) Calculate the amount of sales revenue to be generated per week if a return on equity of 20 per cent is required.

c) If an advertising campaign promoting a '15 per cent off' deal on wet suits at the year-end is launched, how many extra wet suits need to be sold to cover the costs of the promotion which is estimated to cost €5,000.

CHAPTER 5

Relevant Costs and Revenues for Decision-making

Learning Outcomes

By the end of this chapter you will be able to:

❑ Outline what is meant by 'relevant information' within a decision-making context.
❑ Distinguish between quantitative and qualitative information for decision-making purposes.
❑ Understand the principles that apply in determining relevant quantifiable data for decision-making.
❑ Have the ability to apply these principles to decision scenarios.
❑ Apply the principles of relevant cost to decision scenarios involving constraints and scarce resources.
❑ Be aware of the qualitative factors that apply to all decision-making scenarios.

Introduction

The responsibilities of management fall into three main categories, namely planning, decision-making and control. This chapter will focus on decision-making and the relevant information required to inform decision-making. Managers are responsible for every facet of a business and have as their overall objective to increase the wealth of the owners. To effectively carry out this role with any degree of success requires a high degree of planning, effective decision-making and ensuring resources and costs are controlled. Managers strive to achieve planned results using limited resources by making decisions and they require timely and relevant information to do this. Each decision point is a unique opportunity, which often requires relevant specialist information to back the decision. The primary role of the accountant in the decision-making process is to provide this information which may be constructed or revised to fit a specific problem. This chapter will focus on the main principles underlining relevant costs and benefits for decision-making.

Relevant Costs and Benefits in Decision-making

'Costs and revenues appropriate to a specific management decision'
Relevant costs and revenues as defined by CIMA Official Terminology

All decisions relate to the future and thus the past is generally unaffected by a decision. The function of decision-making is to select a course of action for the future that is most likely to satisfy the objectives of the business. Relevant costs and benefits for decision-making can simply be explained as those costs and benefits that will be affected by the decision. The following are the main principles underlying relevant costs and benefits for decision-making. These can be considered under four headings:

- ❏ Historic and sunk costs.
- ❏ Incremental costs.
- ❏ Opportunity costs.
- ❏ Replacement costs.

cost benefits affected by decision making

Historic and Sunk Costs

'Cost that has been irreversibly incurred or committed and cannot therefore be considered relevant to a decision'
Sunk cost as defined by CIMA Official Terminology

can't be relevant to a decision

As mentioned above, decisions affect future costs and revenues and thus past costs and revenues are unaffected. Costs of an historic nature, which are generally referred to as sunk costs, are incurred as a result of past decisions and are therefore irrelevant to the decision-making process. Sunk costs are historical costs which cannot be changed no matter what future action is taken. Sunk costs are easily identifiable as they will have been paid for, or are owed under a legally binding contract, and therefore the company is committed to paying for them in the future.

money already spent

Example 5.1: *Historic/sunk costs*

Food Land Limited has five large freezer display units which were purchased three years ago for €20,000 each. The net book value of the freezers in the last financial accounts of the company was €8,000 each. The company has just purchased new freezers that comply with the latest European safety advice and is faced with a decision to either: *depreciation = €12,000*

a) Sell the existing freezers for €4,000 each,
    or
b) Improve the existing freezers at a cost of €5,000 each and then sell them for €10,000 each.

What should the company do?

Approach

In this situation the focus is on future costs and benefits only. Past costs are ignored. Thus the original cost of the machines and their net book value are irrelevant to the decision. They are sunk costs and should be ignored because they cannot be changed.

The relevant costs and benefits for this decision are as follows:

	Sell now	Alter and sell
Future benefits	€20,000	€50,000
Future costs		€25,000
Future income	€20,000	€25,000

This analysis, which ignores non-quantifiable factors, suggests that Food Land Limited is €5,000 better off by altering rather than selling immediately.

Incremental Costs and Revenues

increase / change by small amounts

'Incremental costs are the changes in future costs and revenues that occur, as a result of decisions'

In the previous example, the focus was on future costs and benefits, ignoring past or sunk costs as irrelevant to the decision-making process. However, not all future costs and benefits are relevant. It is only the incremental future costs that are relevant for decision-making. *costs that will change because of a decision*

Incremental costs and benefits are the changes in future costs and benefits that will occur as a result of a decision. Ultimately if a future cost or revenue is not going to change as a result of a decision, then it is irrelevant to the decision and should be ignored in the decision-making process.

Example 5.2: *Incremental costs and revenues*

The Pleasure Leisure Hotel has 30 bedrooms. The hotel is open all year round and has a capacity of 10,950 (30 x 365) bed-nights. It is anticipated that only 9,000 rooms will be taken up this year. However Duncan Tours Ltd has offered to take up the spare capacity of 1,950 bed-nights for €20 per bed-night. The hotel normally charges €50 a night, with the variable cost per room amounting to €15 and annual fixed costs amounting to €135,000.

The following is a summary profit statement based on selling 9,000 bed-nights:

	Per unit	Total
	€	€
Sales	50	450,000
Less Variable costs	15	(135,000)
Fixed costs (€135,000 ÷ 9,000)	15	(135,000)
Projected net profit		180,000

Should the hotel take up the offer from the tour company?

Approach

At first it would seem foolish to accept the deal offered by Duncan Tours. However on closer inspection, by accepting the tour company's offer, the fixed costs will not change in total. Only sales and variable cost will change. Sales will increase by €20 per bed-night taken up and variable costs will increase by €15 per bed-night taken up. These are the incremental costs and benefits (the future costs and benefits that will change because of the decision) and as the benefits outweigh the costs, the offer should be accepted.

The business would lose out on extra profit of €9,750 (1,950 rooms x €5 (€20 – €15)) if all the spare capacity (rooms) were not taken up by the tour company. The fixed costs are non-incremental and would not change because of the decision and thus are irrelevant. This is presented in the following incremental profit statement.

Incremental Profit Statement

	Per unit	Total
	€	€
Incremental sales	20 x 1,950	39,000
Less		
Incremental variable costs	15 x 1,950	29,250
Contribution	5 x 1,950	9,750
Less		
Incremental fixed costs		0
Incremental profit		9,750

Opportunity Costs

'The value of the benefit sacrificed when one course of action is chosen in preference to an alternative'
Opportunity cost as defined by CIMA Official Terminology

after – if you choose A, you can't the choose B

Opportunity costs occur where there are **mutually exclusive alternatives** from which a business must choose one. **An opportunity cost is the cash benefit sacrificed in favour of a particular course** of action. It is the highest alternative benefit foregone by choosing a specific course of action. Suppose a business has three mutually exclusive options available to it of which the net profits are: option A €100,000, option B €80,000 and option C €60,000. Since only one option can be selected, option A is chosen as it provides the biggest benefit. The opportunity cost associated with this course of action is the benefit foregone by not going with the next best alternative, option B. **Opportunity cost is an economic term** rather than an accounting term. It does not appear in the trading, profit and loss account as an expense because it represents a lost opportunity rather than an outlay cost. It is used in decision accounting as a means of presenting financial information and assessing the financial implications of a decision. For example, the decision to choose option A is not simply because it offers a profit of €100,000 but because it offers a differential profit of €20,000 in excess of the next best alternative.

Example 5.3: *Opportunity costs*

A Leisure Centre runs a small coffee bar which achieves an annual operating profit of €7,000. A coffee franchise company call Moon-Bucks has offered to run the bar and pay the leisure centre an €8,000 annual fee.

Differential profit of 1,000 euro

Approach

The opportunity cost of taking up the Moon-Bucks offer is the €7,000 lost income from operating the coffee bar themselves. The company is €1,000 better off by allowing Moon-Bucks to operate the bar themselves.

Replacement Costs

'Cost of replacing an asset'
Replacement cost as defined by CIMA Official Terminology

This is relevant where an item or resource is purchased for a specific purpose other than the opportunity or decision under consideration. If the resource is used for this new opportunity then it will need to be replaced for its original purpose. The question is 'what is the relevant cost for using the resource under the new opportunity?' Is it the historic cost (what was originally paid for the resource), or is it the replacement cost (the cost of replacing the resource, as it was intended for another purpose)? The answer is the replacement cost. The term replacement cost can refer to any business resource, not just assets, as in the above definition. If for example, manpower (an expense) is transferred from an existing job to a new project, then the replacement cost would be the relevant cost to include in the decision-making process.

Example 5.4: *Replacement cost*

The manager of The Lighting Store has been approached by a local business to install Christmas lights in their complex. The job requires 50 boxes of fancy lights. The lights ^(offered to pay €6 per box) are in stock and cost €5 per box when purchased. The lights are a popular fast moving item in the store and the manager expects all existing stock will be sold well in advance of Christmas. The lights used for the job can be replaced at a cost of €6.50.

What is the cost of materials for the once off special job?

Approach

In this situation the lights will be used for another purpose and 50 boxes will need to be replaced due to the decision to take on this special 'one-off' job. Thus the relevant cost of materials for this special job is the replacement cost of €6.50. You will also note that the historic cost of €5 is a sunk cost as it has been paid for and is unaffected by the decision to undertake the new job.

Accounting for Business Decisions

The following are examples of typical decision situations within the hospitality, tourism and retail sectors whereby the principles of relevant costs can be applied to the decision process.

Decision to outsource

An outsourcing (make or buy) decision, is one every organisation may have to consider. Examples include a hotel contracting a specialist cleaning firm to do all their cleaning, or retailers contracting an external firm to manage security. Decisions like these should not be made based solely on cost and benefit criteria but should also take account of the non-quantifiable factors related to the decision.

Example 5.5: *Outsourcing decision*

A hotel company is deciding on whether to manage their own cleaning or hire in a contracting firm to do it. The cheapest bid of all the contract cleaning companies amounts to €175,000 per annum. The current cost of the cleaning department amounts to €200,000.

These are broken down as follows:

	€
Materials	52,000
Labour	80,000
Supervision	25,000
Apportioned fixed overheads	43,000
	200,000

[handwritten annotations: cost savings/benefit. non-incremental. It won't change, not taken into account]

Approach

Initially the figures would suggest that the company should choose the outsourcing option. However the fixed overhead is an apportionment of the general overheads of the business and would not change irrespective of the decision. Thus the relevant costs in this decision are materials, labour and supervision amounting to €157,000. Comparing this to the cost of outsourcing at €175,000, the hotel should retain its cleaning department.

Suppose however that by outsourcing the work, more space will be come available in the hotel, which could be turned into revenue producing space. For example, storage space used for materials and equipment could become available and this could increase the bedroom capacity of the hotel, generating additional income. This is very relevant to the decision and if the projected extra revenue from this space amounts to €50,000 per annum then the relevant costs and benefits would be as follows:

	€
Cost of outsourcing	(175,000)
Cost savings	157,000
Extra revenues earned	50,000
Benefits exceed costs	32,000

Thus depending on the non-quantitative factors, the business should outsource their cleaning requirements. *[handwritten: make extra profit. other factors - bad will buying materials less local, low morale letting staff go, keep rep]*

Decision to discontinue a department

Any business will need to review its activities on a continuous basis. Part of this review will involve the appraisal of the viability of various departments or divisions. *[handwritten: trained contractors]*

The decision to close any part of a business is a very significant one and thus management must apply the principles of relevant costs to this decision.

Example 5.6: *Closing an unprofitable department*

Irish Pharmacies operate a chain of drug stores. Each store has three departments; medicines, baby products and cosmetics. The performance of the Navan store is under review. The following are the costs and revenues of the three departments:

	Medicines	Baby	Cosmetics	Total
	€'000	€'000	€'000	€'000
Revenues	160	80	120	360
Less Variable costs	60	50	70	180
Less Fixed costs	40	40	40	120
Net profit	60	(10)	10	60

Note: €30,000 of the total fixed costs relates to rent, rates and insurance which the business is under contract to pay. Remaining fixed costs relate to head-office costs that have been apportioned to the three departments.

Discuss the performance of the Navan store with particular reference to closing the baby products department.

Approach

From the information presented, it appears that the baby products department is making a loss and thus is a prime candidate for closure. However, management should look behind the figures and only relevant costs and in particular incremental costs should be used for this decision. Fixed costs of €90,000 relate to head-office which are apportioned to the three revenue producing departments. These costs are non-incremental and will not change whether the baby products department remains open or closed. The rest of the fixed costs relate to rent, rates and insurance, which the business has a contractual obligation to pay. These would be considered sunk or non-incremental. In total, all the fixed costs are irrelevant to the decision. Thus the figures should be presented as follows for the three departments and in particular the baby department.

	Medicines	Baby	Cosmetics	Total
	€'000	€'000	€'000	€'000
Revenues	160	80	120	360
Less Variable costs	60	50	70	180
Contribution	100	30	50	180

The baby department should not be closed as it provides a contribution to cover the fixed costs of the business. If the business were to close the baby department, then the overall profit would be as follows, assuming the fixed costs of the baby department are allocated evenly to the medicines area and the cosmetics department.

	Medicines	Baby	Cosmetics	Total
	€'000	€'000	€'000	€'000
Revenues	160		120	280
Less Variable costs	60		70	130
Contribution	100		50	150
Fixed costs	60		60	120
Net profit	40		(10)	30

By closing the baby department, overall profit has fallen by €30,000 (€60,000 – €30,000) which amounts to the contribution that department provides to the business. A general rule of thumb in decisions like these is, if the department, section or product line provides a positive contribution to fixed costs, then it should not be closed down. Presenting profit statements using a marginal costing approach (where fixed costs are not apportioned) may prevent wrong decisions being made. This is one of the main benefits of marginal costing over the absorption based approach as presented above and discussed in Chapters 3 and 4. The profit statement based on a marginal costing approach is presented below:

Marginal Costing Approach

	Medicines	Baby	Cosmetics	Total
	€'000	€'000	€'000	€'000
Revenues	160	80	120	360
Less Variable costs	60	50	70	180
Contribution	100	30	50	180
Fixed costs				120
Net profit				60

It is important to stress this analysis does not take into account qualitative factors which could sway a decision another way.

Decision for partial closure

In the hospitality and tourism sectors, businesses need to consider on an annual basis whether they should remain open or closed for the off-season. Many hospitality and tourism businesses now have invested to ensure the off-season is not as long as in previous years. The development of local heritage centres and leisure facilities for hotels have had the effect of extending the 'season'. However for smaller businesses, the question still remains.

Example 5.7: *Close in the off-season decision*

The Celtic House Hotel situated in West Mayo is considering the question as to whether to remain open or close during their 'off-season'. Their off-season period runs from 1 November to 1 March. On the basis of past years trading results, the forecast figures for next year are as follows:

	Season	Off-season
	€	€
Sales	90,000	25,000
Cost of sales	20,000	8,000
Wages	20,000	12,000
Manager salary	10,000	5,000
Light and heat	5,000	4,000
Repairs and maintenance	2,000	1,000
Rates	800	400
Depreciation	2,000	1,000
Insurance	4,000	2,000
Sundry expenses	1,000	1,000
Net profit	25,200	(9,400)

Additional relevant information:

❑   If the business closes, a caretaker will be employed at a cost of €2,000.
❑   The general manager is on a basic annual salary of €15,000, which is guaranteed irrespective of whether the business closes in the off-season.
❑   Light and heat, repairs and maintenance and sundry expenses will fall to 20 per cent of the current estimate in the off-season if the hotel closes. Insurance costs will fall by 50 per cent in the off-season if the hotel closes.

Should the hotel close during the four months of the 'off-season', as according to present forecast figures, it would make a net loss of €9,400?

Approach

To answer this we need to take account of the principles of relevant costs, focusing only on the incremental costs. Thus we need to ask 'what costs and benefits will change if the business decides to close?'

		Benefits / costs €
Sales	If the business closes then it loses €25,000 in revenue. Thus it is relevant to the decision.	(25,000)
Cost of sales	If the business closes, this cost will not exist and thus it is incremental and relevant.	8,000
Wages and salaries	If the business closes, a caretaker is required at a cost of €2,000. Thus there is a cost saving of €10,000 due to the decision to close.	10,000
Managers salary	The manager is on a basic annual contract of €15,000. This basic fee will apply irrespective of whether the business closes in the off-season. Thus it is non-incremental and irrelevant to the decision.	
Light and heat	If the business closes, this figure will fall to about 20 per cent of its current estimate, thus ensuring a cost saving of €3,200.	3,200
Repairs and maintenance	This figure will fall to 20 per cent of the current estimate if the business closes, ensuring a cost saving of €800.	800
Rates	This cost is non-incremental and thus will remain irrespective of the decision.	
Depreciation	This cost is non-incremental and will remain irrespective of the decision.	
Insurance	This figure will fall by 50 per cent if the hotel closes, ensuring a €1,000 cost saving.	1,000
Sundry expenses	This figure will fall to 20 per cent of the current estimate if the hotel closes. This will represent a cost saving of €800.	800

The analysis shows that the business should stay open based on financial criteria alone. The cost of closing would be the loss in revenue of €25,000 with the benefits of closing (the cost savings) only coming to €23,800.

Special pricing decisions

Special pricing decisions relate to once-off orders generally at a price below the prevailing market price. The decision facing the supplier is whether they should accept such an order even though it is below market price.

Example 5.8: *Special pricing decisions*

Monaghan Clothing Ltd manufactures and supplies tracksuits to clothing retailers. It has a production capacity of 100,000 tracksuits per month. Expected costs and revenues for the next month at 70 per cent activity level are as follows:

	Unit cost	Total
	€	€
Direct materials	5.00	350,000
Direct labour	10.00	700,000
Variable overhead	2.50	175,000
Fixed overhead (€280,000 ÷ 70,000)	4.00	280,000
Total costs	21.50	1,505,000

Monaghan's supply each tracksuit at €35 to retailers. An event management company has offered to purchase 18,000 tracksuits at a price of €20 each. The company require their company name and logo imprinted on the tracksuits. This is estimated at costing €1.00 per tracksuit. The event management company will cover all distribution costs.

Should Monaghan Clothing accept the order?

Approach

At first it would seem that Monaghan Clothing should reject the order as the offer price of €20 is 43 per cent below their normal supply price and does not exceed the full cost price of producing the tracksuits. However, focusing on the cost estimates, the fixed overhead of €280,000 will not change and the variable overhead will not change as a result of the order. Also direct labour is not expected to change as the company is presently working at 70 per cent of capacity. As these are the non-incremental costs for this order, they should be ignored in the decision process. The only costs that are incremental are the materials cost of €5.00 and the extra adjustment costs of €1.00, thus the company should accept the order. The relevant costs and benefits relating to the decision are as follows:

	Unit cost	Total
	€	€
Materials	5.00	90,000
Extra adjustment costs	1.00	18,000
	6.00	108,000
Selling price	20.00	360,000
Profit	14.00	252,000

Decision-making with Limiting Factors

'Anything which limits the activity of an entity'
Limiting factor as defined by CIMA Official Terminology

Every business has constraints or limiting factors that restrict the activity level in an organisation and prevent it making greater profits. Examples of common limiting factors are:

❑ Sales demand.
❑ Operating capacity.
❑ Shortage of labour.
❑ Shortage of materials.
❑ Lack of available finance.
❑ Limited distribution channels.

Sales demand is an obvious limiting factor for most businesses in the hospitality, tourism and retail sector as capacity is never reached. During the booming 'Celtic Tiger' period, average occupancy for hotels seldom exceeded 80 per cent and although this period was also marked by a huge increase in 'retail therapy', one seldom heard of any stock-outs. However it is rare that there is only one limiting factor for a business. For example, where there are labour or material constraints, then a business is faced with rationing these scarce resources as they do not have the resources to satisfy demand. In this case a decision must be made regarding what products or services should be provided. This type of situation requires management to choose a product mix that will maximise profits within the constraints of the limiting factors. This decision must include an evaluation of the requirements that each product or service has on the scarce resources. Thus in situations where significant limiting factors exist, management should rank products/services according to their 'contribution per limiting factor'. This can lead to the selection of a product/service mix that maximises profit. For example, if labour is the constraint the decision should be based upon contribution per labour hour.

Limiting factors – steps in establishing plan to maximise profits

Step 1	Establish if a constraint actually exists.
Step 2	Establish the contribution per unit.
Step 3	Establish the contribution per limiting factor and rank in order of the highest contribution per limiting factor.
Step 4	Establish the optimum plan.
Step 5	Calculate the profit based on this plan.

Example 5.9: *Limiting factors*

Brophy Craft Sales was set up as a partnership of three local artists to provide a means for selling their hand-crafted products. One of the partners, a ceramic artist, has developed a business plan, which involves creating a workshop at the rear of the store. The artist will run the workshop and provide sessions to groups in the art of ceramic work and painting. It is anticipated that the artist will have only 35 labour hours a week available for the sessions. The following information has been estimated for each of the three groups:

	Adult group €	School group €	Children's party €
Sales (price per group)	120	150	144
Materials	48	60	72
Labour	24	32	16
Total variable cost per group	72	92	88
Labour hours per group (artists time)	1.5 hours	2 hours	1 hour
Estimated number of group bookings per week	8	10	7

The total fixed costs for the workshop per week are estimated at €667.

The artist is concerned that as he needs to be present for the full duration of each workshop, he cannot provide for the estimated number of bookings per week.

Advise the artist on the schedule of bookings to accept in order to maximise profits.

Approach

Step 1 – Establish if a constraint actually exists.

Group	Number of bookings	Hours required	Total hours required
Adult group	8	1.5 hours	12 hours
School group	10	2 hours	20 hours
Children's party	7	1 hour	_7 hours
			39 hours
		Hours available	35 hours
		Hours short	_4 hours

A constraint based on labour hours exists.

Step 2 – Establish the contribution per unit.

	Adult group	School group	Children's party
	€	€	€
Sales	120	150	144
Variable costs	_72	_92	_88
Contribution per group	48	58	56

Step 3 – Establish the contribution per labour hour and rank in order of the highest contribution per labour hour.

	Adult group	School group	Children's party
	€	€	€
Contribution per group	€48	€58	€56
Divide by labour hours	1.5 hours	2 hours	1 hour
Contribution per hour	€32	€29	€56
Ranking	**2nd**	**3rd**	**1st**

As the children's parties have the highest contribution per limiting factor, all of these bookings should be accepted. Also if possible, all adult group bookings should be catered for. Finally the school groups should take up any remaining hours unutilised.

Step 4 – Establish the optimum plan for the artist.

Group	Bookings	Hours	Total hours required	Total hours available 35 hours
Children's party	7	1 hour	7 hours	28 hours
Adult group	8	1.5 hours	12 hours	16 hours
School group	8	2 hours	16 hours	0 hours

The optimum plan requires the number of school groups to be reduced from 10 to 8 because of the shortfall in hours.

Step 5 – Show the profit this plan will earn.

	Adult group	School group	Children's party	Total
Groups	8	8	7	
	€	€	€	€
Sales	960	1,200	1,008	3,168
Variable costs	576	736	616	1,928
Contribution	384	464	392	1,240
Fixed costs				667
Profit				573

Qualitative Factors

Qualitative factors are best described as factors that cannot be quantified in terms of income and costs. In many respects some of the so called qualitative factors could be quantifiable in terms of their effects on the business but this quantification process would be very expensive and not worth the cost. The nature of qualitative factors in decision-making will almost always vary with the circumstances of the decision under review and the options under consideration. The following are some qualitative factors identified by Atkinson, Berry and Jarvis (1995) which can influence the decision-making process:

❑ **Customers:** Management must assess the effects on their customer base of decisions, especially ones that affect product lines and after-sales service. For example, the exclusion of one service from a range because, in financial terms, it is uneconomic to provide and sell, could affect the demand for other services.

Services and products sold by firms are often **inter-dependent** and this should be taken into account in the decision-making process.

❑ **Employees:** Any decision regarding the closure of some product lines or a section of a business or changes in work practices needs to be accepted by employees and their unions. Bad labour relations caused by decisions that involve such changes could lead to inefficiencies and losses. *bad will*

❑ **Competitors:** How competitors will react to any changes should also be taken into account. For example there is no point in reducing a selling price to ensure greater market share if competitors are likely to do the same and maintain the status quo.

❑ **Legal constraints:** Any decision-making process must take into account the legal aspects or consequences of the decision. These can be ignored at the peril of the business. For example, the decision to open a new hotel may be influenced by pending legislation regarding health and safety. Decisions on whether to open a new grocery shop may be influenced by a change in legislation regarding the banning of below cost selling of certain grocery products.

❑ **Creditors/suppliers:** Decisions may affect suppliers and hence this relationship must be taken into account in the decision-making process. *bad will*

Above all, one must be mindful of the fact that the financial projections upon which decisions are made are best estimates, which may fall short of reality.

Summary

This chapter has focused on the rules and principles regarding relevant information for decision-making purposes. The chapter has outlined how to distinguish between relevant and irrelevant costs and the benefits for decision-making.

The main information points covered in this chapter are as follows:

❑ Decisions require accurate and timely information and the likelihood of making a good decision is enhanced by judiciously using the information at hand.

❑ Relevant costs and benefits for decision-making can simply be defined as those costs and benefits that will be affected by the decision.

❑ Decisions affect future costs and revenues, and thus past costs and revenues are unaffected. Costs of an historic nature, which are generally referred to as sunk costs, are incurred as a result of past decisions and are therefore irrelevant to the decision-making process.

❑ Incremental costs and benefits are the changes in future costs and benefits that will occur as a result of a decision. If a future cost or revenue is not going to change as a result of a decision, then it is irrelevant to the decision and should be ignored in the decision-making process.

❑ An opportunity cost is the cash benefit sacrificed in favour of a particular course of action. It is the highest alternative benefit foregone by choosing a particular course of action.

❑ Replacement cost is a relevant cost when a decision opportunity requires the use of resources (materials, labour) which are required for another purpose and thus need to be replaced. The replacement cost, not the historic cost, is the relevant figure to use in this decision.

❑ There are a number of typical decision situations whereby the principles of relevant costs can be applied. For example,
 – Closure of a department or segment of a business.
 – The outsourcing decision.
 – Pricing of a product or service.
 – To open or close in the off-season.

❑ Every business has constraints or limiting factors which restrict the activity level in an organisation and prevent it making greater profits. Examples of common limiting factors are sales demand, operating capacity, labour shortages, materials shortages, and lack of finance. In situations where significant limiting factors exist, management should rank products or services according to their 'contribution per limiting factor'. This can lead to the selection of a product/service mix that maximises profit.

❑ Qualitative factors are best described as factors that cannot be quantified in terms of income and costs. Qualitative factors need to be taken into account and are an integral part of any decision-making process.

Review Questions

Question 5.1

a) Describe the main factors in classifying costs as either relevant or irrelevant for management decision-making purposes.
b) Depreciation is a significant element in the calculation of profit. Justify its classification as an irrelevant cost in decision-making.

Question 5.2

Briefly explain the following financial terms and indicate their relevance in the context of short-term management decision-making.

- ☐ Sunk costs.
- ☐ Incremental costs.
- ☐ Unavoidable costs.
- ☐ Opportunity costs.

Question 5.3

Hobo Hotels plc. are currently assessing whether to carry on managing their own cleaning or contracting out the work. To date they have put out to tender the cleaning contract and the cheapest tender received was from Ciano's Cleaners Ltd at €135,500 per annum. The annual cleaning costs of the hotels are as follows:

	€
Labour	78,500
Supervision	20,500
Materials	23,222
Overhead charge	40,000
	162,222

The overhead charge is a general charge based on labour costs and represents allocated head-office costs including management and administration costs.

If the company decides to contract out the work, spare capacity will be made available in the hotels and this is estimated to lead to additional income of €25,000 per annum.

Required

a) Identify the incremental and unavoidable costs in the above scenario.

b) Advise the company as to whether they should continue to manage their own cleaning or contract out the work.

Question 5.4

Over the last five years, Farley Chemists, a chain of pharmacies, computerised all of their ordering, prescription and accounts processes. As the prescription system is separate from the rest of the processes, it is felt that major modifications are needed. Two options are under review.

Option A – In-house modification

This option requires Farley Chemists to undertake all modification work in-house. A special project team will be created. Five computer programmers will need to be recruited on a one year contract. Salaries are estimated at €50,000 each. Currently one computer technician, on a salary of €44,000 per annum, is employed. He will be transferred to the project and will receive an increase in salary of €4,000 as a result of the transfer. A new employee will be recruited to take over the existing duties of the technician on a salary of €36,000. It is company policy to pay yearly VHI health contributions of €640 for each employee. The costs of both the human resource department and the staff welfare department are charged to other departments at a budgeted rate of €3,000 per employee. Each programmer will require a computer. There are two computers in storage which cost €900 each when purchased last month. These are spare and there is no other use for them in the foreseeable future. The current purchase price of a computer is €1,000. It has been agreed that a printer can be shared and this must be purchased at a cost of €600. Other communications equipment must be purchased for €500 and it will cost €1,350 to install all the equipment. Each worker will require a desk and chair. There are eight spare desks which originally cost €200 each and have a written down value of €80. Special chairs which meet the health and safety requirements will need to be purchased at a cost of €150 each. Tools costing €180 will be required for the technician and consumables are estimated to cost €500.

Option B – Sub-contract the modifications

The work can be subcontracted to a specialist firm. Negotiations have taken place with a suitable organisation and the fee due to the company would be €300,000. In addition, the chain will need to recruit one employee on a salary of €56,000 to oversee the work. This employee will require all the staff benefits of staff in option A plus a computer, printer, desk and chair. Additional modems and communications equipment will also be required costing €3,400.

Both options will take approximately 10 per cent of the administration director's time. The administration director is paid €90,000 per annum. *incremental*

Required

From a financial perspective, advise Farley Chemists on the best option to choose.

Question 5.5

The following are the departmental profit statements for Irish Home Stores Ltd operating in the retail sector. Presently management are considering the closure of department B as it is currently making a loss.

	A	B	C	Total
	€'000	€'000	€'000	€'000
Revenues	320	160	240	720
Less Variable costs	120	100	140	360
Less Fixed costs	80	80	80	240
Total cost	200	180	220	600
Net profit	120	(20)	20	120

The following information is available:

1. The variable costs are directly related to each of the departments.
2. 50 per cent of the fixed costs relate to head-office costs, which are allocated to the three revenue producing departments.
3. 20 per cent of the fixed costs relate to rent, rates and insurance which the business is contractually obligated to pay, irrespective of whether department B remains open or closed.
4. Should department B close, parts of the space could be leased out for the remainder of the year for €5,000.

Required

a) Advise management on whether department B should remain open or closed explaining and justifying your view.
b) Briefly outline the non-quantifiable factors that management should take into account before making a decision.

Question 5.6

A property management organisation runs three shopping complexes in Finglas, Merrion and Baldoyle. The following budget has been prepared for next year:

	Finglas	Merrion	Baldoyle	Total
	€	€	€	€
Rent receipts	920,000	736,000	598,000	2,254,000
Property upkeep	347,000	273,000	341,000	961,000
Wages and salaries	118,000	102,000	74,000	294,000
Overheads	280,000	220,000	180,000	680,000
Total costs	745,000	595,000	595,000	1,935,000
Profit	175,000	141,000	3,000	319,000

Included in the overhead figures are the head–office fixed costs which amount to €500,000. These have been allocated to each complex on the basis of rent receipts. All other costs are direct. Management are concerned that the Baldoyle complex has a profit of only €3,000 which may easily become a loss and are considering closing the complex.

Required

a) Prepare marginal costing statements to show contributions for each complex and the contribution and profit for the whole organisation based on the following:
  i. The original budget.
  ii. If the Baldoyle complex is sold.
b) On the grounds of profitability, should the Baldoyle complex be closed?

Question 5.7

Gerry and Debra Roche recently purchased the Knockwood Hotel for €1.5 million. The hotel has a capacity of 12,000 rooms per annum. In anticipating demand for next year, they feel they will achieve a 75 per cent occupancy level. In addition, a tour operator has offered to take 2,000 rooms for the year at a special price of €25 per room. The acceptance of this special order will not affect regular bookings. Gerry and Debra have agreed an average price per room of €40. The projected costs for next year are as follows:

❑ Variable costs per room sold will amount to €20.
❑ Fixed costs per annum will amount to €90,000. These fixed costs relate to the general running expenses of the hotel and will remain the same whether the hotel is operating at full capacity or at 75 per cent capacity.

Required
a) Identify the sunk, incremental and unavoidable costs in the above scenario.
b) Advise Gerry and Debra whether or not they should take up the offer from the tour company.

Question 5.8

The manager of a small privately owned supermarket has proposed expanding the nature of the outlet to provide customised fresh bread baked in store. The bread will be ordered by the customer before they begin their supermarket shop and will be provided hot from the oven within 45 minutes. The following costs have been estimated:

❏ Budgeted sales amount to 150,000 loaves @ €2.50.
❏ Ingredients on average will cost 85 cent per loaf.
❏ Direct labour is estimated at 5 cent per loaf.
❏ Variable overhead is estimated at 2 cent per loaf.
❏ Fixed costs have been budgeted at €180,000.

Required
a) Comment on the viability of the above proposal.
b) The manager has received a suggestion from a staff member to offer a free cup of tea in the on-site coffee shop while customers wait. This will cost an extra 25 cent per loaf but volume is expected to increase by 15 per cent. Evaluate the new proposal.
c) Should the fresh bread proposal be adopted and if so, should the free cup of tea be included?
d) What other non-financial factors should be considered when evaluating the proposal?

Question 5.9

It is proposed to open a staff crèche for a trial period of ten months, running from September to June. The crèche is to address the needs of staff working in the Western Retail Park. It is planned that 30 children will be catered for in two groups. A fee of €500 per child per month has been agreed.

The crèche will operate in a building currently rented on a long-term lease for €20,000 per annum by the Western Retail Park. The space to be occupied is currently made available to community projects, which currently earns revenue of €3,000 per month.

Other costs have been budgeted at:

Additional insurance and other running costs	€800 per month of operation
Child care workers – two full-time	€25,000 for the trial period
Assistants – four part-time	€10,000 for the trial period
Share of retail park overheads	€28,500
10 per cent of retail park manager's time	€4,200
Purchase of essential materials	€2,000

Required

Based on a financial analysis of the above proposal, recommend whether or not it should be adopted.

Question 5.10

The Detta Hotel is a family owned operation situated in Donegal. The hotel recorded an operating profit for this year of €128,021, however further analysis shows that the business made a loss in the off-season of €27,533. The owners are considering closing for the off-season. The following data is available:

	Season	Off-season
	€	€
Sales	500,365	88,450
Cost of sales	210,153	37,149
Gross profit	290,212	51,301
Less Expenses		
Wages and salaries	73,500	31,200
Light, heat and power	7,850	5,678
Repairs and maintenance	6,670	1,620
Rates	7,000	7,000
Insurance	11,000	11,000
Advertising	2,468	1,456
Staff meals	6,800	4,300
Telephone	6,870	4,580
Depreciation: Premises	6,000	6,000
Depreciation: Furniture and fittings	4,000	4,000
Sundry expenses	2,500	2,000
	134,658	78,834
Net profit	155,554	(27,533)

1. The season runs from 1 April to 30 September and off-season runs from 1 October to 31 March. *6 months*
2. If the hotel closed during the off-season then depreciation on both premises and furniture would fall by 75 per cent.
3. The general manager, whose salary amounts to €40,000 per annum, is employed on an annual contract.
4. The annual rental for telephone amounts to €4,000.
5. Repairs and maintenance costs only arise when the hotel is open.
6. If the hotel is to close, a caretaker's wage will need to be paid, estimated at €10,000 for the off-season.

Required

Advise management on whether the hotel should remain open or closed during the off-season. You should justify your recommendation.

Question 5.11

MDA Group operate within the retail sector, selling food items in five locations across the city. As part of their corporate strategy, MDA Group have decided to launch a 'private label' brand. Bread has been chosen as an initial trial product to investigate if the approach is viable. A senior manager has negotiated with a leading bakery to produce the private label bread for a trial period.

The bakery, currently operating at 80 per cent capacity, makes half a million premium branded loaves per month. The premium branded loaves retail at €1.40 per loaf. MDA Group have established that the bakery has a profit margin of 30 per cent and a contribution sales ratio of 55 per cent when they make half a million loaves.

MDA Group have negotiated the provision of 150,000 loaves per month at a contract price that will give the bakery €0.20 profit per loaf when additional fixed costs of €30,000 per month and any opportunity costs are included.

Required
a) What selling price has been agreed with the bakery?
b) Discuss the qualitative issues the retailer should consider when evaluating the strategy to provide 'private label' items.

Question 5.12

Your business has been invited to supply components to a transport company for a period of one year at a price of €100,000. The costing department has produced the following data and estimates, relating to the manufacture of the component.

1. The component is made up of materials A and B. Material A costs €20,000 for the order whereas material B is already in stock. Material B was originally intended for another product line which has been discontinued. Until the business received this offer, the plans were to dispose of material B at a cost of €1,500.
2. The direct labour cost associated with the manufacture of this component is estimated at €25,000. However some specialist labour will be required which would cost an extra €10,000. They will be transferred from another department which will have to recruit replacement labour at a cost of €13,000.
3. Machinery, currently idle, will be used to manufacture the component. The machinery was purchased five years ago for €50,000 with an estimated life of ten years. Its present estimated realisable value is €15,000 and should it be used for the contract then its estimated realisable value in one year's time is €5,000.
4. It is intended to extend the duties of a foreman currently employed by the firm to include the supervision of the production process. The foreman is paid €20,000 per annum and it is estimated that this extra duty will amount to 10 per cent of his time.
5. General overheads are allocated to the order on the basis of 100 per cent of labour costs.

Required
a) State whether each of the above is relevant or irrelevant to the decision to accept this order.
b) Recommend to the company, based on quantitative information, whether the company should accept this order based on the agreed price of €100,000.

Profit Sensitivity Analysis

Introduction

Profit sensitivity analysis (PSA) is a management information tool that assesses how profit reacts to changes in various key variables that make up the overall profit figure. In essence, profit is a product of a number of variables (revenues and costs) and sensitivity analysis aims to assess and measure the effects changes in each variable have on profit. It can show which factors have the greatest influence on profit and thus is quite a valuable tool in profit planning and decision-making. It is critical in focusing a business' resources on maintaining and increasing profitability.

PSA Key Variables and Procedures

The key variables that affect profit are the variables that make up revenues and expenses in the profit and loss account. These key variables are as follows:

1. Average sales price/average room rate/average spend.
2. Sales volume measured in terms of units, covers, bed–nights, seats sold, etc.
3. Variable cost per unit including cost of sales, food and beverage costs, and the direct cost associated with accommodation providers and travel companies.
4. Fixed costs, which can be categorised into various cost types such as wages and salaries, rent, insurance, advertising etc.

PSA – key variables

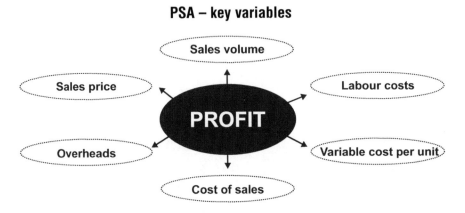

The process in applying PSA is to take any one variable and assess the effect on profit of changes to that variable. For example, should sales volume increase by 10 per cent and the resulting effect on profit is an increase of 15 per cent, then profit is deemed to be sensitive to changes in sales volume. This sensitivity can be measured through the profit multiplier or sensitivity rating which in the above case is 1.5 times (15% ÷ 10%). The profit multiplier or sensitivity rating is calculated as follows:

$$\text{Profit multiplier/sensitivity rating} = \frac{\text{Effect on profit}}{\text{Change in key variable}}$$

A rating of 1.5 tells us that if sales volume increases by 1 per cent, profit will increase by 1.5 per cent. Should sales volume decrease by 5 per cent, profit would decrease by 7.5 per cent. If a small change in a variable (say selling price) causes a huge change in profit, then it can be said that profit is quite sensitive to changes in sales price and that selling price is a critical factor in profitability.

Example 6.1: *Profit sensitivity analysis*

The following forecast information for the next 12 months relates to Celtic Souvenirs Ltd, a chain of souvenir shops in Ireland.

	€	€
Sales		100,000
Cost of sales		50,000
Gross profit		50,000
Other variable costs	10,000	
Fixed costs	20,000	30,000
Net profit		20,000

Management are concerned with the accuracy of these estimates and how sensitive profit is to any change in projected assumptions. They require answers to the following 'what if' questions:

a) Competition is such that sales volume drops by 10 per cent.
b) The business is forced to cut prices by 10 per cent to maintain sales.
c) Cost of raw material increases by 10 per cent.
d) Variable costs increase by 10 per cent.
e) Fixed costs increase by 10 per cent.

Calculate and interpret the sensitivity ratings.

Approach

Each scenario is taken on its own with profit recalculated as follows:

a) Sales volume drops by 10 per cent.
Net profit is recalculated as follows. It is important to remember that when sales volume falls, variable cost will also fall. Fixed costs will remain constant.

	€	€
Sales		90,000
Cost of sales		45,000
Gross profit		45,000
Other variable costs	9,000	
Fixed costs	20,000	29,000
Net profit		16,000

Profit has fallen 20 per cent (4,000 ÷ 20,000) based on a volume decrease of 10 per cent. The profit multiplier or sensitivity rating is 2. In other words, for every 1 per cent increase or decrease in sales volume, net profit is expected to increase or decrease by 2 per cent.

b) Drop in sales price by 10 per cent.

In this situation sales fall, but variable costs and fixed costs remain as before.

	€	€
Sales		90,000
Cost of sales		50,000
Gross profit		40,000
Other variable costs	10,000	
Fixed costs	20,000	30,000
Net profit		10,000

Profit has fallen by 50 per cent (10,000 ÷ 20,000) due to a 10 per cent decrease in selling price. The profit multiplier or sensitivity rating is 5. This means that for a 1 per cent increase or decrease in selling price, profit is expected to increase or decrease 5 per cent. This assumes the drop in selling price has no effect on volume sales.

c) Cost of raw materials increases by 10 per cent.

In this situation the only variable that changes is cost of sales.

	€	€
Sales		100,000
Cost of sales		55,000
Gross profit		45,000
Other variable costs	10,000	
Fixed costs	20,000	30,000
Net profit		15,000

Profit has fallen by 25 per cent (5,000 ÷ 20,000) due to a 10 per cent increase in cost of sales. The profit multiplier or sensitivity rating is 2.5. This means that for a 1 per cent increase or decrease in cost of sales, profit will increase or decrease by 2.5 per cent.

d) Variable costs increase by 10 per cent.

An increase in other variable costs of 10 per cent or €1,000 will cause a fall in profit of €1,000 or 5 per cent (1,000 ÷ 20,000). Thus the profit multiplier or sensitivity rating is 0.5. In other words, for every 1 per cent increase in other variable costs, profit will decrease by 0.5 per cent.

e) Fixed costs increase by 10 per cent.

An increase in fixed costs of 10 per cent or €2,000 will reduce profit by the same amount, €2,000 or 10 per cent (2,000 ÷ 20,000) and hence the profit multiplier or sensitivity rating is 1.

Interpreting the sensitivity ratings

The following table shows the rating for each of the key variables:

Key variable	Sensitivity rating
Sales volume	2 times
Sales price	5 times
Cost of sales	2.5 times
Other variable costs	0.5 times
Fixed costs	1

The following points need to be made:

1. Clearly the project is more sensitive to changes in selling price than to changes in costs and changes in sales volume. This is useful if management consider a strategy of reducing selling price to boost volume sales. The sensitivity rating of 5 times tells us that, should they reduce selling price by 2 per cent, this could reduce profit by as much as 10 per cent. Thus for the strategy to work, it would have to boost sales volume by at least 5 per cent as changes in sales volume have a sensitivity rating of only 2 times.
2. Should the business be focusing on reducing costs, then cost of sales is where they should begin, as any reductions in cost of sales have a greater effect on profit than reductions in fixed and other variable costs.
3. Ultimately, in maintaining satisfactory profit levels, this business should pay particular attention to pricing levels, after which it should focus on cost of sales/ variable costs and sales volume.

PSA and Operating Cost Structures

Most industries have characteristics or norms which distinguish them from other business sectors. The tourism, hospitality and leisure sector is no different. Hospitality, leisure and travel businesses tend to be quite capital and labour intensive with a high fixed and low variable cost structure. Demand for their products and services tends to fluctuate and they also sell a perishable product/service. Cost structure refers to the proportion of fixed and variable costs within the total operating cost structure of the business. A business with a high proportion of fixed costs to total costs would be said to have a high fixed cost structure, sometimes called high operating gearing. Travel agents, although not capital intensive, would have a high fixed cost operating structure. Outdoor catering firms would have a mainly high variable cost structure.

Operating risk is high where a business suffers from profit volatility and this occurs when profit is sensitive to small changes in key variables. Generally a business will have high operating risk or gearing when its cost structure is predominantly fixed. This is due to the fact that the pressure is on the business to achieve a required sales level to cover fixed costs. A business with a predominantly variable cost structure would have low operating risk or gearing as, should the business not achieve expected sales, the variable costs would not be charged.

Cost structure and sensitivity analysis

Businesses with a high fixed cost structure such as hotels, leisure centres, travel agents and airlines can have sensitivity ratings ranging from 0 to 15. For a business with a high variable cost structure, the sensitivity ratings can range 0–7.

In example 6.1 the business would be considered to have a predominantly variable cost structure with variable costs as a percentage of total costs amounting to 67 per cent. You will note the sensitivity ratings varied from 0.5 to 5. Let us now focus on a business with a high fixed cost structure.

Illustration 6.1: *Profit sensitivity analysis*

The following is a projected profit and loss account for Hugh's Hotels Ltd.

	€	€
Sales		100,000
Cost of sales		10,000
Gross profit		90,000
Other variable costs	10,000	
Fixed costs	70,000	80,000
Net profit		10,000

You will note the business has an operating gearing percentage (fixed cost ÷ total costs x 100) of 87.5 per cent. The sensitivity ratings are calculated based on an increase in each key variable of 10 per cent.

❑ An increase in sales volume of 10 per cent would have the effect of increasing profits to €18,000, an 80 per cent increase, resulting in a profit multiplier of 8 times.
❑ An increase in selling price would have the effect of increasing profit to €20,000, a 100 per cent increase, resulting in a profit multiplier of 10.
❑ An increase in cost of sales of 10 per cent would have the effect of decreasing profits to €9,000, a decrease of 10 per cent, resulting in a profit multiplier of 1. This is also the profit multiplier for other variable costs.
❑ An increase in fixed costs of 10 per cent would have the effect of reducing profit to €3,000, a 70 per cent decrease, resulting in a profit multiplier of 7.

Key variable	Sensitivity rating
Sales volume	8
Sales price	10
Cost of sales	1
Other variable costs	1
Fixed costs	7

You will note that overall the sensitivity ratings are higher. This is mainly due to the fact that the business has a high fixed cost structure which results in the following:

1. A higher sales volume sensitivity rating as a high fixed cost structure requires greater sales volume to cover the fixed cost. As sales increase, costs only slightly increase, as they are mainly fixed and thus, profit increases significantly. Profit is more sensitive to sales volume fluctuations for a business with a high fixed cost structure than for a business with a low fixed cost structure.
2. Although the fixed costs sensitivity rating is 7 times higher for the business with the high fixed cost structure, what is significant is that it is less than both the sales volume and price sensitivity ratings. Thus for a business with a high fixed cost operating structure, profit is more sensitive to the revenue side of the profit and loss account than the cost side.

Generally the profit multipliers are high in this company and this indicates a high degree of profit volatility and thus high operating risk. Diagram 6.2 shows graphically the difference between a fixed and variable operating cost structure.

Diagram 6.2: *Fixed and variable cost structures*

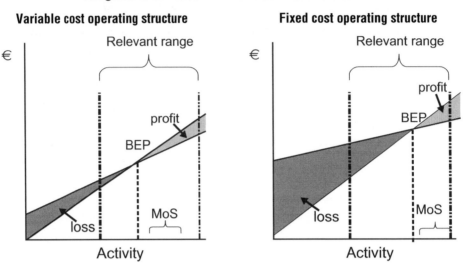

In comparing the graphs, one can see that for businesses with a high variable operating cost structure (low operating gearing), if break-even is not achieved, the extent of the loss is minute compared to the predominantly fixed operating cost structure. Thus the level of risk is lower for businesses with high variable operating cost structures. However to achieve high profit levels, the business must generate high volume sales as the contribution to sales margin is quite low. In contrast, businesses with high fixed operating cost structures (high operating gearing), have high contributions to sales margins and hence, once the break-even point is achieved, these businesses can achieve high levels of profit. However they must achieve higher levels of sales to break even than businesses with a variable cost operating structure.

PSA – Decision-making and Resource Allocation

Below is a comparison of the sensitivity ratings for all the key variables associated with Celtic Souvenirs (with a high variable cost structure) and Hugh's Hotels (high fixed cost structure).

Key variable	Sensitivity rating for high variable cost structure business	Sensitivity rating for high fixed cost structure business
Sales volume	2	8
Sales price	5	10
Cost of sales	2.5	1
Other variable costs	0.5	1
Fixed costs	1	7

High fixed cost operating structure

❑ As already pointed out, the company with high operating gearing representing hotels, airlines, travel agents and most service companies, has quite high sensitivity ratings which indicate that profit is quite sensitive to changes in the various key variables. This implies a high operating risk element. The business has a high level of fixed cost which must be covered before it makes a profit. Thus the pressure is on to generate adequate sales to cover fixed costs and make a profit.

❑ One will also note that the key variables that impact on profit the most are sales price and sales volume. This indicates that this type of business is revenue sensitive, thus management should focus on maximising the revenue side of the profit and loss account.

❑ As the business has few variable costs, this would indicate that it has less latitude in terms of reducing costs, but greater scope to stimulate demand (by reducing prices in off-peak periods) and thus maximise contribution to cover fixed costs. In this regard we see that travel companies, accommodation providers and leisure fitness clubs, during their 'off-peak season', stimulate sales demand by reducing the price. As long as the selling price exceeds the variable costs then the sale makes a positive contribution towards fixed costs and profit. It is important to emphasise that this is not about diluting the importance of cost control, but more about diverting resources into marketing and sales.

❑ Businesses with high fixed cost operating structures tend also to be quite capital intensive (which creates many of the fixed costs such as depreciation, rates, repairs and maintenance). Also, accommodation providers, restaurants and travel companies provide a perishable product (for a hotel, one bed-night lost is lost forever) with fluctuations in demand. Thus in off-peak periods, selling prices can be slashed to ensure a bed-night or air-flight seat makes a positive contribution towards fixed costs instead of a no-sell, zero contribution and a wasted opportunity.

High variable cost operating structure

❑ For the business with a high variable cost structure, the operating risk is significantly lower. If the business suffers from falling sales, then there is the consolation that variable costs are also falling and thus losses would not be as significant as with a business with a high fixed cost structure.

❑ Focusing on the sensitivity ratings, while selling price has still the highest rating, cost of sales and total variable cost have the next highest. This would indicate that the business should focus its attention on price levels, after which attention should focus on reducing costs. The sensitivity ratings would indicate that this business has more scope to reduce costs and less scope to stimulate demand, as the business has high variable costs.

❑ Businesses with relatively low proportions of fixed costs are said to be cost oriented and the presence of high variable costs provides management with the opportunity to improve profits by placing greater emphasis on cost control.

Limitations of Profit Sensitivity Analysis

PSA suffers from two significant limitations.

1. It does not assign probabilities on the possibilities of fluctuations in key variables.
2. It does not consider the effect on projected outcomes of more than one variable at a time.

Summary

Profit sensitivity analysis is a management information tool which helps analyse revenues and costs, providing management with the type of information that helps in planning, resource allocation, decision-making and control. The calculation of profit multipliers can provide management with an insight into the key variables to which profit is most sensitive, thus allowing the allocation of resources to that area to help maximise profits. However the technique does not assign probabilities on the possibilities of fluctuations in key variables, nor does it consider the effect on projected outcomes of more than one variable at a time.

The main information points covered in this chapter are as follows:

❑ The key variables that affect profit are the variables that make up revenues and expenses in the profit and loss account.

❑ The process of applying PSA is to take any one variable, for example sales volume, and change that variable and see the resulting effect on profit. For example, if we increase sales volume by 10 per cent and the resulting effect on profit is an increase of 15 per cent, then profit is deemed sensitive to changes in sales volume. This sensitivity can be measured through the profit multiplier or sensitivity rating which, in the above case, is 1.5 times.

❑ The operating cost structure of a business relates to whether the business' cost structure is mainly fixed or variable. A business with a high fixed cost operating structure has high levels of fixed costs compared to variable. Businesses with high variable cost operating structures have high variable costs compared to fixed costs.

❑ The more sensitive a profit figure is to small changes in key variables, the higher the operating risk to the business. Operating risk is high where a business suffers from profit instability and this occurs when profit is sensitive to small changes in key variables. Generally a business will have high operating risk when its cost structure is predominantly fixed.

❑ For businesses with a high fixed cost operating structure, the key variables that impact on profit most are both sales price and sales volume. This would indicate that this type of business is revenue sensitive. Management should focus on maximising the revenue side of the profit and loss account as well as applying adequate control over costs. Ultimately, the revenue side of the business exerts considerably more influence than the cost side.

❑ For businesses with a high variable cost structure, the key variables that impact on profits are its variable costs and selling price. This would indicate that this type of business is less revenue sensitive than businesses with high fixed costs. Thus to maintain and increase profitability, the company should pay particular attention to pricing levels and after this focus on sales volume and variable costs equally.

❑ PSA does not assign probabilities on the possibilities of fluctuations in key variables, nor does it consider the effect on projected outcomes of more than one variable at a time.

Review Questions

Question 6.1

Discuss the implications of the operating cost structure on profitability in the hospitality and travel sectors.

Question 6.2

Below is a profit statement of Darby's Hotel Group for the year ended 31 December 2005.

Department revenue and expenses:

	Sales	Cost of sales	Payroll	Profit / loss
	€'000	€'000	€'000	€'000
Rooms	2,500		750	1,750
Food and beverage	1,100	450	450	200
Leisure centre	700	50	300	350
	4,300	500	1,500	2300

Undistributed operating expenses:

Marketing	420	
Administration	210	
Maintenance	140	
Power / energy	160	930
		1,370
Fixed charges		700
Net Profit		670

Notes:
❑ Payroll costs have been classified as €1,040,000 fixed and the balance variable.
❑ The undistributed operating expenses contain a fixed element of €800,000 with the balance variable.

Required
a) Present the above information in a marginal costing profit statement format.
b) Calculate the profit multipliers of the hotel based on a 10 per cent change in the following key variables:

    i. Sales price.

   ii. Sales volume.

  iii. Variable costs.

  iv. Fixed costs.

c) Rank the multipliers in terms of their influence on profit.

d) Comment on the profit multipliers calculated.

Question 6.3

The following budgeted profit information relates to the month of January for three companies all operating in different business sectors:

	Company 1	Company 2	Company 3
Budgeted sales (units)	20,000	20,000	20,000
Budgeted selling price per unit	€5.00	€5.00	€5.00
Budgeted variable costs per unit	€4.00	€3.00	€2.00
Budgeted monthly fixed costs	€30,000	€50,000	€80,000

From the above information you are required to compute for each company:

a) Budgeted profit presented in a marginal costing format.

b) The budgeted break-even point in both units and sales value.

c) The impact on profits of an increase of 10 per cent in sales volume and price.

d) The profit multipliers for sales volume and sales price variables.

e) Briefly comment on your answers to (d) in relation to the distribution between each companies fixed and variable expenses.

Question 6.4

The following are the summarised results of a restaurant and outdoor catering company.

	Restaurant	Outdoor Catering
Covers sold	100,000	100,000
Average selling price per meal	€10	€10
	€	€
Sales revenue	1,000,000	1,000,000
Less Variable costs	200,000	600,000
Contribution	800,000	400,000
Less Fixed costs	600,000	200,000
Net profit	200,000	200,000

For both businesses you are required to:

a) Calculate the sensitivity of profit to a 10 per cent change in the following key variables:
   i.   Sales price.
   ii. Sales volume.
   iii. Variable costs.
   iv   Fixed costs.
b) Rank the profit multipliers in order of size.
c) Comment on the profit multiplier profile of the two businesses.

CHAPTER 7

The Pricing Decision and Customer Profitability Analysis

Learning Outcomes

By the end of this chapter you will be able to:

❏ Outline the importance of the pricing decision and the main factors that influence price determination.
❏ Outline pricing theory in economics.
❏ Use cost plus, break–even and profit oriented pricing methods and outline the different situations that would be appropriate for each method.
❏ Appreciate the importance of the external environment in the context of the pricing decision.
❏ Outline the use and value of customer profitability analysis.

Introduction

The selling price to charge for a product or service is one of the most important decisions management have to make. The main aim of a commercial organisation is to make a profit. To do this effectively, a selling price must be set that not only exceeds the direct cost price of the product or service sold, but also is sufficient to cover all overheads and financing expenses. Ultimately, prices must be set in such a way that they help to generate sufficient sales revenue to cover total costs. However, price also has a negative correlation with demand. As price increases, demand in most situations will diminish as customers buy up cheaper substitute products. Price is normally the most influential factor in a customer's decision to buy. Thus one should not set a price that results in demand being too adversely affected. It can also be dangerous to set too low a price, as this creates pressures to either achieve a volume of sales that ensures total contribution covers fixed costs or to reduce costs. This chapter looks at the factors that influence the pricing decision, and the economic theory of pricing, before focusing on the main methods of pricing used in the hospitality, tourism and retail sectors. It also deals with pricing strategies and customer profitability analysis.

Factors that Influence the Pricing Decision

The following are the main factors that must be taken into account before agreeing a price or pricing strategy.

- ❑ Cost of goods sold.
- ❑ Operating cost structure.
- ❑ Nature of the product or service.
- ❑ Competitiveness of the industry.
- ❑ Sensitivity to global issues.
- ❑ Legal and environmental issues.
- ❑ Price elasticity of demand.

Cost of goods sold

For many organisations trading in goods, the cost of goods sold is one of the main factors to be taken into account when establishing a selling price. Cost of goods sold is the invoice cost of the goods plus any additional costs in bringing the goods to the point of sale, such as the cost of transporting the goods to the business and import duty. For a retail organisation it is one of the most significant factors in the pricing decision.

The operating cost structure of the organisation

If an organisation has high levels of fixed costs compared to variable costs, then the organisation has much scope in setting its selling price at a level that can stimulate demand. For example, the hotel industry has a high fixed cost operating structure with quite low variable costs. The variable costs of a room–night may come to only 10 per cent of the selling price. Thus the business has huge scope in setting selling prices that can stimulate demand in off-peak periods and yet provide a positive contribution to fixed costs.

Cost structure in the hospitality sector

The hospitality industry has high levels of fixed costs, thus pricing is an important tool in stimulating sufficient demand to cover fixed costs. Many service industries, particularly tourist attractions, are market driven and seasonal, with great volatility of demand. If a business misjudges its pricing decision, profit levels can plummet.

The nature of the product or service

For most businesses in the retail sector (excluding perishable groceries), if stock is not sold this week it can be sold next week and the product is, within reason, non-perishable. However for the hotel industry and travel sector, a bed-night lost or a flight seat not filled is lost forever and cannot be sold again. Because of the perishability of the product, selling price must be set according to market demand.

The competitiveness and structure of the industry

Should any industry be very competitive, then price reductions are the order of the day as companies compete for the market. Thus competitive pricing comes to the fore. The travel industry is quite competitive with many tour groups constantly under-pricing one another. In the Dublin hotels' market, competition has increased significantly due to the over investment in accommodation in the late 1990s. Since de-regulation the air travel sector has become a very competitive market. The level of competition in the retail sector has increased since the arrival of European competition in the form of Lidl and Aldi.

Discounters drive total Irish store growth

The arrival of German discounters Aldi and Lidl has resulted in the Irish supermarket / discount sector growing almost twice as fast as it would have done in the last six years if they hadn't entered the Irish market. Research was conducted by AC Nielsen on the growth of stores in the period 1998–2004. The four major supermarket operators (Tesco, Dunnes, SuperValu and Superquinn) grew by 16 per cent, with a total of 49 new stores opening. However the arrival of the discounters during this period meant that the total growth rate skyrocketed to 40 per cent. In the six-year period to 2004, the discounters went from having no stores to a total of 74 (53 Lidl stores and 21 Aldi stores). Despite this rapid growth, the discounters' share of the market was static between 2003 and 2004.

Checkout, February 2005

Analysis of Market Share

	February 2004	February 2005
Tesco	24.8%	25.7%
Dunnes Stores	21.9%	22.4%
Superquinn	8.5%	8.5%
SuperValu	19.4%	19.1%
Discounters	5.2%	5.3%
Other operators	7.8%	7%
Other outlets (greengrocers / butchers)	10.6%	10.1%

Source: TNS Worldpanel

Sensitivity to global issues

The sensitivity of a particular sector to international developments can be a factor in pricing decisions. The hospitality, travel and tourism sectors are quite sensitive to international events and are particularly affected by war, natural disasters and terrorism. The effects of September 11 and the Asian tsunami on tourism are well documented.

Legal and environmental constraints

Government policy and legislation can affect the pricing options available to a business. The Groceries Order, when it was in force, prevented retail outlets selling certain grocery items below cost in Ireland. The objective of this order was to provide some protection to small retail businesses from the extensive powers of large multinationals. Thus any special protective covenants in law can influence the pricing of a product or service. This legislation was repealed in late 2005 and it is expected that grocery prices will fall. The *Irish Times* quoted the Minister for Enterprise, Trade and Employment explaining 'The fundamental reason for abolishing the order is that it was keeping prices artificially high. It didn't protect small grocery stores and didn't prevent consolidation of the market. In essence, it was an anti-competitive piece of legislation that created a floor below which prices could not be lowered.'

Air of uncertainty for retailers

In *Checkout* (October 2005), Terence Cosgrave discussed the air of uncertainty for retailers, *'there are issues with regard to increasing costs, the price of oil (and therefore energy), consumer confidence, the difficulty in procuring good staff, and the other worries that are inherent in a business that is 24/7. But the overwhelming concern is how the market will operate following the expected review of the Groceries Order. What change will be enacted (if any) and how will that affect the grocery industry? How will the multiples react? How will consumers react?'*

Source: *Checkout*, October 2005

Price elasticity of demand – N.B.

Price elasticity of demand refers to the relationship between price and demand. It measures the relationship between a change in price and a change in demand for a product or service. Thus it compares the sensitivity of demand for a product or service to changes in its price. It is based on the following formula:

$$\frac{\text{Percentage change in demand}}{\text{Percentage change in price}}$$

Where the numerical value is less than or equal to 1, then the price elasticity of demand is inelastic. In other words, demand is less sensitive to changes in price. For example, if a 4 per cent change in price creates a 2 per cent change in demand, then the numerical value is 0.5 and it can be seen that for every 1 per cent change in price, demand will change by 0.5 per cent. Where the numerical value is greater than or equal to 1, then price elasticity is elastic. In other words demand is sensitive to changes in price. For example, if price falls by 3 per cent and demand rises by 5 per cent then the numerical value is 1.67 and thus, for every 1 per cent change in price, demand changes by 1.67 per cent. This all leads to the theory of setting an optimum price that maximises net profit. If a business can measure its elasticity of demand then it can, in theory, predict demand based on any given price. In this case, management can choose the combination of demand and price that maximises profit.

Illustration 7.1: *Price elasticity of demand*

Brighteeth Ltd specialises in producing and selling one specialised electric toothbrush which is distributed in retail stores throughout Ireland. The following is their estimate of the effect that different prices will have on forecast demand and profitability.

Selling price	€50	€45	€40	€35	€30
Number of units sold	100,000	120,000	130,000	140,000	150,000
	€	€	€	€	€
Revenue	5,000,000	5,400,000	5,200,000	4,900,000	4,500,000
Variable costs €10/unit	1,000,000	1,200,000	1,300,000	1,400,000	1,500,000
Contribution	4,000,000	4,200,000	3,900,000	3,500,000	3,000,000
Fixed costs	3,000,000	3,000,000	3,000,000	3,000,000	3,000,000
Net profit	1,000,000	1,200,000	900,000	500,000	0

From the table, the optimum selling price that maximises operating profit and the operating profit margin is €45.

The main limitation of economic pricing theory is that it assumes there are no other variables that can influence demand. For example it ignores the effects of marketing on sales demand and it effectively assumes that sales volume is solely a function of price. It also assumes that consumers are perfectly informed about the prices of products and services and that price is their sole motivation in changing their spending patterns. The exact shape of a products demand curve is extremely difficult to estimate, thus ensuring that forecast demand at a given price may be misleading. However economic theory in relation to pricing does focus attention on the factors that are important to the pricing decision, namely demand, operating costs and ultimately overall profit.

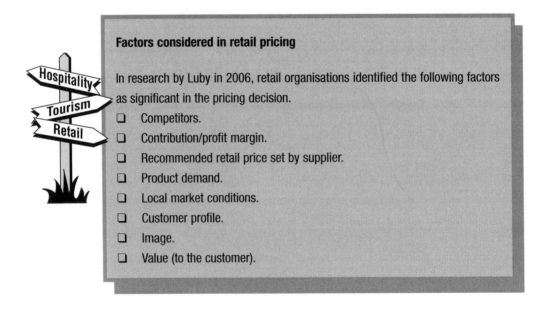

Factors considered in retail pricing

In research by Luby in 2006, retail organisations identified the following factors as significant in the pricing decision.

❑ Competitors.
❑ Contribution/profit margin.
❑ Recommended retail price set by supplier.
❑ Product demand.
❑ Local market conditions.
❑ Customer profile.
❑ Image.
❑ Value (to the customer).

Accounting-based Pricing Methods

Accounting-based pricing methods tend to concentrate on accounting measures such as covering costs and breaking even or achieving a required profit level. They do not focus on the various external factors such as the market, price, elasticity of demand, competition and the economic environment and thus are considered only a good start-off point in tackling the pricing decision.

The three main accounting based pricing methods are:

❑   Cost-based pricing.
❑   Contribution margin pricing.
❑   Profit oriented pricing.

Cost based pricing methods

This is where the pricing decision focuses totally on costs, ensuring that a selling price is set that covers the costs of running the business and will be sufficient to provide a profit. The selling price is arrived at by simply adding a profit percentage to costs. It is based on the following formula:

$$P = C + M (C)$$

Where
P = selling price
C = costs
M = percentage mark-up or profit percentage based on cost.

The percentage mark-up will generally be an industry norm and will vary depending on what actual costs (direct costs only or total costs) are taken into account. Illustration 7.2 shows the various cost based pricing methods commonly used.

Illustration 7.2: *Cost based pricing methods*

1. **Gross margin pricing** is where cost (C) represents just the materials cost or cost of sales. In this situation the mark-up percentage is quite high as it must be sufficient to cover both direct labour and direct expenses as well as overhead expenses and provide a profit.

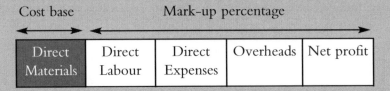

2. **Direct cost pricing** is where cost (C) represents the total direct costs. In this situation the mark-up percentage must be sufficient to cover both overhead expenses and provide a profit.

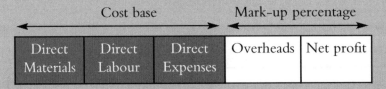

3. **Full cost pricing** is where cost (C) represents total costs of the business. In this situation the mark-up percentage can be quite small as it represents clear profit.

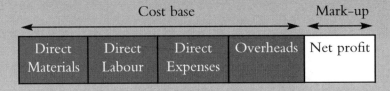

Example 7.1: *Gross margin pricing*

The chief buyer of the Denim Store has negotiated a new consignment of exclusive denim bags at a purchase cost of €10 each which includes shipping and other transport costs. VAT on sales is chargeable at a rate of 21 per cent.

What retail price should the store charge to achieve a gross mark-up of 60 per cent.

Approach

A gross mark-up of 60 per cent means that the profit element on this product needed to cover all other costs and provide a profit amounting to €6 (€10 x 60%). Thus the selling price, excluding VAT, amounts to €16 (€10 + €6) and including VAT amounts to €19.36 (€16 x 1.21).

Profit mark-up and profit margin

Profit mark-up expresses the profit element as a percentage of costs whereas profit margin expresses the same profit element as a percentage of sales.

If the selling price of a product is €100 and the total cost amounts to €80, then the profit element equals €20.

The profit mark-up that expresses profit as a percentage of cost, is calculated as €20 ÷ €80 x 100 = 25%.

The profit margin that expresses profit as a percentage of sales, is calculated as €20 ÷ €100 x 100 = 20%.

Example 7.2: *Direct cost pricing*

The following information relates to the costs of an 8 day coach tour by Cusack International Tours Ltd. The company uses a direct cost-plus approach to pricing their tours, adding a mark-up of 25 per cent to the tour costs. The following are the direct costs of the tour:

	€
Accommodation per person	
Shannon Hotel (1 night – B&B)	34.00
Galway Hotel (1 night – D B&B)	50.00
Killarney Hotel (2 nights – D B&B)	120.00
Cork Hotel (1 night – D B&B)	50.00
Waterford Hotel (1 night – D B&B)	50.00
Dublin Hotel (2 nights – B&B)	80.00
Entertainment per person	
Dinner and cabaret in Dublin (2 nights)	100.00
Medieval banquet Shannon	50.00
Dublin museums	20.00

The cost of a 50 seat coach per day is €500, with guide costs estimated at €90 per day. Also, the company pays a 10 per cent commission on selling price (excluding VAT) to travel agents who promote the tour. The company price all their tours based on a load factor of 80 per cent.

Calculate the cost per person including VAT at 13.5 per cent.

Approach

The total direct costs are added, including agent's commission, to get a total direct cost per person. A mark-up of 25 per cent is added and VAT is charged on this price. The cost base does not represent total cost, only direct costs. The mark-up of 25 per cent must be sufficient to contribute towards the fixed costs/overheads and profit of the business.

	€	
Accommodation costs per person	384.00	
Entertainment cost per person	170.00	
Coach hire per person (€500 x 8 ÷ 50 x 80%)	100.00	
Tour Guide (€90 x 8 ÷ 50 x 80%)	18.00	
	672.00	← 70 %
Agent's commission (672 x 10 ÷ 70)	96.00	← 10 %
	768.00	← 80 %
Mark-up (25% x 768)	192.00	← 20 %
	960.00	← 100 %
VAT (13.5% x 960)	129.60	
Selling price per person	1089.60	

The agent's commission is 10 per cent of the selling price before VAT. However, at the stage of calculating the commission, we only know the direct cost per person. Thus if we assume the selling price before VAT equals 100 per cent and the profit margin equals 20 per cent (profit mark-up of 25 per cent equals profit margin of 20 per cent), then total cost, including commission, equals 80 per cent. If the commission equals 10 per cent of the selling price then total direct costs, excluding commission, equals 70 per cent. Thus in calculating the agent's commission per person, the total direct costs are divided by 70 and multiplied by 10. This amounts to €96 which equals 10 per cent of the selling price before VAT.

Cost based methods

Different business sectors will use different cost based methods. For example, the fast moving consumer goods (FMCG) end of the retail sector tends to use gross margin pricing, whereas other business sectors may use a full costing approach. It all depends on the business sector and the sophistication of the costing system used.

The simplicity of cost based pricing is its main advantage and, as an initial first step in determining a selling price, it is considered quite useful. The main criticism of cost based pricing is that on its own it only focuses on costs and ignores other factors such as the economic environment, competition, and the marketing and sales strategy of the business. It also does not take into account the required level of profitability based on the level of investment in the business.

Contribution margin pricing method

Cost based pricing focuses on covering costs and achieving a target profit. Contribution margin pricing focuses on ensuring that each product or service that a business provides offers a target contribution towards fixed costs and profit. Thus it is important to identify and classify all costs into their fixed and variable components. Contribution margin pricing is based on the premise that prices are set using variable costs as the base and what the market will bear as the ceiling. This ensures that although individual sales may not provide an overall profit, the sum of all sales will provide sufficient contribution to cover fixed costs and provide the required profit. The main focus is on providing a contribution to fixed costs and, should economic conditions and competitive levels be favourable, the contribution can be quite large to ensure the business reaches profitability as early as possible. This method can provide a high discretionary element to price setting and thus can be quite useful for businesses that are sensitive to economic and seasonal factors and have a high fixed cost operating structure, such as hotels and airlines.

Illustration 7.3: *Contribution margin pricing*

The selling price of a hotel bedroom is set at €70 with variable costs per room amounting to €7. In this case, each room sold for €70 provides a contribution of 90 per cent or €63 to cover fixed costs and a required profit. However, as the hotel sector is sensitive to economic and seasonal adjustments and because it sells a perishable product (one bed–night unsold is unsold forever), it has great flexibility/discretion in adjusting the selling price per room to stimulate demand and thus profit. A room sold for €10 will still provide a positive contribution towards fixed costs and thus, in the off-season, stimulate sales and profit.

Contribution margin pricing can also be used to calculate a selling price that will enable the business to break even and thus, any price set above this, will ensure profitability as long as forecast demand is unaffected.

This can be calculated by using the CVP formula below.

Using the CVP formula

$$\pi = P(x) - a + b(x)$$

Where:

π = profit

P = selling price

a = fixed costs

b = variable cost per unit

x = number of units sold

Example 7.3: *Contribution margin pricing*

Abs Crunches Ltd produces and sells a specialised fitness system. It has fixed costs of €900,000 per annum with the variable cost per unit amounting to €10. Estimated demand for the year amounts to 50,000 fitness systems.

Calculate a selling price that ensures the business breaks even.

Approach

The selling price can be calculated by using the CVP formula $\pi = P(x) - a + b(x)$. We need to find P (price) that will ensure π (profit) = 0.

$$0 = P(x) - a + b(x)$$

$$0 = P(50,000) - 900,000 + 10(50,000)$$

$$1,400,000 = 50,000P$$

$$P = €28$$

The price to charge to break even, based on sales of 50,000 units, is €28.
This can also be calculated as follows:

	€
Total variable costs (50,000 x €10)	500,000
Total fixed costs	900,000
Total costs	1,400,000
Add required profit	0
Revenue required to break even	1,400,000
Projected unit sales	50,000
Price per unit (1,4000,000 ÷ 50,000)	€28

The main advantages of contribution margin pricing is that it provides great scope for a pricing policy that is adaptive to changing conditions and takes into account costs and market conditions in setting a selling price. Its main criticisms are those that are associated with the CVP model such as the assumption that all costs can be classified as either fixed or variable. It also requires information on the demand curve and the price elasticity of demand which is quite difficult to predict. As with cost based models, it ignores the level of profitability as a percentage of the capital investment in the business.

Profit oriented pricing

This method focuses on profit and in particular the required level of profit for the amount of investment in the business. The focus is on the return on investment required of a business by its investors. The process involves calculating a total sales figure that should achieve a return on investment that will satisfy investors, assuming forecast costs and demand are accurate. The technique is an extension of the cost based and contribution pricing methods with an extra variable, profit or return, as part of the equation. The total estimated sales figure, divided by expected forecast demand will give a selling price which will ensure the required level of profitability for investors, provided costs and demand levels remain as forecast. Example 7.4 returns to Abs Crunches Ltd to demonstrate how a selling price can be set to ensure a desired return on capital is achieved.

Example 7.4: *Profit oriented pricing*

Abs Crunches Ltd estimate annual fixed costs of €900,000, with variable costs amounting to €10 per unit. Estimated demand for the year amounts to 50,000 fitness systems. A return on capital of 15 per cent is required. The capital employed in the business is €500,000.

Calculate the selling price that ensures the return on capital of 15 per cent is achieved.

Approach

The selling price can be calculated by using the CVP formula: $\pi = P(x) - a + b(x)$. Thus we need to find P (price) that will ensure $\pi = 75,000$ (500,000 x 15%).

$$\pi = P(x) - a + b(x)$$

$$75,000 = P(x) - a + b(x)$$

$$75,000 = P(50,000) - 900,000 + 10(50,000)$$

$$1,475,000 = 50,000P$$

$$P = €29.50$$

The price to charge to achieve a return on capital of 15 per cent based on sales of 50,000 units is €29.50.

This can also be calculated as follows:

	€
Total variable costs (50,000 x €10)	*500,000*
Total fixed costs	*900,000*
Total costs	*1,400,000*
Add required profit	*75,000*
Revenue required to break even	*1,475,000*
Projected unit sales	*50,000*
Price per unit (1,475,000 ÷ 50,000)	*€29.50*

Profit oriented methods are effectively cost based methods taking into account a required rate of return (profitability and investment). Thus their advantages include those of the cost based method with the added advantages that this method focuses on profit and investment. The main criticisms are that, as with cost based methods, it does not focus on the market, price elasticity of demand, competition and the economic environment and thus is considered quite insular. As with the cost based methods, it is considered a good point to start off in tackling the pricing question.

The Hubbard formula

The American Hotel and Motel Association formalised a profit oriented pricing method for all hotel / motels. This method they called the 'Hubbard formula'. It starts with the required profit after tax on capital invested and then adds back taxation, financing costs and all fixed operating costs until total contribution required to achieve such a profit is calculated. The profit contributions of other revenue producing departments in a hotel such as restaurant, bar and banqueting are deducted from this total contribution, to leave the contribution required from accommodation. Adding on variable costs, a total accommodation sales figure is calculated which, when divided by an expected occupancy level, will give an average selling price. The Hubbard formula employs a process that is ultimately designed to set prices that will yield a specified return on capital for the hotel sector.

The following example illustrates how the Hubbard formula works.

Example 7.5: *Pricing hotel accommodation*

A small hotel situated in Dublin has 50 rooms and has recently been purchased for €1.2 million by a small consortium. The new owners are seeking a return of 15 per cent on their investment. The following additional information is available:

Owners' equity	€300,000
Long-term loans with a fixed rate of interest at 9 per cent	€900,000
Annual fixed costs	€280,000
Variable cost per room	€12.00
Expected occupancy rate	70%
Estimated profits from food and bar	€70,000
The hotel will be open 360 days per year.	

a) *Calculate the average room rate the hotel should charge to achieve the required return on capital. You may assume a corporation tax rate of 20 per cent and ignore any problems associated with double or single occupancy.*
b) *If the double rooms are sold at a premium of €15 above the single rooms, what prices should be charged for each single and double to achieve the required rate of return? You may assume that double occupancy as a percentage of overall occupancy is 60 per cent and there is no change to variable cost per room.*

Approach

The starting point under the Hubbard approach is the required return on capital invested. By adding back taxation, finance costs and fixed operating expenses, one arrives at the total contribution required to achieve the return on capital. By deducting the contribution from other revenue producing departments, one arrives at a room's department contribution figure. This figure divided by the forecast number of bed-nights will calculate a contribution per room used. By adding the estimated variable cost per room, an average selling price per room is calculated.

a) *Calculate the average room rate.*

	€		
Net profit to achieve required return			
(300,000 x 15 per cent)	45,000	←	80%
Taxation (45,000 x 20 ÷ 80)	11,250	←	20%
Net profit before tax	56,250	←	100%

Loan interest (900,000 x 9%)	<u>81,000</u>
Net operating profit	137,250
Fixed costs	<u>280,000</u>
Total contribution	417,250
Contribution food and bar	<u>70,000</u>
Room contribution	347,250
No of bed-nights (50 rooms x 70 per cent occupancy x 360 days)	12,600
Contribution per room (€347,250 ÷ 12,600 days)	€27.56
Variable cost per room	€12.00
Selling price per room	€39.56

b) Calculate rates for single and double rooms.

The total sales revenue required amounts to €498,450 (12,600 rooms x €39.56). Use a mathematical equation to find the sales price of a single room.

Let x = price of a single room

	Total sales	**=**	**single room**	**+**	**double room sales**
Room mix	100%	=	40%	+	60%
Bed-nights	12,600	=	5,040	+	7,560
Sales revenue	€498,450	=	5,040x	+	7,560 (x + €15)
	€498,450	=	5,040x	+	7,560x + €113,400
	€385,050	=	12,600x		
	€30.56	=	x		
	Double rooms	=	€30.56 + €15 =		€45.56

Pricing Strategies Involving the External Environment

One element of a pricing strategy is to focus on the needs of the business, its costing structure and profitability requirements. These have been discussed above, however any pricing strategy must also take into account the external market and its require-ments. In any business sector where the level of competition is intense, most pricing strategies are market driven. This certainly is the case regarding the hospitality, tourism and retail sectors. The following are examples of some market based pricing strategies common to these sectors.

Going rate pricing/ competition oriented pricing	This is quite common in the accommodation and travel sectors where price is set close to the level of your main competitor in the market. Competitors' pricing quite often has the most significant influence on the price setting decision. This strategy is often called 'follow the leader' and it is essential that costs and profit are monitored under this strategy.
Perceived value/ psychological pricing	This involves charging what, according to your own research, the market will accept based upon the consumer's perception of the product. Thus understanding the consumer's perceptions of your product or service can provide information regarding their ceiling in terms of what they are willing to pay. This approach recognises that consumers have a predetermined price range within which they are happy to purchase goods and services. Thus price is set within this range.
Loss leader/decoy pricing	An example of a loss leader would be where supermarkets reduce the price of one product to attract customers who will then buy other products. Examples of decoy pricing would be in the restaurant business where the business has high levels of beef in stock compared to chicken. The focus would be to increase the price of chicken to encourage customers to buy the beef.
Two-part pricing	This would be where some tourism organisations may charge a low basic price to gain access but then charge for additional services once the consumer has the basic product. For example in museums there may be a low or zero charge to gain access to the museum but then an extra charge to gain access to specific exhibitions.
Camouflage pricing	This is where businesses try to ensure that customers cannot compare their prices to competitors. This is done by advertising specific packages which include a number of products or services ensuring the consumer will find it hard to compare prices. For example, in the off-season, hotels can offer two nights B & B plus one evening meal or some ferry companies can charge based on one car while others can charge based on a per person rate.

Pricing in a Retail Environment

For a retail organisation, competitive and stable prices are very important. Price is often used by consumers as an indication of quality. Pricing considerations therefore should be prominent in strategy formulation. Research by Luby (2006) investigating pricing strategy found that 56 per cent of retail outlets used a mix between competitive pricing and either cost plus or contribution margin.

A multi-stage approach to setting a retail price incorporates a number of factors in the decision. The approach takes into account cost, demand and competition.

Diagram 7.1: *Multi-stage approach to pricing*

Select the target market	
Determine the floor price (cost price)	◄·········· *This is the cost of goods but could take into account clearance lines and loss leaders.*
Determine the ceiling price (competitors' price)	◄·········· *This is the price charged for the item by competitors. Provides a reasonable upper limit.*
Apply a mark-up	◄·········· *A target mark-up can be applied in order to achieve the required profit objectives.*
Adjust and select the price	◄·········· *If necessary adjust the price (fine tune) to be consistent with store policy.*

The main benefits of the multi-stage approach are that it incorporates more than one factor and allows for adjustments or fine tuning to be made. This fine tuning at the final stage can take into account pricing tactics favoured by the organisation. In a competitive retail environment, organisations can choose from a range of price tactics to entice the consumer into buying their product. These tactics include:

❑ Price lining.
❑ Odd or even pricing.
❑ Multiple unit pricing.
❑ Complementary goods.
❑ Fixed or flexible pricing.

Diagram 7.2: *Pricing tactics*

Price lining
Setting up a number of distinct prices for a product range. Prices could be limited to say €25, €32 and €40.

Odd pricing
Uses prices like €19.95, or €99.99 to give impression of lower price.

Even pricing
Uses prices like €130 to give impression that price is not most important factor and prestige would be tarnished by using odd pricing.

Fixed pricing
The price set is the only acceptable price and will not be bargained down.

Flexible pricing
Allows for the expectation that price can be negotiated down or a bargain struck.

Pricing Tactics

Multiple unit pricing
Providing discount for two or more items

Complementary goods
Promotional price for one item may encourage purchase of complementary products at full price.

Pricing in the Hospitality Sector

In research carried out by Smullan and O'Donoghue (2005) relating to the use and influence of certain financial decision support models used in the hospitality sector, competitors' prices and market research were considered to be the most influential factors in determining hotel accommodation prices. The research showed that nearly 70 per cent of hotel pricing decisions in relation to accommodation are decided on by competitors' prices. This high level of influence has led to a monthly report being distributed to large Dublin hotels giving information on occupancy levels, average room rates and packages on offer. The use of cost information was confined to the food and beverage area in restaurants and pricing for banquets.

These findings are consistent with research carried out by Collier and Gregory on behalf of CIMA in 1995 in a publication entitled *Management Accounting in Hotel Groups*. This stated that pricing policy in hotels was essentially market driven and was a central part of marketing strategy. They found that in general, no cost information was provided by management accounting for either rack rates in individual hotels or promotion prices. The objective of pricing policy was to maximise revenue, with the accounting function concentrating on balancing occupancy with the average room rate in order to maximise revenue, while taking into account the knock-on effect of occupancy on other income streams such as food and beverage and telephone. The use of cost information was restricted to menu pricing.

Hotels now install computerised yield management systems which predict occupancy levels based on past bookings. The system scans historic experience and advises management on the rate to quote on the basis that room rates must fall the nearer the current dates get to the actual date. For example the system may advise that a booking three months in advance gets no discount to the rack rate whereas a booking one day in advance gets a 35 per cent discount. The system requires a minimum of twelve months data and it assumes the past is a reliable guide to the future. Thus the system tells management when to expect low occupancy periods and the price to quote in different time periods leading up this period to maximise occupancy. Hence occupancy is maximised and because variable costs are so low (approx 10% per room), contribution is maximised.

Customer Profitability Analysis (CPA)

Customer profitability analysis (CPA) focuses on how individual customer or customer groups contribute to profit. It is derived from the Pareto principle that about 20 per cent of customers account for 80 per cent of profit. In the past, management accounting reports concentrated on analysing products and product lines and although this information is essential, increasing attention is now being given to analysing profits by customers. The focus of this analysis is to ensure that the most profitable customers or customer groups receive comparable attention from the organisation. This approach can have a two-fold effect:

❏ By focusing on the most profitable customers and providing an improved or commensurate service, customer relations improve and customer retention increases. Also by identifying the attributes of this group, other similar customers may be attracted to the organisation.

❏ By having a knowledge of why certain customers or customer groups do not significantly contribute to profit (and may actually reduce profit), management can assess the difficulties and work on solutions that benefit the organisation as well as the customer.

The process requires the use of an activity based costing system and involves gathering detailed cost and revenue information for each customer or customer group as follows:

a) **Sales details:** These would include the price charged to the customer including any details on cash and quantity discounts.

b) **Cost details:** These would involve focusing on the resources consumed by different customers. These cost drivers (the activities that create the customer cost) need to be separately identified and a cost driver rate associated with the activity. Examples of cost drivers under CPA would include order costs, sales visits, delivery costs, special delivery costs, credit collection and non-standard product requirements.

The following illustration demonstrates the use and importance of CPA.

Illustration 7.4: *Customer profitability analysis*

The following is an analysis of the four main customers of Louth Distributors Ltd. The company uses an activity based costing system to identify costs attributable to each customer.

	Customer 1	Customer 2	Customer 3	Customer 4
Attributable customer costs	€	€	€	€
Sales order	3,000	10,000	5,000	20,000
Sales visits	250	670	320	1,200
Normal deliveries	400	3,500	800	10,000
Special deliveries		800	200	3,250
Cash collection	1,200	2,600	400	8,000
	4,850	17,570	6,720	42,450
Contribution per customer (excluding attributable customer costs)	70,000	60,000	42,000	30,000
Contribution per customer	65,150	42,430	35,280	(12,450)

The above analysis shows that customer 4 is not profitable for the business and makes a negative contribution to fixed costs. Customers 1, 2 and 3 are quite profitable for the business. Louth Distributors Ltd, in striving to improve efficiency, profitability and customer retention, should consider:

❑ Non profitable customers (customer 4): Either an increase in the selling price to this customer or effort to reduce the costs associated with serving this customer is necessary. For example, an increase in order size (reduce the number of orders placed) could be suggested to the customer. Quantity discount here can ensure cost efficiencies for the customer. The period of credit for this customer could be agreed and reduced. The reasons behind special orders and sales visits must be investigated to try and reduce this cost in a way that is beneficial to both supplier and customer.

❑ Profitable customers (customers 1,2,3): Customer 1 is very profitable to the business and thus the company must ensure they retain the goodwill of this customer by ensuring they are happy with the quality of goods and service provided by the company. Special attention must be given to enhancing this relationship. Customers 2 and 3 are also quite profitable and again deserve attention. There may be opportunities to create efficiencies with customer 2 in terms of sales visits and cash collection costs and this should be investigated and discussed with the customer.

Summary

Ultimately the pricing decision is one of the most important decisions taken by management. Any pricing strategy must take into account not just the internal factors such as costs and required profitability, but also the external market, structure of the industry and level of competition. Customer profitability analysis adds to the information required by management to sustain and improve profits into the future.

The main information points covered in this chapter are as follows:

❑ A number of factors must be taken into account before agreeing a price or pricing strategy.
  − The cost of sales.
  − The operating cost structure of the organisation.
  − The nature of the product or service.
  − The competitiveness and structure of the industry.
  − The sensitivity of a particular sector to international developments.
  − Legal and environmental constraints.
  − Price elasticity of demand.
❑ Price elasticity of demand refers to the relationship between price and demand. It measures the relationship between a change in price and a change in demand for a product or service. Thus it describes the sensitivity of demand for a product or service to changes in its price.
❑ Cost plus pricing is where the pricing decision focuses totally on costs, ensuring that a selling price is set that covers the costs of running the business and will be sufficient to provide a profit. The selling price is arrived at by simply adding to costs a mark-up to get the selling price.
❑ Contribution margin pricing focuses on ensuring each product/service that the business offers contributes a target contribution towards fixed costs and profit.
❑ Profit oriented pricing involves calculating a total sales figure that should achieve a return on investment that will satisfy investors, assuming predicted costs and demand are accurate. The technique is an extension of the cost-based and con-

tribution pricing methods with an extra variable, profit or return, as part of the equation.

❑ In any business sector where the level of competition is intense, most pricing strategies are market driven. This certainly is the case regarding the hospitality, tourism and leisure sectors. Examples of market based pricing strategies are going rate pricing, psychological pricing, loss leader pricing, two part pricing and camouflage pricing.

❑ Customer profitability analysis focuses on how individual customers or customer groups contribute to profit. It is derived from the Pareto principle that about 20 per cent of customers account for 80 per cent of profit. The objective of this analysis is to ensure that the most profitable customers or customer groups receive most attention from the organisation and hence are retained.

Review Questions

Question 7.1

A large UK based pharmacy chain is considering expanding into the Irish market. Discuss the main factors to be considered when developing a pricing policy for the Irish outlets.

Question 7.2

a) Distinguish between cost plus and contribution margin pricing.
b) Outline the major criticisms of cost plus pricing.

Question 7.3

a) Distinguish between cost plus pricing and profit oriented pricing.
b) Explain and give examples of market oriented pricing.

Question 7.4

A young clothing designer is considering setting up a retail outlet. Advise the designer of pricing strategies and tactics.

Question 7.5

Seanie Skis Ltd offers all-in package holidays for skiers. The company has reached the end of season where they charged €750 per person per week and sold 1,200 holidays. Fixed overheads amounted to €300,000. Variable costs per holiday were:

Direct materials	€125
Direct labour	€200

The company is now planning for the next season and estimates that direct material costs will increase by 12.5 per cent while direct labour will increase by 9 per cent. Fixed overheads are likely to increase by 5 per cent.

Required

a) The appropriate price to charge per holiday if the number of holidays sold and total profit remain the same for the forthcoming year.

b) The number of holidays which must be sold if the existing selling price and total profit are maintained.

c) The number of holidays which must be sold to break even if the price arrived at in a) is used.

d) The appropriate price to charge per holiday if a profit of €300,000 is required and if they succeed in selling 1,400 holidays.

Question 7.6

Gibson Football Tours Limited are developing a packaged holiday for soccer fans visiting the world cup in the USA. The package includes:

❑ Return flights to New York.
❑ Transfers from airport to hotel.
❑ Hotel accommodation for 10 days.
❑ Tickets to 4 games up to the quarter-final.
❑ Book of vouchers to visit attractions in the locality.

The cost information is as follows:

1) Chartered planes with seating capacity of 150 persons, costing €15,000 per flight, with 3 return flights required.

2) Coaches to transfer holidaymakers from the airport to the hotel and back costing $600 (dollars), with coach capacity at 50 persons.

3) The New York hotel costing $70 per person per night.

4) Tickets to the games with a total cost of $150 for all the games per person.

5) Voucher book costing $40 per book.

Required

Calculate the final selling price for the tour per person assuming the operator requires a mark-up of 40 per cent and the expected load factor is 90 per cent. You can assume an exchange rate of $1.25 to €1.00.

Question 7.7

The following data relate to the Classic Restaurant which provides a standard five course meal:

Days open per year	320
Capacity in covers per day	160
Expected occupancy rate	75%

The following information relates to sales mix and costs:

Course	Percentage of total sales	Food cost percentage	
Appetiser	12	30	
Soup	10	25	
Main course	55	40	
Dessert	15	30	
Coffee	8	5	
Variable costs (excluding food costs) as a percentage of sales			30%
Fixed salaries per annum			€288,400
General fixed overheads, excluding interest, per annum			€180,000

The Balance Sheet shows the business to be financed as follows:

	€
Owner's capital	750,000
Bank loan (interest of 8 per cent)	450,000
	1,200,000

The owners have set a target annual return on their capital of 18 per cent.

Required

a) Set an inclusive price per meal (table d'hote) which will meet the owners' target return.

b) Set prices for the individual courses (à la carte) assuming that à la carte prices are higher than table d'hote prices by 30 per cent.

c) What should be the inclusive price per meal if there was a reduction in occupancy to 70 per cent and if the general fixed overheads increased by 15 per cent.

d) Briefly explain the limitations of your approach.

Question 7.8

A small hotel situated in Dublin has 30 rooms and has recently been purchased for €1 million by a small consortium. The new owners are seeking a return of 15 per cent on their investment. The following additional information is available:

Owners' equity	€200,000
Long-term loans with a fixed rate of interest at 9 per cent	€800,000
Annual fixed costs	€300,000
Variable cost per room	€10
Expected occupancy rate	75%
Estimated profits from food and bar	€80,000
The hotel will be open 360 days of the year.	

Required

a) Calculate the average room rate the hotel should charge to achieve their required return on capital. You may assume a corporation tax rate of 20 per cent and ignore any problems associated with double or single occupancy.

b) If the double rooms are sold at a premium of €20 above the single rooms, what prices should be charged for each single and double room to achieve the owners' required rate of return? You may assume that double occupancy as a percentage of overall occupancy is 60 per cent and there is no change to variable cost per room.

c) What other considerations would you take into account when looking for strategies to improve room occupancy?

Question 7.9

A consortium of investors raised €2,000,000 in capital to finance the building of a wildlife centre outside Galway city. The project, which is near completion, has been financed through equity put up by the consortium of €800,000 and an 8 per cent fixed interest loan of €1,200,000. The following are the projected costs and visitor numbers relating to the first year of operation:

Fixed costs (excluding interest charges)	€150,000
Undistributed operating expenses	€300,000
Estimated profits from non-core activities	
Souvenir shop	€100,000
Café	€150,000
Flume and boat rides	€70,000
Wildlife health, food and care expenses	€100,000

The maximum annual capacity of the centre is estimated at 150,000 visitors with the number of visitors estimated at 45 per cent of capacity. The consortium expects an initial return on capital of 7 per cent after tax.

Required

a) Calculate the average admission fee to achieve the consortiums after tax profit target. (Assume a tax rate of 20 per cent on profits).
b) If a family admission fee (two adults and two children) is set at €16, what should the single visitor admission fee need to be in order to achieve the profit target? (Assume 50 per cent of all visitors would be in families of four).
c) Suggest four other factors which should be taken into account prior to finalising admission prices.

Question 7.10

The University of Athlone offers half-board accommodation to tourists visiting the town during the summer months. Each bed (including breakfast and dinner) is priced at €50 per night. The following figures relate to last year:

Number of guests	5,000
Variable costs per bed-night	
Food	€15
Direct labour	€10
Variable overhead	€5
Fixed costs	€30,000

During the coming year food costs are expected to increase by 5 per cent, direct labour by 10 per cent, variable overhead by 20 per cent and fixed costs by 5 per cent.

Management are presently deciding upon pricing policy for the coming year. Market research has indicated that as long as prices do not increase by more than 10 per cent, demand will remain unaffected. However, it is estimated that should price increase by more than 10 per cent, demand will fall by 5 per cent for every 2 per cent increase in price.

Required

a) Calculate the selling price of a bed-night if the numbers sold and profits earned are to remain the same as last year.
b) The number of bed-nights the university needs to sell to maintain last year's profit if they decide that price is to remain unchanged from last year.

c) Calculate the forecast profit if prices increase by 10 per cent and demand remains the same as last year.

Question 7.11

Outline what you understand by customer profitability analysis and outline the benefits to be achieved for companies undertaking customer profitability analysis.

Budgetary Planning – The Budget Process

Introduction

It is vitally important that a business develops plans for the future. Planning provides a focus for a business. It provides objectives or goals which the business should see as the stepping stones to achieving its strategy. A business is unlikely to be successful unless its managers have a clear plan regarding its future direction. Plans require financial resources (money) and generally the financial resources of a business are limited. Thus it is essential to evaluate the financial implications of pursuing each course of action open to the business. In so doing, a business can select the course that hopefully will achieve its strategic objectives.

Budgets are the most widely used accounting tool for planning, controlling and measuring the financial performance of an organisation. Budgeting has a key role to play in converting the various elements of a strategic plan into periodic forecast financial statements that show how the strategic plan may be achieved. In so doing, these forecast financial statements or budgets provide a benchmark from which actual performance can be compared and the firm's progress in achieving its strategic plans evaluated.

This chapter outlines the whole process of budgetary planning and how it plays a key role in implementing the strategy of a business. It focuses on the role and purpose of budgeting as part of the planning, decision-making and control responsibilities of management. The stages in the budget process and the administration and motivational aspects of budgeting are also covered. Finally the chapter discusses how budgets, coupled with responsibility accounting, provide a focus for managers when interpreting variances.

The Role of Budgeting

'quantitative expression of a plan for a defined period of time'
A budget as defined by CIMA Official Terminology.

The main objective of budgeting is to provide a formal quantitative and authoritative statement of the firm's plans expressed in monetary terms. It acts as a blueprint for a business to follow in future periods. The plan of action selected is termed the master budget for the period. This is what the company wants and reasonably expects to achieve in the time period allotted, based on certain assumptions regarding economic and political conditions. Projected financial statements or budgets portray the predicted financial outcomes of pursuing a particular course of action. The projected financial statements will normally comprise of:

❑   A projected profit and loss account.
❑   A projected balance sheet.
❑   A projected cash budget.

By showing the financial implications of certain decisions, managers should be able to allocate resources in an efficient and effective manner. Where management is considering only one course of action, the preparation of projected financial statements can highlight periods where the business may not have the required resources to sustain the particular course of action. Thus financial plans can warn management of possible future constraints for which they can plan now. For example a projected cash budget can highlight periods when the business may be underfinanced. Management can then take action (arrange a bank overdraft) in anticipation of these events. Financial institutions require financial projections as well as audited accounts when deciding on a business loan application.

Where management require a decision from a range of options, projected financial statements can show the expected revenues and costs associated with each option, as well as the impact each option will have on the future profitability, liquidity, and financial position of the business.

The use of budgeting in hospitality and retail

Collier and Gregory (1995) reported that 'a major part of the day to day operations of the management accounting function in hotel groups is budgetary planning and control' and that 'budgets held the most influence when it came to aiding decision-making'. Research conducted by Smullen and O'Donoghue (2005) found that all hotels surveyed used budgeting in all areas of hospitality decision-making and the budgeting tool is rated as 'the most important decision-making tool available'. In research conducted by Luby (2006), only 45 per cent of retail organisations considered that 'budgeting is the most important tool for decision-making'.

Budgetary Planning

'the establishment of objectives, and the formulation, evaluation and selection of the policies, strategies, tactics and action required to achieve them'
Planning as defined by CIMA Official Terminology

In general, budgetary planning is divided into:

❑ Strategic planning.
❑ Short-term planning.

Strategic planning

Strategic or corporate planning is concerned with the objectives of a business and the long-term plans to achieve these objectives. In the hospitality, tourism and leisure sectors where capital investment is high for new projects, long-term plans for up to 5 to 7 years are made. In general terms however, strategic planning refers to planning periods greater than one year. The level of detail in strategic plans is not as great as in short-term plans. Effectively, short-term plans flesh out the long-term plans of a business.

The following diagram outlines budgeting within a planning, decision-making and control framework. Long-term or strategic planning occurs between stages one and three. An overview of this was provided in Chapter 1.

Diagram 8.1: *Framework for managerial planning, decision-making and control*

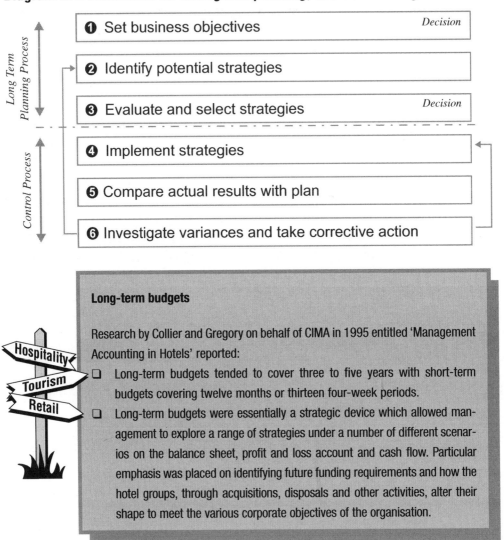

Short-term planning (stages 4 to 6)

This involves preparing projections for the next twelve months. These projections are generally quite detailed and are expected to be reasonably accurate, as the planning period is quite short. Short-term plans are effectively long-term plans broken into smaller time periods and are essential in terms of appraising short-term performance and acting as a benchmark for performance evaluation. The annual budget is generally divided into twelve monthly or thirteen four-weekly time periods. Within the above framework, the short-term or annual budgetary process begins at stage four.

Stage 4   Implement strategies

Implementing strategies involves executing the long-term plans in terms of the annual budget. The real budgetary process begins when a long-term strategy has been selected as the most likely to achieve the firm's objectives. In stage four, a strategic plan is prepared for say five years and this is subdivided into five one-year plans. These annual plans are quite detailed and show exactly how the business is to achieve each annual plan and ultimately the strategic plan. They are prepared based on the differential costs and revenues associated with the particular course of action chosen and although these costs and revenues are estimates, management can apply probabilities to calculate a likely basis for the costs and revenues estimated. Ultimately any annual budget is made up of a number of sub-plans or budgets. For example a projected profit and loss account is made up of a number of sub-budgets such as a sales budget, cost of sales budget, labour cost budget, administration budget, advertising budget etc. As well as these revenue and expense budgets, there would be a capital expenditure budget, a cash budget (showing when monies will be received and spent over the period) as well as estimates regarding debtors, creditors, stock levels etc. These budgets come together to form the master budget. The master budget is a formal document bringing together all the sub-budgets and presenting them in the traditional format of a trading, profit and loss account (income statement), cash budget and balance sheet for the year.

Stage 5   Compare actual results with plan

At this stage the focus is on the whole area of management control. This is where actual performance is monitored to assess if the business is on course to achieve its weekly, monthly and annual targets. This involves either every week or month comparing actual performance against the master/fixed budget. In particular, comparisons are made between budgeted costs and revenues with what is actually happening and variances from budget are calculated. Ultimately this control or monitoring process provides management with reports and regular feedback on key variances (differences between budget and actual performance) to help them decide if any corrective action is required.

Stage 6   Investigate variances and take corrective action

The control process should provide management with relevant, reliable and timely information to help them decide on possible corrective action when variances between budgeted and actual costs and revenues occur. All significant variances must be investigated and this must be done quickly to ensure management have timely information in order to take corrective action.

The Budgetary Process

Every organisation's budgetary process will differ according to its own culture and history. In general however, the following are the most important stages in any budgetary process.

1. Communicate details of budget policy and guidelines

This is where management will communicate the long-term or strategic plan and the consequences of this plan, to those responsible for preparing annual budgets. The consequences for example, may be a focus on different products/markets or contraction and expansion for key activities. Guidelines must also be communicated in terms of what assumptions to make in preparing the annual budget. This can include recommendations on sales prices or wage rates etc.

2. Identify limiting factors

A key task is to identify the principal budget factors, also known as the limiting budget factors. Every organisation has a limiting factor(s), a constraint that prevents it from expanding at the time the budget is prepared. A limiting factor is a variable that impedes the operation or growth of a business. Examples include:

❑   Sales demand.
❑   Labour.
❑   Materials.
❑   Machine capacity.
❑   Finance.

For many organisations operating within the hospitality, tourism and retail sectors, common limiting factors would be sales demand and finance. Constraints, other than sales, within the hospitality industry could include sleeping capacity, bar capacity and restaurant capacity. Manufacturing organisations may have production restrictions and hence can only produce a certain amount of products due to machine availability, scarcity of raw materials or shortage of skilled labour. All budgets must be prepared, mindful of the limiting factors that affect that particular organisation.

3. Preparation of sales budget

This is the most important budget as it determines the level of a company's operations and thus many of its costs and capital commitments. Estimates need to be made on sales volume, sales mix and sales price. This is extremely difficult to do and requires great knowledge of the market and the company's customers. If a constraint other than sales demand exists, it is vital to ensure that the sales budget is prepared with full consideration of the impact of the constraint.

4. First draft preparation of department budgets

This involves each department or cost centre preparing their own budgets based on the activity level agreed in the sales budget, the limiting factors identified and the guidelines set out in stages one, two and three. These budgets will be mainly cost (expense) budgets with various revenue producing departments also showing how they propose to achieve the sales targets set out in the overall sales budget. For example in a hotel, all the departments will produce expense budgets. However only the revenue producing departments such as restaurant, bar, leisure centre or accommodation will also produce sales revenue targets in line with the overall sales target agreed. Budgets laying out capital commitments and spending plans for the period will also be included in the first draft budget. The preparation of the first draft budget should, in so far as possible, be a bottom-up approach, ensuring all managers are involved and are part of the process, thus increasing the probability of acceptance of the budget when finalised.

5. Budget negotiation

In the preparation of budgets there should always be a negotiation procedure. At each stage the budget will be negotiated between the manager who submits and the direct superior. Thus the final agreed figures in the budget are as a result of a bargaining process between a manager and his or her superior. If this bargaining process does not take place then it is likely that managers will be unmotivated in terms of achieving their budget.

6. Co-ordination and review of budgets

The co-ordination of budgets ensures that each budget agreed is likely to ensure the annual target is achievable and that this fits in with the overall strategic plan. If some budgets are out of balance with the overall annual target then these need to be modified and revised so that they are compatible with the overall targets, policies and limiting factors agreed at stages one and two.

7. Final acceptance of budget

When all budgets are prepared, agreed and revised if necessary, they are summarised into the master budget which consists of a budgeted profit and loss account, balance sheet and cash flow statement. Once the master budget is accepted then the various budgets that make up the master budget are passed down through the organisation to the appropriate departments or cost centres.

As the budget control process begins and actual results are compared to budget, it may be necessary to review the assumptions and budget parameters when agreeing the budget at stage 7. This will be necessary where significant variances are occurring and are beyond the control of management. This would occur for example where the original budget was unrealistic, or where actual economic or political conditions differ significantly to the economic and political conditions assumed in the budget. In this scenario it is pointless continuing with the agreed fixed budget. It would be out of line with reality, would distort existing variances and would have an effect on management information and decision-making. Thus the master budget should be revised for the remaining portion of the budget period. Ultimately, budgeting is a continuous process of agreeing plans, comparing actual performance to planned performance and taking corrective action, part of which may be to revise the original plan.

Administration of the Budgeting Process

In order to ensure that the budgetary process operates efficiently, suitable administration procedures should be implemented. These procedures should support management in the preparation of budgets and lay out the process by which budgets are approved. The budget process should have the following administrative supports:

❑ A **budget committee** should consist of senior management who are responsible for the major functions of the organisation. For example management representing such segments as production, administration, finance, marketing and sales etc., should be part of the budget committee. Generally the committee will appoint a budget officer (normally an accountant) who co-ordinates the individual budgets into the master budget. The procedure is that each member of the budget committee is responsible for a segment or department of the business. Each segment submits a budget and thus each member of the budget committee can not only see their budget, but also the other budgets submitted and see the overall effect in the master budget. It is here that the final budgets are agreed and if any budget does not reflect a reasonable level of performance then it will not be approved and will require adjustment and resubmission. The budget committee also sets the guidelines for the preparation of individual budgets and the procedures for negotiating and agreeing budgets.

❑ **Accounting staff** should be available to management as they prepare their individual budgets. Their role is not to determine the content of the budget but to provide advisory, accounting support.

❑ A **budget manual** outlines the objectives, rules, regulations and procedures involved in the budgetary process. It is generally prepared by the company accountant and in addition to the above, would include timetables regarding the process, highlighting important dates as well as identify persons responsible for the various budgets to be submitted.

The use of budget committees and manuals

Research carried out by Smullan and O'Donoghue (2005) found that of all the hotels surveyed, none used a budget committee in formulating budgets and budget policy. The research was based on hotels with a 3-star standard or higher and with 30 or more bedrooms.

Research into budgeting in the retail sector by Luby (2006) reported the following:

The organisation has a budget committee	36%
The organisation uses a budget manual	18%
The budget process is led or driven by an accountant	64%

Budget Considerations

Significant benefits can be achieved for an organisation which implements a well designed budget process. There are also serious implications for an organisation if its management do not fully consider the issues and problems that can arise in the budget process.

Advantages of budgeting

As with any system, the benefits derived tend to correspond with the way in which they are implemented. Where budgets are administered with forethought and sensitivity involving all levels within the organisation, the advantages can be numerous.

❑ A budget gives a firm direction. It forces management to set and prioritise goals which act as a blueprint for the future.
❑ Budgeting compels management to plan and focus on the future, thus gaining an advantage by anticipating future business conditions and otherwise unforeseen problems.
❑ Budgets provide management with a basis on which to measure subsequent performance.

❑ The budgeting process encourages and promotes upward, downward and horizontal communication within the organisation. Thus the budgetary process plays a strong role in the co-ordination of activities and goal congruence. The budget acts as a vehicle through which the activities of the different parts of the organisation can be integrated into an overall plan.

❑ The budgetary process provides a basis for responsibility accounting. Responsibility accounting occurs where managers are identified with their budget centre and are responsible for achieving the budget targets for that centre. Ultimately, responsibility accounting makes managers responsible for the costs, revenues and resources that they actually control. In the context of budgets, responsibility accounting represents the delegation of responsibility to individuals within an organisation.

❑ Control within an organisation is facilitated by the regular, systematic monitoring and reporting of activities and comparison with the budget.

❑ The preparation of a master budget facilitates better cash and working capital management.

❑ Because of the 'exception principle', managers' time can be saved and attention directed to areas of most concern.

The role of budgeting

Research by Collier and Gregory on behalf of CIMA in 1995 entitled 'Management Accounting in Hotels' found that the role of budgeting helped fulfil a number of management functions including:

❑ Acting as a channel of communication and co-ordination.
❑ Forecasting and planning both in the short and longer term.
❑ Motivating staff.
❑ Performance evaluation and control.
❑ Decision-making, especially in relation to investment appraisal exercises.

Research by Luby (2006) in the Irish retail sector found that respondents ranked the uses of budgeting as follows:

1st   For forecasting and planning both in the short and longer term.
2nd   For performance evaluation and control.
3rd   As a tool in motivating staff.
4th   Acting as a channel of communication and co-ordination.
5th   For decision-making, especially in relation to investment appraisal exercises.

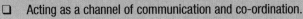

Problems or issues to consider

As with any process, if proper consideration is not given to all potential issues or pitfalls, an organisation can be negatively affected. Issues to be considered include:

❑ Sales demand is the main constraint for many organisations and is also a key budget variable which drives many other budgets, in particular expense budgets. For budgeting to be effective, it requires a reasonably accurate sales forecast. Some organisations may find it difficult to forecast sales with any degree of accuracy as there are many variables to consider and key personnel may lack skills in using sophisticated forecasting software.

❑ It may be difficult for management to estimate the availability of resources for the year ahead. For example, the availability of labour may become an issue as staff may need to be replaced during the year.

❑ Currency fluctuations and inflation may make it difficult to estimate future price levels for materials, expenses and wages.

❑ Badly handled budgetary systems that fail to consider the human aspects involved may dilute the morale of a workforce.

❑ Managers are often made accountable for budget variances that may be caused by factors outside their control. This can have a demotivating effect.

❑ Budget slack, the intentional overstating of expenses, may prevent an organisation from producing accurate budgets and can affect the overall cost competitiveness of an organisation.

❑ For many organisations, budgets are developed around existing organisational structures which may be inappropriate for current conditions and organisational development.

❑ A budget and planning process that is too rigid may hinder the creativity and flexibility in an organisation.

Problems in practice

Research conducted by Luby (2006) identified the following issues in relation to budgeting and the budget process:

❑ It can be a time consuming process tying up considerable resources.
❑ It can take too long to find closure (agreement).
❑ External factors such as movements in exchange rates, competition and political issues are difficult to forecast.
❑ The use of spreadsheets rather than budgeting software makes the process more difficult.

- ❑ Reconciling the budget with management accounts is difficult.
- ❑ There can be a lack of understanding of accounting techniques by non-accounting staff.
- ❑ Sales forecasting can be very difficult.

Approaches to Budget Implementation

While the approach taken towards budgeting can be affected by the nature of the organisation and the economic climate it operates in, there are two main approaches to budget implementation.

- ❑ A top-down (imposed) approach.
- ❑ A bottom-up (participative) approach.

Top-down approach

'a budgeting process where budget allowances are set without permitting ultimate budget holders the opportunity to participate in the process'
Top-down approach to budgeting as defined by CIMA Official Terminology

When a top-down (imposed) approach is adopted, senior management prepare a budget with little or no input from operating personnel. The budget is then imposed on employees who have to work to the budget figures. This imposed approach can be effective in newly formed or small organisations during economic hardship when precise co-ordination is required, or when operational managers lack budgeting skills.

Advantages
- ❑ Senior managers should be aware of the total resources of the organisation.
- ❑ Budgets should be in line with strategic plans.
- ❑ Co-ordination should be enhanced.
- ❑ The approach is quicker and less costly in the short-term.

Disadvantages
- ❑ Imposed approach may result in staff dissatisfaction and poor morale.
- ❑ Can contribute to a lack of team spirit.
- ❑ Limited acceptance of budget by staff which can contribute to poor performance.
- ❑ Budget process may be seen as a punitive device.
- ❑ Unachievable budgets may be set.
- ❑ Lower-level management initiative is stifled.

Bottom-up approach

'a budgeting process where all budget holders have the opportunity to participate in setting their own budgets'
Bottom-up approach to budgeting as defined by CIMA Official Terminology

Where a bottom-up (participative) approach is adopted, budgets are developed by lower-level managers who then submit and agree their budgets with their superiors. This approach can be effective in very large organisations or where operational managers have strong budgeting skills.

Advantages
❑ Budget information comes from those who know at an operational level.
❑ Knowledge used in the process is spread throughout the organisation and should improve the quality and accuracy of budget data.
❑ Morale and motivation may be improved as participation levels increase.
❑ In general, the likelihood of acceptance of the budget is increased.
❑ Generally budgets can be more realistic.

Disadvantages
❑ The approach is more time consuming.
❑ Changes often made by senior managers can cause motivation issues.
❑ Lower level managers may be unqualified to participate.
❑ Budgetary slack may be introduced.
❑ The budget process may be forced to start earlier, therefore more uncertainty exists regarding budget forecasts.

Budget approaches adopted

Research conducted by Smullen and O'Donoghue (2005) into the use and influence of certain financial based decision-making models in the Irish hospitality industry reported that 94 per cent of budgets are constructed using a mixture of a top-down and bottom-up approach. By its nature, this mixed approach was quite iterative and involved lots of interaction between various levels of management. Six per cent used the top-down approach which effectively involved the general manager preparing the figures and distributing them to all department heads without deliberations. This was consistent with the research of Collier and Gregory in 1995 relating to hotel companies in the UK which indicated that hotels use a mixed or interactive approach when it comes to preparing the annual budget.

Research in the retail sector by Luby (2006) found that the approaches to budgeting were adopted as follows:

Top-down approach – budget prepared by senior managers and imposed	27%
Middle managers participate in the budget process	64%
All managers (including lower level and supervisors) participate in the budget process	9%

Motivational Aspects of Budgets

Budgets are intended to motivate the organisation as a whole but specifically to motivate management. In general, research evidence suggests that budgets and the whole budgeting process has a positive motivational effect on management. More specifically, the existence of budgets tends to improve performance in the following circumstances:

❑ When the process involves a bottom-up approach to target setting, management at all levels are involved or have their say in the target setting process.
❑ Where targets are set that are demanding but achievable.
❑ Where the work environment is more relaxed and factors such as staff motivation are considered to be as important as achieving set targets.
❑ Where targets are not achieved, a caring non-personal and non-critical approach is taken.
❑ Where managers are not held responsible for costs and revenues that they are not in a position to control. Thus the existence of responsibility accounting, where departmental managers are only responsible for costs and revenues generated within their control.

The existence of budgets can demotivate management in the following circumstances:

❑ Where the process of target setting is a top-down approach with management deciding targets for their subordinates.
❑ Where unrealistic targets are set resulting in an idealistic budget rather than an attainable or realistic budget.

❑ Where the expectation in the work environment is that targets must be met above all other things. In this instance managers will introduce 'slack' into the target setting process to ensure the target is achieved.

❑ Where a critical approach is taken when targets are not achieved.

Overall it would seem that budgeting thrives in motivating management where a culture of a 'human approach to man-management' exists, involving 'real' participation and a bottom-up approach. The existence of responsibility accounting with assigned cost centres also supports a management motivating budget process.

Budgeting and Responsibility Accounting

Budgeting works best where a clear organisation structure exists and where clear lines of responsibility are laid out. An organisation structure is an arrangement of lines of responsibility within the company or department. Each manager within the organisation is in charge of, or responsible for, a part or segment of the organisation and thus that part could be called a responsibility centre. There are effectively four major types of responsibility centres:

Cost centre

This is where the manager is responsible for costs only. An example would include the maintenance or cleaning department of a hotel which only deals with costs and expenditure and thus would be a cost centre.

Revenue centre

This is where managers are only responsible for the revenues earned. An example would include the sales reservations of a hotel or leisure centre.

Profit centre

This is where the manager is responsible for both the revenues and costs of a section or segment of the organisation. An example would include a leisure centre as part of a chain or a retail outlet as part of a chain of outlets or a restaurant within a hotel. Here the budget represents both revenues and costs.

Investment centre

This is where a manager is responsible for investments as well as revenues and costs. The regional manager of a retail chain would for example, be responsible for not just how each of the outlets have performed from a profit (revenues less costs) perspective, but for the level and quality of the investment and the level of return on investment achieved within the region.

Responsibility accounting measures actual results with budgeted for every responsibility centre and ultimately helps to trace costs and revenues to the person who has the most knowledge of, and who is responsible for, those costs and revenues. Budgets coupled with responsibility accounting, provide a focus for managers when interpreting variances. Variances, whether positive or negative, should prompt questions and subsequent investigation, not blame. Thus responsibility accounting identifies a person who can properly explain a variance. It is of utmost importance with responsibility accounting that all non-controllable costs within a responsibility centre are separately identified and not included as part of any performance review of that centre.

Summary

This chapter has dealt with the overall framework for planning, controlling and decision-making and has outlined the role of budgeting within that framework. It has focused on the various stages of the budget process, distinguishing between short-term and long-term planning and the link between budgetary planning and control. It has focused on the administrative back-up and detailed organisational structures required to ensure an efficient budgetary system incorporating responsibility accounting. Finally budgeting, as with any evaluation tool, has enormous motivational consequences for employees. A budgetary system can have a motivating or de-motivating effect depending on how it is used.

The main information points covered in this chapter are as follows:

❏ Budgets are the most widely used accounting tool for planning, controlling and measuring the financial performance of an organisation. Budgeting has a key role to play in converting the various elements of a strategic plan into periodic forecast financial statements that show how the strategic plan may be achieved.

❏ The main objective of budgeting is to provide a formal quantitative and authoritative statement of the firm's plans expressed in monetary terms. A budget is a quantitative expression of a proposed future plan put forward by management for a limited period. It acts as a blueprint for a business to follow in future periods. The plan of action selected is termed the 'fixed budget' or 'master budget' for the period.

❏ In general, budgetary planning is divided into two time periods, long-term and short-term. Long-term planning is defined as greater than one year, however, in reality, companies plan up to seven years in advance. Short-term planning relates to periods of one year or less.

❑ In order to ensure that the budgetary process operates efficiently, suitable ac _istration procedures should be implemented. These procedures should support management in the preparation of budgets and lay out the process by which budgets are approved.

❑ There are two main approaches to budget implementation.
  – A top-down (imposed) approach.
  – A bottom-up (participative) approach.

❑ Budgeting works best where a clear organisation structure exists and where clear lines of responsibility are laid out.

❑ Responsibility accounting is a system that measures actual results against the budget for every responsibility centre and ultimately helps to trace costs and revenues to the person who has most knowledge of them and who is responsible for them. Budgets coupled with responsibility accounting provide a focus for managers when interpreting variances.

Review Questions

ᴴe main objectives of budgetary planning.

b)   ᵍuish between budgetary planning and budgetary control.

Question 8.2

a)   Distinguish between short-term and long-term planning.

b)   What is the master budget and describe its role in relation to other budgets.

Question 8.3

1. indentily   idea

a)   Identify the key steps in the development of a financial plan.

b)   Outline the administrative back-up procedures that need to be implemented to ensure the budget process works effectively.

Question 8.4

each manager responsible for meeting centres budget

What do you understand by the term 'responsibility accounting' and how does it help the budget process.

Organisation divided into responsibility centr 1.

Question 8.5

Outline the circumstances which could cause the whole budgeting process to have a demotivating effect on management and employees within an organisation.

Question 8.6

Distinguish between a bottom–up and a top–down approach to budget implementation.

CHAPTER 9

Budgetary Planning – Preparation of the Master Budget

Learning Outcomes

By the end of this chapter you will be able to:

- ☐ Outline the role of the master budget within an organisation.
- ☐ Distinguish between operating and capital budgets.
- ☐ Outline key forecasting variables used in developing projected financial statements and the factors to consider when forecasting these variables.
- ☐ Describe the various approaches to budget preparation including zero-based budgeting, incremental budgeting, activity based budgeting and rolling budgets.
- ☐ Prepare a forecast profit and loss account and balance sheet for a business based on key forecast assumptions.
- ☐ Outline the importance of cash budgeting and be able to prepare monthly budgeted cash projections.
- ☐ Outline how management use forecast financial statements for decision-making.

Introduction

Chapter 8 discussed the theory of budgeting and the budget process within the framework of planning, decision-making and control. In this chapter we now turn our attention to the preparation of the master budget for an organisation. The chapter also outlines the various types of budgets and the approach to forecasting key variables.

The Fixed or Master Budget

'budget set prior to the control period and not subsequently changed in response to changes in activity, costs, or revenues'
Fixed Budget as defined by CIMA Official Terminology

The fixed or master budget sets out the plans for the business for the next accounting period based on various assumptions of sales and sales growth, inflation (in particular labour inflation), interest rates, taxation and capital expenditure. This master budget is known as the fixed budget as it is based on these fixed assumptions of trading performance and financial outlook. Its chief role is at the planning stage, in setting the overall direction or plan for the business.

There are three summary budgeted statements that are the end result of any budgetary planning process and that make up the master budget.

❑ **The trading, profit and loss account** (also known as the income statement). This is made up of a number of operating budgets such as sales, cost of sales, payroll, operating expenses budgets, and fixed expenses budgets.
❑ **The balance sheet.** The balance sheet is influenced by the capital expenditure budget, stock budget, debtors budget and creditors budget. Collectively these budgets are known as the capital budgets.
❑ **The cash budget.** This budget is primarily concerned with the timings of future cash inflows and outflows and is based on data from the operating and capital budgets. The cash budget assists in the management of company finances by disclosing the cash peaks and troughs within the budget period indicating when extra funds will be needed. If the extra funding is required only for a number of months and thereafter the situation becomes self-financing, then the shortfall may be met with short-term sources of finance such as bank overdraft. Otherwise long-term funding is preferable as it gives the business more cash leeway and will not require the business to start refinancing a few months later should anything unexpected happen. The cash budget is normally presented in two formats:
 – A cash flow statement as per FRS 1 and IAS 7 (normally used for more strategic planning).
 – A month by month cash budget showing all cash inflows (both of a revenue and capital nature) and cash outflows (both capital and revenue expenditure). This is normally used for the short-term planning cycle.

The above budgets come together to form the fixed or master budget which is the projected profit and loss, balance sheet and cash flow of the business. The diagram below outlines this relationship.

Diagram 9.1: *The master budget*

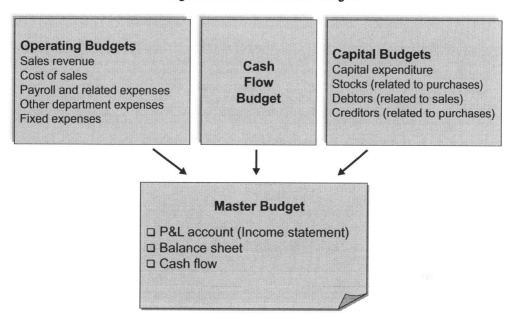

The master budget brings together all the financial projections from the various operating and capital budgets within an organisation for the period. It embraces the impact of both operating decisions (running the business) and investment and financing decisions that the business has planned for the next time period (usually 12 months). It sets out the organisation's targets for the coming period in a quantifiable and easily understood format, helping to provide direction and ensuring goal congruence.

It is vitally important to understand the purpose and the relationship that exists between the profit and loss account, the balance sheet and the cash budget.

Diagram 9.2: *The master budget statements*

Profit and Loss Account	**Balance Sheet**	**Cash Budget**
A projected profit and loss account (income statement) includes all the revenues and expenses anticipated for the budget period under review.	A projected balance sheet is a statement of the expected position of an entity at the end of the budget period. It contains the expected monetary value of assets, liabilities and capital at the end of the budget period.	Cash budgets are prepared in order to ensure that there will be sufficient cash in hand to cope adequately with budgeted activities. They must contain every type of cash inflow (money received) and every type of cash outflow (money paid).

When preparing the profit and loss statement, the normal rules of accounting (accruals and matching concepts) must be followed. This results in, for example, sales revenue recorded in the profit and loss statement including all sales incurred irrespective of receipt of income. The cash budget is concerned with cash inflows and outflows, therefore only cash received in the period will be recorded in the cash budget. Thus cash receipts and payments in the cash budget are not the same as the sales, cost of sales and expenses in the profit and loss statement.

Example 9.1: *The effect of sales in the master budget*

Joseph Flynn is in the process of setting up a new business enterprise which involves selling quality music products from an outlet in Galway Retail Park under the banner 'Flynn Music Sales'. Joseph anticipates sales in the first month to be €80,000, rising to €100,000 per month thereafter. As Joseph plans on attracting corporate business, he expects 10 per cent of each month's sales to be given one month's credit.

You are required to demonstrate to Joseph how sales representing the first three months of trading will be recorded in a master budget.

Approach

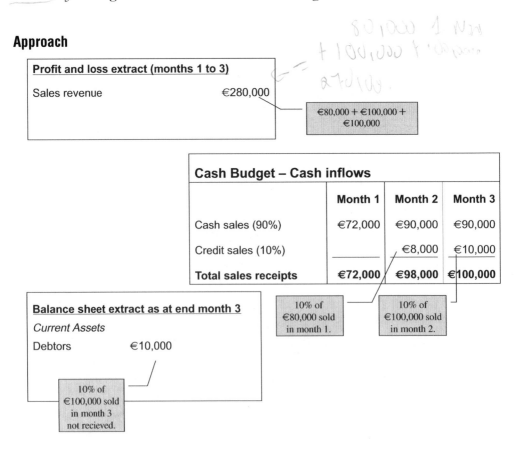

The total cash received in the first three months of trading should amount to €270,000 (€72,000 + €98,000 + €100,000) and can be seen in the cash budget above. In accordance with accounting concepts, the sales revenue in the profit and loss statement is recorded at €280,000, representing both cash and credit sales achieved during the period. The balance sheet shows the amount of cash outstanding from debtors at the end of the period at €10,000 (10 per cent of month 3 sales of €100,000).

The recording of sales transactions is not the only cause for differences between the profit and loss statement and the cash budget. Similar to sales revenue, purchases may be on credit and the full cost of purchases should appear in the profit and loss statement while the cash budget will only include the amount paid in the period.

Example 9.2: *The effect of purchases and stock in the master budget*

Pauline Murphy is about to operate a souvenir shop in a transport museum. She has estimated that €50,000 of goods will be purchased each month for the first three months of trading, and has negotiated one month's credit with all suppliers. At the end of this period she expects to have stock of €20,000.

Show how purchases and stock will be recorded in a master budget representing the first three months of trading.

Approach

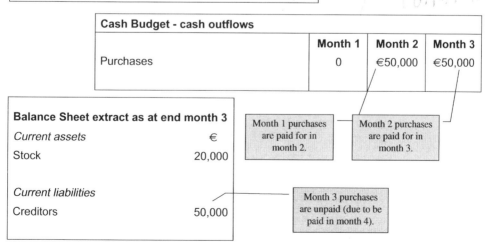

Profit and loss extract for (months 1 to 3)	€
Opening stock	0
Purchases (€50,000 x 3)	150,000
Closing stock	(20,000)
Cost of goods sold	130,000

Cash Budget - cash outflows	Month 1	Month 2	Month 3
Purchases	0	€50,000	€50,000

Balance Sheet extract as at end month 3	€
Current assets	
Stock	20,000
Current liabilities	
Creditors	50,000

Month 1 purchases are paid for in month 2.

Month 2 purchases are paid for in month 3.

Month 3 purchases are unpaid (due to be paid in month 4).

One can see that due to the timing differences between receiving and paying for purchases and the movement in stock, cost of goods sold amounts to €130,000 in the profit and loss account, whereas only €100,000 is recorded as purchases in the cash budget.

Other differences between the profit and loss account and cash budget can be due to:

❑ The purchase cost or sales proceeds of fixed assets not being shown in the profit and loss statement but appearing in the cash budget. The profit and loss statement will only contain the profit or loss on disposal of fixed assets.
❑ Depreciation appearing in the profit and loss statement but not in the cash budget as it does not give rise to a movement in cash.
❑ The fact that not all cash flows are presented in the profit and loss statement. For example, the proceeds from the issue of shares are recorded in the cash budget and balance sheet.

Forecasting Key Variables

'A prediction of future events and their quantification for planning purposes'
A forecast as defined by CIMA Official Terminology

Three essential elements are required before one can begin to prepare projected financial statements. These are:

❑ Forecast of sales.
❑ Forecast of costs/expenditure.
❑ Forecast of the required investment in net assets to achieve these sales.

The following are the main issues which should be considered when developing these forecasts.

Forecasting sales

When preparing projected financial statements, the forecast of sales is the initial task or starting point. A reliable sales forecast is essential as many items such as cost of goods sold, other variable costs, stock levels, fixed assets and capital requirements will be significantly influenced and determined by the level of sales forecast.

Forecasting future sales is not an easy task. It is made up of three variables namely sales volume, sales price and sales mix. These variables are influenced by a number of factors that should be taken into account when forecasting sales.

Factors influencing sales

Past sales volume and mix	Level of competition
Quality of the product or service	Consumer behaviour
Strength of the brand name	State of the economy
Planned advertising expenditure	Political and industrial outlook
Pricing policy	Local activities and events
Capacity	Seasonality
Advance bookings	Demand analysis

Forecasting issues in retailing

Research by Luby (2006) identified the following issues in relation to forecasting sales demand in the retail sector:

❑ Weather can influence shopping patterns and have a significant impact on sales. It is difficult to forecast weather.

❑ Macro-economic factors such as interest rates and petrol prices affect retail sales demand and can be difficult to determine.

❑ The level of competition. A competitor who changes pricing policy or opens a new store can have a significant effect on sales demand which is difficult to forecast.

❑ For retail outlets targeting tourists, it can be difficult to predict accurately the number of tourists visiting the area.

❑ Some respondents reported that sales forecasting 'can be almost useless' and that sales forecasting relating to new outlets 'is virtually impossible'.

In practice, sales forecasts can be developed in a number of ways such as:

1. To aggregate projections made by the sales force on the basis of their assumptions of the market and changes in market conditions. On one hand this can be quite a subjective approach, however a good sales team should know its market well and should anticipate any significant changes that could affect sales.
2. Using market research techniques would be particularly appropriate when considering the launch of a new product.
3. Large businesses sometimes develop economic models to predict sales. These models would incorporate a number of the variables identified above and take into account the relationship between them and their effect on sales.

Forecasting sales is extremely difficult and the costs and benefits of each method must be properly assessed. For example, for small businesses the cost of developing a complex economic model would probably outweigh the benefits of such a model.

Sales structure in hotels

Hotel operations employ a complicated sales structure. Sales includes rooms, catering, telephone, club and other services. Catering sales can involve the same food items sold at different prices if served in the bar compared to the restaurant. Thus prices and margins vary throughout the hotel. However according to B.S. Wijeysinghe in his article 'Break-even Occupancy for a Hotel Operation' (*Management Accounting*, February 1993), catering, telephone, club and other sales are largely dependent on room-sales and thus have a fairly consistent sales to room-sales ratio. Thus a reasonably accurate calculation of occupancy can lead to an accurate assessment of sales from other products and services offered by a hotel due to this relationship or level of dependence.

Forecasting costs

To accurately estimate future costs, it is important to understand cost behaviour patterns and how some costs are affected by fluctuating sales activity levels. Costs may be classified into the following categories:

❏ **Fixed costs:** These are costs which are not expected to vary with sales. For example if sales increase by 10 per cent, fixed costs would remain fixed and not increase in proportion to sales. Examples are rent, rates, depreciation, salaries and insurance. From a forecasting perspective, the level of sales activity forecast will not significantly influence these costs unless the sales forecast is beyond the relevant range of sales activity for these costs. Thus the main factors that influence fixed costs are inflation, legal agreements, economic outlook and national wage agreements, as labour costs are a major element of the fixed costs of any business.

❏ **Variable costs:** These are costs that are expected to vary with sales. Thus if sales increase by 10 per cent, these costs are expected to increase proportionately. Examples would include cost of sales, sales commissions and part-time labour. In reality, although these costs should increase as sales increase, it may not be strictly proportionate because factors such as suppliers' prices, commissions and part-time labour rates may vary.

❏ **Semi-variable costs:** These have both a fixed and a variable element and so may vary partially with sales. Such costs may be identified by examining the past records of the business. For example, light and heat costs could be classified as a semi-variable cost as a certain amount of light and heat will be incurred irrespective of the level of sales. However if sales increase significantly, then more rooms will be used requiring extra power. Semi-variable costs can be broken down into their separate fixed and variable components (through the use of the high-low method, scatter-graph approach and statistical techniques such as regression analysis covered in Chapter 2). By doing this, one can establish the total variable and total fixed costs of a business.

The analysis of costs into fixed and variable components is vitally important when forecasting future costs. Variable costs will increase in relation to sales whereas fixed costs may only increase with the rate of inflation (unless there is evidence to the contrary such as a new leasing agreement or new wage agreements).

Forecasting the balance sheet (net assets requirement)

Sales activity will also have a significant effect on the balance sheet. A number of items on the balance sheet of a company will increase as sales increase. For example a significant increase in sales will most likely lead to increases in the following balance sheet items:

- ❏ **Debtors:** Debtors tend to increase as sales increase.
- ❏ **Stock levels:** More stock is required to meet increased demand.
- ❏ **Cash:** More cash is required to meet increased costs associated with the increase in sales.
- ❏ **Creditors:** More credit is required from suppliers as purchases increase in line with sales.
- ❏ **Accrued expenses:** More accrued expenses occur as a result of increased overheads.
- ❏ **Bank overdraft:** A bank overdraft is frequently used to bridge any financing gaps caused by increases in activity.
- ❏ **Fixed assets:** As the business expands new fixed assets are required. (Note that fixed assets will not increase as sales increase, but only as the business reaches capacity and requires expansion). Hence there is a long-term relationship between sales and the fixed assets requirement.
- ❏ **Long-term finance:** As fixed assets expand, one will also expect long-term finance in the form of equity and more likely long-term debt to increase.

The relationship between sales and balance sheet items must be taken into account when forecasting balance sheet items. A simple approach to forecasting some balance sheet items is to express the balance sheet items as a percentage of forecast sales. To use this method requires management to examine past records to see the effect fluctuations in sales have on various balance sheet items. For example, if past records indicate that trade debtors levels amount to 10 per cent of sales, then if forecast sales amount to €10m, debtors levels could be taken as €1m unless management have a policy or cap on maximum debtor levels. This method is quite simple and assumes a linear relationship between sales and the balance sheet item. Other more sophisticated methods involving statistical analysis (regression analysis) can also be used. In forecasting balance sheet items, one must be aware of the policies of a business. For example, has the company set maximum levels for loan capital, fixed assets, debtors, creditors etc.? The commitments and policies of a business and their influence on forecasting are discussed below.

Other forecasting issues

Forecasting involves an awareness of the economic environment and government policy. These influence the following items:

❑ Taxation and rate of corporation tax.
❑ Variable interest rates on borrowings.
❑ The rate of inflation.
❑ The policies and commitments of the business.

All financial projections will be based on assumptions made on these items. The rate of corporation tax is a significant item in the profit and loss account as well as a significant item in current liabilities in the balance sheet. For long-term financial forecasting it is important to be aware of government policy in relation to rates of taxation. For example, it is government policy at present to maintain the rate of corporation tax at 12.5 per cent for the foreseeable future.

Generally, interest rates track inflation and as inflation increases interest rates increase. It is important to be aware of where the economy is in relation to its economic cycle. Is it on the rise with increased production and growth? If so this would indicate possible increases in inflation in the future with the associated increases in interest rates. If it is in a depressed state then this would indicate low inflation with a monetary policy of low interest rates to try and boost the economy and domestic demand. Most businesses lock themselves into fixed interest debt as it is easier to plan for and is less risky. However if the long-term view of interest rates is that they will fall, then the temptation would be to ensure the cost of debt is based on variable rather than fixed rates.

With regard to the effect of inflation on individual items of expense, each category should be dealt with separately. Using an average rate of inflation for all items in the profit and loss account is usually inappropriate, as the level of inflation can vary significantly between individual items.

The policies and existing commitments of a business must also be considered when preparing projected financial statements. These may relate to such matters as:

❑ Capital expenditure.
❑ Financing methods (debt or equity).
❑ Dividends.

The level of capital expenditure is directly influenced by the strategic plan. Financing is a direct result of the level of capital expenditure planned. Financing methods are influenced by the level of existing debt in the business as well as company policy on debt levels. The costs and risks associated with equity and debt levels must be taken into account in this decision.

For dividend payments, there is no problem determining the rate of preference dividend as this is generally specified in the share agreement. However, ordinary share dividends are decided on by the directors of a company who propose dividends based on annual results. This indicates that ordinary share dividends fluctuate with the fortunes of the company. However evidence suggests that directors have usually a target rate of dividend and are generally reluctant to deviate from this level. Remember, dividends tell the market a lot about the directors' confidence in the future of the company and a sudden reduction or even increase can affect share price. Generally the target level of dividends is linked to the level of profit for the period.

Dividend policy

Jurys Doyle plc. tend to ensure their rates of dividend are in excess of 30 per cent of profits available for dividend. For the years 2002 and 2003, the company declared dividend amounting to 33 per cent and 39 per cent respectively of profits available for dividend.

Ryanair plc. has not declared any dividends since it floated on the stock exchange as it is a young company experiencing rapid growth and thus all profits are retained in the company for expansion. However at present (November 2005), there are indications that Ryanair may relax this policy.

Preparation of Projected Financial Statements

Let us now take the following comprehensive example of an existing business and develop projected financial statements from their forecast budget figures. An existing business will always have an actual balance sheet at the beginning of the budget forecast period.

Example 9.3: *Projected financial statements*

The following is the balance sheet for Equip Suppliers Ltd as at 31 December. The company supplies fitness equipment to hotels and leisure centres.

Balance Sheet as at 31st December

		€
Fixed assets (net book value)		120,000
Current assets		
Stock	10,200	
Trade debtors	19,800	
Cash	5,600	35,600
Current liabilities		
Trade creditors	14,700	
Accruals	20,000	(34,700)
Long-term liabilities		
10% fixed interest loan	25,000	(25,000)
		95,900
Financed by		
Share capital		70,000
Profit and loss account		25,900
		95,900

The following data has been agreed by the budget committee for the next four months. The committee believe the company will experience increased demand for its products and are keen to plan for this expansion.

1. Sales, labour and overheads have been forecast as follows:

Month	Budgeted sales	Labour costs	Overheads
	€	€	€
January	55,000	14,500	11,580
February	60,500	15,950	12,738
March	68,063	17,545	14,012
April	76,911	19,300	15,413

2. Stock is sold at a 68 per cent gross profit margin and management policy is to hold sufficient stock on hand to meet 50 per cent of sales demand for the next month.
3. On average, 60 per cent of the sales are cash sales with debtors on average paying the following month.
4. Suppliers of materials offer one month's credit for purchases.
5. Labour costs are paid in full by the end of each month.

6. Overheads which are paid as incurred include depreciation of €2,500 per month, but exclude the rental charge for the company's premises. This is an annual charge of €36,000 paid in two equal instalments on 1 January and 1 July.
7. The accruals figure in the balance sheet at 31 December represents arrears of VAT and corporation tax. The company have come to an agreement with the Revenue Commissioners that the amount will be paid by 28 February. This figure is inclusive of penalties and interest.
8. There will be a repayment of €5,000 on the existing loan on 31 March. Interest on the loan is paid at the end of each month.

a) *Prepare a budgeted trading, profit and loss account for the three months ended 31 March.*
b) *Prepare a monthly forecast cash budget for January, February and March.*
c) *Prepare a forecast balance sheet as at 31 March.*

Approach

The budgeted trading, profit and loss account, cash budget and balance sheet are presented below with detailed notes showing workings and explaining the figures.

a) Budgeted Trading, Profit and Loss Account for three months ending 31 March

	January	February	March		Total	
	€	€	€	€	€	
Sales	55,000	60,500	68,063		183,563	Note 1
Less Cost of goods sold						
Opening stock	10,200	9,680	10,890	10,200		
Purchases	17,080	20,570	23,196	60,846		Note 4
Closing stock	(9,680)	(10,890)	(12,306)	(12,306)		Note 3
Cost of goods sold	(17,600)	(19,360)	(21,780)		(58,740)	Note 2
Gross profit	37,400	41,140	46,283		124,823	Note 2
Less Expenses						
Labour costs				47,995		Note 5
Overheads				30,830		Note 5
Depreciation				7,500		
Rent				9,000		Note 5
Loan interest (€25,000 x 10% x 3/12)				625		Note 5
					95,950	
Net profit					28,873	

b) Cash Budget

	January €	February €	March €	Total €	
Cash inflow – income					
Cash sales (60% current month)	33,000	36,300	40,838	110,138	
Credit sales (40% previous month)	19,800	22,000	24,200	66,000	**Note 6**
Total	52,800	58,300	65,038	176,138	
Cash outflow – expenditure					
Purchases	14,700	17,080	20,570	52,350	**Note 7**
Rent	18,000			18,000	**Note 8**
Labour	14,500	15,950	17,545	47,995	**Note 9**
Overheads	9,080	10,238	11,512	30,830	**Note 10**
Taxation		20,000		20,000	**Note 11**
Loan repayment			5,000	5,000	**Note 12**
Loan interest	208	208	209	625	**Note 12**
Total expenses	56,488	63,476	54,836	174,800	
Net inflow / (outflow)	(3,688)	(5,176)	10,202	1,338	**Note 13**
Opening balance	5,600	1,912	(3,264)	5,600	**Note 13**
Closing balance	1,912	(3,264)	6,938	6,938	

c) Balance Sheet as at 31 March

	Cost €	Depreciation €	NBV €	
Fixed assets	120,000	7,500	112,500	**Note 14**
Current assets				**Note 15**
Stock		12,306		
Trade debtors		27,225		
Prepayments (Rent 3 months x €3,000)		9,000		
Bank		6,938	55,469	
Current liabilities				**Note 16**
Trade creditors		23,196	(23,196)	
Long-term liabilities				
10% Loan		20,000	(20,000)	**Note 17**
			124,773	
Financed by				
Share capital			70,000	**Note 18**
Profit and loss reserve (€25,900 + €28,873)			54,773	**Note 18**
			124,773	

Notes explaining the figures:

The projected profit and loss account

Note 1: Sales

The trading, profit and loss account is based on the following simple formula:

> **Sales – expenses = net profit**

It is important to remember that in preparing the profit and loss account, we are only concerned with revenues earned and expenses charged for the forecast period. The profit and loss account is not concerned with whether or not we have received these monies, or when we will pay the various expenses. Thus sales are simply the forecast figures for January, February and March of €55,000, €60,500 and €68,063.

Note 2: Gross profit and cost of sales

The gross profit of a business is simply the difference between the selling price and the cost price of goods sold, multiplied by the quantity of goods sold. Most businesses will be able to calculate an average gross profit margin. In the above example we are told in point (2) of the example that the company's stock (goods) is sold at a 68 per cent gross profit margin. This tells us that on average, for every €100 sales, the business will make a gross profit of €68 and thus the cost of buying the goods will amount to €32. In this example, we calculate gross profit per month by simply multiplying sales by the gross profit margin of 68 per cent and cost of sales is simply the difference between sales and gross profit.

Gross profit margin and gross profit mark-up

Gross profit margin

The gross profit margin, (sometimes called the gross profit percentage), is calculated as follows:

$$\frac{\text{Gross profit} \times 100}{\text{Sales}}$$

This tells us that if the gross profit margin is 68 per cent, then gross profit equals 68 per cent and sales equals 100 per cent (the denominator in the fraction). Hence cost of goods sold will equal 32 per cent. Gross profit and cost of sales can be calculated by simply multiplying sales by 68 per cent and 32 per cent respectively.

Gross profit = sales multiplied by the gross profit percentage

Cost of sales = sales multiplied by the cost of sales percentage

Gross profit mark-up

Sometimes a business will express its gross profit percentage in terms of gross profit mark-up. This percentage expresses gross profit as a percentage of cost of sales as follows:

> ### Gross profit x 100
> ### Cost of sales
>
> For example, a gross profit mark-up of 70 per cent would imply that gross profit is 70 per cent and cost of sales is 100 per cent (the denominator in the fraction). Hence sales will equal 170 per cent. We can calculate gross profit by simply dividing sales by 170 and multiplying by 70. Cost of sales can be calculated by dividing sales by 170 and multiplying by 100. Gross profit mark-up is sometimes called gross profit as a percentage of cost or as a percentage of cost of sales.

Note 3: Stock figures

Most businesses that sell goods will have a policy of holding a certain amount of stock. Some businesses will try and ensure stock levels stay within a certain range. Stock levels are generally dependent on sales demand. If sales are expected to increase, then stock levels tend also to increase. Depending on the business sector, stock levels can be extremely high (manufacturing and retail) to very low (restaurants, hotels). However they are a product of demand. In this example we are told in point (2) that it is management policy to have sufficient stock in hand to meet 50 per cent of sales demand for the next month. In other words the closing stock at the end of January should equal 50 per cent of February's projected sales. Closing stock at the end of January should equal €30,250 (€60,500 multiplied by 50 per cent). However, the €30,250 figure values stock at selling price. The cost concept requires that stock should be valued at cost price unless selling price is less than cost price. We do know that the cost of sales percentage equals 32 per cent (100 per cent minus 68 per cent). Thus we need to mark down the stock valuation to cost price by multiplying €30,250 by 32 per cent to get €9,680. Remember, closing stock at the end of January is the opening stock for February.

Calculation of closing stock

> ### Next month's sales x stock percentage required x
> ### cost of sales percentage

Closing stock end of January   €60,500 x 50% x 32% = €9,680
Closing stock end of February   €68,063 x 50% x 32% = €10,890
Closing stock end of March   €76,911 x 50% x 32% = €12,306

Opening stock of €10,200 at the beginning of January is provided in the balance sheet at 31 December.

Note 4: Calculation of purchases figures

At this stage we have calculated sales, cost of sales, opening stock and closing stock for each of the months. The figure that is missing is that for purchases, which is simply calculated as the balancing figure. Let us look at January again.

		€	€
Sales			55,000
Less Cost of sales			
Opening stock		10,200	
Purchases		?	
Less Closing stock		(9,680)	
Cost of goods sold	(32% x 55,000)		17,600
Gross profit	(68% x 55,000)		37,400

Sales of €55,000 are provided in the example. The gross profit is found by applying the gross profit margin. The cost of goods sold is the difference between sales and gross profit. Purchases can be calculated using the following formula:

Calculation of purchases

> **Purchases = cost of goods sold + closing stock – opening stock**

	Sales (given)	Cost of sales (sales x 32%)	+ Closing stock	– Opening stock	= Purchases
	€	€	€	€	€
January	55,000	17,600	9,680	10,200	17,080
February	60,500	19,360	10,890	9,680	20,570
March	68,063	21,780	12,306	10,890	23,196

It is important to calculate the purchases figures for each month as there is a time lapse of one month between receiving the goods and paying for them. Thus purchases in January will be paid for in February. We need to know the purchases figure for each month to know when it is paid, as this information is required for the cash budget.

There are many calculations involved in preparing a forecast trading account. The following step by step approach may be helpful.

Preparing trading accounts

Step 1	*Outline the trading account, inserting the figures given in the question. These are generally the sales and opening stock figures.*
Step 2	*Identify the gross profit and cost of sales percentages and calculate these figures.*
Step 3	*Calculate the closing stock figure.*
Step 4	*Calculate the purchases figures. In the above example, purchases is the balancing figure, however, one should note that in some questions, the purchases figures will be given, with closing stock acting as the balancing figure. (See question 9.9)*

Note 5: Expenses

In the profit and loss account we are concerned with expenses charged and not if, or when, they are paid. Labour costs and overheads are as given for each month. Depreciation of €2,500 per month was included in overheads but is shown separately in the profit and loss account.

The rental charge on the company's premises, point (6) in the example, is €36,000 per annum. As we are only preparing the profit and loss account for three months then only 3/12 of €36,000 will be charged to the profit and loss account irrespective of what is paid.

There is a repayment of €5,000 on a loan. This is a capital transaction affecting the balance sheet, not the profit and loss account. However the cost of a loan is the interest charged and this should appear as an expense in the profit and loss account. We are told from the balance sheet, and point (8) in the example, that loan interest is charged at 10 per cent on the amount of the loan. The amount of the loan has been €25,000 for the period and thus interest is charged to the profit and loss account for each month as €208 (€25,000 x 10 per cent x 1/12).

The projected cash budget

Here we are concerned with when revenues are received and expenses are paid. There is no distinction between revenues and expenses of a capital or operating nature. For example, if a business had sales for January of €5,000 and also received a loan of €10,000, then in the profit and loss account we would only take into account the sales figure as the loan would appear as a liability in the balance sheet. However in the cash budget, there is no distinction between transactions of a capital or revenue nature and hence we would show both on the income side of the cash budget.

The cash budget is the same as a bank or cash account and is governed by the formula:

> **Receipts – payments = net cash inflow / (outflow) +**
> **opening cash balance = closing cash balance**

It is generally presented in a monthly or quarterly format. It shows for each period whether the business has a shortfall or an excess of cash. The following are examples of typical cash inflows and outflows for a business:

Cash inflows	Cash outflows
Cash sales	Expenses paid
Cash received from debtors	Cash purchases
Cash from issue of shares	Payments to creditors
Loans received	Dividend
Cash from the sale of fixed assets	Loan repayments
Tax refunds	Purchase of fixed assets
	Payments to Revenue Commissioners

Note 6: Income/receipts

Income or receipts would include income from sales as well as any monies received from the sale of fixed assets or any monies received by way of loans to the business. In this example, the only income for the business is its trading income or monies received from sales. The income section of the cash budget is reproduced below, with the calculation of each figure outlined:

Cash Budget

	January	February	March	Total
	€	€	€	€
Cash inflow – income				
Cash sales (60% current month)	33,000	36,300	40,838	110,138
Credit sales (40% previous month)	19,800	22,000	24,200	66,000
Total	52,800	58,300	65,038	176,138

In point 3 of the example, we are told that on average, 60 per cent of the company's sales are cash with debtors paying the balance (40 per cent) one month later. Thus 60 per cent of January's sales of €55,000 will be received in January, amounting to €33,000, with the balance of €22,000 received in February. Regarding February's sales of €60,500, 60 per cent will be received in February amounting to €36,300 with the balance of €24,200 received in March. Regarding March's sales of €68,063, 60 per cent will be received in March amounting to €40,838 with the balance amounting to €27,225 received in April. Thus at the end of March, debtors will be shown in the balance sheet as €27,225.

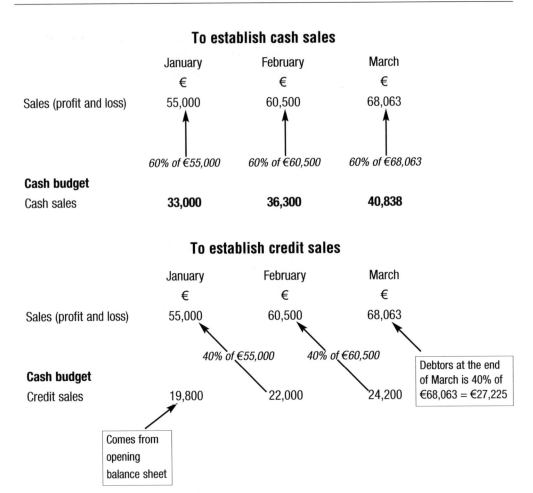

It is important to note that the debtors figure in the balance sheet at 31 December of €19,800 represents monies that it is assumed will be received in January and hence it is recorded in the cash budget for that month.

Note 7: Expenditure (purchases)

We have calculated the purchases figures in the profit and loss account, but for the cash budget we need to know when they are paid. We are told in point (4) of the example that suppliers of materials offer one month's credit for purchases. In other words January's purchases are paid in February (€17,080) and February's purchases are paid in March (€20,570). March's purchases are paid in April. Thus at the end of March, trade creditors will amount to March's purchases of €23,196. In the opening balance sheet at 31 December, under current liabilities, creditors amount to €14,700. These represent December's purchases which will be paid in January.

Note 8: Expenditure (rent)

We are told in point (6) that the annual charge for rent is €36,000, which is paid in two equal instalments on 1 January and 1 July. Hence €18,000 will come out of the bank account in January. It is important to note that at the end of March we will have prepaid three month's rent as we have paid rent up until the end of June. Thus at the end of March there is three month's rent prepaid and this should appear in the balance sheet as a prepayment under current assets amounting to €9,000.

Note 9: Expenditure (labour)

Labour is paid as incurred by the end of each month (point (5) in the example) hence the figure for labour costs in the profit and loss account is the same as in the cash budget.

Note 10: Expenditure (overheads)

We are told in point (7) that overheads are paid as incurred, hence there is no timing difference between overheads being charged and paid. However overheads do include depreciation which is a non-cash transaction and does not affect the cash budget. Thus we need to take depreciation of €2,500 per month out of overheads and charge the balance to the cash budget.

Note 11: Expenditure (taxation)

In point (7) we are told that the accruals figure in the opening balance sheet at 31 December represents arrears of taxation which will be paid in February. This €20,000 is treated as an outflow / expenditure in the cash budget in February. It is important to note that this taxation figure does not appear in the profit and loss account for January, February or March as it represents tax unpaid from previous years and has already been charged in the profit and loss account in previous years.

Note 12: Expenditure (loan repayment and loan interest)

In point (8) we are told that there will be a repayment of the existing loan of €5,000 in March. This is a cash outflow to be recorded in the cash budget in March. It does not appear in the profit and loss account as it is a transaction of a capital nature. The loan interest is paid as charged in the month and thus is treated as an outflow in the cash budget.

Note 13: Opening and closing balance

The opening balance of €5,600 is the money in the bank account at 31 December (see opening balance sheet). As January's expenditure exceeded income by €3,688, the cash balance at the end of January amounts to €1,912. As expenditure exceeds income in February by €5,176, the business' bank balance goes into the red. Management should ensure the company has a bank overdraft facility. In March, income exceeds expenditure by €10,202 and the business bank account balance goes back into the black.

The balance sheet

Note 14: Fixed assets
There were no increases to fixed assets during the three month period, hence the fixed assets cost figure stays the same at €120,000. Three month's depreciation of €2,500 per month is deducted to get the net book value of fixed assets which amounts to €112,500.

Note 15: Current assets
❑ **Stock:** This is the closing stock figure at the end of March. (See note 3)
❑ **Debtors:** This figure represents 40 per cent of March's sales. Payment will be received in April, but at the end of March it is owed to the business. (See note 6)
❑ **Prepayments:** This represents three months rent prepaid. By the end of March the business had already paid rent up until the end of June and thus is prepaid by three months. (See note 8)
❑ **Bank:** This is the closing balance in the cash budget at the end of March.

Note 16: Current liabilities
These are trade creditors representing monies owed for purchases. It represents March's purchases unpaid at the end of March. (See note 7)

Note 17: Long-term liabilities
This is the loan which has fallen to €20,000 due to a repayment of €5,000 at the end of March. (See note 12)

Note 18: Share capital and reserves
There were no new issues of share capital thus it remains unchanged. Reserves represent the amount of profit retained in the business (not given out as dividend). Up to 31 December, reserves amounted to €25,900 (see opening balance sheet). Add to that the projected profits from the profit and loss account of €28,873 and reserves stand at €54,773 on 31 March.

Projected Financial Statements and Decision-making

Projected financial statements, once prepared, must be critically examined by management as to their reasonableness and reliability. Management must assess the reasonableness of the assumptions underlying the projections and also whether all relevant items have been accounted for. They must attain a sense of whether the projected targets are overambitious or too easily attainable. The use of techniques such as sensitivity analysis (Chapter 6), and probability analysis (Chapters 5 and 14) can be useful in developing a feel for the reliability of these projections.

Once management are satisfied as to the reasonableness and reliability of the projections, they can then be used to inform management decision-making on the following issues:

1. Is the projected profit satisfactory in relation to the risks involved and the required return on capital? If not, what can be done to improve this?
2. Are sales and individual expense items at a satisfactory level?
3. How adequate are the projected cash flows of the business and can they be improved?
4. Should management consider additional financing?
5. What type of financing is required, long, medium or short-term financing?
6. What type of financial instruments are appropriate, debt or equity?
7. Will there be surplus funds and, if so, what plans do the company have as regards investing these funds?
8. Is the business overly financed through debt?
9. How liquid is the business?
10. Is the financial position at the end of the period acceptable?

Alternative Approaches to Budget Preparation

There are a number of different approaches or techniques used to formulate and prepare budgets. These are considered under the following headings:

❑ Incremental budgeting.
❑ Zero-based budgeting.
❑ Activity based budgeting.
❑ Rolling budgets.

Incremental budgeting

> **'Method of budgeting based on the previous budget or on actual results,
> adjusting for known changes and inflation'**
> Incremental budgeting as defined by CIMA Official Terminology

This is where the current budget and actual figures act as the starting point or base for the new budget. The base is adjusted for forecast changes to, for example, the product mix, sales volume, sales price, expenses and capital expenditure that are expected to occur over the next budget period. It is called incremental budgeting as the approach does not focus on the base, but focuses on the increment (the changes from the base). An example would include increasing last year's operating expenses by the rate of inflation to calculate the new budgeted figure. The major disadvantage of this is that the major part of the expense (the base) does not change and in fact is overlooked and not questioned under this approach. For example the base figure may be distorted due to extraordinary events in the previous period which are not expected to reoccur. Thus if this is not taken into account, the budget could be misleading.

Zero-based budgeting

> *'Method of budgeting that requires all costs to be specifically justified by the benefits expected'*
> Zero-based budgeting as defined by CIMA Official Terminology

This approach requires that every year, all costs and capital expenditure are questioned and require justification and prioritising before any decision is taken regarding the allocation of resources. Thus a zero base is adopted which effectively means that both the base and the increment are questioned. In fact the whole activity that leads to the item of expenditure is questioned and requires justification. Zero-based budgeting changes the approach of traditional or incremental budgeting from focusing on changes in expense items from year to year, to an approach that looks at each department budget as if it were undertaking its activities or programmes for the first time. It requires a detailed justification and cost-benefit approach to each expense item in the department budget. It forces managers to prioritise activities and related expenses based on a value for money concept. In effect, it overcomes the limitations of incremental budgeting.

Advantages
❑ It fosters a questioning attitude to all revenues and costs in preparing operating budgets.
❑ It focuses attention on the value for money concept.
❑ It can help identify inefficient work processes and operations.
❑ It helps minimise waste.
❑ It should result in more efficient allocation of resources.

Disadvantages
❑ It is a costly and time consuming approach.
❑ It may require management to develop and learn new skills.

Many companies today do not apply a full-scale zero-based approach to their budgeting process but only apply it to selected revenue and expense items or departments within an organisation. These expense items would often include advertising, research and the costs associated with developing new products and product lines.

Activity based budgeting

'Method of budgeting based on an activity framework and utilising cost driver data in the budget setting and variance feedback processes'
Activity based budgeting as defined by CIMA Official Terminology

Activity based budgeting (ABB) involves the build up of budgeted costs using an activity approach. All the activities that are undertaken in the organisation, function or department are defined, and costs attributed to that activity are established. Resources are allocated according to activity levels. ABB can be used in all types of organisations. For example, ABB in the front office of a hotel would involve ascertaining such activities as answering customer queries, processing a reservation, preparing a quotation and updating customer accounts. The costs of each activity would then be established and resources would be allocated based on the planned level of activity.

ABB is an extension of the zero-based budgeting approach and goes into far greater detail in identifying value and non-value activities. It can be more effective than zero-based and incremental budgeting because:

❑ It avoids slack that is often included in the incremental approach.
❑ ABB focuses attention on each activity, highlighting those that do not add value.

Rolling budgets

'Budget continuously updated by adding a further accounting period (month or quarter) when the earliest accounting period has expired'
Rolling budgets as defined by CIMA Official Terminology

A rolling budget is a twelve month budget which is prepared several times each year (say once each quarter). The purpose of a rolling budget is to give management the chance to revise its plans, but more importantly, to make more accurate forecasts and plans for the next few months. When rolling budgets are used, the extra administration costs and effort of producing several budgets instead of just one, should be balanced with more accurate forecasting and planning.

Advantages

❑ Budgets are reassessed regularly and thus should be more realistic and accurate.
❑ Because rolling budgets are revised regularly, uncertainty is reduced.
❑ Planning and control is based on a recent updated plan.
❑ The budget is continuous and will always extend a number of months ahead.

Disadvantages

❑ Rolling budgets are time consuming and expensive as a number of budgets must be produced during the year.

❑ The volume of work required with each reassessment of the budget can be off-putting for managers.

Budget approaches in practice

In research conducted by Smullen and O'Donoghue (2005) into the use and influence of certain financial based decision-making models in the Irish hospitality industry, it was found that 12 per cent of hotels surveyed used the zero-based approach to forecasting whereas 23 per cent used the incremental approach. However 65 per cent of hotels used a balance of zero-based and incremental for different forecast variables. The research was conducted in early 2005 and was based on hotels with a 3-star standard or higher and with 30 or more bedrooms.

Research by Luby (2006) found the following uptake on the budgeting approaches in the retail sector:

Incremental budgets	55%
Flexible budgets	36%
Rolling budgets	27%
Activity based budgets	27%
Zero-based budgets	0%

Summary

The preparation of projected financial statements is based on the same principles as the preparation of historic financial statements. The only difference is that projected data is employed in their preparation rather than actual data. Projected statements are only useful if the projections made are reliable. Hence the starting point in any evaluation of projected financial statements is to examine the underlying assumptions on which the data is prepared.

The main information points covered in this chapter are as follows:

❑ The master budget contains three summary budgeted statements that are the end result of any budgetary planning process.

- The profit and loss account, made up of a number of budgets such as sales, cost of sales, payroll, operating expenses budget, and fixed expenses budget. Collectively, these are known as the operating budgets.
- The balance sheet, made up of the capital expenditure budget, stock, debtors and creditors budgets.
- The cash budget, which is primarily concerned with the timings of future cash flows and is based on data from the operating and capital budgets.

❏ The master budget brings together all the financial projections from the various operating and capital budgets within an organisation for the period. It embraces the impact of both operating decisions (running the business) and investment or financing decisions that the business has planned for the next time period (usually twelve months). It sets out the organisation's targets for the coming period in a quantifiable and easily understood format, helping to provide direction and ensuring goal congruence.

❏ Three essential elements are required before one can begin to prepare projected financial statements. These are:
- Forecast of sales.
- Forecast of costs.
- Forecast of the required investment in net assets to achieve these sales.

❏ Forecasting involves an awareness of the economic environment and government policy. These influence the following items:
- Taxation and rate of corporation tax.
- Interest rates for borrowings with variable interest rates.
- The rate of inflation.
- The policies and commitments of the business.

❏ There are a number of different approaches or techniques used to formulate and prepare budgets. These are considered under the following headings:
- Incremental budgeting.
- Zero-based budgeting.
- Activity based budgeting.
- Rolling budgets.

❏ After projected financial statements have been prepared, they must be critically examined by management as to their reasonableness and reliability. Management must assess the reasonableness of the assumptions underlying the projections and also assess whether or not all relevant items have been accounted for. They must attain a sense of whether the projected targets are overambitious or too easily attainable.

Review Questions

Question 9.1

a) Distinguish between operating and capital budgets.
b) What are the main advantages of preparing monthly cash budgets?
c) Outline the main objectives of budgetary planning.

Question 9.2

a) Outline the main factors that influence sales.
b) Why is the sales forecast of critical importance to the preparation of projected financial statements?
c) Outline the main ways in which a business can forecast its operating costs.

Question 9.3

Briefly outline the following approaches to budget preparation:
a) Incremental budgeting.
b) Zero-based budgeting.
c) Activity based budgeting.
d) Rolling budgets.

Question 9.4

Maura Young is considering leaving the health and fitness centre where she is employed as a yoga instructor and starting a new venture. Maura plans on providing yoga instruction for clients in their own homes, commencing in January. Maura will charge a fee of €450 for a course of eight weekly sessions. The fee includes a DVD and a book. Half the fee will be payable upfront, the remainder will be due at the beginning of the following month. The following details have been estimated:

1. Cash of €20,000 and some equipment worth €500 will be invested in the business by Maura before January. The equipment will be depreciated at a rate of 10 per cent per annum, straight-line.

2. A second hand jeep will be purchased at the commencement of business for €13,000 and will be paid for in cash. This will be depreciated at a rate of 25 per cent per annum, straight-line.

3. Maura will take on 30 clients in January and work with them for January and February. As a promotion, the first 10 clients to sign up will receive a 10 per cent discount. In March, 40 new clients will be taken on and trained in the period from March to the end of April.

4. The DVDs cost €15 each and the books €12 each. Maura will buy the amount required at the beginning of January and March and has negotiated one month's credit.

5. Office services will be provided by a local agency. Initial set-up costs will amount to €500 in the first month and €200 thereafter. Office services must be paid in the month the service is provided.

6. Insurance of €750 per quarter will be payable in advance.

7. General overheads of €100 per month will be payable as incurred.

8. Maura will receive wages of €2,500 per month.

Required
a) Prepare a cash budget outlining the first four months of trading.
b) Prepare a profit and loss account for the first four months ending 30 April.
c) Prepare a balance sheet as at 30 April.

Question 9.5

Collins Solutions, a small business wholesaling stationery items, is just reaching the end of its first year in operation. Data is currently being gathered in preparation for budgets for the first quarter of the next financial year. The financial year-end is 31 December. The following information is available:

Balance Sheet as at 31 December

Fixed Assets	Cost	Accumulated depreciation	N.B.V.
Equipment	€250,000	€25,000	€225,000
Furniture & fittings	€165,000	€16,500	€148,500
	€415,000	€41,500	€373,500
Current Assets			
Stock	€ 30,000		
Debtors	€180,000		
Bank	€ 10,000	€220,000	
Current liabilities			
Creditors		(€130,000)	€90,000
			€463,500
Financed by:			
Capital			€463,500
			€463,500

Projections for first quarter are detailed below:

	January	February	March	Total Quarter
Sales	€240,000	€256,000	€252,000	€748,000
Purchases	€140,000	€150,000	€148,000	€438,000

Other information available:

1. 20 per cent of sales are for immediate payment, the balance is received one month following the sale.
2. All purchases benefit from 30 days credit.
3. Wages have been estimated at €60,000 for January with a 5 per cent increase planned from the 1 February. Wages are paid in the month due.
4. Expenses of €25,000, payable in the month incurred, have been estimated for each of the first three months.
5. Purchases have been planned to facilitate an increase in stock levels of 25 per cent by the end of the first quarter.
6. All depreciation is at a rate of 10 per cent per annum straight-line, calculated on the basis of one month's ownership equals one month's depreciation. Depreciation is included in the expenses above.
7. A new piece of equipment will be purchased on 1 January for €35,000.

Required

a) Prepare a profit and loss account for the quarter ending 31 March.
b) Prepare a cash budget for January, February and March.
c) Prepare a balance sheet as at 31 March.

Question 9.6

The Ballyyahoo Tourism Co-operative, as part of its overall strategy to attract more tourists to the locality, has finalised plans to open a restaurant on its riverbank in part of an old renovated warehouse leased to the co-operative and which will eventually consist of a heritage centre with restaurant and bar. The opening date of the restaurant is 1 July with pre-opening expenditure estimated as follows:

Furniture and equipment	€38,000
Stock of food and beverages	€2,000
	€40,000

The initial requirements will be financed through the issue of 40,000 €1 shares in the co-operative. Any additional needs will be financed with the aid of a bank overdraft. The shares will be issued and paid for by early June with the equipment and stock purchased and ready by 1 July.

Meals are expected to be sold at 150 per cent above food cost and it is estimated that 10 per cent of sales will be paid for in the month after sale. Expected sales revenue is €5,000 for the first three months and €6,000 thereafter.

One month's credit is expected from the suppliers of food, with the initial stock, along with the furniture and equipment, being paid for in June. Monthly overheads are expected to amount to €1,200 per month (including depreciation of €200 per month). This does not include leasing and insurance of €5,000 for the first year which will be paid quarterly in advance from 1 July. Advertising for the first six months costing €1,600 will be paid in July.

The restaurant expects to receive a refund of VAT of €3,210 in September and a VAT payment of €1,210 will be paid in November. Wages and salaries are estimated at €1,500 per month, paid in the month charged. However, €300 of the €1,500 relates to PAYE and PRSI which is paid in the following month. It is agreed that there should be sufficient stock in hand at the end of each month to meet 50 per cent of the following month's demand.

Required

a) Prepare a projected profit and loss account for the 5 month period ending 30 November.
b) Prepare a monthly projected cash budget for the 5 month period ending 30 November.

Question 9.7

The following is the balance sheet for McQuaid Leisure Suppliers Ltd at the beginning of the year. The company is involved in supplying the leisure industry with leisure and fitness systems.

Opening Balance Sheet

		€
Fixed assets (net book value)		100,000
Current assets		
Stock	9,000	
Debtors	24,000	
Cash	2,500	35,500
Current liabilities		
Creditors	15,000	
Accruals	25,000	(40,000)
Long-term liabilities		
10% fixed interest loan		(19,500)
		76,000
Financed by		
Share capital		57,000
Profit and loss account		19,000
		76,000

The following data has been agreed by the budget committee for the next six months. The committee believe the company will experience increased demand for its products during this period and are keen to plan for this expansion.

1. Sales, labour and overheads have been forecast as:

Month	Budgeted sales	Labour costs	Overheads
	€	€	€
January	60,000	15,000	12,000
February	66,000	16,500	13,200
March	72,600	18,150	14,520
April	79,860	19,965	15,972

2. The company's stock is sold at a 65 per cent gross profit margin and management's policy is to have sufficient stock in hand to meet sales demand for the next month.

3. On average, 50 per cent of the company's sales are cash sales with debtors, on average, paying the following month.

4. Suppliers of stock offer one month's credit for purchases.

5. Labour costs are paid in full by the end of each month.

6. Overheads include depreciation of €2,000 per month but exclude the rental charge for the company's premises. This is an annual charge of €24,000 paid in advance in two equal instalments, on 1 January and 1 July.

7. The accruals figure in the opening balance sheet represents arrears of VAT and corporation tax. The company have come to an agreement with the Revenue Commissioners that the amount will be paid by 28 February. This figure is inclusive of penalties and interest.

8. The company expects to invest in new plant and equipment in March. The investment will amount to €30,000 and will be paid in March.

9. The fixed interest loan is repaid on a quarterly basis with equal instalments of capital plus interest outstanding at the end of the three month period. The capital repayment, excluding interest, amounts to €300 per month. The next payment date is 28 March.

Required

a) Prepare a budgeted trading, profit and loss account for the three months ended 31 March.

b) Prepare a monthly cash budget for January, February and March.

c) Prepare a balance sheet as at 31 March.

Question 9.8

The following is the balance sheet for Leisure Hire Ltd at the end of August. The company is involved in hiring out all leisure, catering and party equipment for all social occasions.

Opening Balance Sheet

	€	€
Fixed assets (net book value)		268,000
Current assets		
Debtors	22,000	
Cash	3,560	
Rent prepaid	2,000	27,560
Current liabilities		
Creditors	15,000	
Accruals	15,000	(30,000)
Long-term liabilities		
10% fixed interest loan		(33,000)
		232,560
Financed by		
Share capital		205,000
Profit and loss account		27,560
		232,560

The following data has been agreed by the budgeting committee for the next six months. The committee believe the company will experience increased demand for its products during this period.

1. Sales, labour and overheads have been forecast as:

Month	Budgeted sales	Labour costs	Overheads
	€	€	€
September	66,000	16,500	13,000
October	72,600	18,150	14,300
November	79,860	19,965	15,730
December	87,846	21,961	17,303

2. The direct cost of equipment hire and set-up generally, amounts to 10 per cent of the contract price (sales). These direct costs are paid as incurred.
3. On average, 50 per cent of the company's sales are cash sales, with debtors on average paying the following month.
4. Labour costs are paid in full by the end of each month.
5. Overheads include depreciation of €2,000 per month, but exclude the rental charge for the company's premises, which is an annual charge of €24,000, paid in two equal instalments in advance on 1 April and 1 October.

6. The accruals figure in the opening balance sheet represents monies owed for accounting services which will be paid by 28 October.
7. The creditors figure in the opening balance sheet represents the amount due for equipment purchases made in August. These will be paid in September.
8. The company expects to invest in new plant and equipment in November. The investment will amount to €30,000. This will not be paid until December.
9. Interest will accrue on the loan as usual, based on the amount outstanding at the beginning of September. A capital repayment of €3,000 plus the interest accrued for the three months will be paid on 30 November.

Required
a) Prepare a budgeted trading, profit and loss account for the three months ended 30 November.
b) Prepare a budgeted monthly cash budget for September, October and November.
c) Prepare a forecast balance sheet as at 30 November.

Question 9.9

The following is the summarised balance sheet of the 'Hendy' Sports Bar and Restaurant at their financial year-end 31 May.

Balance sheet as at 31 May

		€
Fixed assets		
Leasehold property		200,000
Furniture and equipment		50,000
		250,000
Current assets		
Stock Beverage	800	
Food	500	
Trade debtors	1,000	
Bank	2,360	4,660
Current liabilities		
Trade creditors	2,230	
Rent received in advance	1,000	
Preliminary tax due	10,000	(13,230)
Long-term liabilities		
Loan capital		(43,430)
		198,000
Financed by		
Share capital		150,000
Reserves		48,000
		198,000

The following are forecast figures and information relating to the next three months to 31 August.

Month	Food Sales	Beverage Sales	Food Purchases	Beverage Purchases	Wages	Expenses	Depreciation
	€	€	€	€	€	€	€
June	24,000	8,800	13,000	4,000	10,000	6,000	850
July	30,000	10,000	14,000	4,400	12,000	7,000	850
August	36,000	11,200	17,000	5,000	12,500	7,500	850

The following additional information is also available:

1. 90 per cent of sales of both food and beverages are for cash, with the balance settled in the month following the transaction.
2. All stock purchases are on credit with payment made in the month following the date of transaction.

3. The bar works on a gross margin of 55 per cent and the restaurant on a gross margin of 60 per cent.
4. 70 per cent of wages are paid in the month worked, with 30 per cent representing PAYE and PRSI paid the following month.
5. Expenses are paid as incurred, except insurance premiums (included in expenses) of €3,000 per annum which are paid in advance on 1 of June each year.
6. The business sublets part of its premises and receives rent at quarterly intervals in advance on 1 August, 1 November, 1 February and 1 May each year.
7. Capital repayments on the loan amount to €1,200 per month with interest charges amounting to €450 per month. Both these items of expenditure are paid for as incurred.
8. Preliminary corporation tax due for last year's profits of €10,000 will be paid in August.
9. The depreciation charge of €850 per month can be broken down into depreciation of leasehold €600 and furniture and equipment of €250.

Required
a) Prepare a budgeted departmental trading, profit and loss account for the three months ended 31 August.
b) Prepare a monthly forecast cash budget for June, July and August.
c) Prepare a budgeted balance sheet as at 31 August.

Question 9.10

The following information is available regarding 'Play World', a family run children's play centre with coffee shop and fast food outlet.
1. The bank balance on 1 June is €10,000.
2. Sales are expected to be €10,000 per month for the quarter ended 31 August and €9,000 per month for the following quarter. 10 per cent of sales are estimated to be on credit, with the monies received in the month following the sale.
3. The gross profit margin for the business is expected to be 30 per cent for the budget period.
4. Insurances are €1,900 per annum, payable annually in advance on 1 June.
5. Rates are €450 per annum, payable half yearly in advance on 1 August and 1 February.
6. Stock costing €500 is on hand at 1 June and will be maintained at this level throughout the period.
7. A 12 per cent mortgage of €100,000 exists at 1 June, with nine years to run from that date. It is being repaid on a quarterly basis by equal instalments of capital plus

interest outstanding at the end of each quarter. The next repayment is due on 1 August.

8. Part of the premises is sublet on a five year lease at €250 per month payable quarterly in advance from 1 May.

9. Trade creditors will allow accounts to be settled in the month following that in which goods are supplied.

10. Other business expenses are expected to be €950 per month, to be paid at the end of the month following that in which they are incurred.

11. Private drawings are estimated to be €800 in total per month.

Required

a) A forecast trading, profit and loss account for the period 1 June to 30 September inclusive.

b) A forecast monthly cash budget for the above period.

c) Relevant extracts from the balance sheet as at 30 September.

Question 9.11

A new hotel company, Shamrock Ltd, has been formed and will commence business on 1 January. The following forecast data for the first three months has been prepared:

1. Share capital to be issued   €250,000
2. Bank loan to be raised, at an annual interest rate of 6%   €180,000
3. Equipment and furniture to be purchased   €384,000
    The amount is payable 50% in January and 50% in March.
    The annual depreciation charge is on a straight-line basis at 12.5%.
4. Budgeted Monthly Data:

Month	Sales	Closing stock	Wages and salaries	General expenses
	€	€	€	€
January	50,000	70,000	12,000	6,000
February	60,000	80,000	13,500	6,500
March	80,000	96,000	15,500	7,500

5. Cash sales as a percent of total sales will be 30 per cent.
6. The period of credit allowed to debtors will be two months.
7. The gross profit margin is expected to be 70 per cent.

8. Monthly purchases will depend on the level of sales and stocks. The period of credit received from suppliers will be one month.
9. Wages and salaries will be paid in the month incurred.
10. Annual rent of premises, payable six months in advance, amounts to €150,000.
11. General expenses, which exclude rent and depreciation, are payable one month in arrears.
12. The bank loan of €180,000 will be repaid over 10 years in equal monthly instalments.

    Loan interest will be paid each month, based on the balance at the start of the year.

Required

a) A forecast profit and loss account for the three months ending 31 March.
b) A monthly cash budget for the three months from January to March.
c) A forecast balance sheet at 31 March.

Budgetary Control

'Knowledge is control'

Introduction

The two previous chapters focused on budgetary planning and the preparation of the master budget for the forecast accounting period. The master budget sets out the plans for the business for the next accounting period based on various assumptions of sales and sales growth, inflation (in particular labour inflation), interest rates, taxation and capital expenditure. This master budget is known as the fixed budget as it is based on these fixed assumptions of trading performance and financial outlook. However budgetary planning is only one part in the overall budgetary process. Actual performance needs to be monitored and compared to the budgeted targets set to evaluate the performance of the business. Actual performance will always differ from the fixed budget as the business environment is quite dynamic and thus events and conditions may not turn out as anticipated in the budget. It is important that actual events in a budget period are monitored against the budget plan so that timely action can be taken to remedy or improve the situation. Thus in budgetary control we are concerned with the manner in which budgets are used as a tool of management. This chapter focuses on the budgetary control process which involves the preparation of flexible budgets and the calculation of variances. These provide management with information to monitor performance. The need to investigate variances (difference between actual and budgeted performance) and take corrective action is also explained.

The Budgetary Control Process

Returning to the budget framework presented in earlier chapters, the focus has moved to the control process which deals with stages four and in particular stages five and six. Stage four deals with implementing the decisions made and hence preparing an annual budget based on the course of action selected. This was covered in detail in Chapter 9. This stage is also part of the control process as budget targets can be adjusted or influenced by actual performance feedback. However the main focus in budgetary control is on stages five and six. These stages provide the feedback to influence the budget setting process.

Diagram 10.1: *Budgeting within a planning, decision-making and control framework*

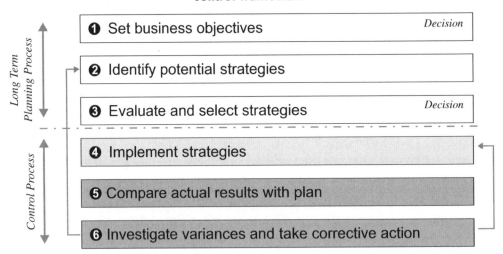

In stage five, the process by which actual results are compared with budgeted can be divided into two distinct activities namely;

❑ Measure actual performance. Actual performance needs to be measured frequently to ensure any differences with budget are identified. This can ensure early detection of problems and hence ensure timely corrective action is taken. Actual performance can be measured on a daily, weekly, monthly or quarterly basis depending on the size of the business and its control system.

❑ Compare actual results with budgeted. As actual performance is measured, it must be compared to budgeted targets with variances (differences) identified and categorised as favourable or adverse. Management must consider which variances are significant and thus require further investigation and action.

The final stage (stage 6) involves the investigation of significant variances and initiating corrective action which again can be divided into two distinct activities namely:

❑ Investigate differences (variances). Management must understand and be able to explain the causes of significant variances and decide whether or not they are within their control. For example variances may be due to:
  – Unreasonable targets set in the budget.
  – Once-off or random events that distort actual performance.
  – Inefficiencies within the organisation.
  Many variances will be insignificant and thus will only require monitoring, however management must be clear on what is a significant variance. For example, a labour cost variance of €1,000 may be immaterial when budgeted labour costs are €250,000. However if budgeted labour costs are €30,000, this could constitute a significant variance and hence require investigation and corrective action. Management must decide on the correct type of action to remedy the situation. This leads to the fourth activity, the control action.

❑ Take corrective action. In investigating variances and taking corrective action, it is most important that a business is organised into various decision centres where costs and revenues can be traced to individual managers who are primarily responsible for making the decisions and controlling the costs and revenues of these departments or cost centres. This ensures that managers, who know the particular costs and revenues they are responsible for, can take appropriate corrective action. It must be kept in mind that if any variance is due to an unreasonable target or standard, then management should review and set a more appropriate target level. If however the variances are caused by inefficiencies within the organisation, corrective action should be taken to limit these inefficiencies.

This process of monitoring performance, comparing actual results with budget, identifying and investigating variances and taking corrective action is at the core of the control activities of any organisation. It is very unlikely that actual performance will be the same as budgeted, thus the comparison of actual performance to budget will result in differences, commonly known as variances. These variances can be further analysed and broken down into their component parts. For example, a sales variance of €10,000 negative (actual sales were €10,000 less than budgeted sales) should be analysed into its component parts namely, sales volume, sales price and sales mix. Was the variance due to the business selling less or due to the company not achieving its budgeted selling prices, or due to the company selling less of its more profitable items (sales mix)? The use of flexible budgeting can help in analysing and investigating differences between budgeted and actual performance.

Flexible Budgets and Budgetary Control

'Flexing variable costs from original budgeted levels to the allowances permitted for actual volume achieved while maintaining fixed costs at original level'
Flexible budgets as defined by CIMA Official Terminology

As mentioned earlier, the master budget is a fixed budget as it is based on fixed assumptions regarding economic conditions, forecast sales and sales growth. However it is seldom that forecasters get these predictions right as the business environment is quite a dynamic one. It can be meaningless to compare a budget based on certain economic conditions to actual performance based on completely different economic conditions. It is far more informative for the business to compare performance under similar conditions. Thus the use of flexible budgets allows the fixed budget to be adjusted (flex the fixed budget) to allow for actual activity in making the comparison between actual and budgeted performance. For example, there is little value in comparing a hotel's performance based on forecast sales of 80,000 bed-nights compared to actual sales of 120,000 bed-nights. We are not comparing like with like. Not alone will sales be different, but also variable costs will differ as they will vary with sales. Fixed costs may be greater than budgeted due to the fact that the hotel's sales performance has exceeded the relevant range. Part of the process of comparing budgeted performance with actual involves flexing the fixed budget to the same activity level as actual, and then comparing actual sales and costs with the flexible budget. It is important to remember that there is still a positive volume variance of 40,000 bed-nights, but once this is identified, it is important to go on and compare costs and revenues under similar conditions. It is also important to remember that the fixed budget still remains as the target for the year. The flexible budget is only used as a tool to improve management control information.

Three points must be made regarding the whole budgetary control process.

❑ The control process must take place at frequent intervals. With the advent of computers and sophisticated management information systems, many large firms compare actual results to budgeted on a daily, weekly or monthly basis.
❑ The business should be organised into various decision centres where costs and revenues can be traced to individual managers with responsibility for making the decisions and controlling the costs and revenues of these departments or cost centres.

❑   Any investigation of variances should also be directed at the planning process and the realism of the budget target. If the budgetary planning process is predominantly a downward communication of targets by senior management without involving the whole management team, then the risk of unrealistic targets being set increases. Also, junior and middle management will be demotivated due to their diminished role in the target setting process. This can influence performance and result in unachieved targets and negative variances.

It is important to understand the process of flexing a budget and establishing the variances for each item in the budget. The steps involved in this process are:

Flexible budgeting steps

Step 1 – Measure actual performance.
Step 2 – Compare actual results with budgeted.
Step 3 – Calculate and investigate differences (variances).
Step 4 – Take corrective action.

Example 10.1 illustrates each step of the budgetary control process.

Example 10.1: *The budgetary control process*

The following information relates to the restaurant and café bar of the exclusive Country Leisure Club for the first quarter of its financial year:

Budget

Number of covers	50,000
Average spend	€10
Materials (food & beverages) as a percentage of sales	40%
Direct labour costs as a percentage of sales	10%
Fixed labour costs	€98,000
Fixed overhead costs	€62,000

Actual results

Number of covers	60,000
Sales	€540,00
Materials	€243,000
Direct labour costs	€57,000
Fixed labour costs	€105,000
Fixed overhead costs	€58,000

a)   *Prepare a statement showing the fixed budget, flexible budgets, actual results and variances for the quarter.*

b)   *Prepare a statement reconciling actual net profit to budgeted net profit.*

Approach

Step 1: Measure actual performance

The information in the example focuses on budget targets set as well as the actual performance for the first quarter of the Country Leisure Club's financial year. Thus actual sales and costs have been measured for the period and a comparison can be made between budgeted and actual performance.

Step 2: Compare actual results with budgeted

The comparison of actual results with budgeted involves the following steps:

a)   Prepare the fixed budget based on the data given. It is best to use the marginal costing profit statement format, classifying costs into fixed and variable categories, calculating contribution and net profit. Generally, most companies will give very detailed breakdowns of the various categories of expenses. However this example is kept simple to enhance understanding.

b)   Prepare the flexible budget. As budgeted and actual performance figures are based on two different sales activity levels, the fixed budget is flexed to the actual level of activity achieved. In this example the actual level of activity of 60,000 covers is used to prepare the flexible budget. Thus sales and variable costs will reflect the new sales activity level, with fixed costs remaining as per the fixed budget. In preparing the flexible budget figures for sales and variable costs, the formula to use is budgeted price multiplied by actual volume. The difference in sales, expenses and ultimately profit between the fixed budget and the flexible budget, is due to volume sales differences. It is important to remember that the flexible budget is still a budget and hence fixed costs will remain the same, even though volume is different. Exhibit 10.1 illustrates this step.

Exhibit 10.1: *Fixed and flexible budgets*

		Fixed budget	**Flexible budget**	
Sales (units)	1 unit	50,000	60,000	
		€	€	
Sales	10.00	500,000	600,000	=60,000 covers x €10
Less Variable costs				
Materials 40%	4.00	200,000	240,000	= 60,000 x €4.00
Direct labour 10%	1.00	50,000	60,000	= 60,000 x €1.00
	5.00	250,000	300,000	The total of above
Contribution		250,000	300,000	= €600,000 – €300,000
Less Fixed costs				
Labour		98,000	98,000	All fixed costs remain
Overheads		62,000	62,000	unchanged
		160,000	160,000	
Net Profit		90,000	140,000	

c) Enter the actual results in the same marginal costing format as the fixed and flexible budgets. Exhibit 10.2 illustrates this step.

Exhibit 10.2: *Fixed and flexible budgets and actual performance*

		Fixed budget	**Flexible budget**	**Actual results**
Sales (units)	1 unit	50,000	60,000	60,000
		€	€	€
Sales	10.00	500,000	600,000	540,000
Less Variable costs				
Materials 40%	4.00	200,000	240,000	243,000
Direct labour 10%	1.00	50,000	60,000	57,000
	5.00	250,000	300,000	300,000
Contribution	5.00	250,000	300,000	240,000
Less Fixed costs				
Labour		98,000	98,000	105,000
Overheads		62,000	62,000	58,000
		160,000	160,000	163,000
Net Profit		90,000	140,000	77,000

Step 3: Calculation of variances

Variances occur when actual costs and revenues differ from budget. Variance analysis is the processes of breaking down variances to find the true cause for the deviation with a view to improving efficiencies within the business. Sales and costs figures will be influenced by three elements, and hence variances are caused by fluctuations in these elements. They are:

1. Volume of activity.
2. The cost of the various expense items as well as the prices of goods and services sold.
3. The sales mix of the business.

Sales mix is the term used to describe the mix of products/services that a business sells. Many of these different products have different prices and profit margins. For example in a hotel, accommodation would average a gross margin of 90 per cent with food closer to 64 per cent and beverages around 60 per cent. Thus if sales volume increases, but actual accommodation sales have fallen, then overall profit could fall. Hence differences between budgeted and actual sales mix will cause differences between budgeted and actual net profit.

If we make the simplifying assumption that all products, both food and beverages, in the above example are sold at the same profit margin, then we need not concern ourselves for the moment with the sales mix. Thus sales and expenses are made up of two variables, volume and price. For example, total sales will be made up of sales volume multiplied by sales price. The cost of materials (food and beverages) will be made up of volume of materials used multiplied by cost price. Labour costs will be made up of rate multiplied by labour hours worked. Overheads, for example light and heat, will be made up of rate multiplied by usage. By comparing the fixed budget with actual results, we can calculate what are called static or overall variances.

However a deeper analysis through the use of flexible budgets can categorise variances into volume and price/cost variances as illustrated below in diagram 10.2 and exhibit 10.3.

Diagram 10.2: *Levels of variance analysis*

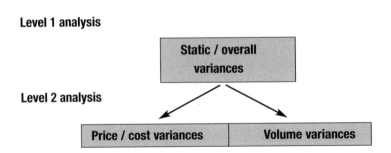

Exhibit 10.3: *Fixed and flexible budgets versus actual performance*

	Fixed budget	Flexible budget	Actual results	Static variance Actual v Fixed	Volume variance Fixed v Flexible	Price/cost variance Actual v Flexed
Sales (units)	50,000	60,000	60,000	10,000	10,000	10,000
	€	€	€	€	€	€
Sales	500,000	600,000	540,000	40,000 F	100,000 F	60,000 A
Less Variable costs						
Materials	200,000	240,000	243,000	43,000 A	40,000 A	3,000 A
Direct labour	50,000	60,000	57,000	7,000 A	10,000 A	3,000 F
	250,000	300,000	300,000	50,000 A	50,000 A	0
Contribution	250,000	300,000	240,000	10,000 A	50,000 F	60,000 A
Less Fixed costs						
Labour	98,000	98,000	105,000	7,000 A	0	7,000 A
Overheads	62,000	62,000	58,000	4,000 F	0	4,000 F
	160,000	160,000	163,000	3,000 A	0	3,000 A
Net profit	90,000	140,000	77,000	13,000 A	50,000 F	63,000 A

F denotes favourable variance
A denotes adverse variance

Volume and price / cost variance for each item equals the static variance

1. Volume variances

The volume variances reflect the difference between budgeted and actual profit caused by the fact that the fixed budget is based on a sales activity level of 50,000 covers, whereas actual sales activity was 60,000 covers. Sales and variable costs differ as a result of these different sales activity levels. Thus volume variances can be isolated by comparing the fixed and flexible budgets, as any differences between these two budgets reflect the different sales activity levels. These volume variances are calculated as follows:

Volume variances

Sales volume variance	(€500,000 – €600,000)	€100,000 F
Materials volume variance	(€200,000 – €240,000)	(€40,000) A
Direct labour volume variance	(€50,000 – €60,000)	(€10,000) A
Sales margin volume variance	(€250,000 – €300,000)	€50,000 F

F denotes favourable variance (sales increased by €100,000)
A denotes adverse variance (food cost increased by €40,000)

The volume variances are all caused by the fact that the fixed budget is based on sales of 50,000 covers, whereas the actual sales activity was 60,000 covers. The sales margin volume variance is the summary variance and it informs management that profit increased by €50,000 compared to budget, due to the fact that actual sales volume was greater than budgeted. The sales margin volume variance can be calculated in two ways:

Sales margin volume variance

> **Sales revenue volume variance – variable cost volume variance**
>
> or
>
> **Fixed budget contribution – flexible budget contribution**

Note: there are no fixed cost variances as fixed costs are not expected to fluctuate with sales volume.

2. Price/cost variances (flexible budget variances)

The price/cost variances are often called the flexible budget variances as they are calculated by comparing actual results to the flexible budget. The flexible budget represents the budget forecast based on the actual level of activity. If the difference between the fixed budget and flexible budget is due to the volume variance, then the differences between the flexible budget and actual budget are due to price or cost variances. These are calculated as follows, starting with the sales revenue figures and working down through the various costs.

Price/cost variances

Sales price variance	(€600,000 – €540,000)	(€60,000) A
Materials cost variance	(€240,000 – €243,000)	(€3,000) A
Direct labour cost variance	(€60,000 – €57,000)	€3,000 F
Fixed labour cost variance	(€98,000 – €105,000)	(€7,000) A
Fixed overhead cost variance	(€62,000 – €58,000)	€4,000 F

❏ **The sales price variance** is the difference in profit caused by fluctuations in the selling price. There are no volume implications as the volume variances have been taken out in the flexing process. In this case the average spend per customer fell to €9 (€540,000 ÷ 60,000), €1 less than budgeted.

❏ **The materials cost variance** is €3,000 adverse. In this business, materials represent the cost of food and beverages. Overall, food and beverage cost was expected to be €240,000 at the actual level of activity. The €3,000 variance represents a 1.25 per cent (3,000 ÷ 240,000) increase on this cost. This variance, if it was significant, could be further investigated and broken down into a usage variance and a price variance. Usage represents the wastage or theft element in production, whereas price variances can tell management if the company is getting price value from its suppliers. This can help indicate whether the company has proper purchase specification procedures in place for insuring competitive pricing from its suppliers. To further analyse the materials cost variance into usage and price, more information based on standard costing procedures would need to be available. This is dealt with in Chapter 11. Overall, the materials cost variance tells us the difference between budgeted and actual profit, caused by either increases in suppliers' prices, inferior food, poor production control or unrealistic budget targets.

❑ **The direct labour cost variance** is €3,000 favourable. It is favourable because the actual spend on direct labour costs was €3,000 less than budgeted, based on the actual level of activity. Direct labour variances are similar to those for materials in that they can be further analysed. For example, is the variance due to a reduction in the rate of payment or an increase in employee efficiency? To further analyse the direct labour cost variance into rate and efficiency, more information based on standard costing procedures would need to be available. This is dealt with again in Chapter 11. One could note that the fixed labour cost variance is an adverse variance of €7,000. Could this be due to the fact that some part-time labour was re-classified as full-time?

❑ **The fixed labour variance** is €7,000 adverse and is the difference between the flexible budget and actual figures. It is adverse because more was spent on labour costs than was anticipated. This variance represents a difference of 7 per cent (7,000 ÷ 98,000) and would be considered significant. This would require further investigation into the reasonableness of the budget figure to ascertain whether unforeseen or random circumstances or inefficiencies caused this variance.

❑ **The fixed overhead variance** is €4,000 favourable and is the difference between the flexible budget (or fixed – as they will be the same) and actual figures. It is favourable because less was spent on overheads than anticipated in the budget. Fixed overheads generally do not react to sales increases in the short-term and thus tend not to fluctuate significantly. If they do, it is generally for reasons outside the control of management. For example, increases in fuel and energy prices, insurance, audit and legal fees all tend to be outside the control of management. A detailed breakdown of each cost within this category will help in the analysis.

A budgetary control statement, as in exhibit 10.4 below, showing the fixed budget, the flexible budget, actual results and variances can now be prepared. The figures in bold show the make-up of each variance.

Exhibit 10.4: *Budgetary control statement*

	Fixed budget	Flexible budget	Actual results	Variances	
Sales (units)	50,000	60,000	60,000		
	€	€	€		
Sales	500,000	**600,000**	**540,000**	(60,000) A	SPV
Less Variable costs					
Materials	200,000	**240,000**	**243,000**	(3,000) A	MCV
Direct labour costs	50,000	**60,000**	**57,000**	3,000 F	DLCV
Contribution	**250,000**	**300,000**	240,000	50,000 F	SMVV
Less Fixed costs					
Labour	98,000	**98,000**	**105,000**	(7,000) A	FLCV
Overheads	62,000	**62,000**	**58,000**	4,000 F	FOCV
Net profit	90,000	140,000	77,000	(13,000) A	

SPV = *sales price variance*

MCV = *material cost variance*

DLCV = *direct labour cost variance*

SMVV = *sales margin volume variance*

FLCV = *fixed labour cost variance*

FOCV = *fixed overhead cost variance*

Note: There is one summary volume variance (the sales margin volume variance) whereas the price or cost variances are categorised into type. This is because of the wide range of possible reasons that cause different price or costs variances. The fluctuations in the sales activity level is the only reason for the volume variance.

A statement reconciling the budgeted net profit with actual net profit can be prepared as follows:

Statement reconciling budgeted net profit to actual net profit

	€	€
Budgeted net profit		90,000
Sales margin volume variance	50,000	
Sales price variance	(60,000)	
Materials cost variance	(3,000)	
Direct labour cost variance	3,000	
Fixed labour cost variance	(7,000)	
Fixed overhead variance	4,000	(13,000)
Actual net profit		77,000

Step 4: Take corrective action

After investigating the main significant variances, the focus is on taking corrective action. This very much depends on the business, the sector, the problems experienced and whether or not it is within the control of management. In general, the causes of variances can be categorised into the following:

1. **Operating variances:** These variances are caused by operating issues within a business and are usually controllable by management. Examples include human resource issues or technical issues regarding plant and equipment.
2. **Planning variances:** These are variances that are caused by targets that are either unrealistic and unachievable, resulting in high adverse variances, or, too easily achieved, resulting in high favourable variances. This again is under the control of management and they must ensure proper target setting procedures are in place. If the budgetary planning process is predominantly a downward communication of targets by senior management without involving the whole management team, then the risk of unrealistic targets being set increases. In investigating any variances, management must always look at the realism of the forecast target.
3. **Random variances:** These variances are caused by chance and management have no means of controlling them. For example, the airline industry will have a fuel requirement which can be affected by adverse or fair weather conditions. Unusual wind patterns on a given route may result in the actual consumption of fuel being very different from that budgeted. Oil price increases affect most businesses and again is outside management control.

From example 10.1 the following points can be made:

❑ The sales variances are the largest and have the most significant impact on profits. Did the business reduce prices to boost sales? If they did why did it not work? Although sales volume increased, it did not increase enough to compensate for the decrease in the average spend. Should the business continue with this policy or should prices be increased slightly as profit can be more sensitive to price changes than to volume changes? This is very much a decision point and requires knowledge of the company's consumer base and existing and potential markets.
❑ The materials variance is not significant and should only be monitored. It is essential in any business to maintain procedures to ensure competitive pricing from its suppliers. Portion control, wastage and risk of theft should be monitored.
❑ The direct labour cost variance is €3,000 favourable representing a 5 per cent (3,000 ÷ 60,000) difference between budgeted and actual. Management must investigate this variance and understand why it occurred.
❑ The fixed labour cost increased by over 7 per cent (7,000 ÷ 98,000). Reasons for this increase should be forthcoming. Was the budgeted figure unrealistic and, if so, why?

❏ The fixed overhead variance is €4,000 favourable, representing a 6.5 per cent (4,000 ÷ 62,000) difference between budgeted overhead figure and actual. What caused this reduction? Is the budgeted figure unrealistic and if so why? A detailed breakdown of what constitutes fixed overhead costs should uncover reasons for this favourable variance. A favourable variance should also initiate questions such as, 'did the company cut back on expense items such as repairs to the property to achieve short-term savings?' This action could result in more costly repairs next year and hence is an example of poor decision-making. It is important to be aware that so called favourable cost variances could lead, in the long-term, to large adverse cost variances.

It is important to analyse variances accurately to establish their true cause and effect on an organisation's overall performance. Corrective action can only come about as a result of exhaustive investigations into significant variances. The identification of the problem and its causes will help decide what corrective action to take.

The Control Process

The control process outlined above is known as *feedback control*. Its main objective is to assess whether a business' performance is in line with budget and to get operations back on track as soon as possible, if it is not. There is an alternative type of control known as *feed-forward control* where, in the planning process, information may come to light regarding what is likely to go wrong in the future and hence steps can be taken now to avoid this scenario. An example of feed-forward control would be where a detailed forecast cash budget shows cash shortages during the forecast period. Management can respond to this warning by arranging suitable finance to eliminate the problem. Essentially feedback control focuses on correcting actual problems, whereas feed-forward control focuses on predicting and eliminating possible future problems. In practice, businesses in the hospitality, tourism and retail sector tend to use both control forms.

The Sales Mix Variance

In example 10.1 it was assumed that the Country Leisure Club sold all its products or services at the same profit margin and hence there were no sales mix implications or variances. However, in reality most businesses sell a number of products or services, all at different profit margins. A business can be in the situation where, although sales increased from a volume perspective, profits fell due to the company selling less of its more profitable items. Thus changes in sales mix will result in differences between budgeted net profit and actual net profit. The fixed budget will assume a certain sales mix. For example, a hotel's budgeted sales mix could be 60 per cent revenue from accommodation, 20 per cent from food and 20 per cent from beverages and banqueting. If this differs from actual performance (as it is almost certain to do), then profit will be affected. From a management information viewpoint, it is important to distinguish the sales mix variance from sales volume and sales price variances. In calculating the sales mix variance, we are asking the question, 'how much did actual profit differ from budget due to differences between budget and actual sales mix?'

In separately calculating the volume, sales mix and price or cost variances, we need to go through the following steps:

Steps in calculating volume, mix and price or cost variances

1. Prepare the fixed budget. All the figures in the fixed budget are based on the original budget assumptions about sales price, sales volume and sales mix.

   budgeted price x budgeted volume x budgeted mix (BP x BV x BM)

2. Prepare the flexible budget (flexible budget 1). This budget is based on actual volume sales, but at the original budgeted mix and budgeted prices. Any difference in contribution between the fixed and the flexible budget is due to the volume variance and hence this variance is isolated.

   budgeted price x actual volume x budgeted mix (BP x AV x BM)

3. Prepare a second flexible budget (flexible budget 2). This budget is based on actual volume and the actual sales mix but at budgeted price. The difference in contribution between the first and second flexible budgets is due to the sales mix variance and hence this variance is isolated.

   budgeted price x actual volume x actual mix (BP x AV x AM)

4. Enter the actual figures.

   actual price x actual volume x actual mix (AP x AV x AM)

5. Find the price or cost variance. This is the difference between flexible budget 2 and actual figures.

Summary of the variances

Fixed budget	Flexible budget 1	Flexible budget 2	Actual
BP x BV x BM	**BP x AV x BM**	**BP x AV x AM**	**AP x AV x AM**
Fixed budget	Flexed budget 1	Flexed budget 2	Actual results

Sales volume variances   Sales mix variances   Sales price and cost variances

Example 10.2 outlines the process of calculating the sales mix variance along with price and volume variances.

Example 10.2: *Calculation of sales mix variance*

The following information relates to Ski Slopes Tour Operators Ltd who offer three different seven night packaged deals for their customers. The following information relates to their budget for the first three months of the winter season:

Budget information

Package	Sales mix	Selling price per package	Variable cost as a per cent of selling price
Budget	50%	€1,500	35%
Mid-range	35%	€2,000	30%
Luxury	15%	€3,000	25%

The company estimates that for the first three months of the season they will sell 1,000 packages. Fixed costs for the three months are estimated at €500,000.

Actual results

❑ For the first three months actual packages sold amounted to 900.
❑ The actual sales mix was budget, 40 per cent; mid-range 30 per cent; and luxury 30 per cent.
❑ The company generated €1,800,000 from the sale of its holiday packages for the period.
❑ Actual variable costs amounted to €500,000.
❑ Actual fixed costs amounted to €520,000.

a) *Prepare a statement showing the fixed budget, flexible budget, actual results and variances for the year.*
b) *Prepare a statement reconciling actual net profit to budgeted net profit.*

Approach

From the data it can be seen that actual sales volume was less than budgeted and thus an adverse volume variance is expected. Actual sales mix is also different to budgeted, with the company selling more of its luxury packages. These packages generate a higher profit or contribution margin than the budget or mid-range packages and thus the sales mix variance is expected to be positive.

In separately calculating the volume and mix variances, we need to go through the following steps:

	Step 1	Step 2	Step 3	Step 4	Step 5
	Fixed budget 1,000 holidays **BP x BV x BM**	**Flexible budget 1** 900 holidays **BP x AV x BM**	**Flexible budget 2** 900 holidays **BP x AV x AM**	**Actual** 900 holidays **AP x AV x AM**	**Price / cost variance**
Sales					
Budget	750,000	675,000	540,000		
Mid-range	700,000	630,000	540,000		
Luxury	450,000	405,000	810,000		
Total sales	1,900,000	1,710,000	**1,890,000**	1,800,000	(90,000) A
Variable costs					
Budget (35%)	262,500	236,250	189,000		
Mid-range (30%)	210,000	189,000	162,000		
Luxury (25%)	112,500	101,250	202,500		
Total var costs	585,000	526,500	**553,500**	500,000	53,500 F
Contribution	**1,315,000**	**1,183,500**	**1,336,500**	1,300,000	
Fixed costs	500,000	500,000	**500,000**	520,000	(20,000) A
Net profit	815,000	683,500	836,500	780,000	

Sales margin volume variance €(131,500) A	Sales margin mix variance €153,000 F

Note: The make-up of the variances are in bold on the statement.

Some of the calculations for the above statement are quite complex. The following shows how both the sales and variable costs figures are computed:

Budget type	Package sales		Variable costs
Fixed:			
BV x BM x BP	Budget:	1,000 holidays x 50% x €1,500 = €750,000	€750,000 x 35% = €262,500
	Mid-range:	1,000 holidays x 35% x €2,000 = €700,000	€700,000 x 30% = €210,000
	Luxury:	1,000 holidays x 15% x €3,000 = €450,000	€450,000 x 25% = €112,500
Flexible 1:			
AV x BM x BP	Budget:	900 holidays x 50% x €1,500 = €675,000	€675,000 x 35% = €236,250
	Mid-range:	900 holidays x 35% x €2,000 = €630,000	€630,000 x 30% = €189,000
	Luxury:	900 holidays x 15% x €3,000 = €405,000	€405,000 x 25% = €101,250
Flexible 2:			
AV x AM x BP	Budget:	900 holidays x 40% x €1,500 = €540,000	€540,000 x 35% = €189,000
	Mid-range:	900 holidays x 30% x €2,000 = €540,000	€540,000 x 30% = €162,000
	Luxury:	900 holidays x 30% x €3,000 = €810,000	€810,000 x 25% = €202,500

- ❏ The sales volume margin variance is an adverse variance of €131,500 due to the fact that the company sold less package holidays than anticipated. This variance is simply the difference between contribution in the fixed and first flexible budget.
- ❏ The sales margin mix variance is €153,000 favourable. This variance tells us that actual profit was greater than budgeted due to the fact that the company sold more of its most profitable holiday packages (luxury) and less of the least profitable packages (budget and mid-range) than anticipated in the budget. This variance is simply the difference between contribution in flexible budgets 1 and 2.

A statement reconciling budgeted net income with actual net income can be prepared as follows:

Statement reconciling budgeted net income to actual net income

	€	€
Budgeted net profit		815,000
Sales margin volume variance	(131,500) A	
Sales price variance	(90,000) A	
Sales margin mix variance	153,000 F	
Variable cost variance	53,500 F	
Fixed cost variance	(20,000) A	(35,000)
Actual net profit		780,000

Summary of reasons for variances

Variance	Reasons
Sales price variance	❑ Fluctuations in demand not detected when preparing budget. ❑ Increased or reduced competition. ❑ Economic and social factors. ❑ Political factors. ❑ Unrealistic budget.
Sales volume variance	❑ Price too high or too low. ❑ Unrealistic budget. ❑ Increased or reduced competition. ❑ Poor performance from sales team. ❑ Cutbacks in advertising and marketing.
Sales mix variance	❑ Unrealistic budget. ❑ Poor pricing strategy. ❑ Increased competition in a particular product line.
Direct materials variance	❑ Poor or excellent usage of materials. ❑ Less waste or increased waste. ❑ Suppliers increasing prices or reducing prices. ❑ Quantity discounts availed of or not availed of. ❑ Poor materials leading to increased waste. ❑ Poor equipment resulting in increased waste.
Direct labour variance	❑ Unrealistic budget not taking into account rate increases. ❑ Unrealistic budget targets in terms of efficiency. ❑ Poor supervision. ❑ High staff turnover resulting in efficiency problems. ❑ Poor quality materials resulting in labour time wasted. ❑ Increased equipment breakdowns resulting in labour time wasted. ❑ Customer issues resulting in wasted time. ❑ Supply issues resulting in wasted labour time. ❑ Using a higher grade of worker than budgeted for.
Fixed overheads	❑ Increased costs of overheads not taken into account in the budget. ❑ Lack of control of overheads.

Budgetary control in hospitality

Research conducted by Smullen and O'Donoghue (2005) into the use and influence of certain financial based decision-making models in the Irish hospitality industry showed the following in relation to budgetary control:

❑   All hotels used budgets as a control device and regularly compared actual performance to budget.
❑   Only 11 per cent of hotels prepared flexible budgets.
❑   The most popular timeframe for comparison of actual performance to budget was on a monthly basis with some preparing on a daily, weekly and quarterly basis.
❑   Variance analysis greatly influenced decisions relating to staff performance, capital investment and resource allocation.

The results are consistent with a Collier and Gregory study in 1995 which showed that variances were calculated on a line-by-line comparison between actual and the fixed budget with no flexing of budgets to calculate volume variances. This lack of flexing of budgets reflects the low variable costs and the high fixed costs structure of the hotel sector and a view that revenue maximisation is priority.

Summary

Budgetary control is a vital part of the whole budgetary process. Without regular comparisons of budget with actual performance, one cannot judge how effectively an organisation is operating. Variance analysis provides managers with information upon which to base corrective action procedures. Ultimately, any budgetary information system must provide timely, relevant, reliable and accurate information to ensure management make timely and informed decisions.

The main information points covered in this chapter are as follows:

❑   Budgetary control is concerned with the manner in which budgets are used as a tool of management. It is important that actual events in a budget period are compared against the budget plan so that timely action can be taken to remedy or improve the situation.
❑   The budgetary control process can be divided into four distinct activities:
    – Measure actual performance.

- Compare actual results with budgeted.
- Investigate differences (variances).
- Take corrective action.

❏ The use of flexible budgets allows the fixed budget to be adjusted to allow for actual activity in making the comparison between actual and budgeted performance. Budgeted sales prices and variable unit costs are applied to actual activity leaving fixed costs unaltered.

❏ Variances occur when actual costs and revenues differ from the budget. Variance analysis is the process of breaking down variances to find the true cause for the deviation with a view to improving efficiencies within the business.

❏ Variances result from differences between actual performance and budget and are categorised into three types:
- Volume variances, which measure the difference between budgeted and actual net profit caused by the difference in volume sales. It is normally calculated as one summary variance called the sales margin volume variance.
- Price or cost variances measure the difference between budgeted and actual net profit caused by differences between the selling and cost prices agreed in the budget and actual selling and cost prices. This variance category can have many causes and thus price/cost variances are calculated for each type of revenue and expense item.
- Sales mix variances measure the difference between budgeted and actual net profit caused by the differences between the assumed sales mix in the fixed budget compared to the actual sales mix. As there is only one reason for this variance, a summary variance is calculated called the sales margin mix variance.

❏ The causes of variances can be categorised into the following:
- **Operating variances:** These variances are caused by operating issues within a business and are usually controllable by management. Examples include human resource issues or technical issues regarding plant and equipment.
- **Planning variances:** These are variances that are caused by unrealistic targets being set and hence are unlikely to be achieved.
- **Random variances:** These variances are caused by chance and management has no means of controlling them. For example the airline industry will have a fuel requirement which can be affected by adverse or fair weather conditions.

❏ The main variances calculated in this chapter are:
- Sales price variance.
- Sales margin volume variance.
- Sales mix variance.
- Materials cost variance.
- Labour cost variance.
- Fixed overhead cost variance.

Review Questions

Question 10.1

a) Distinguish between fixed and flexible budgeting.
b) What are the main features of a control system?

Question 10.2.

a) Explain what is meant by the term variances and distinguish between favourable and adverse variances.
b) Explain the three variances that can be applied to the analysis of sales.

Question 10.3

a) Outline the roles of both flexible and rolling budgets in an organisation, explaining clearly the differences between both approaches.
b) Outline how flexible budgets assist in analysing variances.

Question 10.4

Paul Collins operates a successful business selling and installing home computers. Paul purchases each computer from a leading manufacturer for €500. An agreement has been reached with the company to deliver the computers for a fixed charge of €1,000 for the period and a variable charge of €5 per computer. It takes approximately two hours to install and provide initial training. Paul pays a technician €40 per hour to provide the installation and training. Overheads are all fixed in nature. The report presented below shows the total or static variances calculated from comparing actual performance to the fixed budget for the last three months.

Management Report

	Fixed budget	Actual	Variance
Sales volume	1,000	1,200	
Purchases	€500,000	€576,000	€76,000 Adverse
Installation costs	€80,000	€97,000	€17,000 Adverse
Delivery	€6,000	€7,000	€1,000 Adverse
Overheads	€120,000	€123,000	€3,000 Adverse
Total cost	€706,000	€803,000	€97,000 Adverse
Revenue	€900,000	€960,000	€60,000 Favourable
Profit	€194,000	€157,000	€37,000 Adverse

Paul is concerned about the fact that the €60,000 extra revenue was eliminated by an over-run in costs of €97,000. He requires more information that may explain the situation.

Required

a) Prepare a budgetary control statement that enables identification of volume and price or cost variances.

b) Discuss the position revealed by the statement.

Question 10.5

The following data relates to a three month forecast period for Reilly's Good Grub Restaurant.

Budget information

Number of covers sold	60,000
Average selling price per cover (including VAT at 12.5%)	€9
Variable costs per meal	€3.20
Budgeted fixed costs for the first 3 months	124,750

The actual results for the three months were as follows:

Actual results

Number of covers sold	65,000
Sales revenue (including VAT at 12.5%)	€562,500
Variable costs	€220,000
Fixed overhead	€120,000

Required

a) Prepare a statement showing the fixed budget, flexible budget, actual results and variances for the three month period.

b) Comment on the results.

Question 10.6

The following information relates to the E.U. Restaurant and Café Bar, for the previous three months trading.

Budget

Number of covers	75,000
Average spend per cover including VAT at 12.5%	€11.25
Food and beverage costs as a percentage of sales	40%
Other variable costs as a percentage of sales	12%
Fixed labour costs	€158,000
Fixed overhead costs	€78,000

Actual

Number of covers sold	82,000
Sales revenue (including VAT at 12.5%)	€732,000
Food and beverage costs	€270,500
Other variable costs	€85,000
Fixed labour costs	€165,000
Fixed overhead costs	€65,000

Required

a) Prepare a statement for the period showing the fixed and flexible budgets with actual results and variances.

b) Prepare a statement reconciling the actual net profit with the budgeted net profit.

c) Prepare a report evaluating the results you have prepared and suggesting possible causes for the variances.

Question 10.7

The following budget analysis report for the month of May relates to Power Appliances Limited, a chain of retail outlets supplying electrical appliances. The general manager is concerned with the actual performance and the level of adverse variances that have occurred during the period.

Power Appliances Limited – Budget Analysis
Period: May

	Fixed budget	Actual	Variance
Volume	435,000	475,000	
	€	€	€
Sales	5,133,000	5,557,500	424,500 F
Cost of sales	1,022,250	1,102,000	79,750 A
Variable labour	717,750	798,000	80,250 A
Operational overhead*	1,305,000	1,348,000	43,000 A
Sales commission 5%	256,650	277,875	21,225 A
Administration **	865,000	878,000	13,000 A
Marketing **	350,000	341,400	8,600 F
Total costs	4,516,650	4,745,275	228,625 A
Profit	616,350	812,225	195,875 F

* 20% of budgeted operational overhead is variable. Actual fixed operational overhead is exactly as budgeted.

** Administration and marketing costs are both fixed.

Required

Prepare an alternative presentation for the budget above that provides more meaningful information for control purposes.

Question 10.8

Jack Harris operates a successful business selling and installing garden sheds. Jack purchases each shed as a wooden kit which is then installed on site by experienced workers. Currently there are two shed options, the small shed accounting for 60 per cent of the budgeted sales volume and a medium sized shed.

Jack has budgeted on the following:

	Sales price	Purchases cost	Installation time at €50 per hour
Small shed	€520	€250	2 hours
Medium shed	€700	€400	3 hours

An agreement has been reached with a distribution company to deliver the sheds for a fixed charge of €1,000 for the period and a variable charge of €20 per shed. All overheads are unaffected by volume changes.

Management Report

	Fixed budget	Actual	Variance
Sales volume	1,000	985	
Purchases	€310,000	€311,725	€1,725 Adverse
Installation costs	€120,000	€122,750	€2,750 Adverse
Delivery	€21,000	€20,700	€300 Favourable
Overheads	€95,000	€97,500	€2,500 Adverse
Total cost	€546,000	€552,675	€6,675 Adverse
Revenue	€592,000	€594,650	€2,650 Favourable
Profit	€46,000	€41,975	€4,025 Adverse

Having reviewed the management report (shown above), Jack is concerned about the lower profit figure achieved and how the adverse costs have wiped out his additional revenue. As the sales mix he achieved is significantly different to budget mix, he finds the report of little use. Jack negotiated a lower purchase cost for the medium shed which he passed on to his customers in a reduced selling price. The reduction in selling price of the medium shed made it more attractive and displaced some of the small shed sales. During the period, 500 small sheds and 485 medium sheds were actually sold and installed.

Required
a) Prepare a budgetary control statement showing fixed and flexible budgets with actual results and variances.
b) Discuss the position revealed by the statement.

Question 10.9

Funcity Ltd has a leisure games complex which has three separate revenue producing streams: bowling, snooker and play area. The following data relates to its budgeted sales and actual sales for the month of August.

	Original budget		Actual results	
	Quantity	Price €	Quantity	Price €
Bowling	22,000	6.00	25,000	5.50
Snooker	6,000	8.00	5,000	8.50
Play area	12,000	4.00	14,000	4.50

Required

a) Prepare a statement showing the fixed and flexible sales budgets, actual revenue and variances.

b) Prepare a statement reconciling the budgeted sales revenue to the actual sales revenue.

Question 10.10

The following information relates to the budgeted and actual trading performance of Doyle's Hotel and Leisure Centre for the previous quarter.

Budget information

Accommodation type	Sales mix	Selling price per room-night	Direct costs to sales percentage
Luxury	8%	€160	20%
Mid-range	50%	€80	15%
Budget	42%	€50	10%

The forecast number of bed–nights sold for the period was 1,200.
Other variable costs including part-time labour were estimated at 10 per cent of sales.
Budgeted fixed costs were set at €50,000 for the quarter.

Actual results

Actual activity as a percentage of budget activity was 90 per cent.
Actual sales mix

Luxury	10%
Mid-range	60%
Budget	30%

Total sales for the period amounted to €112,500 including VAT at 12.5 per cent.
Total direct costs amounted to €41,000.
Other variable costs amounted to €13,000.
Fixed costs for the period amounted to €45,000.

Required

a) Prepare a statement showing the fixed budget, flexible budgets, actual results and variances for the quarter.

b) Prepare a statement reconciling the budgeted net profit to the actual net profit.

c) Write a short report to the directors of the Doyle's Hotel and Leisure Centre evaluating the results you have produced and suggesting possible reasons for the variances.

Question 10.11

The following is the forecast budget of Sunshine Resorts Ltd, a holiday resort complex with a total of 300 self-catering accommodation units made up of studios, duplexes and chalets. The company has a 44 week season for which its units are available for let, ensuring a rental capacity of 13,200 accommodation weeks. The remaining eight weeks of the year are required for maintenance and repairs.

Budget information for the year

Accommodation category	Sales mix	Selling price per week €	Percentage contribution after direct costs
Studios	35%	400 (excl VAT)	90%
Duplex	50%	600 (excl VAT)	85%
Chalets	15%	800 (excl VAT)	80%

The budget is based on an activity level of 60 per cent of its capacity.
Budgeted fixed costs were set at €720,000 for the quarter.

Actual results for the period

Actual activity was 10 per cent below budgeted.

Actual sales mix	
Studios	15%
Duplex	60%
Chalets	25%

Total sales for the period amounted to €4,500,000 including VAT at 12.5 per cent.
Total direct costs amounted to €680,000.
Fixed costs for the period amounted to €690,000.

Required

a) Prepare a statement showing the fixed budget, flexible budgets, actual results and variances for the year.
b) Prepare a statement reconciling the budgeted net profit to the actual net profit.
c) Write a short report to the general manager of the Sunshine Resorts Ltd evaluating the results you have produced and suggesting possible reasons for the variances.

Standard Costing and Variance Analysis

Introduction

Standard costing is a system where preset standards are used in the estimation of costs. This can provide more detailed variance analysis information for managers. It involves the setting of detailed predetermined standard product costs, so that a business can accurately estimate, based on the standards set, what the cost of a product or service should be. By comparing this standard to the actual cost of a product, more detailed information is available to enhance cost control. This is part of the whole process of cost accounting whereby a business should be able to calculate the expected cost of producing a product or service. It is particularly applicable to the manufacturing and processing business sectors. Businesses in the hospitality, tourism and retail sectors rarely use standard costing although it is applicable and used in the fast food and food processing sectors, as well as in the mass production of tourist souvenirs. This chapter focuses on how a standard costing system can provide management with extra information to be used for analysing and investigating variances and taking corrective action.

Standards

*'Benchmark measurement of resource usage or revenue or profit generation,
set in defined conditions'*
Standard cost as defined by CIMA Official Terminology

A standard cost is a predetermined calculation of what a cost should be under specified working conditions. Standards can be set for materials, labour and overheads. Setting a standard involves the establishment of two components for each cost type, the volume required and the unit cost attached to that volume. By multiplying the amount of raw material required to produce one unit of product by the cost per kilo or litre, we are able to estimate the standard direct material cost per product. The same applies to labour, with the standard hours required to produce one unit multiplied by the labour rate per hour, giving the standard direct labour cost per unit. Standards are generally agreed and set based on observing past performance. It can be a subjective process. However the standard becomes the benchmark against which comparisons are made with actual materials and labour costs and thus, more detailed variances are calculated.

Variance Analysis

*'Evaluation of performance by a means of variances, whose timely reporting should
maximise the opportunity for managerial action'*
Variance analysis as defined by CIMA Official Terminology

In the previous chapter, through the use of flexible budgets, volume and price variances were calculated. However the materials, labour and overhead cost variances could have been analysed even further if a standard costing system had been in use. The following example shows how this works.

Illustration 11.1: *Budgetary control worksheet*

The following worksheet shows the fixed and flexible budgets as well as actual results and variances for a food production facility.

	Unit cost	Fixed budget	Flexible budget	Actual results	Variances
Sales (units)		50,000	60,000	60,000	
		€	€	€	€
Sales	10.00	500,000	**600,000**	**540,000**	(60,000) A
Less Variable costs					
Materials (food)	4.00	200,000	**240,000**	**243,000**	(3,000) A
Direct labour	1.00	50,000	**60,000**	**57,000**	3,000 F
Variable overhead	0.10	5,000	**6,000**	**8,000**	(2,000) A
	5.10	255,000	306,000	308,000	
Contribution	4.90	**245,000**	294,000	232,000	49,000 F
Less Fixed overheads		160,000	**160,000**	**163,000**	(3,000) A
Net profit		85,000	134,000	69,000	(16,000) A

The bold figures identify the make-up of each variance.
This production facility does not use a system of standard costing.

A statement reconciling the budgeted net profit with the actual net profit can be prepared as follows:

Statement Reconciling Budgeted Net Profit to Actual Net Profit

	€	€
Budgeted net profit		85,000
Sales margin volume variance	49,000 F	
Sales price variance	(60,000) A	
Materials variance	(3,000) A	
Direct labour variance	3,000 F	
Variable overhead variance	(2,000) A	
Fixed overhead variance	(3,000) A	(16,000) A
Actual net profit		69,000

Focusing on the materials variance of €3,000 adverse, if a standard costing system was in place then this variance could be further analysed into its two component parts:

❑ **Materials price variance:** This variance reflects the difference between the actual purchase price of materials (food) and the standard purchase price set.
❑ **Materials usage variance:** This variance reflects the difference between the actual quantity of materials used and the quantity allowed for the various products produced.

Focusing on the direct labour variance of €3,000 favourable, if a standard costing system was in place this could be further analysed into its two component parts:
❑ **Labour rate variance:** This is caused by differences between the actual labour rate and the standard rate set in the budget.
❑ **Labour efficiency variance:** This is due to the differences between the actual time spent in producing the products and the standard time allowed or set in the budget.

Focusing on the variable overhead variance of €2,000 adverse, if a standard costing system was in place this variance could be further analysed into its two component parts:
❑ **Rate:** Caused by the difference between the actual variable overhead rate and the budgeted rate.
❑ **Efficiency:** Caused by the difference between the actual variable overhead usage and the standard usage allowed in the budget.

Variable overhead relates to a number of factory overheads such as production power, or wear and tear on machinery etc. Thus a standard would be set for the amount of power required to produce a product and the rate charged for this.

Finally, focusing on the fixed overhead variance of €3,000 adverse, standards are not normally set for fixed overhead because they are a product of time and not of efficiency or production. For example, salaries or administration expenses are fixed costs that do not vary according to production schedules and thus this variance is simply the difference between what was spent on fixed overhead and what was budgeted.

Standard Costing and Variance Analysis

A standard costing system ensures that more detailed analysis and information is available to support management decision-making on costs and cost control. It does not provide any extra analysis regarding sales and sales variances. This chapter will focus on the additional cost variances relating to materials, labour and overheads.

The following pyramid depicts the range of variances that can be produced from a standard costing system. The additional variances provided through the use of standard costing are highlighted in bold.

Summary of variances

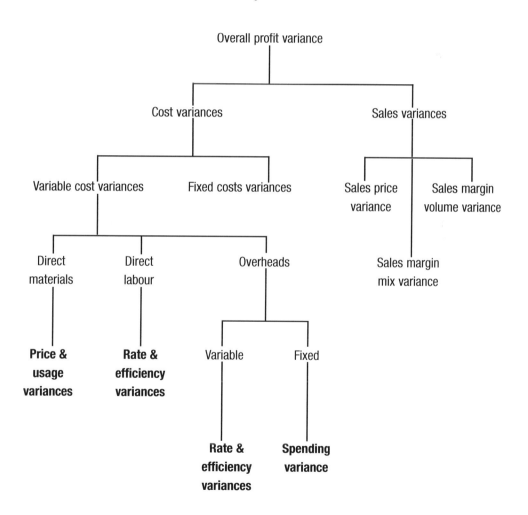

Key Variances in Standard Costing

Material cost

The difference between the actual materials cost incurred and the standard material cost of what was actually produced.

Material price *(standard cost per unit – actual cost per unit) x actual quantity used*

The difference caused by paying more or less than the standard price per item of materials.

Material usage *(standard quantity used – actual quantity used) x standard price per item*

The difference between what was actually used and what should have been used for the actual production volume, based on standard cost per item of materials.

Direct labour cost

The difference between actual labour cost incurred and the standard labour cost of what was actually produced.

Direct labour rate *(Standard rate per hour – actual rate per hour) x actual hours worked*

The difference caused by paying more or less than the standard labour rate per hour.

Direct labour efficiency *(Standard hours allowed – actual hours) x standard rate per hour*

The difference caused by using more or less labour hours than the standard labour hours allowed for the actual production volume, based on the standard rate.

Variable overhead cost

The difference between the total actual variable overhead cost incurred and the standard cost of what was actually produced.

Variable overhead rate *(standard hourly rate – actual hourly rate) x actual hours worked*

The difference between what was actually paid and what was absorbed.

Variable overhead efficiency *(standard hours – actual hours) x standard overhead hourly rate*

The difference between the amount that was actually absorbed and what should have been absorbed.

Example 11.1: *Standard costing*

The following information relates to Tourism Products Ltd, a company that specialises in producing plaster souvenirs for the tourism market. The information relates to its most popular product range called the 'Stiletto in the Ghetto', a miniature replica of the Spire in O'Connell Street, Dublin.

Unit cost information	Cost	Production time
Materials 1 kg plaster	€10 per 10 kg	
Standard wage rate	€10 per hour	6 minutes
Standard power cost	€2 per hour	6 minutes

Budgeted sales are estimated at 20,000 units per week at a price of €3.00 and fixed costs are estimated at €8,000 per week.

Actual results for the week were as follows:

		€	€
Sales	22,000 units sold		60,000
Direct costs			
Material	22,040 kgs	20,497	
Labour	2,250 hours	23,130	
Variable overhead / power	2,250 hours	4,207	
Fixed costs		8,500	

a) Calculate the standard variable cost of a single souvenir unit.
b) Prepare a worksheet showing the fixed budget, flexible budget, actual results and variance for the period.
c) Further analyse the materials, labour and overhead variances into the following sub-variances:
   ❑ Materials price variance.
   ❑ Materials usage variance.
   ❑ Labour rate variance.
   ❑ Labour efficiency variance.
   ❑ Overhead rate variance.
   ❑ Overhead efficiency variance.
d) Prepare a statement reconciling the budgeted net profit with actual net profit.

Approach

a) The standard variable cost of a single souvenir.

		€
Materials	€10 ÷ 10 kgs	1.00
Labour	$\left(\dfrac{€10}{60\ min}\right)$ x 6 min	1.00
Overhead	$\left(\dfrac{€2}{60\ min}\right)$ x 6 min	0.20
Total standard variable cost per unit		2.20

b) Preparation of budgetary control worksheet.

	Unit cost	Fixed budget	Flexible budget	Actual	Variances
Sales units		20,000	22,000	22,000	
Sales price	€ 3	€ 3	€ 3		
	€	€	€	€	€
Sales revenue	3.00	60,000	66,000	60,000	(6,000) A
Variable costs					
Materials cost	1.00	20,000	22,000	20,497	1,503 F
Labour	1.00	20,000	22,000	23,130	(1,130) A
Overhead	0.20	4,000	4,400	4,207	193 F
Total variable costs	2.20	44,000	48,400	47,834	
Contribution	0.80	16,000	17,600	12,166	1,600 F
Fixed costs		8,000	8,000	8,500	(500) A
Net profit		8,000	9,600	3,666	

c) Calculation of detailed cost variances.

Materials variances

The materials variance is €1,503 favourable and is a significant variance, as actual profit would be 41 per cent (1,503 ÷ 3,666) less if this variance did not exist. The variance can be further analysed by dividing it into its two component parts.

1. Materials price variance

This variance is caused by the difference between the actual price per kg charged for materials and the standard price per kg set in the budget. If the company achieves a lower purchase price than budget, then this will lead to a favourable price variance. The formula to calculate this variance is as follows:

> (Standard cost per kg – actual cost per kg) x actual quantity used
> (€1.00 – €0.93) x 22,040 kg
> €1,543 Favourable

Note: the actual cost per kg of €0.93 is calculated by simply dividing the actual materials cost by the actual amount of materials used (€20,497 ÷ 22,040 kg).

2. Materials usage variance

This variance is created when the business uses more or less materials than envisaged in the budget. If more materials are used then this leads to an adverse variance. The materials usage variance is calculated by using the following formula:

> (Standard usage allowed – actual usage) x standard price
> (22,040kg – 22,000kg) x €1.00
> €40 Adverse

This variance can be caused by a number of different factors:

❑ The purchase of poor quality materials which can result in a favourable price variance but also an adverse usage variance.
❑ Greater levels of waste in the production process. Poor quality materials as well as old, inefficient equipment can cause this.
❑ Poor performance by production staff resulting in increased waste.
❑ Theft of materials by staff or others.

The total of the price and usage variances amounts to the total materials variance of €1,503 favourable.

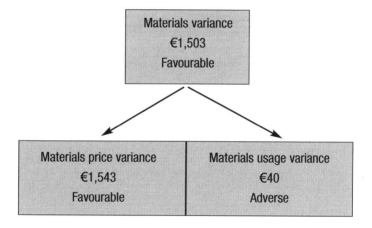

Materials variance
€1,503
Favourable

Materials price variance
€1,543
Favourable

Materials usage variance
€40
Adverse

Labour cost variances

The labour cost variance is €1,130 adverse and is a significant variance, as actual profit would be 31 per cent (1,130 ÷ 3,666) greater if this adverse variance did not exist. It can be further analysed by dividing it into its two component parts.

1. Labour rate variance

The labour rate variance is created when the actual labour rate per hour differs from the standard rate set in the budget. This variance is calculated using the following formula:

> (Standard wage rate per hour – actual wage rate per hour) x actual hours worked
> (10.00 – 10.28) x 2,250 hours
> €630 Adverse

Note: the actual wage rate of €10.28 is calculated by dividing the actual labour costs by the actual labour hours (€23,130 ÷ 2,250 hours).

The actual rate of payment will differ from the standard due to a number of reasons:

❑ An unexpected wage agreement not included in the standard.
❑ More over-time worked than was envisaged.
❑ More staff hired than envisaged when preparing the budget.
❑ Using a higher grade of worker than planned.

2. Labour efficiency variance

This variance occurs when the actual hours worked is different to the standard used in the budget. The variance is calculated using the following formula:

> (Standard hours allowed – actual hours) x standard wage rate per hour
>
> (2,200 hours – 2,250 hours) x €10
>
> €500 Adverse

The variance is influenced by the following factors:

❑ Employee efficiency is affected by a range of issues including the quality of management, levels of motivation, staff turnover, management and staff relations.
❑ Delays in the production process causing employees to be idle.

The total of the labour rate and efficiency variances amounts to the total of the labour cost variance of €1,130.

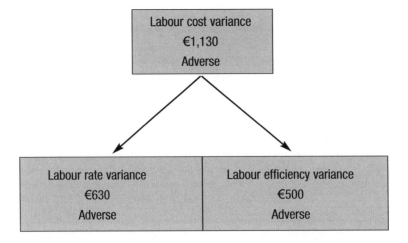

Variable overhead variances

In this example, variable overhead is represented by power costs associated with the production process. The total variable overhead variance amounts to €193 favourable. It can be divided into its two component parts as follows:

1. Variable overhead rate variance

This variance occurs when the actual variable overhead rate differs from the standard set in the budget. This variance is generally caused by fluctuations in the price per hour of power and is calculated as follows:

> (Standard hourly rate – actual hourly rate) x actual hours
> (€2.00 – €1.87) x 2,250 hours
> €293 Favourable

Note: the actual variable overhead cost per hour of €1.87 is calculated by dividing actual overhead costs by actual hours (€4,200 ÷ 2,250 hours).

2. Variable overhead efficiency variance

It is important to remember that production overheads cannot be traced directly to any single product or unit of production. In management accounting, the technique of overhead absorption is used to assign variable overhead costs to units of production on an activity basis, such as direct labour costs or direct machine hours. Thus the variable overhead efficiency variance is linked to the basis on which overheads are assigned to units of production. In the previous example, variable overheads are assigned to units of production based on labour hours worked and hence the difference between actual labour hours worked and the standard used in the budget will determine the significance of this variance. Thus if there is an adverse labour efficiency variance (taking longer than anticipated to complete the job), then there will also be an adverse variable overhead efficiency variance. This makes sense because the longer it takes to complete a job, the longer the machines are running and thus more power is used up. It is calculated as follows:

> (Standard hours allowed – actual hours) x standard overhead hourly rate
> (2,200 labour hours – 2,250 labour hours) x €2.00
> €100 Adverse

Note: the standard time to produce one unit is 6 minutes, or 10 units per hour and thus the standard time to produce 22,000 units is 2,200 hours.

The total of the rate and efficiency variance amounts to the total overhead cost variance of €193 favourable.

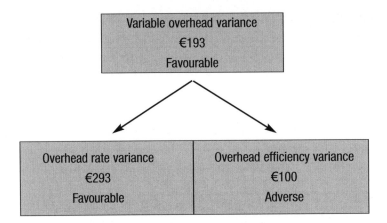

The reconciliation below shows all the variances that make up the difference between budgeted net profit and actual.

d) Reconciliation of budgeted net profit to actual.

Statement Reconciling Budgeted Net Profit to Actual Net Profit

		€	€	€
Budgeted net profit				8,000
Sales variances	Price		(6,000) A	
	Volume		1,600 F	
Materials variance	Price	1,543 F		
	Usage	(40) A	1,503 F	
Labour variance	Rate	(630) A		
	Efficiency	(500) A	(1,130) A	
Variable overhead variance	Rate	293 F		
	Efficiency	(100) A	193 F	
Fixed cost variance			(500) A	€4,334
Actual net profit				€3,666

Interpretation of the Cost Variances

The additional variances that are calculated under a standard costing system need to be interpreted and evaluated. Example 11.1 will now be used to illustrate the interpretation and evaluation of standard cost variances.

Interpreting the materials variances

The overall materials cost variance is €1,503 favourable. This is made up of a materials price variance of €1,543 favourable and a usage variance of €40 adverse.

1. Materials price variance

The main cause of the materials price variance is that the company was able to purchase cheaper material supplies and this was not reflected in the standard. This would lead us to ask two questions:

1. How often are the standards reviewed to reflect reality?
2. What is the actual cause of this variance? Did the purchasing manager seek competitive pricing to ensure the best value is obtained in purchasing? Did the company avail of quantity discounts or was there simply a general reduction in the price of raw materials?

Variances direct management in their investigations to improve the standard setting process, control procedures, and overall efficiency within the organisation.

2. Materials usage variance

The materials usage variance of €40 adverse indicates that the organisation used more materials than was budgeted for. This variance is very insignificant. If the variance was greater it should lead management to investigate the following areas:

1. The standard of quality of the materials purchased. Poor quality materials can lead to greater materials wastage. This could be in conjunction with a favourable materials price variance, as cheap materials could give rise to greater waste and inefficiencies.
2. The quality and age of the equipment used. If the company is using old machinery, this can lead to greater levels of wasted materials.
3. The levels of labour efficiency which, if quite poor, would lead to greater levels of waste. Again this could be in conjunction with a favourable labour cost variance reflecting cheaper, less skilled labour.
4. The theft of materials.
5. The accuracy of the standard for materials usage.

Overall, actual profit would be 41 per cent less (1,503 ÷ 3,666 x 100) if there was no materials variance. This is very significant and management must assess whether these are genuine savings or inappropriate standards set in the budget.

Interpreting the labour cost variances

The overall labour cost variance is €1,130 adverse. This represents 31 per cent of actual profit. In other words actual profit would be 31 per cent greater if this variance did not exist. It also represents 26 per cent of the difference between budgeted and actual profit and hence would be classified as a very significant variance. This variance is made up of the labour rate variance and labour efficiency variance.

1. Labour rate variance

The labour rate variance is €630 adverse. Thus the actual payment rate that applied to direct labour is greater than that budgeted for. The budget figure was €10 per hour, however the actual rate increased to €10.28 per hour. Reasons for this 2.8 per cent increase would include an unexpected wage deal that applied retrospectively, increased levels of overtime, or maybe the rate of employers' PRSI increasing. The possible increase in overtime levels could indicate a lower level of efficiency and hence an adverse efficiency variance.

2. Labour efficiency variance

This is a variance of €500 adverse and is caused by lower levels of efficiency in production by direct labour employees. Management must investigate the following areas:

1. The skills level of staff. For example a favourable labour rate variance could be part of the reason for an adverse efficiency variance, as lower skilled workers are employed at lower rates of pay.
2. Motivational factors such as rate of pay, working conditions, career prospects, training or participation in the standard setting process.
3. The quality of materials used may also be reflected in an adverse efficiency variance.
4. The quality and age of equipment. Frequent machinery breakdowns can have an adverse effect on the labour efficiency variance with increased idle labour time.
5. Problems with the supply of materials can cause an adverse labour efficiency variance.
6. The accuracy of the original standard used in the budget.

Interpreting the variable overhead variances

The variable overhead variance is €193 favourable. Actual profit would be 5 per cent less (193 ÷ 3,666 x 100) if this variance did not exist. These overheads such as power, light and heat etc. cannot be traced directly to a single unit of production. Thus for accounting purposes, the technique of overhead absorption is used which assigns variable overheads to units of production on an activity basis, such as direct labour hours or direct machine hours. For example, assume variable overheads are assigned to units of production based on a rate of €2.00 per direct labour hour. Thus the standard variable overhead per unit is based upon the charge multiplied by the number of direct labour hours worked per unit. Should there be a variance, then this could be due to a change in the overhead price (variable overhead rate variance) or a change in the rate of usage/efficiency (variable overhead efficiency variance), which is connected to the absorption method, which in this case is direct labour hours.

1. Variable overhead rate variance

In this case there is a favourable variance of €293 due to the fact that the budgeted rate was €2.00 per hour and the actual rate was €1.87 per hour (€4,207 ÷ 2,250 hours). This favourable variance suggests that the rate for power fell in this case by 6.5 per cent.

2. Variable overhead efficiency variance

This variance is an adverse variance of €100 and is due to a less efficient use of overhead (power) than forecast in the budget. As stated above, this variance is related to the labour efficiency variance and is effectively influenced by the same factors that affect the labour efficiency variance. In this case, because the labour efficiency variance is adverse (it is taking longer to produce the products), it is expected that the overhead efficiency variances will also be adverse.

Summary of reasons for adverse standard cost variances

Materials Price	❑ Changes in market price between the agreeing of standards and actual performance. ❑ Poor performance by the purchasing department staff in not achieving better value purchasing. ❑ Unrealistic standards not regularly reviewed.
Materials Usage	❑ Poor quality materials purchased, leading to high levels of waste. ❑ Faulty equipment leading to higher levels of waste. ❑ Poor levels of labour efficiency. ❑ Unrealistic standards not reviewed.
Labour Rate	❑ Standard not reflecting changing rates of pay. ❑ Unanticipated increases in overtime levels. ❑ Unanticipated increases in labour taxes (employers PRSI).
Labour Efficiency	❑ Poor staff motivation. ❑ High staff turnover and hence an increase in staff training. ❑ Poor quality materials. ❑ Faulty equipment. ❑ Delays in material supplies resulting in wasted labour time.

Interrelationship of variances

When investigating the causes of a variance, it is important to consider the interrelationship of variances. For example:

❑ The purchase of cheap and inferior materials will lead to a favourable materials price variance but can cause an adverse materials usage variance, due to increased waste associated with the inferior materials. It can also lead to an adverse labour efficiency variance as employees may require added time as a result of the inferior materials.

❑ Cheaper labour costs will lead to a favourable labour rate variance but can cause an adverse labour efficiency variance due to the requirement for training and the effects of the learning curve. This can also cause an adverse materials usage variance.

❑ Adverse labour efficiency variances can also create adverse variable overhead efficiency variances.

❑ Not reinvesting in equipment can create favourable capital spending variances. However this can lead to adverse variances in materials usage, labour efficiency and variable overhead.

The Standard Setting Process

Crucial to a system of standard costing is the setting of standard costs that can be used as a benchmark against which actual performance can be measured. Before a system of standard costing can be implemented, a range of information must be collected from various departments to be analysed. Examples would include:

1. Purchasing costs of direct materials from the purchasing department.
2. Wage rates and productivity agreements from the personnel department.
3. Details of overhead costs from the accounting/production department.

Ultimately, for each product type, management must set standards for direct materials, direct labour and variable overheads.

Direct materials standard costs

❑ **Standard price:** This is determined based on prices agreed and negotiated with suppliers and should take into account any pending short-term increases. Ultimately, the standard price should be the average price the firm expects to pay during the life of the standard.

❑ **Standard usage:** This is based on product specifications derived from an intensive study of the make-up of each product. It must take into account losses that may be caused by wastage, pilferage and deterioration of materials while in stock. Ultimately the business needs to set a standard that will indicate that if they plan to produce 50 units of production, then 1,000 kgs of material X will be needed. Thus they need to take into account the quality of the materials purchased, the quality of equipment used to develop the materials (which is related to the level of waste), the storage conditions and security.

Direct labour standard costs

❑ **Standard rate:** This is effectively the wage rate as agreed in any trade union agreement. In Ireland, with national wage agreements lasting over two years, it has become easier to budget for and agree standards.
❑ **Standard efficiency:** This is effectively the average time a direct labour employee takes to perform tasks related to a unit of production. This is quite difficult to establish as a number of tasks may have to be separately identified in the preparation of a unit of production. Also, other more subjective variables need to be considered such as skill, experience, motivation, working conditions and training. Generally, each operation is studied and an allowed time agreed, usually after a time and motion study is carried out.

Variable production overhead standard costs

❑ **Variable overhead rate standard:** A firm will have quite detailed historic information about its variable overhead costs and, along with information from department projections, can work out a standard rate.
❑ **Variable overhead efficiency standard:** As stated above, this variance is very much tied into the basis on which overheads are absorbed into a single unit of production cost. This is generally either direct labour hours or direct machine hours. Effectively, the drivers of these two variables (labour costs or machine hours) will also be the main drivers in setting overhead efficiency standards.

Ultimately management should keep in mind the following when setting standard costs:
1. Standards should be attainable and should not assume perfect or ideal conditions. This would lead to unrealistic standards and large adverse variances as well as demoralised staff. This can happen when standards are set from the top down in an autocratic styled organisation.
2. Built into any standard should be certain allowances for what is termed 'normal loss'. This could include factors such as machine breakdowns and unavoidable material wastage.

3. Standards, although realistic and with allowances built in, should also have a motivating effect on employees. In performing different tasks, different employees will have different levels of ability and motivation. If standards are perceived to be unfair then employees may be unmotivated to achieve the standard.

4. Employees must be involved in the standard setting process where it affects them, especially in terms of the efficiency standards. This can ensure a fairer and more motivating standard is set.

5. In setting standards, management must accept and anticipate some degree of variability between actual performance and the standard set. These variations or variances can be positive or negative. However what is important is the degree of variation or variance. This will dictate the level and extent of investigations. For example, should a variance be only 1 per cent of the standard, then it may be ignored. However with extremely large positive or negative variances, it should be asked whether standards were set either too high or too low. Also management must be aware that departments can show extremely large positive variances by cutting training or research budgets which might affect the long-term profitability of the business.

6. Standards have to be revised, especially if the level of variance is extreme, as this would indicate the standard is meaningless. Also should there be any change in work practices, materials used, materials cost or wage rates, then standards need to be adjusted. Ideally, any revisions should take place when the business is preparing its annual budget.

Advantages of Standard Costing

Introducing a standard costing system into a business is expensive. Thus before any business embarks on this, management should prepare a detailed cost-benefit analysis. Advantages of a standard costing system include:

1. More accurate pricing of products based on detailed cost analysis.
2. Carefully planned standards are an aid to more accurate budgeting.
3. The business will have a more simplified stock control system, as all materials purchased are valued at standard cost rather than LIFO or FIFO value systems.
4. More detailed variance analysis leading to a deeper level of investigation and better management decision-making.
5. A target of efficiency is set for employees and cost consciousness is stimulated.
6. The setting of standards involves determining the best materials and practices, which may lead to economies.
7. An overall improvement in the financial control of the business.

Summary

Standard costing is part of the whole budgetary control system that contributes to better quality information which enhances management control and decision-making. It can be expensive and time consuming to set up, however, it also provides a greater level of financial control and is quite suited to certain automated type businesses. Organisations in the tourism, leisure and hospitality sectors rarely use standard costing, although it is used in fast food retailing and the manufacturing of retail souvenirs, where a uniform product or service is produced in controlled circumstances, with a high volume output.

The main information points covered in this chapter are as follows:

❑ Standard costing involves the setting of detailed predetermined standard product costs so that a business can accurately estimate, based on the standards set, the detailed cost of any one product. By comparing this standard to the actual cost of a product, more detailed information on variances can be calculated.

❑ Standards are set, based on observations from past production runs of the amount of materials used for each product and the labour time spent in manufacturing each product.

❑ A standard costing system can help provide more detailed information for managers when comparing actual performance to budget, for example:
   – Materials variances can be broken into price and usage variances.
   – Labour variances can be broken into rate and efficiency variances.
   – Variable overhead variances and be subdivided into rate and efficiency variances.

❑ The materials price variance is caused by the difference between the actual purchase price paid for materials and the standard purchase price set in the budget.

❑ The materials usage variance is created when the business uses more or less materials than envisaged in the budget. Using more materials leads to an adverse variance.

❑ The labour rate variance is created when the business pays more or less per hour than envisaged in the budget. Paying a higher rate leads to an adverse variance.

❑ The labour efficiency variance occurs when the actual hours worked are different to the standard allowed in the budget. The variance is influenced by employee efficiency as well as delays in the production process.

❑ The variable overhead rate variance occurs when the actual variable overhead rate differs from the standard set in the budget.

❑ The variable overhead efficiency variance is linked to the basis on which overheads are assigned to units of production.

❑ Crucial to a system of standard costing is the setting of cost standards that can be used as a benchmark against which actual performance can be measured.

❑ Introducing a standard costing system into a business is expensive. Thus before any business embarks on this, management should prepare a detailed cost benefit analysis. However a standard costing system can provide significant advantages.

Review Questions

Question 11.1

What are standard costs and why is a standard costing system considered more useful than comparing actual costs to budget?

Question 11.2

a) Briefly explain the following terms:
   i.   Standard cost.
   ii. Materials usage variance.
   iii. Labour rate variance.
   iv. Labour efficiency variance.
b) Outline the process for developing standards of efficiency and usage for both direct labour and direct materials.

Question 11.3

a) Outline the advantages of standard costing.
b) Briefly outline the problems involved in setting standards.

Question 11.4

Cian Foods Ltd, a fast food restaurant, operates a standard costing system in relation to its raw material inputs. The following is the budget based on standards set and the actual results for the month of March:

	Budgeted			**Actual**		
	Quantities / covers	Price €	Total €	Quantities / covers	Price €	Total €
Sales	3,000	5.00	15,000	3,500	5.20	18,200
Cost of sales			12,750			14,538
Gross profit			2,250			3,662

The standard cost per dish is based on three main ingredients as follows:

Ingredient A	500g @ €5.00 per kg
Ingredient B	250g @ €3.00 per kg
Ingredient C	400g @ €2.50 per kg

The actual costs and quantities used were as follows:

	Price per kg	Quantities used
Ingredient A	€5.50	1,400 kgs
Ingredient B	€3.50	925 kgs
Ingredient C	€2.40	1,500 kgs

Required

a) Prepare a work sheet showing the fixed and flexible budgets, actual results and variances for March.
b) Calculate the materials price and usage variances.
c) Prepare a statement reconciling the budgeted gross profit to actual.
d) Briefly comment on the significance of the variances calculated.

Question 11.5

Celtic Leisure offers a standardised leisure experience and operates a standard costing system. The following budgeted information is available for August:

The budgeted number of visitors is 120,000.

Standard cost per visitor

Food costs etc.	1.50 kgs at cost per kg of €2.80
Direct labour	0.40 hours at cost per hour of €11.00
Variable overheads	0.40 hours at cost per hour of €3.50

Budgeted fixed overheads for month is €150,000.

Actual results for August

Number of visitors			115,000
			€
Food	165,000	kgs	528,000
Direct labour	47,000	hours	493,500
Variable overheads			178,600
Actual fixed overheads			144,300

Required

a) Prepare a statement showing, *for expenses only*, fixed and flexible budgets, actual expenses, and variances, for the month.
b) Calculate all relevant standard cost variances.
c) Prepare a statement reconciling budgeted and actual expenses.
d) Give possible reasons for the variances.

Question 11.6

The Knock Souvenir Production Company uses a standard direct costing system in accounting for direct materials and labour. The standard cost of a souvenir unit based on normal production output of 1,000 units is as follows:

	€
Material X (100 feet @ €0.15 per foot)	15.00
Direct labour (4 hours @ €5.00 per hour)	20.00
	35.00

In addition, variable overheads are budgeted to be €6 per unit and fixed overheads at €30,000 per month. The budgeted level of sales at a standard selling price of €50 was 1,000 units. The actual costs for the month of January based on a production run of 1,200 units were as follows:

	€
Material X (132,000 feet @ €0.12 per foot)	15,840
Direct labour (5,100 hours @ €5.50 per hour)	28,050
Variable production overhead	7,800
Fixed production overhead	32,310

Actual sales for January amounted to €100,000.

Required

a) Prepare the fixed and flexible budgets, actual results and variances, for the month of January.
b) Calculate the following sub-variances:
   i.   Materials price variance.
   ii. Materials usage variance.
   iii. Labour rate variance.
   iv. Labour efficiency variance.
c) Briefly discuss the above materials and labour variances and state how, in many respects, they are related.

CHAPTER 12

Performance Appraisal

Learning Outcomes

By the end of this chapter you will be able to:

❑ Outline the need for performance appraisal.
❑ Describe the role of both benchmarking and inter-firm comparison as performance appraisal tools.
❑ Prepare key performance ratios from financial statements under the headings of profitability, efficiency, operations, liquidity and capital structure.
❑ Prepare and interpret key operating and efficiency ratios unique to the hospitality, tourism and retail sectors.
❑ Write reports analysing the financial performance of a commercial organisation within the hospitality, tourism and retail sectors.

'If you cannot measure it, you cannot manage it'

(Eccles 1991)

Introduction

Performance measurement and appraisal is a central component of a management control system. Making good planning and control decisions requires information about how an organisation as a whole has performed, as well as how each subunit has performed. The whole focus of performance measurement and appraisal is to ensure the business is following its strategies and that each element or unit within the organisation is contributing to the overall objectives of the business. Performance appraisal of managers is instrumental in decisions regarding salaries, bonuses, future assignments and career advancement. Good performance measurement promotes goal congruence with the organisation's objectives and facilitates comparison across different subunits. There are many different financial and non-financial performance appraisal techniques such as:

1. Budgetary control and variance analysis (covered in Chapters 10 and 11).
2. Key internal financial performance indicators such as:
   - Return on investment.
   - Profitability and asset utilisation ratios.
   - Residual income.
3. Inter-firm comparisons or benchmarking performance against other companies regarded as best performers in the sector.
4. Various non-financial performance indicators such as levels of innovation, customer satisfaction and staff morale, all of which affect profitability.

This chapter focuses on the key financial performance indicators used across different business sectors and specifically the hospitality, tourism and retail sectors, to appraise the performance of an organisation. It concentrates on showing how these financial indicators are used in benchmarking and inter-firm comparisons. Effectively, this chapter examines the key financial ratios used for external comparative purposes and hence mainly focuses on centralised organisation structures. Chapter 13 will focus on the specific financial performance measures used within a divisionalised organisation structure. It concentrates on large divisionalised businesses that decentralise decision-making and responsibility. Performance needs to be measured for each division to ensure that it is achieving its objectives and the objectives of the organisation as a whole.

Centralised and divisionalised organisations

The distinction between divisionalised and centralised organisations will be covered in greater detail in Chapter 13. For the moment the main distinction is that divisionalised organisations are those that decentralise decision-making power and responsibility to sub-units or divisions, whereas centralised organisations centralise decision-making and responsibility. The distinction is important in relation to performance appraisal, as additional performance measures are required for decentralised organisations to ensure that their individual divisions are performing and making decisions in line with the goals and objectives of the whole organisation.

Performance Measurement and Evaluation

'Before it can be evaluated it must be measured'

Performance measurement and evaluation involves an organisation monitoring how it is achieving its predetermined goals and fulfilling the requirements of its stakeholders. To be successful, an organisation must be able to measure its performance and, through the appraisal process, identify areas that need improvement while building on achievements. A technical briefing by CIMA relating to the 'Latest Trends into Corporate Performance Measurement' identified the following factors that are required for a successful performance measurement system:

1. It must be integrated with the overall strategy of the business.
2. There must be a system of feedback and review.
3. The performance measurement system must be comprehensive.
4. The system must be owned and supported throughout the organisation.
5. Performance measures must be fair and achievable.
6. The system needs to be simple, clear and understandable.

The objectives of measuring performance are as follows:

❑ To assess and ensure that management's actions and decisions are in line with strategic objectives.
❑ To act as a motivational tool in providing a framework to guide and measure managers' decisions.
❑ To help in improving decision-making across an organisation by ensuring that decisions are informed and based on key performance indicators.
❑ To provide timely, relevant information on areas needing management attention, thus acting as a control mechanism.
❑ To enable managers to understand the needs and expectations of the various stakeholders in an organisation.

Performance evaluation requires three key elements:

1. Clearly defined and articulated strategic objectives which are used in assessing whether a strategy or business performance has achieved its primary goals.
2. Clear frameworks and performance indicators to measure performance, assess strategy, explore threats and weaknesses and ultimately provide information for management to take corrective action.
3. Regular feedback, which ensures that management appreciates the impact of their decisions on the overall strategy of an organisation. It also provides early warning to management where the objectives are not going to be achieved.

Benchmarking and Inter-firm Comparisons

'Establishment, through data gathering, of targets and comparators that permit relative levels of performance (and particularly areas of underperformance) to be identified'
Benchmarking as defined by CIMA Official Terminology

Benchmarking is a continuing activity where a business or division seeks to copy or become like another successful business and achieve a similar level of success. It involves identifying a successful business or part of a business and using that business as a standard to follow. There are three principal approaches to benchmarking:

1. **Competitor benchmarking** is a process of comparing one's financial performance with that of direct competitors.
2. **Process benchmarking** where data is exchanged between companies with similar operating and administrative systems, with the objective of learning from one another and improving efficiencies.
3. **Strategic benchmarking,** which compares businesses that possess similar organisational structures and implement similar business strategies.

The benefits of competitor benchmarking

The annual report of New Look plc. (a clothing retail chain) for 2002/2003, shows how their cost of sales percentage decreased by 2 per cent. This was credited in the main to efficiencies which came about after benchmarking against better businesses in the sector.

Inter-firm comparison is the process of comparing the performance of different companies, subsidiaries and investment centres. Performance is compared by preparing key accounting ratios to assess the businesses that are performing above average and those that are not. This can provide good control information for managers of poor performing companies to initiate appropriate measures to improve performance. For managers of companies performing above average, the challenge is to try and continue this performance level. To be informative and to ensure management receive realistic control information, inter-firm comparisons require that the comparative process only involves:

1. Businesses within the same sector.
2. Businesses of similar size.
3. Businesses that employ similar accounting policies.

Both benchmarking and inter-firm comparisons are extremely effective ways of appraising and improving the performance of a business. One of the key elements in both procedures is the preparation and interpretation of key financial performance measures.

Key Financial Performance Measures

Financial performance measures are generally expressed as ratios. Ratios measure the relationship between figures and express that relationship as a percentage or ratio. Ratios are useful in that they provide a means of comparison of actual results with:

❑ A budget or desired target.
❑ Ratios of previous years in order to detect trends.
❑ Ratios of other companies or divisions in a benchmarking and inter-firm comparative appraisal process.
❑ Industry norms or indices.

The following pyramid shows the relationship between the various ratios used for evaluating financial performance. This was first developed by the Du Pont organisation in America. It commences with the primary ratio, return on capital employed (ROCE), before dividing it into its two main determinants:

1. Profitability and cost/sales ratios.
2. Capital employed/asset turnover ratios.

Diagram 12.1: *The Du Pont pyramid*

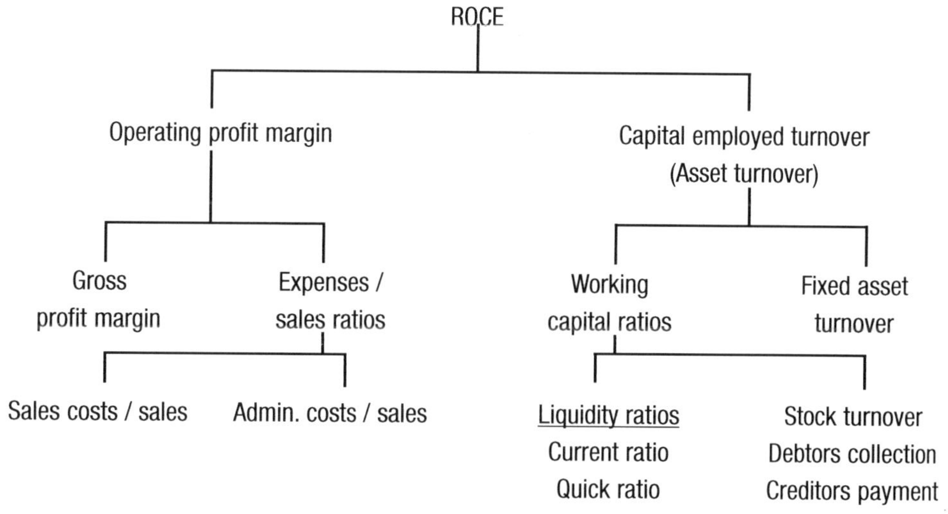

ROCE

Operating profit margin — Capital employed turnover (Asset turnover)

Gross profit margin — Expenses / sales ratios — Working capital ratios — Fixed asset turnover

Sales costs / sales — Admin. costs / sales — Liquidity ratios, Current ratio, Quick ratio — Stock turnover, Debtors collection, Creditors payment

As can be seen from above, the ROCE is made up of two ratios, the operating profit margin and the capital employed turnover ratio. Thus a ROCE of 20 per cent can be due to a net operating margin of 20 per cent multiplied by a capital employed turnover of one. The key ratios identified above are grouped under the following headings:

❑ Profitability.
❑ Efficiency or use of assets.
❑ Liquidity.
❑ Capital structure or gearing.

Ratios Appraising Profitability

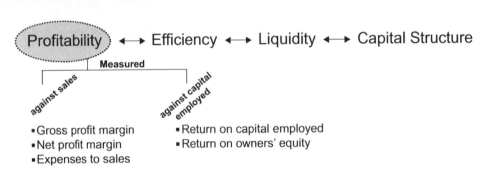

Profit is the excess of revenues over expenses and is the ultimate measure of the success of a business. However the profit figure on its own can only say so much about an organisation. What is more informative to users of accounts is to compare profit with the level of sales and investment required to achieve these profits.

As can be seen from the diagram above, profitability is normally measured in two ways:

1. Against sales.
2. Against capital employed.

The gross profit margin indicates the margin of profit between sales and cost of sales. A gross profit percentage of 60 per cent tells us that for every €100 of sales, a gross profit of €60 is earned and cost of goods sold will amount to €40.

The gross profit percentage can fluctuate and management should be aware of the main reasons for the fluctuation. A fluctuating gross profit percentage can be caused by:

Reduction	Increase
❑ Reduction in selling price. ❑ Increase in the cost price of stock purchases. ❑ Changes in the product sales mix with the business selling a higher proportion of goods with a lower gross profit margin. ❑ Theft of cash or stock. ❑ Waste.	❑ Increase in selling price. ❑ Reduction in cost price of stock purchases. ❑ Changes in the product sales mix with the business selling a higher proportion of goods with a higher gross profit margin.

An increase in sales volume will lead to an increase in gross profit but NOT necessarily to an increase in the gross profit percentage.

The hospitality sales mix

The sales mix represents the mix of products or services that make up the total sales generated by a business. The sales mix within the hotel sector can be made up of revenues from accommodation, bar, restaurant, leisure facilities, and conferencing and banqueting. These elements are all interrelated. For example, revenues from bar and restaurant tend to be dependent on accommodation sales. Accommodation sales are influenced by conference and banqueting functions.

Each element within the sales mix tends to have different pricing strategies and achieves different gross profit margins. For example the gross profit percentage for accommodation can be as high as 90 per cent, whereas restaurants can achieve gross profit margins of between 64 per cent and 68 per cent. The gross profit margin from the sale of beverages can be as high as 70 per cent for nightclubs and high profile bars, however in general it would average around 60 per cent. Obviously management will seek to maximise revenues from accommodation as this provides the highest profit margins and also creates sales in the bar and restaurant functions, as well as other revenue streams such as telephone. Due to the perishability of the accommodation product (one bed-night lost, is lost forever) and the fact that margins are so high, management can stimulate demand by reducing accommodation prices significantly while still making a profit and boosting sales from other revenue streams.

Accommodation sales can be classified according to the type of customer. Thus accommodation sales could be divided into those that relate to business, tourism or recreation, banqueting and tour groups. Business customers would tend to achieve the highest margins whereas tour groups would achieve the lowest. During the 'Celtic Tiger' period, hotel operating profit margins increased by up to 40 per cent due in part to increased business occupancy.

It is important to remember that many companies in the tourism and leisure sector provide services rather than sell a tangible product and thus do not calculate a gross profit and gross profit margin. Examples include sectors such as airlines, accommodation providers, and tour operators.

Operating profit margin	$\dfrac{\text{Operating profit (PBIT)} \times 100}{\text{Sales}}$

The operating profit margin expresses an organisation's operating profit as a percentage of sales. The percentage shows how much a company's sales revenue remains as profit, after all operating expenses have been deducted. Operating profit is the net profit before interest and tax. A fluctuating operating profit margin can be caused by:

Reduction	Increase
❑ Decrease in gross profit margin.	❑ Increase in gross profit margin.
❑ Increase in the expenses to sales percentage.	❑ Decrease in the expenses to sales percentage.

The optimal gross and operating profit percentage will vary from industry to industry. What is of particular importance is that an organisation reviews trends in its gross and operating profit percentages over time and investigates any significant changes.

'People look at 20 per cent margins in the airline business and they assume you are smuggling drugs or doing something naughty with the figures'

A cock-a-hoop Michael O'Leary (CEO Ryanair plc.) after announcing operating margins of 26 per cent in 2002, an increase from 23 per cent in 2001. They reached 36 per cent in 2003.

Source: Siobhan Creaton (2004), *Ryanair*

'We work on the basis that we net 8 per cent of the price of every pint'
Oliver Hughes

Oliver Hughes is the owner of the Porterhouse chain of niche pubs in Dublin and London. He also commented that the net margins in London are far higher than in Dublin at 20 per cent, or 2.5 times the Dublin margins. The main reasons are that staff costs and insurance are significantly higher in Dublin than in London.

Source: *Sunday Times*, 28 November 2004

Expenses to sales	$\dfrac{\text{Expenses} \times 100}{\text{Sales}}$

The expenses to sales ratio examines the amount of sales required to cover the running costs or expenses of the business. It is simply expenses divided by sales expressed as a percentage.

A significant decrease in the operating profit percentage, which is not accompanied by a similar change in the gross profit margin, may indicate that an organisation needs to improve control of its expenses. Any areas where significant increases in expenses have occurred need to be examined. Wages can be an area of particular concern and a review of the level of overtime payments and the grade and numbers of staff employed could be considered.

The expenses to sales percentage can be further analysed by calculating each category of expense to sales, for example, labour costs to sales percentage or advertising to sales percentage as the following diagram illustrates. The expense categories can be further analysed into each element that makes up each category as illustrated under marketing and labour costs below:

Diagram 12.2: *Breakdown of expenses to sales*

Expenses to sales percentage

$\dfrac{\text{Administration}}{\text{Sale}}$	$\dfrac{\text{Marketing costs}}{\text{Sales}}$	$\dfrac{\text{Quality costs}}{\text{Sales}}$	$\dfrac{\text{Labour costs}}{\text{Sales}}$	$\dfrac{\text{Property costs}}{\text{Sales}}$
$\dfrac{\text{Advertising}}{\text{Sales}}$	$\dfrac{\text{Selling expenses}}{\text{Sales}}$	$\dfrac{\text{Recruitment costs}}{\text{Sales}}$	$\dfrac{\text{Staff training}}{\text{Sales}}$	$\dfrac{\text{Salaries}}{\text{Sales}}$

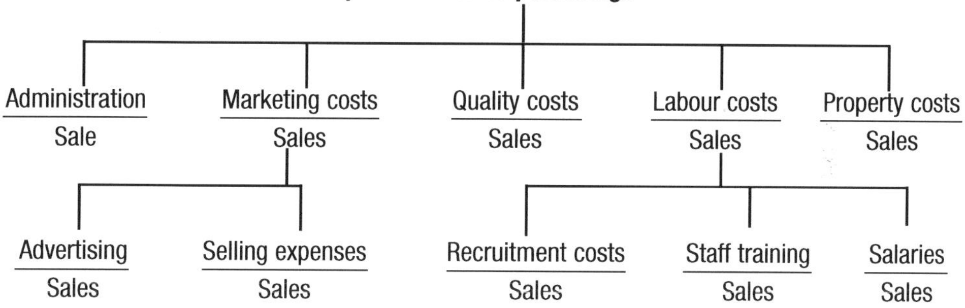

Expenses can also be analysed as a percentage of total expenses as illustrated below.

Diagram 12.3: *Breakdown of expenses to total costs*

Expense items as a percentage of total costs

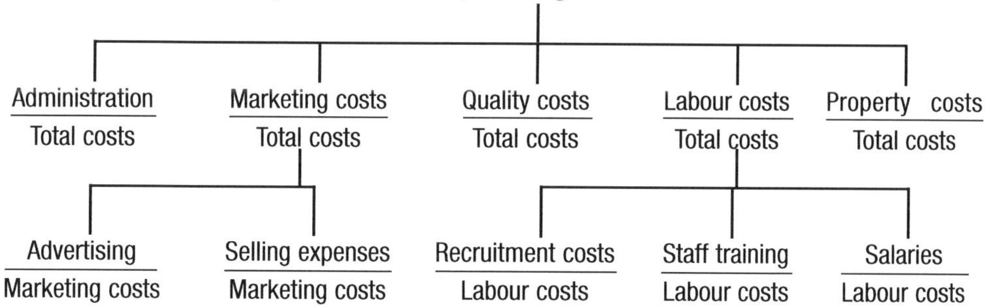

$\dfrac{\text{Administration}}{\text{Total costs}}$	$\dfrac{\text{Marketing costs}}{\text{Total costs}}$	$\dfrac{\text{Quality costs}}{\text{Total costs}}$	$\dfrac{\text{Labour costs}}{\text{Total costs}}$	$\dfrac{\text{Property costs}}{\text{Total costs}}$
$\dfrac{\text{Advertising}}{\text{Marketing costs}}$	$\dfrac{\text{Selling expenses}}{\text{Marketing costs}}$	$\dfrac{\text{Recruitment costs}}{\text{Labour costs}}$	$\dfrac{\text{Staff training}}{\text{Labour costs}}$	$\dfrac{\text{Salaries}}{\text{Labour costs}}$

Expenses can also be analysed by department or cost centre. Also different sectors will use expense efficiency ratios unique to that particular sector. For example within the hospitality, tourism and retail sectors, measures commonly used to analyse expense categories would be:

❑ Cost per square foot.
❑ Cost per employee.

The analysis of costs is a very important part of the control function of management. Essential to this analysis is the ability to trace costs to departments and cost centres and to identify at an early stage those costs that are out of line with cost target. This is done by analysing and comparing the above ratios to previous years, to industry norms and to budget targets.

RAI Gross profit margins

According to the Restaurants Association of Ireland (RAI), the average gross profit margin achieved by restaurants in Ireland was 64.4 per cent, with operating margins at 3.5 per cent.

The association's 'Do you know' card, published in June 2005 outlines the following average expense percentages:

	Percentage of sales net of VAT
Food and drink	35.6
Wages and salaries	35.6
Overheads	25.3
Total expenses	96.5

Return on capital employed (ROCE)

$$\frac{\text{Net profit (PBIT)} \times 100}{\text{Capital employed}}$$

This ratio measures the net profit before interest and tax (operating return) that a business is achieving for the total amount of capital employed (both equity and debt). Capital employed is defined as *'share capital plus reserves plus loan capital'*. It can also be calculated as *'fixed assets plus current assets less current liabilities'*. Effectively it is the total capital required to finance the assets of the business. Net profit before interest and tax is the operating profit of the business that is attributable to the total capital employed (debt and equity) in the business. Return on capital employed is the return before any payments are made to providers of capital (loan interest and dividends) and the Revenue Commissioners (corporation tax).

The ROCE is an important measure of profitability for a number of reasons.

1. The ultimate measure of a business' profitability and sustainability is whether it can consistently achieve high returns on its capital employed. If this is achieved, then the business is, in effect, creating real shareholder wealth, which is the ultimate objective of a business.
2. It can serve as a guide to the company and to potential investors in assessing a possible acquisition and in considering the start up of new activities. If their potential ROCE is not attractive they should be avoided. Similarly, a persistently low ROCE in any part of the business suggests it could be a candidate for disposal if it is not an integral part of the business.

The calculation of capital employed can be quite complex and different companies calculate it in different ways. Some companies include short-term loans and overdrafts as part of the capital employed and some do not. Others deduct cash balances from the overdrafts before including them in capital employed. Some include government grants, others do not. Ultimately one should state clearly the basis on which the ratio is calculated to ensure the same basis is used when making inter-firm comparisons.

Return on owners' equity before tax (ROOE)	$\dfrac{\text{Net profit before tax} \times 100}{\text{Shareholders' funds}}$
or	
Return on owners' equity after tax	$\dfrac{\text{Net profit after tax} \times 100}{\text{Shareholders' funds}}$

The ROOE assesses the return before tax for the ordinary (equity) shareholders alone. Thus we exclude loan capital or debt finance from the denominator and for the numerator we deduct loan interest charges from net profit before interest and tax. This ensures we only take account of the profit before tax available to equity shareholders. This ratio should also be calculated using profit after tax, as this is the overall return or profit that belongs to shareholders. It is important to point out that ROOE after tax is of more interest to shareholders than management, as management have little input and control over tax liability computations.

Both ratios (ROCE and ROOE) indicate how efficiently an organisation is using the resources invested in it, expressing its profit as a percentage of the capital employed to achieve that profit. It is important for investors to compare their return on capital with other returns within the industry. How high the return should be is really a matter of opinion for the investor. It depends on a number of factors such as the current economic situation, other investment opportunities available to the investor, the current expected returns from the sector concerned and the risk of the company. The following table should be used as a rule of thumb:

Percentage return	Comment
< 5 per cent	Poor
Between 5 and 10 per cent	Fair
Between 10 and 15 per cent	Good
Greater than 15 per cent	Excellent

Ryanair – The envy of the world

By the year 2000, Ryanair was one of the most profitable airline companies in the world. Its ROCE in 2003 reached 18 per cent with every indication this would improve even further. These figures were the envy of the air-travel sector. Ryanair achieved these returns through the successful implementation of the following strategies:

1. **Good investment strategies:** This was implemented through the purchase of new efficient aeroplanes at low cost. The September 11 crisis hit airlines and aircraft manufacturers very hard. During this period Ryanair decided to place an order for 100 new Boeing 737 aircraft with options for 50 more. As Boeing were desperate to get the contract (Boeing had just laid off 30,000 workers worldwide) it was speculated that Ryanair managed to negotiate a discount of between 30 per cent and 50 per cent off the 'catalogue price' which amounted to $9.1 billion.

2. **Utilising assets more efficiently:** This policy of working assets harder to increase sales was achieved through perfecting the 25 minute turnaround of aircraft at airports. This could only be achieved at uncongested airports and this time efficiency allowed the company to schedule two more flights per day per aircraft.

3. **Maximising operating margins:** Ryanair achieved operating margins of 23 per cent in 2002 and this increased to 36 per cent in 2003. These record margins could not be matched even with other successful low cost airlines such as Southwest airlines, which achieved margins of between 15 per cent and 19 per cent in periods of economic growth. These margins were achieved through the following:
   - ❑ The development of their on-line booking service which ensures no commissions need to be paid to travel agents.
   - ❑ The strict no refunds policy to customers for delayed or cancelled flights.
   - ❑ The policy of flying into obscure airports, which ensures much lower airport landing charges.
   - ❑ The 'no-frills' policy and the 'pay for everything' policy while flying ensure lower costs and higher revenues. For example in 1998, cabin crew were alerted to Ryanair's 'ice ban' in a memo that explained how the initiative would save the airline £40,000 per year. This was due to a dispute with Ryanair's supplier Gate Gourmet who were attempting to put up their charges. Ryanair did not want to accede to this as it would only encourage other suppliers to do the same. The dispute was eventually resolved, the ice flowed again and according to Ryanair, there were no increased payouts to Gate Gourmet.

❑ Staff numbers kept to a minimum, with just two flight attendants serving passengers on each 130-seater flight.

❑ Dispensing with air-bridges ensured further cost savings. Passengers now had to walk onto the tarmac and climb the steps onto the plane.

Ratios Appraising Management Efficiency

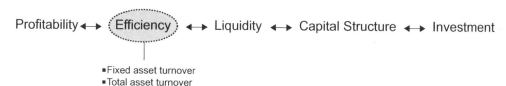

Profitability ⟷ (Efficiency) ⟷ Liquidity ⟷ Capital Structure ⟷ Investment

- Fixed asset turnover
- Total asset turnover
- Stock turnover/stock days
- Debtors days
- Creditors days

Several ratios are used to indicate how efficiently an organisation is utilising its assets. Assets generate sales and profits and the more efficiently assets are used, the greater the level of sales and profits for a business. It is also important that a business has an appropriate level of investment in assets for the level of business it can generate. For example, a 500 bedroom hotel in a remote area may not be able to sustain the occupancy levels required for such investment. Management may be unable to generate enough sales to cover costs and make the required return on such assets.

The following are the main ratios used to evaluate management's efficiency in utilising the assets of the business.

Fixed asset turnover

$$\frac{\text{Sales}}{\text{Fixed assets}}$$

The fixed asset turnover compares sales with the fixed assets that generated the sales and measures the utilisation a firm is obtaining from its investment in fixed assets. It indicates how much each €1 invested in fixed assets generates in sales. In general, a higher ratio of sales to fixed assets indicates that fixed assets are being utilised more efficiently.

Capital employed turnover (total asset turnover)

$$\frac{\text{Sales}}{\text{Capital employed}}$$

This ratio is calculated in the same way as the fixed asset turnover except capital employed is used. Capital employed is calculated as *'fixed assets plus current assets less current liabilities'* or alternatively, *'share capital plus reserves plus loan capital'*. As per the fixed asset ratio, it shows the amount of sales generated per €1 invested in the total assets of the company.

This ratio is an important determinant of ROCE. The overall return on a business is made up of two essential components which are the operating margin (operating profit ÷ sales) and the capital employed turnover (sales ÷ capital employed).

$$\text{ROCE} = \frac{\text{Operating profit}}{\text{Capital employed}} = \frac{\text{NPBIT}}{\text{Sales}} \times \frac{\text{Sales}}{\text{Capital employed}}$$

N.B. *Operating profit represents the net profit before interest and tax*

A ROCE of 20 per cent could be due to the fact that the company makes an operating profit margin of 10 per cent, and for every €1 invested in the company, it generates €2 sales. Thus the company makes a return of 20 per cent per €1 invested.

$$\text{Stock turnover} \quad \frac{\text{Cost of sales}}{\text{Average stock}} \qquad \text{Stock days} \quad \frac{\text{Average stock} \times 365}{\text{Cost of sales}}$$

One ratio is simply the inverse of the other and is just a different way of expressing the same thing. Stock turnover is a measure of how many times stock is sold during an accounting period. It can be measured in terms of the number of days it takes to sell stock or the number of times stock is sold in a period.

For example, if it takes a company on average 30 days to sell its stock (stock days) then its stock turnover rate is 12 times per annum.

A fluctuating stock turnover ratio indicates the following:

Decrease in stock turnover	Increase in stock turnover
❏ A fall in sales demand.	❏ An increase in sales demand.
❏ A policy to increase stock levels.	❏ A policy to lower stock levels.

It is important to be mindful that as well as tying up an organisation's resources, holding unnecessarily high levels of stock is expensive in terms of storage, insurance and security. Also the longer an organisation holds stock, the greater the risk that the stock will perish or become obsolete. Thus companies should have a policy which minimises stock holding while at the same time ensuring no stock–outs occur.

In calculating the stock turnover ratio it is important to use the stock figure that is representative of the average stock held during the year. If stock is seasonally high or low at the balance sheet date, then the ratio may be distorted, thus the average stock figure may have to be computed. Average stock is calculated as opening stock plus closing stock divided by two. If it is impossible to calculate the average stock, the closing stock figure can be used.

What is Stock?

Hotels, airlines and tour bus companies all deal in stock that is classified as fixed assets. A hotel's largest stock is its stock of bedrooms which it rents out. This stock is classified as a fixed asset. The same applies to airlines and tour bus companies that sell or rent out seats.

This is in marked contrast to the retail sector that deals in 'goods' that are classified as current assets. This is because once the item is sold it does not belong to the company whereas for hotels, airlines and tour bus companies they rent out the rooms or seats.

Debtors days

$$\frac{\text{Trade debtors x 365}}{\text{Credit sales}}$$

The debtors collection period (debtors days) indicates the average number of days between a credit sale taking place and an organisation receiving payment from a customer. The shorter the collection period the better, since liquidity will improve and the risk of bad debts will be reduced. Credit control is essential in an organisation, especially one that has a high proportion of credit sales. If debtors take too long to pay, an organisation will struggle to meet its own credit payments as they fall due. The ratio refers to trade debtors (customers) not to loan debtors. If the credit sales figure is not available, then one should use the total sales figure.

Decrease in debtors days	Increase in debtors days
❑ Risk of bad debts reduce. ❑ Liquidity improves.	❑ Risk of bad debts increase. ❑ Liquidity may worsen. ❑ Better control over debtors is required.

Creditors days

$$\frac{\text{Trade creditors x 365}}{\text{Credit purchases}}$$

The creditors payment period (creditors days) shows the average number of days that a business takes to pay its suppliers for goods purchased on credit. Although some organisations see trade credit as an interest free form of funding (with no collateral involved), it does in fact have a cost. Delays in paying suppliers will result in an organisation foregoing discounts for prompt payment. Trade creditors are used for this ratio, not loan creditors or preferential creditors i.e. VAT and PAYE/PRSI. Should the credit purchases figure not be available then one should use the total purchases or cost of goods sold figure. It is important to keep in mind that to maintain supplier's goodwill, a company should try to pay its bills reasonably promptly.

Decrease in creditors days	Increase in creditors days
❑ Paying suppliers quicker and availing of discounts. ❑ Goodwill of suppliers is maintained. ❑ Losing a form of interest free credit.	❑ Taking longer to pay suppliers and not availing of discounts. ❑ Risk of losing the goodwill of suppliers. ❑ Are there liquidity issues?

Ratios Appraising Liquidity

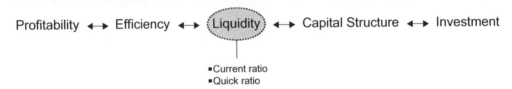

Profitability ⟷ Efficiency ⟷ Liquidity ⟷ Capital Structure ⟷ Investment

- Current ratio
- Quick ratio

Liquidity refers to the ability of a company to meet its liabilities as they fall due. It is not uncommon for a business, which on paper is making a profit, to experience severe liquidity problems. There are two key ratios to calculate when appraising liquidity, the current ratio and the quick–acid test ratio.

Current ratio $$\frac{\text{Current assets}}{\text{Current liabilities}}$$

The current ratio measures a business' ability to pay its debts over a 6–12 month period. There is no standard or recommended current ratio (except the standard text book conservative rule of thumb of 2 times (2:1), mainly recommended for wholesale businesses) since it will vary depending upon the sector in which the organisation operates. The following table outlines the current ratio norms for various business sectors.

Expected sector liquidity ratios

Industry Type	Current ratio
Manufacturing	2.5 – 4.5 : 1
Wholesalers	2 : 1
Retail, including supermarkets	0.8 : 1
Hotels, restaurants, fast food	0.4 : 1

Generally, manufacturing and wholesalers will have higher current ratios due to the high levels of stock and debtors that are the norm for these sectors. Retail outlets and hotels operate with lower current ratios due to the low levels of stock and debtors that apply in these sectors. In such organisations, cash, and not credit is the currency and hence low current ratios are the norm.

Quick-acid test ratio $$\frac{\text{Current assets} - \text{stock}}{\text{Current liabilities}}$$

This ratio measures a business' ability to pay its debts immediately i.e. within a few weeks. It thus ignores stock and concentrates upon those assets which can be converted into cash quickly. In the event of severe liquidity difficulties, an organisation can encourage debtors to pay more quickly, while short-term investments can be sold and converted into cash. However, stock takes longer to convert and thus is excluded from the ratio. Once again the minimum safe ratio will vary from sector to sector. As hotels, restaurants and fast food outlets can operate with low stock levels, there is often no significant difference between the quick and current ratios of these business types. Football clubs are other organisations that operate with low current and quick ratios for exactly the same reason. Tottenham Hotspur's current ratio is normally around 0.17: 1. **Note:** *The ratio can also be simply expressed as 0.17.*

A current or acid test ratio that differs significantly to that of other organisations of similar size and nature might indicate a number of problems and should be investigated further.

❏ Ratios significantly lower than those of other organisations within the same sector can indicate the organisation is too dependent upon short-term borrowings (creditors, bank overdrafts, short-term loans) for the funding of its day to day operations.

❏ High current and acid test ratios indicate that cash flow is not a problem, however they might suggest that an organisation is not using its resources as efficiently as it could be. This can result in lower than expected rate of return, displeasing current and potential shareholders.

   – High liquidity ratios can indicate consistently high cash and bank balances which may need to be invested elsewhere to gain a higher return.

   – High liquidity ratios can indicate excessively high stock levels which may prompt management to improve their system of stock control, or may help to identify slow moving or obsolete items which require revaluation (lowering of cost and net realisable value).

   – High liquidity ratios can indicate poor credit control and the need for management intervention to review its credit control policy and minimise the threat of bad debts. This would not be a problem however for cash based businesses.

A business should maintain its working capital elements at optimum levels. This implies that stock levels should be kept to a minimum to reduce costs and risk of deterioration. Debt should be collected promptly, mindful of not losing customer goodwill, and cash should not lie idle in a current account. If a company's liquidity ratios are too high, resources, which should be invested in income-producing fixed assets, are invested in non-productive stock and debtors and high cash balances. It is the equivalent of an individual investing their savings in a current account that earns no interest compared to a long-term deposit account that earns a fixed rate of interest.

Ratios Appraising Capital Structure

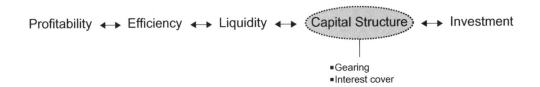

Every business must decide how it is to finance its fixed assets and working capital requirements. In general, this is down to a choice (after grant aid) between debt or equity, or a mixture of both. Debt is where finance is borrowed from third parties who are not owners of the business. Equity relates to the owner's contribution or investment in the business. Capital structure measures the funding mix of a business. At this stage it is important to be aware of the characteristics of both debt and equity funding. The following points should be understood:

❑ Each source of finance has a cost to it. Interest is the cost of debt while dividends are the cost of equity.

❑ Debt as a source of finance is cheaper than equity for a business. This is due to the following reasons:

  – Loan interest is tax deductible (reduces the tax charge on profits) whereas dividends are not. In other words, loan interest reduces profits on which taxes are based, thus reducing the tax liability. Dividends are paid out of profits after tax and thus have no effect on the tax liability.

  – Loan interest is paid for the term of the loan whereas dividends are paid forever.

  – Equity shareholders take a greater risk than providers of debt capital. In theory, they require a greater return for taking that risk. It is important to remember that profit is a payment for risk-taking.

❑ Debt is a riskier source of finance for the business because when a company experiences difficult trading conditions and cash flow is a problem, debt interest still has to be paid. On the other hand, dividends can be deferred or cancelled. Also at some stage, debt will need to be repaid whereas equity will not.

Financing through debt	Financing through equity
❏ Interest must be paid on the debt. ❏ Interest is tax deductible. ❏ Debt generally cheaper. ❏ Debt is risky because interest must be paid. ❏ Loan must be repaid.	❏ Dividends will be paid to shareholders. ❏ Dividends are not tax deductible. ❏ Equity requires higher returns to compensate for the extra risk. ❏ The rate of dividend is at discretion of management and may be deferred. ❏ Equity does not require repayment.

Investors, potential investors and other lenders will be particularly interested in an organisation's long-term funding arrangements. The higher the ratio of debt to equity, the more dependent the organisation is upon borrowed funds and the greater the risk that it will be unable to meet interest payments on these funds as they fall due. This is what is known as financial risk (as distinct from commercial risk) and is measured through the gearing ratio.

$$\text{Gearing ratio – debt to equity} \quad \frac{\text{Fixed interest debt}}{\text{Shareholders funds}}$$

The term fixed interest debt includes preference share capital, debentures, loan capital, and any leasing liabilities. Bank overdrafts and short-term loans may be included on the assumption that the bank overdrafts are effectively a permanent source of finance and that short-term loans may be renewed or replaced when they mature. If short-term loans and bank overdrafts are included as part of debt, then any existing cash balances should be deducted from debt to get the *net debt*. Capital and reserves are normally taken as equity share capital and reserves. For example, if fixed interest debt is €200,000 and equity capital is €300,000 then the gearing ratio is €200,000 divided by €300,000 which equals 0.67:1 or 67 per cent. If one measures gearing as a proportion of total capital (debt + equity), then the ratio is €200,000 divided by €500,000 which equals 40 per cent. This text will concentrate on the debt to equity ratio and the following table acts as a guide to interpreting this ratio.

Low Gearing = debt is less than capital and reserves ⇒ less than 100%
High Gearing = debt is greater than capital and reserves ⇒ greater than 100%

Effect of property revaluations

The hotel sector would be characterised by having high value properties in their balance sheets. Once a company decides to value its properties at current value, these assets must be revalued over time. The effect of a revaluation is to increase property asset values and to show this profit as an unrealised reserve in the balance sheet. Thus assets and shareholders' funds increase as a result of a revaluation. According to FRS 15, a full property valuation is required at least every five years and must involve an external qualified valuer. Should a significant revaluation occur, this can significantly reduce the following key ratios:

❑ ROCE and ROOE.

❑ Capital employed turnover and the fixed asset turnover.

❑ Debt to equity ratio.

It is important when interpreting ratios that revaluations of property assets do not distort the trend analysis. Thus it is important to be aware of the effects of revaluations on key ratios.

Another ratio that helps assess the appropriate level of debt for a business is the interest cover ratio.

$$\text{Interest cover} \qquad \frac{\text{Operating profit (PBIT)}}{\text{Interest}}$$

Interest cover indicates how many times interest payments on debt are covered by profit before interest and tax. The higher the interest cover, the less likely that interest payments will not be met and hence the lower the level of financial risk associated with the organisation. If the interest cover is low, there is a greater chance that a decline in profits will result in either:

1. Interest payments not being met.
2. Profits available for distribution to shareholders being very small resulting in small or zero dividend payments.

Financial institutions generally require a minimum level of cover of 3 times. If lenders were not happy with the capital structure ratios calculated (in other words they are too high), an organisation would find it difficult to raise additional, long-term finance or would have to pay a premium (risk premium) for such funds in the form of higher interest rates.

BWG sells Bargain Booze chain for €93m to clear debts

Spar owner BWG has cleared its debts after realising £63.5m (€93m) from the sale of its Cheshire based, off-license chain, Bargain Booze, to ECI partners. Although the price was well below the £70–£80m range mooted last June, chief executive Leo Crawford stated *'we are pleased with the sale. It strengthens our balance sheet and leaves us effectively debt free.'* Bargain Booze is the second largest off-license chain in Britain with 565 stores. The chain had wholesale sales of £329 million in 2004 generating profits of £8 million. BWG signaled last March that Bargain Booze was not core to its strategy and that it wanted to concentrate on its food distribution and retail business.

Source: *Irish Times*, 17 January 2006

Key Operating Ratios – Hospitality Sector

Every business sector will have its own specific or unique performance measurements. The hospitality sector is no different, with a number of key ratios or measurements that are important in comparing performance within the industry. The following are the key efficiency or operating ratios unique to the hospitality industry.

Name	Calculation	Meaning/Use/Interpretation
Occupancy ratios 1	$\dfrac{\text{Rooms occupied} \times 100}{\text{Rooms available}}$	Where a hotel has 100 rooms of which 65 are occupied, then the occupancy ratio is 65 per cent. The ratio is important when comparing the performance of a hotel from year to year or in an inter-firm comparative analysis. Its main criticism is that it does not take into account price per room, as this has a direct effect on the occupancy levels of a hotel.
2	$\dfrac{\text{Number of guests} \times 100}{\text{Guest capacity}}$	This occupancy ratio measures guest capacity to the number of guests staying in the hotel. It is

		considered to be more accurate than 1 above as it takes into account the possibility that some double rooms could be sold as single.
3	$\dfrac{\text{Actual room revenue} \times 100}{\text{Potential room revenue}}$	This is known as room sales potential and takes into account the lowering of prices to boost occupancy. Thus a hotel with a high occupancy level could have a low room sales potential due to the lowering of prices to boost occupancy.
Average room rate (ARR)	$\dfrac{\text{Annual room revenue}}{\text{Rooms occupied} \times 365}$	This ratio measures the relationship between room sales and the number of rooms occupied. It gives an average room sales rate.
Revenue per available room (RevPAR)	$\dfrac{\text{Annual rooms revenue}}{\text{Rooms available} \times 365}$ or ARR x Occupancy rate	Both formulae will calculate RevPAR which is considered a more important ratio than the ARR as it takes into account the occupancy levels of a hotel. For example, a guest house of 10 rooms with an average occupancy of 70 per cent achieves, on average, daily sales of €700. The ARR equals €100 (€700 ÷ 7). RevPAR equals €100 x 70 per cent = €70 or alternatively this could be calculated as €700 ÷ 10 = €70. A hotel may have a high ARR and a low RevPAR due to the company not achieving its occupancy rates in part due to the high ARR.
Average rate per guest	$\dfrac{\text{Room revenue}}{\text{Number of guests}}$	This gives the average rate per guest staying in the hotel and again is essential in interpreting any occupancy ratios, as the rate may fall in order to boost room sales.

Average spend	$$\frac{\text{Sales}}{\text{Number of covers}}$$	This is a useful ratio for restaurants as it calculates the average spend per cover/customer. This can be done separately for lunch and dinner (à la carte) menus. It is an important ratio in terms of budgeting and planning.
Sales mix	$$\frac{\text{Rooms revenue x 100}}{\text{Total hotel revenue}}$$ $$\frac{\text{Food revenue x 100}}{\text{Total hotel revenue}}$$ $$\frac{\text{Bar revenue x 100}}{\text{Total hotel revenue}}$$	This tells us the percentage of total sales that is made up from room revenue, restaurant revenue, bar revenue and any other revenue streams a hotel may have.
Total sales per room **Sales per seat** **Sales per employee** **Operating profit per employee**	$$\frac{\text{Total hotel revenue}}{\text{Room sales}}$$ $$\frac{\text{Total restaurant revenue}}{\text{No. of seats}}$$ $$\frac{\text{Total sales}}{\text{No. of employees}}$$ $$\frac{\text{Operating profit}}{\text{No. of employees}}$$	These ratios are generally used to spot trends in hotel or restaurant revenue. They make up part of the performance statistics for the business and can be quite useful in measuring performance and forecasting sales.
Labour costs as a percentage of sales	$$\frac{\text{Labour costs x 100}}{\text{Sales}}$$	This indicates the extent to which revenue is being absorbed by staff costs. As labour costs are mostly fixed, this ratio will fall as the business experiences an increase in sales. The ratio will increase as sales fall.

Ratios such as occupancy rates, average spend, revenue per available room (RevPAR) and average room rate (ARR) can help explain changes in asset turnover and profit margin ratios and thus help explain a fluctuating ROCE. These ratios provide management with more relevant information to inform decision-making. Example 12.1 illustrates.

Example 12.1: *Operating ratios for hotels*

The directors of Joshua Hotels Ltd are concerned about the falling ROCE between 2004 and 2005. The hotel achieved a ROCE of 17.6 per cent in 2004 but that has fallen to 15.94 per cent in 2005. The following key financial indicators have been provided by the financial controller.

Explain in as much detail as possible, reasons for the falling ROCE.

	2005	2004
Operating profit margin	24%	30%
Gross profit margin	66%	70%
Expenses to sales percentage	40%	38%
Capital employed (total asset) turnover	0.664	0.585
Occupancy	76.67%	68.3%
ARR	€75	€85
RevPAR	€57.5	€58.06
Room sales as a percentage of total sales	73%	75%
Labour costs as a percentage of total sales	33%	30%
Profit per employee	€7,250	€7,900

Approach

From the data given, ROCE has fallen from 17.6 per cent to 15.9 per cent, a fall of 1.7 per cent. The first step is to break the ROCE into its two component parts, capital employed turnover and operating profit. The capital employed turnover ratios have improved, however the operating profit margin fell from 30 per cent to 24 per cent. From the data given, the main reasons for this fall are:

❑ The fall in the gross profit percentage from 70 per cent to 66 per cent. The main reasons for this are:
   – The company not maintaining its average room rate of €85. The average room rate fell to €75. This resulted in a reduced gross profit percentage and will affect the operating profit margin. Management must ascertain why this has occurred and assess how to rectify the situation. Although the average room rate fell by 12 per cent (10 ÷ 85), RevPAR fell by only 1 per cent suggesting that occupancy rates improved due, in part, to the lower ARR.
   – The room sales as a percentage of total sales has fallen from 75 per cent to 73 per cent. Room sales are the most profitable part of a hotel's sales mix and thus any proportionate change can reduce gross and operating profit margins.

❑ The expenses to sales percentage has increased from 38 per cent to 40 per cent. From the information given, labour costs have increased from 30 per cent of sales to 33 per cent. Labour cost makes up a major part of the expenses to sales percentage and this is the main reason for the increase in the expenses to sales percentage. This is further backed up by a fall in the profit per employee ratio from €7,900 to €7,250.

On the positive side, the capital employed turnover ratio has improved and the company is achieving more sales from capital employed. This is also reflected in the increased occupancy ratio, which was possibly influenced through the reduced average room rate. Ultimately, management must reassess its pricing strategy to maximise profit per room and at the same time maintain occupancy levels. Labour costs must also be examined to assess value and efficiency.

Key financial performance indicators for hotels

According to research by Smullan and O'Donoghue (2005) into *'the use and influence of financial support decision models within the Irish hospitality sector'*, the following financial performance indicators were considered the most commonly used.

1. Labour cost as a percentage of sales.
2. Occupancy rate and percentage change in turnover.
3. Operating margins.
4. Operating cost as a percentage of sales.
5. Average room rate and RevPAR.
6. Return on investment.

These findings are backed up by research undertaken by Flanagan into *'performance measurement practices of Irish hotel companies (2005)'*, which showed that the main financial performance indicators used were:

1. Growth in sales measured on a daily basis.
2. Costs as a percentage of sales, which are measured on a weekly or monthly basis.
3. Operating margins, which are measured on a monthly basis.

The research however clearly showed that the preparation and analysis of key financial ratios is only one element of financial performance appraisal within the hotel sector. The use of budgets and the calculation of variances are the most popular financial performance evaluation tools used in the sector.

Key Operating Ratios – Retail Sector

Diagram 12.4 illustrates a pyramid of ratios that relate specifically to the retail sector. The pyramid shows the various profitability and asset turnover ratios relevant to the sector. As with any business, the pyramid starts with the return on assets (ROCE) and analyses it into its two component parts, namely profitability and capital employed turnover. The total expenses can be further categorised according to type or department.

Diagram 12.4: *Ratio pyramid for a retailer*

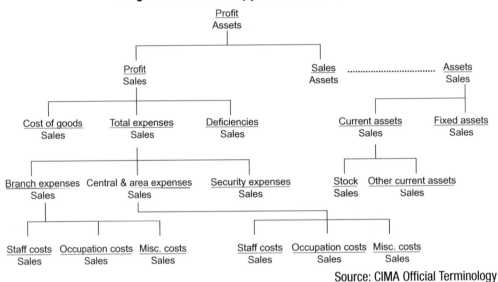

Source: CIMA Official Terminology

In addition to the ratio pyramid presented above, there are a number of other operating ratios, unique to the retail sector, that assist in assessing the performance of a retail outlet, as the following table illustrates:

Additional ratios used in the retail sector

Ratio	Formula	Use
Sales per square foot	$\dfrac{\text{Sales revenue}}{\text{Sales floor area}}$	This ratio is particularly useful in assessing the performance of different branches.
Operating profit per square foot	$\dfrac{\text{Operating profit}}{\text{Sales floor area}}$	Useful in assessing the profitability of different branches.
Sales per checkout	$\dfrac{\text{Sales revenue}}{\text{Number of checkouts}}$	Useful in assessing if the retail outlet has an acceptable number of checkouts.
Sales per assistant	$\dfrac{\text{Sales revenue}}{\text{Number of staff}}$	Useful in judging labour productivity.
Stock turnover	$\dfrac{\text{Cost of sales}}{\text{Average stock}}$	An important measure in establishing how effective an organisation is in managing stock and converting stock into cash.

These ratios provide additional measures for evaluating the operating efficiency and the performance of a retail outlet as illustrated in example 12.2.

Example 12.2: *Retail ratios*

The details presented below relate to B&M Department Stores.

	2005	2004
Sales revenue	€87,500,000	€83,200,000
Cost of sales	€56,875,000	€54,100,000
Operating profit	€13,125,000	€12,150,000
Average stoc	€8,500,000	€8,300,000
Square feet	180,000	180,000
Number of checkouts	40	40
Number of shop assistants	165	169

Calculate key operating performance measures for B&M that relate to the retail sector.

Approach

The figures given in the example can be applied to the formulae presented above to arrive at the ratios for the year.

		2005		2004	
Operating profit margin	$\dfrac{\text{Net profit x 100}}{\text{Sales}}$	$\dfrac{13{,}125 \times 100}{87{,}500}$	= 15%	$\dfrac{12{,}150 \times 100}{83{,}200}$	= 14.6%
Sales per square foot	$\dfrac{\text{Sales revenue}}{\text{Sales floor area}}$	$\dfrac{87{,}500}{180}$	= €486.11	$\dfrac{83{,}200}{180}$	= €462.22
Operating profit per square foot	$\dfrac{\text{Operating profit}}{\text{Sales floor area}}$	$\dfrac{13{,}125}{180}$	= €72.92	$\dfrac{12{,}150}{180}$	= €67.50
Sales per checkout	$\dfrac{\text{Sales revenue}}{\text{No. of checkouts}}$	$\dfrac{87{,}500}{40}$	= €2,187.50	$\dfrac{83{,}200}{40}$	= €2,080
Sales per assistant	$\dfrac{\text{Sales revenue}}{\text{No. of staff}}$	$\dfrac{87{,}500}{165}$	= €530.30	$\dfrac{83{,}200}{169}$	= €492.31
Stock turnover	$\dfrac{\text{Cost of sales}}{\text{Average stock}}$	$\dfrac{56{,}875}{8{,}500}$	= 6.7 times	$\dfrac{54{,}100}{8{,}300}$	= 6.5 times

Overall the performance has improved in 2005. Both sales revenue and operating profit have increased by 5 per cent and 8 per cent respectively. This is reflected in increases in both sales and operating profit per square foot as there was no increase in floor area. Similarly, there is a healthy increase in sales per checkout due entirely to the increase in sales revenue. The increase in sales per assistant is due to the increase in revenue, as well as the reduction in the number of assistants employed. There is also improved efficiency in handling stock, with stock turnover increasing from 6.5 to 6.7 times.

Many of the ratios presented in the retail pyramid and in the example above are calculated and used by internal management in assessing the operating efficiency of the organisation. These ratios are predominantly management operating ratios which help management in identifying areas where efficiencies and improvements can be made. They ultimately help to ensure costs are controlled and cost value is maximised and reflected in the overall return on capital ratios. These ratios are not available to shareholders and other external users of accounts.

Setting a Context for Financial Statement Analysis

When analysing and comparing financial statements of businesses, one should always keep in mind the following factors that provide a context from which to analyse the financial statements.

The age of the business: Any young business is quite vulnerable to the many internal and external factors or shocks that can occur. Many young businesses are highly financed by debt and will be vulnerable to interest rate and exchange rate movements as they try to develop a brand name and reputation. Providers of finance are known to add a premium to the loan interest charge for young companies as they would view them as high risk. It stands to reason that a new business, compared to an established business, will always have a greater level of business risk.

The size of the business: The larger the business, the less vulnerable it is to external factors. Providers of finance will always ensure cheaper finance for a sound large company in existence for a number of years, as they would perceive the business risk to be less. Also larger businesses may have diversified their investments and this again protects them or reduces their business risk.

Xtra-vision Diversifies

Sales at Xtra-vision, Ireland's biggest DVD and video rental chain, rose by 25 per cent last year to €89m as the company diversified into providing snacks, mobile phones, computer games and computer electronics. A small number of stores also sell DVD players, televisions, camcorders and home cinema systems. Pre-tax profits rose by 17 per cent to €7.5m ensuring a net profit before tax margin on sales of 8.4 per cent. Xtra-vision, one of the high flyers of the 1980s with more than 300 stores, now operates from 147 stores.

Source: *Sunday Times,* 12 December 2004

The economic and political environment: The economy both local and global, inflation, exchange rates and interest rates, all affect a business. Should the euro strengthen against the dollar or sterling then tourism will be affected as it becomes more expensive for tourists to travel. If an economy has spiralling inflation then the products and services produced in the economy will have a high cost base and thus will not be competitive in comparison to other countries. From a tourism and business perspective, this can ensure reduced tourist numbers and reduced direct foreign investment. Any country experiencing political upheaval and uncertainty will always find it difficult to entice business and tourism investment. In interpreting any financial statements, one must take into account the prevailing economic and political circumstances. The effects of the 11 September terrorist attacks have to be taken into account when comparing a company's performance over the period 1999 to 2003. The effects of inflation must be taken into account when looking at a company's performance over a few years. For countries experiencing high inflation, any profit made could be wiped out in real terms.

'The Travel Agents feel the Chill'

Despite Stein Travel having a healthy trade in flight only packages to Alicante and Malaga, their accounts for the 12 months ended 31 October 2003 showed a fall in turnover of almost 20 per cent to €47.1m from €57.1m in 2002. The company went from a pre-tax profit of €3.4m in 2002 to a pre-tax loss of €1.8m. Possible reasons given for this decrease were:

❑ Increased competition with Aer Lingus offering direct flights to Alicante and Malaga.

❑ The number of people who have bought second homes abroad and who offer them to friends and family has hit the core package holiday market.

Source: *Sunday Tribune*, 17 October 2004

Industry Trends: Technology innovation and deregulation are just two examples of industry trends. In the hospitality industry, technological innovations such as central reservation systems (CRS) have ensured that unless they keep up with international industry trends, businesses can be left behind. In interpreting any financial statements, one must be aware of the trends and pressures within the specific industry. For example the increased phenomenon of disintermediation (booking holidays direct and leaving out the middle-man e.g. travel agents) presents new challenges to travel agents and tour operators. The increased popularity and success of low-cost airlines and the success of the low-cost Jurys Inns model point to changes within the hospitality, travel and tourism sectors. According to Fáilte Ireland's end of year review for 2005, 21 per cent of B&Bs closed during the period 1999 to 2004 with the main reason given as increased competition due to the growth in low cost hotel accommodation.

'Don't just blame the internet'

Profits at JWT, the biggest Irish owned tour operator and travel agent, more than halved in 2003 as increasing numbers of holiday-makers booked their flights and accommodation direct from airlines and hotels via the internet. The firm suffered a 14 per cent slump in sales with accounts for the year to the 31 December 2003 showing pre-tax profits falling to €136,596 from €283,814 in 2002. However it is not only the internet that is to blame. Travel agents have also felt the heat as Aer Lingus and Ryanair slashed the commissions they pay to agents on ticket sales. Now Budget Travel has decided from January 2005 to slash the commission it pays to travel agents selling its holidays from 10 per cent to 5 per cent. Budget has said that the decision is partly in light of the impact that Ryanair and Aer Lingus are having on its sales as both airlines offer direct flights to many sun destinations, previously the preserve of chartered carriers. One worry for travel agents could be that other tour operators such as Panorama and Falcon might also decide to cut commissions.

Source: *Sunday Times*, 24 October 2004

The trend towards deregulation of various business sectors has happened particularly in the travel sector with air travel and taxi deregulation. The bus market could be next for deregulation where bus operators could compete for city and nationwide bus routes.

The retail sector responded to the changes created by the prospering economy in the later half of the twentieth century. The makeup of the sector shifted from small independent stores, to larger retail outlets, particularly in the food sector. This movement led to the development of a range of retailers who are larger than many of the manufacturers (suppliers). Within the supply chain, the power has shifted from manufacturing to retailing. Diversification and improved customer services are other trends that have developed in the retail sector today. The retail industry and the groceries sector in particular, has faced growth and increased competition from globalisation. Discounters in the form of German operators Aldi and Lidl have entered the Irish market. In addition, the grocery sector faces uncertainty due to the repeal of the Groceries Order.

Discounters drive total Irish store growth

The arrival of German discounters Aldi and Lidl meant that the Irish supermarket /discount sector grew almost twice as fast as it would have done in the last six years if they hadn't entered the Irish market. According to exclusive research from AC Nielsen revealed at the Checkout Conference, in terms of store number growth in the period 1998–2004, the four major supermarket operators (Tesco, Dunnes Stores, SuperValu and Superquinn) grew by 16 per cent with a total of 49 new stores opening. However the arrival of the discounters during this period meant that the total growth rate skyrocketed to 40 per cent. In the six-year period to 2004, the discounters went from having no stores, to a total of 74, with 53 Lidl stores and 21 Aldi stores. Despite this rapid growth, the discounters' share of the market was static between 2003 and 2004.

Checkout, February 2005

Analysis of Market Share

	February 2004	February 2005
Tesco	24.8%	25.7%
Dunnes Stores	21.9%	22.4%
Superquinn	8.5%	8.5%
SuperValu	19.4%	19.1%
Discounters	5.2%	5.3%
Other operators	7.8%	7%
Other outlets (greengrocers, butchers)	10.6%	10.1%

Source: TNS Worldpanel

Key Factors in Evaluating Financial Performance

When scanning a set of financial statements, the following key factors should be quickly assessed before preparing financial ratios. This may only take a few minutes, but is vital in gaining a feel for the financial performance and position of the business.

When comparing the year to year performance of one company over a number of years, the following initial queries should be made:

❑ Have sales increased or decreased and by what percentage? In calculating a percentage increase in sales between two years, find the difference and divide it by the base (earlier) year, multiplying by 100 to get the percentage.

❑ Has operating profit increased or decreased and by what percentage?

❑ Has loan interest increased or decreased and by what percentage? Check also the long-term loans in the balance sheet to see if they have increased or decreased.

❑ Compare profit after tax to see if it has increased or decreased.

❑ Calculate the percentage increase or decrease in fixed assets. If assets have been increased, has this been financed through increased loans or issued share capital?

❑ Check to see if the business has cash or is in overdraft and if this is increasing or decreasing.

❑ Check current assets and liabilities for any major increases, for example a doubling in stocks, debtors or creditors.

When comparing two separate businesses, the following queries should be made:

❑ Check both businesses are in the same industry or sector.

❑ Compare the size of each business. This is normally done by comparing the total asset levels to capital employed in the balance sheet.

❑ Compare sales and profit levels.

❑ Compare financing. For example, is one company high geared and the other low geared?

❑ Compare cash balances or overdraft levels.

❑ Compare accounting policies to ascertain if they are similar and assess whether the property assets of either company have been revalued recently.

Summary

This chapter focused on financial performance appraisal for functional organisational structures. It outlined the process of inter-firm comparison and benchmarking before concentrating on key financial performance indicators used within the hospitality, tourism and retail sectors.

The main information points covered in this chapter are as follows:

❑ Performance measurement is a central component of a management control system. Making planning and control decisions requires information about how an organisation as a whole has performed, as well as the performance of the subunits within the organisation.

❑ There are many different financial performance measurement techniques such as:
   – Budgetary control and variance analysis.
   – Key internal financial performance indicators including return on investment, profitability and efficiency ratios.
   – Inter-firm comparisons or benchmarking performance against other companies regarded as best performers in the sector.
   There are also non-financial performance indicators such as customer satisfaction.

❑ Inter-firm comparison is the process of comparing the performance of different companies, subsidiaries and investment centres. Performance is compared by preparing key accounting ratios to assess the businesses that are performing above average and those that are not.

❑ Benchmarking is a continuing activity where a business or division seeks to copy or become like another successful business and achieve a similar level of success. It involves identifying a successful business or part of a business and using that business as a standard to follow.

❑ The Du Pont pyramid shows the relationship between key ratios and the overall goal of providing a return on capital.

❑ Ratio analysis is usually carried out under the following headings as the performance of an organisation is appraised:

   Profitability: Is the business profitable, both as to return on capital invested and as to the proportion of sales revenue remaining as profit? The key ratios under this heading are ROCE, ROOE, operating profit margin, gross profit margin and expenses to sales ratios.

   Efficiency or asset utilisation: Are the assets generating sufficient turnover and sufficient profits for the business? Is the business over- or under- capitalised? The key ratios under this heading are fixed asset turnover, total asset turnover, stock turnover, debtor collection period and creditor payment period.

   Liquidity: Is the business on a sound financial footing, able to pay its creditors and other obligations as they fall due? The key ratios under this heading are the current and the quick (acid-test) ratios.

   Capital structure: What are the organisation's long-term financing arrangements and how dependent is the organisation on borrowed funds (financial risk)? The key ratios under this heading are the debt to equity ratio and the interest cover ratio.

❑ Each sector has its own individual efficiency or operating ratios quite apart from the generic ones used across all business sectors.

Review Questions

Question 12.1

a) Outline the main reasons why the operating profit margin of a hotel would increase from one year to the next.
b) Outline the effect each of the following decisions would have on the return on capital employed ratio:
   i.   Increasing sales price.
   ii. Paying off a long-term loan with cash in hand.
   iii. Reducing fixed costs in the profit and loss account.
   iv. Arranging an overdraft facility.

Question 12.2

a) Outline the objectives of performance evaluation.
b) Distinguish between inter-firm comparisons and benchmarking as a form of performance appraisal.

Question 12.3

The following information relates to two pub restaurant businesses in Dublin for the month of December:

Summary Trading, Profit and Loss Account

		Daly's		Mulligan's	
		€	€	€	€
Sales					
	Bar	10,000		40,000	
	Restaurant	30,000	40,000	80,000	120,000
Cost of sales					
	Bar	5,000		14,000	
	Restaurant	12,000	17,000	29,000	43,000
Gross profit			23,000		77,000
Expenses					
	Labour	12,000		30,000	
	Overheads	9,000	21,000	20,000	50,000
			2,000		27,000

The following additional information is available for both businesses:

Capital employed	€120,000	€400,000
Average stocks	€1,000	€3,000
Number of employees	10	20
Sales mix: Bar	25%	33%
Restaurant	75%	67%

Required

Analyse and compare the profitability and operating performance of both businesses.

Question 12.4

Management of Collins Tours Limited is concerned about the falling ROCE between 2004 and 2005. The company focuses exclusively on providing tours of Ireland to Italian visitors. The business achieved a ROCE of 14.9 per cent in 2004 but that has fallen to 10.5 per cent in 2005. The key financial indicators for both 2004 and 2005 are provided below. You are required to explain in as much detail as possible, reasons for the falling ROCE.

	2005	2004
Operating profit margin	10%	12%
Capital employed	€950,000	€930,000
Number of tourists per annum	2,000	2,100
Average price per person per tour	€500	€550
Revenue per seat available	€350	€440
Direct costs as a percentage of sales	50%	48%
Labour costs as a percentage of sales	30%	28%
Overheads as a percentage of sales	10%	12%
Number of employees	300	280

Question 12.5

NEXT plc. is a major clothing retailer trading in high quality clothing. The success of NEXT is, in part, down to knowing their customers and what they like to buy.

Consolidated Profit and Loss Account

For the financial year ended 31 January

	2004 £m (Unaudited)	2003 £m
Turnover	2,516.0	2,202.6
Profit before interest	370.6	301.5
Net interest payable	(17.3)	(0.3)
Profit on ordinary activities before taxation	353.3	301.2
Taxation on profit on ordinary activities	(108.1)	(90.7)
Profit on ordinary activities after taxation	245.2	210.5
Dividends	(89.3)	(86.0)
Profit for the year transferred to reserves	155.9	124.5
Earnings per share	92.1p	68.7p
Diluted earnings per share	91.2p	68.1p

Consolidated Balance Sheet

As at 31 January

	2004 £m (Unaudited)	2003 £m
Fixed assets		
Goodwill	36.2	31.0
Tangible assets	355.7	323.1
Investments	1.0	0.5
Investment in own shares	65.9	47.0
	458.8	401.6
Current assets		
Property development stocks	5.9	9.1
Stocks	263.5	234.9
Debtors	378.5	318.1
Cash at bank and in hand	62.3	32.6
	710.2	594.7
Current liabilities		
Creditors: amounts falling due within one year	576.6	664.9
Net current assets/(liabilities)	133.6	(70.2)
Total assets less current liabilities	592.4	331.4
Creditors: amounts falling due after more than one year	352.7	37.0
Provision for liabilities and charges	18.7	19.3
Net assets	221.0	275.1
Capital and reserves		
Called up share capital	26.5	28.7
Share premium account	0.6	-
Revaluation reserve	14.0	14.8
Capital redemption reserve	3.4	1.2
Other reserves	(1,448.9)	(1,448.9)
Profit and loss account	1,625.4	1,679.3
Shareholders' funds	221.0	275.1

From the Notes

For the financial year ended 31 January

	2004 £m (Unaudited)	2003 £m
Turnover	2,516.0	2,202.6
Cost of sales	(1,762.5)	(1,548.1)
Gross profit	753.5	654.5
Distribution	(158.9	(145.0)
Administration	(226.0)	(210.7)
Group operating profit	368.6	298.8
Share of profit in association undertaking	2.0	2.7
Profit before interest	370.6	301.5
Trade debtors	303.0	248.3
Trade creditors	131.9	108.0

(Closing stock in 2002 amounted to £165.6 million)

Required

Use the extracts above from the published accounts of NEXT plc. to calculate the key performance ratios for the years 2004 and 2003.

Question 12.6

Outline the operating ratios and performance measures that are specific to *either* the retail or hospitality sector.

Question 12.7

The following balance sheet and profit information has been prepared for the Cahirsiveen House Hotel at the end of its trading year 2006. The hotel has a room capacity of 100 and achieved an occupancy rate of 76 per cent in 2006. It employed on average 45 persons throughout the year.

Balance Sheet at 31st December 2006

Fixed assets at net book value	€'000
Premises	12,960
Furniture and fittings	2,560
Licence	100
	15,620
Current assets	250
Current liabilities	350
	15,520
Financed by	
Capital	9,000
Retained profits	3,520
Loan capital	3,000
	15,520

Departmental Trading Profit and Loss Account

	Rooms	Restaurant	Bar		Total
	€'000	€'000	€'000	€'000	€'000
Sales	2,950	1,800	1,200		5,950
Cost of sales		774	636		1,410
Gross profit	2,950	1,026	564		4,540
Department expenses					
Wages	300	70	60		430
Other expenses	90	30	24		144
Departmental profit	2,560	926	480		3,966
Undistributed operating expenses					
Labour costs				1,750	
Property expenses				250	
Accounting and admin				120	
Advertising and sales				90	
General overheads				120	2,330
Operating profit					1,636

The hotel's performance evaluation system consists of the comparison of actual performance to key budget targets. The following targets were set at the beginning of the year:

		Rooms	Restaurant	Bar	Total
		€'000	€'000	€'000	€'000
1.	Sales revenue targets	2,550	1,800	1,100	5,450
2.	ROCE				8.75%
3.	Operating profit margin				25%
4.	Capital employed turnover				0.35
5.	Occupancy				74%
6.	ARR				€94
7.	Rooms revenue per available room (RevPAR)				€69.80
8.	Total sales per room available				€54,500
9.	Total cost per available room				€40,875
10.	Gross profit %				75%
11.	Departmental expenses as a percentage of sales				9%
12.	Labour costs as a percentage of sales				35%
13.	Departmental contribution as a percentage of total contribution				
	Rooms				60%
	Restaurant				25%
	Bar				15%
14.	Undistributed operating expenses as a percentage of sales				41%
15.	Total sales per employee				€121,111
16.	Operating profit per employee				€30,277

Required
a) Calculate the above financial indicators for 2006.
b) Evaluate the performance of the hotel in comparison to the budget targets.

Question 12.8

The following are the summarised accounts of Gibson Resorts plc., a company specialising in the hotel, tourism and leisure sector.

Profit and Loss Account

	€'000	2004 €'000	€'000	2003 €'000
Turnover		6,254		4,584
Cost of goods sold		1,814		1,146
Gross profit		4,440		3,438
Property expenses	1,100		650	
Wages and salaries	1,414		1,050	
Administration expenses	175		155	
Selling and distribution expenses	250	2,939	200	2,055
Operating profit		1,501		1,383
Interest		384		322
Net profit before tax		1,117		1,061
Corporation tax		350		320
Net profit after tax		767		741

Balance Sheet

	2004		2003	
	€'000	€'000	€'000	€'000
Fixed assets at N.B.V.		10,190		8,503
Current assets				
Stock	167		120	
Debtors	32		25	
Short-term investments	25		12	
Prepayments and accrued income	12		10	
Bank	10		120	
		246		287
Current liabilities				
Trade creditors	290		340	
Accruals and deferred income	15		12	
Taxation	460		320	
Dividends	150		250	
Bank loans and borrowings	100		10	
		1,015		932
Long-term liabilities Debentures	4,000		3,200	
Bank loans	800	4,800	1,400	4,600
Total net assets		4,621		3,258
Capital and Reserves				
Called up Share Capital				
Ordinary shares nominal value 0.25 per share		2,100		2,000
Reserves Share premium		371		
General reserve		1,000		500
Revaluation reserve		500		
Retained profits		650		758
		4,621		3,258

Additional information:

	2004	2003
Average number of employees	280	300
Breakdown of sales Rooms	3,440	3,438
Bar	1,564	550
Restaurant	1,250	596
Average daily number of rooms available	120	120
Average daily number of rooms occupied	92	85

Required

a) Calculate key accounting and operating ratios for Gibson Resorts plc. for the years 2003 and 2004 under the headings of profitability and efficiency. You are required to include in your calculations efficiency/operating ratios unique to the hotel sector.

b) From the information available to you including the ratios calculated in part (a) of the question, write a report to the directors of Gibson Resorts plc. on their operating performance for 2004.

Question 12.9

The following balance sheet and profit information has been prepared for Terri's Tours Ltd, a tour operator specialising in ski holidays. The company offers a similar package experience to three different locations, the French Alps, Italy and Andorra. Their accounting system shows the revenues and direct costs associated with each location. In previous years the company has found that the most profitable venue per package is Andorra, with France and Italy having higher direct costs.

Balance Sheet at 31 December 2006

	€'000
Fixed assets at net book value	20,960
Current assets	2,100
Current liabilities	2,300
	20,760
Financed by	
Capital	10,240
Retained profits	3,520
Loan capital	7,000
	20,760

The company sold 9,700 packages for 2006 and employed, on average, 80 persons. The following is the profit and loss account for 2006, showing sales, less the direct costs based on location.

	France	Italy	Andorra		Total
	€'000	€'000	€'000	€'000	€'000
Sales	2,100	1,800	3,400		7,300
Less Direct costs					
Materials (accom, flights, lessons)	900	850	750		2,500
Labour	350	325	225		900
Overheads	100	70	60		230
	1,350	1,245	1,035		3,630
Gross profit	750	555	2,365		3,670
Undistributed operating expenses					
Labour costs				1,750	
Accounting and admin expenses				120	
Advertising and sales				90	
General overheads				120	2,080
Operating profit					1,590
Loan interest					560
Net profit before tax					1,030

The company's performance evaluation system consists of the comparison of actual performance to budget targets. The following targets were set as part of the budget at the beginning of the year.

1	Forecast packages sold		9,810
2	Sales revenue targets	France	€2,224,908
		Italy	€1,748,142
		Andorra	€3,973,050
			€7,946,100
3	ROCE		8.75%
4	Operating profit margin		25%
5	Capital employed turnover		0.35
6	Average price per package		810
7	Labour costs as a percentage of sales		32%
8	Direct costs as a percentage of sales	France	60%
		Italy	70%
		Andorra	25%
9	Undistributed operating expenses as a percentage of sales		27%
10	Total sales per employee		€99,351
11	Operating profit per employee		€24,831
12	Interest cover		3 times

Required

a) Calculate the above financial indicators for 2006.

b) Write a report on profitability and operating performance of Terri's Tours in comparison to the budget targets set.

Question 12.10

The following are the summarised accounts of Faraway and Getaway Ltd, two companies specialising in the hotel and leisure sector for a number of years.

Profit and Loss Accounts for the year ended
31 December 2004

	Faraway	Getaway
	€'000	€'000
Turnover	25,250	19,280
Food and beverage costs	6,370	4,640
Gross profit	18,880	14,640
Wages and salaries	7,550	5,380
Property expenses	2,080	1,550
Administration expenses	880	830
Selling and distribution expenses	1,020	780
	11,530	8,540
Operating profit	7,350	6,100
Interest	1,360	1,050
Net profit before taxation	5,990	5,050
Corporation tax	1,310	1,210
Net profit after tax	4,680	3,840

Additional Information

	Faraway	Getaway
Breakdown of sales – Rooms €'000	14,800	14,300
Bar €'000	5,700	2,400
Restaurant €'000	4,750	2,580
Average daily number of rooms available	490	410
Average daily number of rooms occupied	350	320
Average number of employees	450	310

Balance Sheets at 31 December 2004

	Faraway €'000	Getaway €'000
Fixed assets at Net Book Value	51,130	35,150
Current assets		
Stocks	1,450	1,040
Trade debtors	2,100	1,280
Prepayments and other debtors	660	330
Bank		520
	4,210	3,170
Current liabilities		
Trade creditors	1,110	1,230
Accrued expenses	190	150
Taxation	1,470	1,310
Dividends	900	950
Bank overdraft	440	
	4,110	3,640
Long-term liabilities		
Debentures	16,800	10,600
Bank loans	3,600	4,600
	20,400	15,200
Total net assets	30,830	19,480
Capital and reserves		
Ordinary share capital		
(nominal 25c each)	3,600	2,200
Share premium account	5,100	2,700
Reserves	13,350	9,250
Retained profits	8,780	5,330
	30,830	19,480

Required

a) Calculate 12 key ratios for each company for the year ended 31 December 2004, under the headings of: profitability, efficiency, operations, liquidity and gearing.

b) From the information available to you, including the ratios calculated in part (a) of the question, write a report comparing the performance of the two companies for 2004.

Question 12.11

The following are the summarised accounts of the Dunne Hotel Group and Gibson Hotels for the year ended 31 December 2005. Both companies are resident in Ireland with a property portfolio mix of three and four star hotels. Both companies have recently decided to use one another in an inter-firm comparative analysis and bench-marking exercise in an effort to develop efficiencies and maximise returns. Both companies operate similar accounting policies.

Profit and Loss Accounts for year ended 31 December 2005

	Dunne Group		Gibson Group	
	€'000	€'000	€'000	€'000
Turnover		15,222		17,589
Cost of goods sold		5,360		6,012
Gross profit		9,862		11,577
Administration expenses	3,125		3,598	
Selling and distribution expenses	2,598	5,723	3,012	6,610
Operating profit		4,139		4,967
Interest		356		923
Net profit before tax		3,783		4,044
Corporation tax		811		1,023
Net profit after tax		2,972		3,021

Balance Sheet as at 31 December 2005

	Dunne Group	Gibson Group
	€'000	€'000
Fixed assets at NBV	21,250	30,017
Current assets		
Stock	270	227
Debtors	56	60
Bank	382	33
	708	320
Current liabilities		
Trade creditors	300	290
Taxation	800	1,023
Dividends	770	1,015
Bank loans and borrowings	11	145
	1,881	2,473
Long-term liabilities		
Debentures	7,520	12,125
Total net assets	12,557	15,739
Capital and reserves		
Ordinary shares nominal value		
€0.50 per share	8,750	10,750
Reserves Share premium		
General reserve	2,000	2,000
Retained profits	1,807	2,989
	12,557	15,739

Additional information:	Dunne Group	Gibson Group
Number of rooms available per day	350	400
Average rooms occupied per day	263	280
Sales mix percentages		
Rooms	65%	62%
Food and beverages	20%	20%
Banqueting and conferences	15%	18%
Number of employees	300	350

Required

Analyse and compare the operating performance of both hotel groups under the headings of profitability, asset utilisation, operating performance, liquidity and capital structure. Your report should outline where and how each company could generate efficiencies and improve returns due to this inter-firm comparison and benchmarking exercise.

CHAPTER 13

Strategic and Divisional Performance Appraisal

Learning Outcomes

By the end of this chapter you will be able to:

❑ Distinguish between functional and divisional organisational structures.
❑ Distinguish between cost centres, profit centres and investment centres.
❑ Calculate and interpret the return on investment and residual income measures of divisional performance and be aware of the problems associated with both.
❑ Outline non-financial performance indicators used by companies.
❑ Outline the balanced scorecard approach to performance evaluation.

'What gets measured gets attention particularly when rewards are tied to the measures'
(Eccles 1991)

Introduction

In the previous chapter the focus was on performance evaluation, directed at centralised organisation structures, with an emphasis on key financial measures that enable good inter-firm comparisons and performance benchmarking. This chapter focuses on divisionalised organisation structures and the various levels of decentralisation that can occur and the key financial measures appropriate for each level. The chapter also introduces non-financial performance measures used in both centralised and decentralised business structures. It concludes with an overview of performance measurement frameworks that integrate the use of financial and non-financial performance measures. These frameworks translate the aims and objectives of a business into a series of performance targets that can be measured. Thus performance is measured through the use of financial and non-financial performance targets that are directly linked to the strategic objectives of the organisation. This helps ensure that as a strategy evolves, management can judge whether strategic objectives are being, or are likely to be, achieved.

Organisation Structure and Performance Appraisal

Performance measurement is directly linked to the organisational structure of a business. For example, a small family owned retail business that functions through the involvement of one or two family members can have the relevant performance statistics at their finger tips as the business is small and the owners are directly involved in all aspects of it. However, as a business grows, organisation structures develop and this requires more sophisticated information systems supplying key performance measures. Although the key financial performance indicators covered in Chapter 12 are relevant to all businesses and business structures, a distinction can be made between two categories of organisational structure for performance appraisal:

1. Functional organisation structures.
2. Divisionalised organisation structures.

Functional organisation structures

A functional organisation structure is where a business is divided into separate departments such as operations and purchasing along with separate support departments such as administration, accounting, marketing and sales. The managers of each department are only responsible for their part in the process of ensuring the provision and sale of a product or service. For example, a purchasing manager is responsible for ensuring the raw materials or products purchased are of good quality and meet the required specifications for the best possible price. Marketing and sales managers are responsible for total sales revenue and the costs associated with selling. The revenues from the marketing department and the costs from the other departments (cost centres) are combined only at managing director or CEO level. This would occur where a company produces a similar type of product or service in the same location.

Diagram 13.1: *Functional Organisation Structure (retail)*

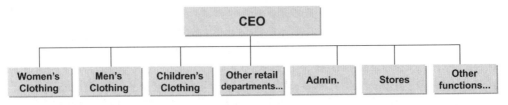

Divisionalised organisation structures

A divisionalised or decentralised organisation structure occurs where the organisation is broken into divisions in accordance with the products or services offered. Each divisional manager is responsible for all the operations relating to their particular product or service. Thus the autonomy experienced at CEO level in a functional organisation is similar to that experienced by a divisional head in a decentralised organisation structure. An example would be a large hotel chain where the general manager heading up each hotel has decision-making responsibility over costs and revenues and an input into investment decisions. Decentralisation is the delegation of decision-making responsibility and is a necessary response to the increasing complexity of the business environment that organisations face and the increasing size of many organisations. Today it is impossible for one person to make all the decisions involved in the operation of even a small company, hence senior managers delegate decision-making responsibility to subordinates.

Diagram 13.2: *Divisionalised Organisation Structure (retail)*

Divisional performance at NEXT

When David Jones took over as CEO of NEXT in 1988, his life was dominated by the task of saving the business. He was amazed to find that nobody at a retail board meeting knew how many retail stores were making a loss. Four weeks later it was established that 200 of the 428 stores had not made a profit.

Financial Management, October 2005.

Performance Measurement in a Divisionalised Setting

One danger of decentralisation is that divisional managers may make decisions that can be in their interest but not in the best interests of the overall company (dysfunctional decisions). To redress this problem, senior managers introduce systems of performance measurement to help ensure that decisions made by divisional managers are in the best interests of the company as a whole.

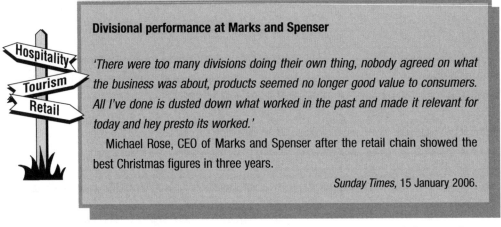

These performance measurement systems depend on the degree of decentralisation involved. There are four recognised levels of decentralisation as follows:

❑ Cost centres.
❑ Revenue centres.
❑ Profit centres.
❑ Investment centres.

Diagram 13.3: *Centres within a divisionalised structure*

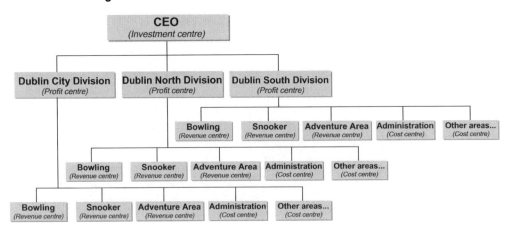

Cost centres

This is where the manager of such a centre or division is responsible for the costs associated with that centre and hence the main focus is cost minimisation. This level of decentralisation occurs normally in functional organisation types. The key measures used in appraising performance for a cost centre would be cost variances from budget and individual cost items (labour for example), as a percentage of total costs.

Revenue centres

This is where the manager is totally concerned with raising revenue with no responsibility for costs. The key measures used in appraising performance would be monitoring sales variances from budget.

Profit centres

This is where the manager of such a centre or division has responsibility for both revenue and costs for the assets assigned to the division. Thus performance is measured in terms of the difference between the revenues and costs that relate to a profit centre. A profit centre is like a separate company with its own profit and loss account and the manager's decisions relate to the revenue and costs that make up the division's profit statement. The main performance measures focus on cost and revenue variances to budget, as well as the preparation of key profit ratios such as gross profit percentage, operating profit percentage and expenses to sales percentages. Divisional profit statements are commonly used in profit centres and mainly distinguish between costs that are controlled by the division and costs that are controlled by head-office. However not all costs can be easily divided into these two categories. Thus a third category of cost called traceable divisional costs exists. This category relates to those costs where the divisional manager may have some influence but not control. Illustration 13.1 below outlines a typical format for such a statement.

Illustration 13.1: *Divisional profit statement*

		€'000	€'000
Sales	(external customers)	450	
	(internal customers)	90	
Total sales revenue			540
Controllable divisional variable costs			(100)
Controllable divisional fixed costs			(150)
Controllable divisional profit			290
Other traceable divisional variable costs			(40)
Other traceable divisional fixed costs			(50)
Divisional profit			200
Apportioned head-office cost			(50)
Net profit			150

An example of traceable divisional costs would be depreciation on divisional machinery. This would not be categorised as controllable as the divisional manager has no control over investment in fixed assets. However in practice, divisional managers would have some input and influence in investment decisions and hence, to recognise this level of influence, it is considered a traceable cost in assessing the performance of the division.

With any divisionalised organisation, the major difficulty when appraising performance is deciding what is controllable and traceable to that particular division. When assessing the performance of a divisional manager, one should judge the manager on controllable profits and hence only consider costs and revenues under the control of that manager. When assessing the performance of a division, the focus should be on costs and revenues that are traceable to the division and hence judge the division on traceable profit.

Investment centres

This is where the manager has responsibility for not just the revenues and costs relating to the centre, but also the assets that generate these costs and revenues and the investment decisions relating to disposal and acquisition of assets. For managers of investment centres, the main performance measures used will be based on return on investment and breaking that down into its two component parts namely operating profit margin and capital employed turnover (asset turnover). Two measures of divisional performance most commonly used are:

❑ Return on investment (ROI).
❑ Residual income.

Return on investment (ROI) is very similar to return on capital employed (ROCE) which was discussed in Chapter 12, except the focus is on controllable and traceable revenues, expenses and assets. The following formula is used:

$$\text{Return on investment (ROI)} = \frac{\text{Divisional net profit x 100}}{\text{Divisional net assets}}$$

The residual income is profit earned less interest on the capital that has been employed to generate the profit. The residual income formula is:

$$\text{Residual income} = \text{Divisional net profit less an imputed interest charge on divisional investment}$$

Example 13.1: *ROI and residual income*

The Millenium Cinema Group opened a new division in Limerick. The investment in the Limerick division amounted to €5m and profit of €900,000 was generated in the first year of trading. The weighted average cost of capital for the group is 10 per cent.

Measure the performance of the Limerick division using return on investment and residual income.

Approach

Return on investment	$\dfrac{\text{Divisional net profit} \times 100}{\text{Divisional net assets}}$	$\dfrac{€900 \times 100}{€5,000} = 18\%$

Residual income	Divisional net profit	€900,000
	Imputed interest (€5m x 10%)	(500,000)
	Residual income	400,000

What is important under all four divisionalised structures (cost centre, revenue centre, profit centre and investment centre) is that the centre and manager is appraised on the costs, revenues and assets that are wholly under their control and for which they are fully responsible.

Table 13.1 below summarises the typical financial performance measures under the various divisionalised approaches.

Table 13.1: *Financial performance measures in divisionalised organisations*

Responsibility structure	Manager's area of responsibility	Typical financial performance measure
Cost centre	Decisions over costs	Standard costing variances
Revenue centre	Decisions over sales and revenue	Sales variances from budget
Profit centre	Decisions over costs and revenues	Controllable profit
Investment centre	Decisions over costs, revenues and assets	Return on investment and residual income

A good performance measure should:

❑ Provide incentive to the divisional manager to make decisions which are in the best interests of the overall company (goal congruence).

❑ Only include factors for which the divisional manager can be held accountable.

❑ Recognise the long-term objectives as well as short-term objectives of the organisation.

Return on Investment and Residual Income

Return on investment (ROI) and residual income measures have been used in performance appraisal of investment centres for many years. The approaches, while simple to calculate, have drawbacks that must be considered when appraising performance. The following example demonstrates their calculation and some of the drawbacks associated with the return on investment measure.

Example 13.2: *ROI and residual income in project appraisal*

Supershop Galway is a division of Supershop Ireland plc. Net assets are currently €20 million, earning a profit of €4.5 million per annum. Supershop Galway has a minimum required return on capital of 10 per cent. The division is considering two proposals:

> Proposal 1: Investing a further €2 million in fixed assets to earn an annual profit of €0.30 million.

> Proposal 2: Disposal of assets at their net book value of €4.6 million. This would lead to a reduction in profits of €0.6 million.

Proceeds from the disposal of assets would be credited to head-office.

Calculate the current return on investment and residual income for Supershop Galway and show how they would change under each of the two proposals.

Approach

The current situation and the two proposals should be evaluated using return on investment and residual income.

Current situation	**Return on investment is 22.5 per cent** Divisional net profit of €4.5 million divided by divisional net assets of €20 million equals 22.5 per cent. **Residual income €2.5 million** Profit of €4.5 million less imputed interest charge of €2 million (€20 million multiplied by 10 per cent) equals €2.5 million. **Comment** ROI exceeds the cost of capital and residual income is positive. The division is performing well.

Proposal 1	**Return on investment is 21.8 per cent**
	The investment increases to €22 million with profits increasing to €4.8 million. This gives a return on investment (divisional net profit of €4.8 million divided by divisional net assets of €22 million) for the division of 21.8 per cent, a reduction of 0.7 per cent.
	Residual income €2.6 million
	Profit of €4.8 million less imputed interest charge of €2.2 million (€22 million multiplied by 10 per cent) equals €2.6 million.
	Comment
	This project is acceptable to the company as it offers a rate of return of 15 per cent (€0.30 ÷ €2) which is greater than the cost of capital. However, divisional ROI falls and this could lead to the divisional manager rejecting proposal 1. This would be a dysfunctional decision. Residual income increases if proposal 1 is adopted and this performance measure should lead to goal congruent decisions.
Proposal 2	**Return on investment is 25 per cent**
	Under this proposal the net assets of the business would fall to €15.4 million and profits would decrease to €3.9 million giving a return on investment of 25.3 per cent (divisional net profit of €3.9 million divided by divisional net assets of €15.4 million).
	Residual income €2.36 million
	Profit of €3.9 million less imputed interest charge of €1.54 million (€15.4 million multiplied by 10 per cent) equals €2.36 million.
	Comment
	The disposal of assets is not acceptable to the company as these assets have a rate of return of 13.0 per cent (€0.6 million ÷ €4.6 million), which is greater than the cost of capital and hence should not be disposed of. However, divisional ROI rises and this could lead to the divisional manager accepting proposal 2. This would be a dysfunctional decision. Residual income decreases if proposal 2 is adopted and once again this performance measure should lead to goal congruent decisions. It is important to note that this analysis ignores the possible returns that head-office could achieve from the sale of the assets and how this could impact on the decision to dispose of the assets.

Advantages and disadvantages of return on investment

Return on investment is a common measure in performance evaluation. Its advantages include:

1. It is a financial accounting measure that is understandable to managers.
2. ROI can be further analysed into its component parts of capital employed turnover (asset turnover) and operating profit margin. These ratios can be further divided into their component parts. This can help management understand the drivers behind ROI and hence work to improve the ROI.
3. ROI is a common measure and thus is ideal for comparison across corporate divisions for companies of similar size and in similar sectors.

There are a number of disadvantages associated with return on investment.

1. The level of investment or capital employed can be difficult to measure and this can distort inter-firm comparisons. For example, comparing ROI for hotels that periodically revalue their property assets to those that don't, can be misleading. The companies with the revalued properties will have a higher asset base and hence a lower return on investment. If assets are valued at net book value, ROI and residual income figures generally improve as assets get older. This can encourage managers to retain outdated plant and machinery.
2. Different accounting policies will affect both profits and asset or investment values. Thus inter-firm comparisons can be very misleading if the companies involved do not have similar accounting policies with regard to fixed assets, stocks and certain intangible assets such as research and development.
3. The use of ROI can lead to dysfunctional decisions made by managers as illustrated in example 13.2.

Advantages and disadvantages of residual income

Residual income is considered a better overall performance measure as it is an absolute measure, whereas return on investment is a relative measure and suffers accordingly. As illustrated in example 13.2, the use of ROI can lead to dysfunctional decisions. Residual income, being an absolute measure, can lead management to make decisions that maximise the wealth of the business.

The main disadvantages of residual income as a performance measure are:

1. It can be difficult to calculate a minimum required return (cost of capital) for a business or division.
2. As with the return on investment, identifying the appropriate value for investment or assets can be difficult and subjective.

3. Residual income is not as well understood and known by managers as return on investment.

Divisional performance evaluation measures

Surveys of methods used to evaluate the performance of divisional managers indicate a strong preference for ROI over residual value. For example, the UK survey by Drury et al. (1993) reported the following measures were used:

A target ROI set by the group	55%
Residual income	20%
A target profit before charging interest on investment	61%
A target cash flow figure	43%

Source: Drury (2001), *Management Accounting for Business Decisions*

Transfer Pricing

Transfer pricing occurs where an organisation structures itself into separate independent divisions. When separate divisions within the organisation buy and sell to and from one another, then transfer pricing occurs. The transfer price is the cost of buying the product in the buying division and is the sales revenue for the selling division. The level of the transfer price will affect the profitability of both divisions and thus has performance appraisal implications. For example, should the selling division set a high transfer price then its profits will increase, but the profits of the buying division will decrease. Thus some agreed price must be found that is fair to both divisions.

The alternatives are:

1. Set full cost price as the transfer price. This however is very harsh on the selling division and undermines its profitability and hence its performance appraisal.
2. Set cost plus a mark-up as the transfer price. This system would help ensure the selling division has some element of profit on the transaction.
3. Set market price as the transfer price. This is a feasible option where prices would be set, based on listed prices of identical products or services, or, on a price a competitor is quoting.
4. Set a transfer price based on negotiation between the managers of the buying and selling divisions. This option often has behavioural benefits, as managers develop an understanding of each others' problems.

Transfer pricing basis

A UK survey by Drury et al. in 1993 showed that market price was the most common basis on which to agree a transfer price, with negotiated pricing coming a close second and cost plus mark-up coming third.

In the USA, a survey by Borkowski in 1990 showed that 32.7 per cent of those surveyed used market price, 22.6 per cent used negotiated and 41.1 per cent used full cost basis for agreeing a transfer price.

Source: Drury (2001), *Management Accounting for Business Decisions*

Transfer pricing is important as the transfer price affects both the buying and selling divisions profits. If unrealistic transfer pricing exists within an organisation, it can result in divisions reporting misleading profits, which can have negative motivational consequences.

Limitations of Traditional Financial Performance Measures

Traditional measures of performance focus on the financial performance measures covered thus far in both Chapters 12 and 13. These approaches have significant limitations and hence should not be used as the only basis for measuring and evaluating performance.

The following are the main criticisms of traditional financial performance measures:

1. Accounting measures are historical and backward looking in nature and although they can indicate future trends, they can also be misleading.
2. Accounting measures only present a limited picture of a business' performance. For example, they do not highlight the fact that a business may be overly dependent on one customer, one product line, or one supplier.
3. Accounting indicators can focus too much on the short-term and can give rise to short-term decisions that could have a harmful effect on the business in the future. For example, management may cut back on research and training to ensure profit targets are reached.
4. Traditional financial measures tend to be quite inward looking and not focused on external factors such as customers and competitors.

'If you look into an organisation you will see only costs, you have to be an insider looking out to be aware of value'

Peter Druker

5. Financial analysts and capitalists are increasingly taking the view that the intangible assets of a business are more likely to create future value. For example, the value of goodwill, a strong brand, an innovative organisation culture, a quality management team and work-force, are all intangible assets that can create value and competitive advantage in the future. However, these assets are so subjective to measure in financial terms, that they are often ignored.

6. Accounting measures can ensure the focus is on cost rather than value.

> *'Too many accountants conform to Oscar Wilde's definition of a cynic –*
> *knowing the cost of everything and the value of nothing'*
>
> David Allen, *Management Accounting*, April 1994

7. Single factor measures are capable of distortion by unscrupulous managers for example, undertaking proposal 2 in example 13.1 above.

8. They are of little use as a guide to action. If ROI or residual income fall, they simply indicate that performance has decreased, without indicating why.

Non-Financial Performance Indicators

In recent years, the trend in performance measurement has been towards a broader view of performance, covering both financial and non-financial indicators. By focusing solely on financial performance measures, it is unlikely that a full picture of divisional performance can be obtained.

Non-financial performance indicators in hospitality, tourism and retail

Examples of non-financial performance indicators within the hospitality, tourism and retail sectors would be:

❑ **Travel sector:** Safety standards, level of delays, level of comfort, efficiency and friendliness of staff and market share.

❑ **On-line travel booking:** Accessibility of service and ease of use.

❑ **High street travel agent:** Efficiency and friendliness of staff and market share.

❑ **Restaurants and pubs:** Quality of food, beverages and service, atmosphere and friendliness and efficiency of staff.

❑ **Hotels:** Quality of accommodation, efficiency and friendliness of staff, atmosphere, quality of food and beverages, quality of service, hygiene standards, market share, occupancy and flexibility.

❑ **Retail:** The frequency of stock-outs, quality of products (freshness of groceries), number of customer complaints, efficiency and friendliness of staff, average wait at checkout queue, and availability of parking.

Since the late 1980s there have been many publications on performance measurement systems or frameworks. These suggest a more holistic and systematic approach to performance measurement that integrates financial and non-financial performance indicators. Fitzgerald et al. (1991), focusing on service businesses, identify six dimensions upon which measurement of business performance can take place:

❑ **Financial performance,** focusing on profitability, liquidity, efficiency, capital structure and market ratios.
❑ **Competitiveness,** which measures market share, position and sales growth.
❑ **Resource utilisation,** focusing on productivity, efficiency and asset utilisation.
❑ **Quality of service,** which focuses on several measures of service quality including reliability, responsiveness, cleanliness, comfort, friendliness, courtesy, communications and competence security.
❑ **Innovation,** measuring the proportion of new to old products and services, as well as new products and service sales levels.
❑ **Flexibility,** measured in terms of volume as well as delivery speed, and product or service specification flexibility.

The research suggests that every service organisation needs to develop its own set of performance measures to ensure it gains and retains competitive advantage.

The end of the last century saw a move towards using a more balanced approach to performance appraisal by including non-financial performance indicators in the appraisal assessment. The most well known of these approaches is the balanced scorecard proposed by Kaplan and Norton, based on a research project in 1990 and published in the *Harvard Business Review* in 1992.

The Balanced Scorecard

The balanced scorecard system was developed from research undertaken by Professor Robert Kaplan (Harvard Business School) and David Norton (management consultant). The research was based on the belief that managers need a broad range of performance measures in order to manage their businesses and that existing financial performance measures were not enough and actually limited a business' ability to create economic value. The balanced scorecard provides a framework that translates the aims and objectives of a business into a series of performance targets that can be measured. Thus performance is measured and the link to strategy ensures that management can see if strategic objectives are being achieved. The balanced scorecard measures a company's performance from four different perspectives namely:

❑ **The financial perspective,** focusing on traditional financial measures such as sales growth, profit, return on capital and shareholders' value.

❑ **The customer perspective,** focusing on corporate customer service objectives in terms of measures that correspond to customers' priorities. Performance measures for customers would include customer satisfaction levels, customer retention and growth in customer numbers.

❑ **The internal business processes perspective,** focusing on what the business must excel at and on the internal processes, decisions and actions, if the business is to meet customer requirements.

❑ **Innovation and learning perspective,** focusing on how a business can continue to improve and create value. It measures how a business seeks to learn, innovate and improve every aspect of the organisation. The fact that it exists and is being measured, forces businesses to become aware of and to monitor their propensity to innovate, retrain, up-skill and improve performance in the face of competition.

Diagram 13.4: *The balanced scorecard*

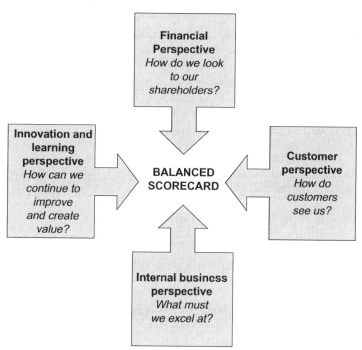

The term 'balanced' is used because managerial performance is assessed under all four headings and it implies that each quadrant is of equal importance and deserves equal weighting. This can help senior management evaluate whether lower level managers have improved one area at the expense of another. For example, a manager at risk of not meeting operating profit margin targets may start to ship high margin products and delay deliveries of low margin ones. The balanced scorecard will recognise the improvement in financial performance but will also reveal that this was achieved by sacrificing 'on-time' performance targets.

Critical success factors (CSF) and key performance indicators

When using the balanced scorecard, an organisation has to decide which performance measures to use under each heading. Areas to measure should relate to an organisation's critical success factors. Critical success factors (CSFs) are performance requirements which are fundamental to an organisation's success (for example innovation in a consumer electronics company) and can usually be identified from an organisation's mission statement, objectives and strategy. Key performance indicators (KPIs) are measurements of achievement of the chosen critical success factors. Key performance indicators should be:

1. **Specific:** For example, measure profitability rather than 'financial performance', a term which could mean different things to different people.
2. **Measurable:** Key performance indicators must be capable of having a measure placed upon them, for example, number of customer complaints rather than the 'level of customer satisfaction'.
3. **Relevant:** Key performance indicators must relate to and measure the achievement or non-achievement of a critical success factor.

Illustration 13.2 outlines a generic balanced scorecard with typical critical success factors and key performance indicators.

Illustration 13.2: *A generic balanced scorecard*

BSC perspective	Critical success factors	Performance measures
Financial	Sales growth	Sales volume trends
		Sales price
	Operating margins	Gross margin
		Operating profit margins
		Operating costs to sale percentage
	Asset utilisation	Total asset turnover
		Fixed asset turnover
	Cash-flow	Operating cash to operating profit
		Debtors days
		Creditors days
Customer	Number of new customers	Number of new customers and sales value
	Customer retention	Number of repeat customers and sales value
	Customer satisfaction	Customer survey, number of complaints
Internal	Efficiency ratings	Level of wastage
		Number of defective products
		Production average cycle time

	After sales service	Number of visits to customers
		Number of complaints of faulty products
Innovation and learning	New innovations	Percentage sales from products less than one year old
		Number of new accounts opened
		Number of new innovations
		New product sales
		Work in progress for new product or service ideas
	Learning	Staff training courses offered
		Staff training courses taken up

Balanced scorecard in practice

Research conduced by CIMA for 'A Practical Guide to the Balanced Scorecard', surveyed 60 UK companies and identified that the following measures were commonly adopted.

'Commonly Used Measures' (KPI) in *Balanced Scorecard* (UK)

Performance measure	No of companies	% of companies	Performance measure	No of companies	% of companies
Profitability	59	93.3	Supplier service levels	28	46.7
Revenue growth	54	90.0	Process statistics	28	46.7
Return on investment/capital	48	80.0	Process quality	27	45.0
Market share	45	75.0	Customer retention	22	36.7
Customer satisfaction	45	75.0	Economic value added	21	35.0
Cost reduction	44	73.3	Customer profitability	20	33.3
Share price	43	71.7	Brand Value	19	31.7
Customer service level	43	71.7	Customer acquistion	15	25.0
Productivity	36	60.0	Employee profitability	8	13.3
Employee satisfaction	34	56.7	Human capital	4	6.7
Employee retention	30	50.0	Intellectual capital	3	5.0
Employee training/competency levels	30	50.0			

Source: *A Practical Guide to the Balanced Scorecard* (CIMA)

Example 13.3: *Balanced scorecard*

Management at Express Supermarkets are concerned about the performance of the group. The group consists of ten supermarkets operating in key locations in Ireland. Each supermarket provides a good range of grocery items at affordable prices with attention directed at customer service and quality. The financial director has suggested introducing the balanced scorecard approach to performance appraisal.

For each perspective within the balanced scorecard, identify one suitable critical success factor and for each critical success factor, two related performance measures.

Approach

A balanced scorecard should be drawn up with columns for critical success factors and performance measures.

BSC perspective	Critical success factors	Performance measures
Financial	Profitability	Gross profit margin Return on capital employed
Customer	Customer retention and satisfaction	Number of repeat customers / total customers Number of complaints / total customers
Internal	Efficiency ratings	Average wait at checkout Stock replenishment cycle times
Innovation & learning	Innovation	Number of new products stocked Number of staff initiatives or suggestions adopted

Use of CSF/KPI and the balanced scorecard in retail

Research by Luby (2006) concluded that while 82 per cent of respondents used critical success factors and key performance indicators in performance appraisal, only 18 per cent used a balanced scorecard. The research covered Irish retail outlets.

The balanced scorecard in hospitality

Louvieris et al. (2003) translated the four quadrants of the balanced scorecard into critical success factors and related performance measures specifically for the hotel sector. This interpretation of the framework was developed in consultation with general managers of hotels.

The Balanced Scorecard – Hotel Sector (Louvieris et al.)

BSC perspective	Critical success factors	Performance measures
Financial	Profitability	Gross operating profit
		Net operating profit
	Budgetary control	Sales achieved
		Adhering to budget
		Meeting financial targets
		Achieving predicted occupancy rates
		Revenue per available room
		Cash-flow
Customer	Quality of service	Guest surveys
		Mystery guest
		Participation in grading schemes
	Customer profiling	Feedback via staff
		Customer satisfaction levels
	Customer relationship management	Average spend
		Customer satisfaction levels
		Customer retention rate
Internal	Having clear objectives	Meeting financial targets
	Tracking objective	Internal auditing
		Completion of capital projects
	Investing in staff	Staff satisfaction surveys
		Staff development reviews
		Staff retention rate
		Staff incentive schemes
	Productivity	Ratio of wages to turnover
Innovation and learning	Staff as drivers of innovation	Number of new products or services
		Process improvement initiatives
	Cross sector comparison	Networking relationships
		Membership of trade / professional bodies
		Participation in grading schemes
		Courses completed by staff
	Encouraging staff	Level of multi-skilling Productivity

Performance measurement practices in Irish hotel groups

Research conducted by Flanagan (2005) into the performance measurement practices of Irish hotel groups found the following rankings in terms of the most popular critical success factors and key performance indicators:

Rank	Critical success factors
1	Sales growth
2	Increase revenue
3	Improve hotels financial position
4	Win new or retain existing customers
5	Maintain product or service standards
6	Manage assets and staff efficiently
7	Improve satisfaction or quality ratings
8	Cost / benefit management
9	Motivate or improve morale
Rank	**Key performance indicators**
1	Total revenue
2	Cost as percentage of sales
3	Customer feedback and satisfaction
4	Compliance with regulatory body
5	Operating margins
6	New suggestions from customers
7	Best practice
8	Up-selling and cross-selling
9	Numbers of new customers
10	Benchmark against competitors or industry

The main conclusions of the research were:

1. Irish general managers broadly agree on the factors that are critical to their success. However critical success factors from the financial perspective of the balanced scorecard were considered more important. CSFs from the innovation and learning perspective were considered least important.

2. While Irish general managers broadly agree on the choice key performance indicators, these indicators did not directly relate to the most popular critical success factors.

Advantages of the balanced scorecard approach

The balanced scorecard approach to performance measurement offers several advantages:

1. It measures performance in a variety of ways, rather than relying on one figure.
2. Managers are unlikely to be able to distort the performance measure as bad performance is difficult to hide if multiple performance measures are used.
3. It takes a long-term, strategic approach to business performance.
4. Success in the four key areas should lead to the long-term success of the organisation.
5. It is flexible, as what is measured can be changed over time to reflect changing priorities.
6. 'What gets measured gets done'. If managers know they are being appraised on various aspects of performance, they will pay attention to these areas, rather than simply paying 'lip service' to them.

Disadvantages of the balanced scorecard approach

The main difficulties with the balanced scorecard approach are:

1. Setting standards for each of the key performance indicators can prove difficult where the organisation has no previous experience of performance measurement. Benchmarking with other organisations is a possible solution to this problem.
2. Allowing for trade-offs between key performance indicators can be problematic. How should an organisation judge a manager who has improved in every area apart from, say, financial performance? One solution to this problem is to require managers to improve in all areas and not allow trade-offs between the different measures.

Summary

This chapter focused on performance appraisal within divisionalised organisation structures. It also concentrated on non-financial performance indicators and the approach of a balanced framework for appraising performance, including a system put forward by Kaplan and Norton called the balanced scorecard. The balanced scorecard provides a framework which translates the aims and objectives of a business into a series of performance targets that can be measured.

The main information points covered in this chapter are as follows:

❑ A functional or centralised organisational structure is where a business is divided into separate departments. Each department is only responsible for a part of the process of turning raw materials into a finished product that is sold on to the consumer.

❑ A divisionalised or decentralised organisational structure occurs where the organisation is broken into divisions in accordance with the products produced. Each divisional manager is responsible for all the operations relating to their particular product or service. An example would be a large hotel chain where the general manager heading up each hotel has decision-making responsibility over costs and revenues and has an input into investment decisions.

❑ Decentralisation is the delegation of decision-making responsibility. The following levels of decentralisation exist:
   − Cost centre.
   − Revenue centre.
   − Profit centre.
   − Investment centre.

❑ In an investment centre, managers are responsible for a profit centre as well as for capital investment. Two measures of divisional performance are commonly used:
   − Return on investment.
   − Residual income.

❑ In recent years, the trend in performance measurement has been towards a broader view of performance, covering both financial and non-financial indicators. The most well known of these approaches is the balanced scorecard proposed by Kaplan and Norton. The balanced scorecard approach measures a company's performance from four different perspectives namely:
   − The financial perspective.
   − The customer perspective.
   − The internal business processes perspective.
   − The innovation and learning perspective.

Review Questions

Question 13.1

a) Distinguish between functional and decentralised organisational structures.
b) Distinguish between cost centres, profit centres and investment centres from a management accounting perspective.
c) The managers of the Athlone division of 'Looking Good plc.', a retail chain dealing in cosmetic products, has decision-making authority over selling price and has responsibility for controlling costs. Decisions on fixed asset acquisitions and disposals are made at head-office. Is the Athlone division a profit centre, a cost centre or an investment centre?

Question 13.2

a) Compare and contrast the return on investment and residual income measures of divisional performance.
b) Outline three reasons why return on investment may be an unreliable measure of divisional performance.

Question 13.3

Outline what you understand by the term 'transfer pricing' and explain how the existence of transfer pricing can distort performance appraisal within a divisionalised organisation structure.

Question 13.4

Leisure Gear plc. operates several retail divisions, all treated as profit centres. The following information relates to the financial performance of the Mayo division for last month.

	€
Sales	350,000
Cost of sales	55,000
Other variable costs	71,000
Fixed costs	100,000
Depreciation	50,000

20 per cent of the fixed costs are non-controllable and 30 per cent of the depreciation charge relates to fixed assets over which the division has complete control. The head-office allocation for the month is €40,000.

Required

a) Prepare a divisional performance statement for the Mayo division.
b) Outline what financial measures can be used to evaluate divisional performance.

Question 13.5

Cinema Ireland plc. is organised on a divisional basis. The company uses ROI to evaluate managerial performance. The budgeted results for its Munster and Leinster divisions are as follows:

	Munster	Leinster
	€	€
Fixed assets	1,000,000	320,000
Current assets	1,000,000	750,000
Net profit	400,000	325,000

Both divisions are considering new projects which they hope will prove to be profitable for the division and the company as a whole. The financial information is as follows:

1. Management at the Munster division feels it can create additional sales of €100,000 and achieve a contribution margin of 15 per cent on these sales if they undertake a special advertising campaign which they have costed at €8,000. This project requires an investment of €50,000 per annum in additional stocks.
2. Management at the Leinster division has plans to invest in a new food outlet in its cinema at a capital cost of €100,000. The division expects this initiative to improve company profits by €10,000.

Cinema Ireland plc. uses a cost of capital of 12 per cent.

Required

a) Calculate the return on investment and residual income for each division before incorporating the new projects.
b) Calculate the return on investment and residual income for each division after incorporating the new projects into the respective budgets.
c) Based on the calculations in (a) and (b), discuss the extent to which the ROI and residual income financial performance measures encourage divisional managers to pursue a corporate profit objective.

Question 13.6

O'Sullivan Hotels plc. own and operate two hotels located in Galway and Cork. The following is the summarised financial performance of both hotels for the most recent year ending 31 December 2004.

Profit Statement

	Galway	Cork	Total
	€'000	€'000	€'000
Hotel revenues	700	1,593	2,293
Variable costs	(188)	(498)	(686)
Contribution	512	1,095	1,607
Fixed costs	(362)	(840)	(1,202)
Operating profit	150	255	405
Loan interest			(225)
Net profit before tax			180
Corporation tax			(90)
Net profit after tax			90

Other operating information

	Galway	Cork
Breakdown of sales	€'000	€'000
Rooms	560	955
Bar	75	240
Restaurant	65	397
	Rooms	Rooms
Average daily rooms available	100	150
Average daily rooms occupied	53	105

Balance Sheet

	Galway	Cork	Total
	€'000	€'000	€'000
Fixed assets	750	1,200	1,950
Current assets	250	300	550
Current liabilities	75	150	225
	925	1,350	2,275
Long-term debt			1,275
Shareholders funds			1,000
			2,275

The company requires a return on capital of 12 per cent.

Required
a) Prepare the following key operating ratios for both hotels:
    i.   ROCE.
    ii. Asset turnover.
    iii. Operating profit margin.
    iv. Contribution to sales ratio.
    v.   Fixed costs as a percentage of sales.
    vi. Residual income.
    vii. Occupancy rates.
    viii. Average room rate (ARR).
    ix. Sales mix percentage.
    x.   Revenue per available room (RevPAR)
b) From the information above and the ratios calculated in part (a), justify your opinion as to which hotel is the best performing in the group.

Question 13.7

Andrews Hotels plc. own and operate three hotels located in Dublin, Galway and Cork. The following is the summarised financial performance of all three hotels for the most recent year ending 31 December 2004.

Profit Statement

	Dublin	Galway	Cork	Total
	€ '000	€ '000	€ '000	€ '000
Hotel revenues	1,200	1,400	3,185	5,785
Variable costs	(310)	(375)	(995)	(1,680)
Contribution	890	1,025	2,190	4,105
Fixed costs	(650)	(725)	(1,680)	(3,055)
Operating profit	240	300	510	1,050
Loan interest				(450)
Net profit before tax				600
Corporation tax				(180)
Net profit after tax				420

Other operating information

	Dublin	Galway	Cork
	€'000	€'000	€'000
Breakdown of sales			
Rooms	900	1,120	1,911
Bar	200	150	480
Restaurant	100	130	794
	Rooms	Rooms	Rooms
Daily rooms available	70	150	200
Average rooms sold per day	60	80	140

Balance Sheet

	Dublin	Galway	Cork	Total
	€ '000	€ '000	€ '000	€ '000
Fixed assets	600	1,500	2,400	4,500
Current assets	400	500	600	1,500
Current liabilities	50	150	300	500
	950	1,850	2,700	5,500
Long-term debt				4,500
Shareholders funds				1,000
				5,500

The company requires a return on capital of 12 per cent.

Required

a) Prepare the following key operating ratios for the three hotels:
  i. ROCE.
  ii. Asset turnover.
  iii. Operating profit margin.
  iv. Contribution to sales ratio.
  v. Fixed costs as a percentage of sales.
  vi. Residual income.
  vii. Occupancy rates.
  viii. Average room rate (ARR).
  ix. Sales mix percentage.
  x. Revenue per available room (RevPAR).

b) Compare and evaluate the operating performances of each hotel.

Question 13.8

a) Explain the advantage of a balanced scorecard approach to divisionalised per-
    formance measurement.
b) Suggest for each of the following headings, two critical success factors for a health
    and leisure company.
    i.   Financial success.
    ii.   Customer satisfaction.
    iii. Process efficiency.
    iv.   Organisational learning growth.

Question 13.9

Perry plc. is a large conglomerate company structured on a divisional basis. It seeks
to maximise investor's wealth. Head-office avoids day to day involvement in divisional affairs and only intervenes if performance is considered unsatisfactory.
Divisional performance is measured by residual income.

   One of Perry's divisions operates a chain of high class hotels throughout the United
Kingdom. The division's mission statement is *'to be the hotel of first choice for business
users and tourists'*. Although the chain has generally been popular with tourists, it is not
proving quite so popular with business users and conference organisers. Competition
in the top segment of the hotel market is fierce with customers expecting the highest
standards of facilities, services and catering. Over the last two years, the division has
invested a lot of money in modernising its hotels, including the improvement of
bedrooms and public rooms, installation of gymnasia and swimming pools, and the
information technology features required by business travellers. A large amount of
money has also been spent on staff training to improve service levels and on a
television advertising campaign to promote the improved hotels to business users.

   Head-office is concerned that the performance of the hotels appears to have
declined over the last few years despite this expenditure.

The following figures are available:

	£ Millions		
	2001	2002	2003
Capital employed	50	70	90
Operating profit	15	16	17

The cost of capital applicable to the hotel division is 20 per cent per annum.

Required

a) Calculate residual income for the hotel chain for each of the years.

b) Discuss the advantages and disadvantages of residual income as a divisional performance measure.

c) Explain the advantages to Perry plc. of a balanced scorecard approach to divisionalised performance measurement.

d) Suggest for each of the following headings, two critical success factors suitable for the hotel chain:

   i.   Financial success.

   ii. Customer satisfaction.

   iii. Process efficiency.

   iv. Organisational learning growth.

   For each critical success factor, suggest one key performance indicator suitable for the hotel chain.

(The Association of Chartered Certified Accountants)

Question 13.10

The Quality Plus Group own a chain of successful supermarkets. The group prides itself on providing top quality goods and superior service to customers. The group is quick to adopt technological developments and consumer requirements. In recent times the group has introduced a 'home shopping' option, where customers can order over the internet and have goods delivered directly to their homes. Because of the growth in home shopping, the group has created a home shopping division and appointed a manager responsible for all aspects of home shopping. The management of deliveries has been targeted as a key area for improvement. Significant improvement in costs is anticipated if a system of effective route planning and scheduling is introduced.

Required

a) Discuss the value of using a balanced scorecard approach to evaluate the performance of the new division.

b) Suggest two critical success factors and accompanying performance indicators for each of the headings:

   i.   Financial perspective.

   ii. Customer perspective.

   iii. Internal business processes perspective.

   iv. Innovation and learning perspective.

Question 13.11

The Nugget Group plc., your employer, operates two divisions, one in food production and the other in catering and leisure. You do not yet have full information in relation to last year's performance of the two divisions.

From various memoranda and conversations, you have been able to extract the following:

- ❑ The food production division made a profit (before interest and tax) of €12 million. This represented an average margin of operating profit to sales of 10 per cent. The rate of turnover of investment to sales during the last year was two.
- ❑ The catering and leisure division achieved sales of €80 million. The return on investment of the division was 32 per cent, achieved with an operating profit (before interest and tax) to sales ratio of 20 per cent.
- ❑ The Nugget Group uses a cost of capital of 18 per cent in all its calculations.

The in-tray of a colleague who deals with group purchases contains a letter, the abbreviated contents of which are:

> Included in the reported profits of the food production division is €4 million made from inter-divisional sales of €22 million to the catering and leisure division. An outside supplier is offering to undertake this supply in the future. Its price for supplies equivalent to the above would be €19 million. Funds invested would not be affected significantly by such an event.

Required
a) From the information on last year's performance, calculate other appropriate measures or ratios in order to determine which division you consider to be the more profitable. Give your reasons and any qualifications you may have. For this part, ignore all reference to the outside supplier.
b) Briefly examine the implications for each division and the group of the outside supplier's offer. For any numerical illustrations, you should use the figures relating to last year, assuming such a situation would also be repeated in the current year.

(The Association of Chartered Certified Accountants)

Capital Investment Appraisal

Introduction

A very important objective of management accounting is to provide information which will assist management decision-making in relation to the investment of capital funds. Capital investment involves the sacrifice of current funds in order to obtain the benefit of future wealth. It involves investing now in the hope of generating future cash flows which will exceed the initial investment. Investment in capital projects involves large initial financial outlays, with long waiting periods before these funds are repaid from future cash flows or profits. Decisions regarding capital projects significantly influence the direction and success of a business. In order to minimise the risk of poor decision-making in this regard, it is essential that management are aware of the main techniques used to evaluate capital projects.

This chapter focuses on the features and characteristics of capital investment projects before describing in detail the main financial techniques used in their evaluation. As capital projects involve waiting (sometimes for long periods) before repayment, the chapter focuses on this cost of waiting and the time value of money. It also incorporates risk into the investment appraisal process before concluding with a review of the non-financial considerations to be taken into account when evaluating capital investment projects.

Features of Capital Investments

Capital investment involves the use of significant levels of finance to acquire assets for long-term use in an organisation with the desire to increase future revenues and profits.

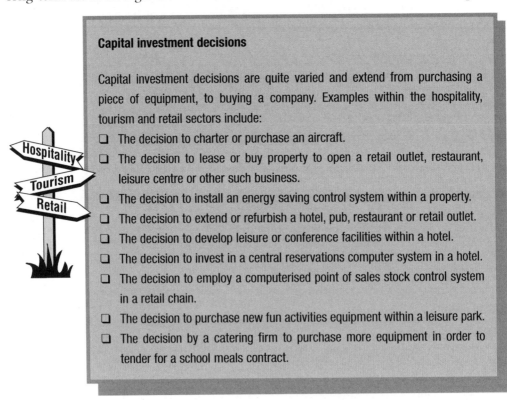

Capital investment decisions

Capital investment decisions are quite varied and extend from purchasing a piece of equipment, to buying a company. Examples within the hospitality, tourism and retail sectors include:

❏ The decision to charter or purchase an aircraft.
❏ The decision to lease or buy property to open a retail outlet, restaurant, leisure centre or other such business.
❏ The decision to install an energy saving control system within a property.
❏ The decision to extend or refurbish a hotel, pub, restaurant or retail outlet.
❏ The decision to develop leisure or conference facilities within a hotel.
❏ The decision to invest in a central reservations computer system in a hotel.
❏ The decision to employ a computerised point of sales stock control system in a retail chain.
❏ The decision to purchase new fun activities equipment within a leisure park.
❏ The decision by a catering firm to purchase more equipment in order to tender for a school meals contract.

Capital investments have very distinct features which make it worthwhile developing and applying a special set of techniques to appraise these decisions. These features are:

❑ The sums involved are relatively large. Bad decisions can have very serious long-term consequences.

❑ The timescale over which the benefits will be received is relatively long, with greater risks and uncertainty in forecasting future revenues and costs.

❑ The nature of a business, its direction and rate of growth is ultimately governed by its overall investment programme.

❑ The irreversibility of some projects due to the specialised nature of certain assets for example, some plant and machinery bought with a specific project in mind could have little or no scrap value.

❑ In order to complete projects on time and within budget, adequate continuous control information is required.

❑ Capital investment is long-term and the recoupment of investment may involve a significant period of time. This waiting period has a cost because the money tied up could be used elsewhere to generate a return or earn interest. This is an important principle of financial management which recognises that monies receivable in the future, have less value than if they were received immediately. This is because:

  – By waiting for cash, one is foregoing the opportunity to invest and earn interest or a return on the investment.

  – The buying power of €1 received today is greater than €1 received in 12 months time due to inflation.

Investment failures

The Austrian Hotel and Tourism Bank has estimated that 53 per cent of business failures are due to poor planning during the initial stage of business set-up. 10 per cent of that 53 per cent was down to mistaken investment. They have also estimated that causes of business failure due to overruns in construction amount to 17 per cent.

Factors to Consider in Assessing Capital Projects

When considering any capital investment projects, there are a number of factors that need to be considered before making a decision.

❑ The size of the investment. Companies should ensure that they do not overextend their capacity and take on a project that they cannot properly operate and finance.

❏ The phasing of the investment expenditure. This can help reduce the risks involved in a project as it involves less time waiting for the recoupment of expenditure.

❏ The period between the initial investment and the asset actually generating revenues and profits for the business. As mentioned above, cost over-runs are expensive, not just in terms of extra investment, but also in lost revenue as the asset is not generating income. Also, a venture that offers significant profits towards the end of its life is obviously higher risk than one that offers profits and positive cash flows earlier.

❏ The economic life of the project. Ultimately, management will desire as short as possible a period before repayment of capital, with a long lifespan thereafter contributing to the company's profits.

❏ The level of certainty regarding the projected cash flows. How accurate are the projected cash flows for the investment?

❏ The working capital required.

❏ The degree of risk involved in the project. This factor relates to both the level of certitude in the projections and the cost of waiting for financial recoupment. It also includes other characteristics such as type of investment in terms of the sector, location, political and economic environment, all of which influence the risk profile of the investment.

Achieving a higher return on property investment

German discounters Aldi and Lidl have had to adjust business strategies in response to market conditions in Ireland. As property is extremely expensive in Ireland, both companies, in an effort to maximise returns, are becoming property developers. A prime example of this is Aldi's outlet on the Fonthill Road. Stephen Murray was quoted in an article in the *Irish Times* as saying 'Aldi and Lidl want to ensure they get a good return on their investment. Since site costs are extremely high, both companies are increasingly developing the associative uses of their land. This means they don't just build their own stores but add more retail units which they can then either sell on or lease.'

Source: www.ireland.com

Capital Appraisal Methods

As capital investment decisions usually involve significant amounts of finance, it is important to fully evaluate each decision using sound appraisal techniques. The main methods used to evaluate investment in capital projects are:

- ❑ Accounting rate of return.
- ❑ Payback method.
- ❑ Net present value.
- ❑ Internal rate of return.

These methods use different approaches to evaluating the value of an investment for an organisation. While three of the methods focus on cash flow, the accounting rate of return uses accounting profit in its appraisal calculation, providing a view of the overall profitability of the investment.

Diagram 14.1: *Approaches to investment appraisal*

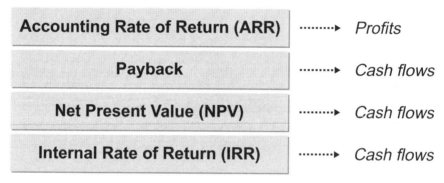

The accounting rate of return is based on the use of *operating profit*. The operating profit of a project is the difference between revenues earned by the project, less all the operating costs associated with the project, including depreciation. Note: the revenues and expenses must be directly related to the project and would exclude any element of fixed costs apportioned from elsewhere in the business.

All other appraisal methods use net cash flows as the basis for appraising capital projects. This is due to the nature of assessing capital investment projects where one must spend cash now and reap the cash rewards later. Financial theory tells us that waiting for money has a cost. For example the cost of waiting for a customer to pay their account is the interest charge on a bank overdraft used while waiting. To take account of this cost of waiting, it is important to be mindful of the timing of the cash inflows and outflows of a business. The calculation of accounting profit is not concerned with the timing of cash flows. This is due to its adherence to the accruals concept whereby profits are calculated by deducting expenses charged from revenues earned.

Net cash flow is calculated as follows:

Net cash flow = operating cash flows + / − capital cash flows

❑   Operating cash flow is the difference between the cash received (cash inflow) less the cash payments (cash outflow), as a result of the project. It has often been described as the cash contribution the project makes to the overall cash flow of the business, before tax. Depreciation is ignored as it is a method of spreading the original capital expenditure to the profit and loss account over its useful life. It is not a cash outlay, as this occurs when the asset is originally purchased.

❑   Capital cash flows include the original cost of the asset and any estimates of residual value, where the asset is disposed of at the end of the project. It also includes any initial investment in working capital required for the project.

❑   The cash inflows and outflows must be directly related to the investment project and would exclude for example, any element of fixed costs apportioned from elsewhere in the business.

Thus in calculating net cash flow, no distinction is made between receipts and expenditure of an operating nature and receipts and expenditure of a capital nature. This would also be the case with any other cash receipts associated with the project. For example, the sale of any existing assets made redundant by the new investment would be relevant and would be included in the cash flow projections.

Net profit	Net cash flow
Related revenue earned	**Related cash inflows (operating + capital)**
less	*less*
All related costs	**Related cash outflows (operating + capital)**
(including depreciation)	(NOT including depreciation)
equals	*equals*
Profit	**Net cash flow**

The Accounting Rate of Return (ARR)

The accounting rate of return method calculates the estimated overall profit or loss on an investment project and relates that profit to the amount of capital invested and to the period for which it is required. It is the profit that is directly related to the investment project that is used in the appraisal process and thus costs or revenues generated elsewhere in the business are excluded. A business will have a required minimum rate of return for any investment. This is related to the cost of capital of the business. If an investment yields a return greater than the cost of capital, then the investment would be considered suitable and profitable. The accounting rate of return is an average rate of return calculated by expressing average annual profit as a percentage of the average value of the investment.

$$\text{ARR} = \frac{\text{Average annual profit}}{\text{Average investment}}$$

Average annual profit	Average investment
Total project profit after depreciation and before interest, tax and dividends, divided by the estimated life of the project.	Initial investment, plus value of investment at project-end, divided by two

The accounting rate of return is also known as the return on investment (ROI) or average net income as a percentage of capital employed (ROCE). The variety of names for this method reflects the variety of possible ways of calculating both 'profit' and 'capital employed'. Profit is normally calculated as shown above, however, capital employed can be calculated using just the opening capital employed figure (the initial investment) alone and not the average capital investment. In general however, the most popular method is as given above.

Calculating operating profit from operating cash flow

Many investment appraisal questions show the operating and capital cash flows relevant to a project. Thus in calculating operating profit one must adjust the operating cash flows back to operating profit. Over the life of a project, the key difference between operating profit and operating cash flow is depreciation. This is due to the fact that depreciation is deducted in the calculation of operating profit but is a non-cash item and thus is not deducted in calculating operating cash flow. This is because the cash outlay for any asset is treated as capital expenditure and is thus part of the capital cash flows. Also, delays between receiving and paying for goods (resulting in debtors and creditors) can cause differences between operating profit and operating cash flow. However these tend to even themselves out over the life of a project, thus it is fair to assume that depreciation is the main difference between operating cash flow and operating profit.

Operating cash flow – Depreciation = Operating profit

Operating profit + Depreciation = Operating cash flow

Example 14.1: *Accounting rate of return*

Newport Leisure Park Ltd. is considering investing €135,000 in a new flume ride. The ride has an estimated life of six years, at the end of which it is estimated it will be sold for €10,000. The following cash flows and profits have been estimated:

Year	Net operating cash flow	Depreciation	Operating profit
	€	€	€
1	14,000	20,833	(6,833)
2	25,000	20,833	4,167
3	35,000	20,833	14,167
4	36,000	20,833	15,167
5	30,000	20,833	9,167
6	25,000	20,833	4,167
Total	165,000	125,000	40,000

Using the accounting rate of return appraisal method, advise the company on whether or not they should make this investment.

Approach

As the accounting rate of return is based on profit, not cash flow, it is first necessary to calculate the profit on the project. This requires the cash flow to be adjusted to take depreciation into account. Depreciation is the reduction in the value of the asset (€135,000 – €10,000) over its useful life and needs to be considered when calculating profit and in order to comply with accounting concepts.

The accounting rate of return for Newport Leisure Park is calculated as follows:

		€
Total profit for the project	€165,000 – (€135,000 – €10,000) *Operating cash flow less depreciation*	40,000
Average annual profit	€40,000 ÷ 6 years *(Total profit divided by life of the project)*	6,667
Average investment	(€135,000 + €10,000 ÷ 2) *(Initial value + residual value ÷ 2)*	72,500
Average annual return	€6,667 ÷ €72,500 x 100 *Average profit divided by average investment*	9.2%

If the company has a cost of capital of 12 per cent, then this project should not be undertaken, as it is forecast not to be economically profitable.

Accept or reject criteria for ARR method

Accept the project	Reject the project
Project ARR greater than the minimum required return.	Project ARR less than the minimum required return.

Advantages of ARR
❑ It takes account of the overall profitability of the project.
❑ It is simple to understand and easy to use.
❑ Its end result is expressed as a percentage, allowing projects of differing sizes to be compared.

Disadvantages of ARR
❑ It is based on accounting profits rather than cash flows. The calculation of profit and capital employed depend on which items of expenditure are treated as capital (on the balance sheet) and as revenue (charged to the profit and loss account). Despite guidelines in this area, it can be quite subjective. Also different accounting policies (depreciation) can produce different profit and capital employed figures, thus allowing the profit and balance sheet figures to be somewhat manipulated. It is for this reason that capital projects are also evaluated in terms of cash flows.
❑ The ARR does not take into account the timing of cash flows. For example, project A may give an ARR of 20 per cent compared to project B's 18 per cent. However project A may be an eight year project whereas project B may be a five year project. Investors may choose a project that is slightly less profitable but which generates cash earlier.
❑ The ARR does not take into account the time value of money. It does not take into account the cost of waiting to recoup the investment.
❑ The ARR takes no account of the size of the initial investment. A five per cent return on an investment of €25,000 might be acceptable, however it may not be an acceptable return on an initial investment of €10 million.

The Payback Method

This method of investment appraisal simply asks the question *'how long before I get my money back?'* In other words how quickly will the cash flows arising from the project exactly equal the amount of the investment. It is a simple method, widely used in industry and is based on management's concern to be reimbursed on the initial outlay as soon as possible. It is not concerned with overall profitability or the level of profitability.

We can now return to the Newport Leisure Park scenario to demonstrate the payback method.

Example 14.2: *Payback*

Newport Leisure Park Ltd is considering investing €135,000 in a new flume ride. The ride has an estimated life of six years at the end of which it is estimated it will be sold for €10,000. The projected operating net cash flows are as follows:

Year	Net operating cash flow
1	14,000
2	25,000
3	35,000
4	36,000
5	30,000
6	25,000
	165,000

Establish the payback period for this investment.

Approach

In the present year (year zero) there is a cash outflow of €135,000 with projected cash inflows for years one to six. The payback method answers the question, 'when in this six year period will the company get its €135,000 back?'

Year	Cash flow	Cumulative cash flow
	€	€
0	(135,000)	(135,000)
1	14,000	(121,000)
2	25,000	(96,000)
3	35,000	(61,000)
4	36,000	(25,000)
5	30,000	5,000
6	35,000 *	40,000

⋆ Operating cash flow of €25,000, plus residual
value of the investment €10,000.

As can be seen from the above table, at the end of year four a further €25,000 is needed for the initial investment to be fully recovered. By the end of year five the initial investment is fully recovered and the project is showing a surplus of €5,000. Thus the payback period is between four and five years. If we assume that cash flows are earned evenly throughout the year then, by interpolation, we can calculate the number of months or days it will take in year five to recover the full amount.

This is calculated as follows:

$$\text{The annual period} \times \frac{\text{Cash required to payback}}{\text{Total net cash flow for the period}}$$

$$12 \text{ months} \times \text{€}25{,}000 \div \text{€}30{,}000 = 10 \text{ months}$$

The payback period is 4 years 10 months

If the company have a maximum payback period of 4 years then the project will be rejected.

Accept or reject criteria for payback method

Accept the project	Reject the project
Payback period is less than that required by investors.	Payback period is greater than that required by investors.

Advantages of payback
❑ It is simple to understand and apply.
❑ It promotes a policy of caution in investment.

Disadvantages of payback
❑ It takes no account of the timing of cash flows (€100 received today is worth more than €100 received in 12 months time). This is known as the time value of money and will be considered in more detail below.
❑ It is only concerned with how quickly the initial investment is recovered and thus it ignores the overall profitability and return on capital for the whole project. The accounting rate of return incorporates the overall profitability of the investment.

The Time Value of Money

The final two methods of investment appraisal are more sophisticated than those already discussed since they take into consideration the time value of money concept. Discounted cash flow methods (DCF) are capital appraisal techniques that account for the fact that €1 earned or spent sooner, is worth more than €1 earned or spent later. The earlier positive cash flows are generated, the sooner they can be used to make a further contribution to profit. Thus the time value of money concept plays an important role in appraising capital projects because the time lag between the initial investment and payback can be quite long. However the difficulty lies in comparing €1 cash flow received today with €1 received in the future, as the two cannot be equal to each other given they are received in different time periods. Thus to evaluate any project taking into account the time value of money, the cash flows received in the future must be reduced or discounted to a present value, so that all relevant cash flows are denominated in today's value (present value). This discount factor represents the cost of waiting, or the time value of money.

The reasons why cash flows received in different time periods have different values are:

❑ **Uncertainty:** Monies invested in projects run the risk of not being refundable. Ultimately, investors take this risk and profit is a payment for risk-taking. The greater the risk an investor takes, the greater will be the required return from the project to compensate for this risk-taking. The business world is full of uncertainty and risk, thus investors will require the promise of significant returns to entice them to take on extra risk. Although there might be a promise of future cash flows, it can never be certain that the money will be received. For example the massive investment in the 'dot.com' sector in the late 1990s ensured massive valuations for these companies before they even made a profit. However, as many investors will now testify, most did not make and never will make a profit.

❑ **Interest or returns lost:** Monies received earlier can be invested to earn extra income for a business. Monies received earlier can be used to reduce bank overdrafts and thus reduce the associated interest cost. Having to wait for cash is an opportunity cost as it results in these type of opportunities being lost to a business. DCF therefore takes into account the notional interest lost because of the time delay in receiving cash flows.

❑ **Inflation:** General price inflation ensures that €1 now purchases more and is worth more than €1 received in the future. It is important to know that even if there was a period of zero inflation, the time value of money would still be a relevant concept and DCF would still be used for investment appraisal.

Uncertainty and risk, inflation, and the interest or return lost by not receiving cash earlier, all ensure that waiting for future cash flows has a cost and hence money has a time value. The difficulty for every business is to evaluate their cost of waiting or their time value of money, as it will be different for every business due to the following:

❑ The differing levels of uncertainty and risk that applies to different business sectors, as well as to different businesses within a sector.
❑ The inflation rate that applies to the specific business sector that the company operates in.
❑ The opportunity cost of waiting is related to the interest foregone by not having the money earlier. This is certainly easier to evaluate than inflation or risk.

In reality, these three elements make up the cost of capital of a business and hence the discount factor to use in evaluating capital projects should be the cost of capital that applies to that business.

The Cost of Capital

All investment projects require funding. Generally, funding can be classified into:

❑ Equity funding, where investors buy an equity or ownership share in a project. This is done through the issue of shares or by retaining profits in the business.
❑ Debt, where the company can borrow or issue its own debentures.

Each source of finance has a cost. The cost of debt is the interest rate that applies to the debt. The costs of equity finance are the dividends and increases in share price expected by shareholders. This cost of capital becomes the benchmark or minimum required return on a project. Thus a project is only truly profitable when its actual return on assets is greater than the company's cost of capital.

Example 14.3: *Cost of capital*

Graham's Limo Services Ltd has invested €150,000 in two second-hand limousines. The investment has been financed through a bank loan of nine per cent. In its first year, the cars generate €60,000 in revenues and €40,000 in operating expenses, including chauffeurs wages, cleaning, petrol, insurance, advertising and depreciation.

Is this business generating a return greater than the cost of capital?

Approach

Ignoring corporation tax, the project achieved an operating profit of €20,000 and hence the return on assets (ROCE) is 13.33 per cent (€20,000 ÷ €150,000). This is greater than the cost of capital of nine per cent and thus the project is truly profitable.

Another way to look at this is that the business must make at least €13,500 (€150,000 x 9%) profit to meet the cost of capital.

The cost of capital of nine per cent could be made up of 2 per cent compensation for loss of interest, three per cent for inflation and four per cent risk premium.

Weighed average cost of capital

If a project is funded by more than one method of financing, the weighted average cost of capital (WACC) should be calculated. The following demonstrates this:

Loan finance €100,000 at 9%.

Equity finance €50,000 at 12%.

$$
\begin{array}{llll}
\text{Debt} & \text{€100,000 x 9\%} & = \text{€9,000} \\
\text{Equity} & \underline{\text{€50,000}} \text{ x 12\%} & = \underline{\text{€6,000}} \\
& \text{€150,000} & \text{€15,000}
\end{array}
$$

Thus the WACC is 10% (15,000 ÷ 150,000 x 100)

In this case the WACC is the minimum required return on the project.

In summary then, the business cost of capital is the discount factor to use when discounting future cash flows to present values, as it represents the minimum required return for investors to compensate them for the interest lost, inflation, and risk inherent in any investment. Should a business be financed through a mixture of equity and debt, then a weighted average cost of capital should be calculated and this should be the factor used in discounting future cash flows to present value.

Discounting cash flows

The following exercises focus on the theory and techniques of discounting future cash flows to present values.

❑   A business requires a rate of return of 10 per cent on its capital. A certain investment promises to pay us €1,000 in one year's time. Thus the amount we would need to invest now to amount to €1,000 is €909. Thus €909 is considered to be the present value of receiving €1,000 in one year's time, based on a cost of capital of 10 per cent.

The formula for this calculation is:

$$PV = \frac{FV \times 1}{(1 + r)^n}$$

Where r = cost of capital

n = the number of years

FV = the future sum

$$\frac{1,000 \times 1}{(1+0.1)^1}$$

1,000 x .9091 = €909

❑ If the €1,000 is expected to be received in two years time, then the present value of that future sum of money can be calculated as:

$$\frac{1,000 \times 1}{(1+0.1)^2}$$

$$1,000 \times .826 = €826$$

❑ This calculation can be done for any amount and for any time period. €1,000 received in three year's time equals €751.

$$\frac{1,000 \times 1}{(1.1)^3}$$

❑ An easier way of calculating the present value of a future sum based on a certain cost of capital, is to use what is known as present value tables. These give the present value of €1 to be received in n years' time, given a rate of interest of r % for a wide range of values for both r and n (see appendix C).

Try the following:

1. Calculate the present value of €2,000 received in three years at a discount rate of 10 per cent.

(Answer = €1,502)

2. Calculate the present value of €1,000 received in year two and €3,000 received in year three using a discount factor of 9 per cent.

(Answer = €3,158)

3. Calculate the present value of receiving €3,000 in year one, €4,000 in year two and €5,000 in year three, using a discount rate of 8 per cent.

(Answer = €10,176)

❑ If one was to receive €5,000 each year for the next five years then a short-cut in calculating the present value of each of the sums is to use the annuity tables (see Appendix C). The present value of receiving €5,000 each year for five years at a discount rate of 10 per cent is €5,000 x 3.791 = €18,955. (Go to the 10 per cent column and take the fifth year.)
This factor of 3.791 is the sum of the individual present value discount factors at a rate of 10 per cent (0.909 + 0.826 + 0.751 + 0.693 + 0.621). Thus it represents a quicker way of discounting once the annual cash flows are the same.

❑ Finally calculate the present value of receiving an annuity (annual payment) of €1,000 for the rest of your life using an interest rate of 11 per cent. This is simply calculated as €1,000 ÷ 0.11 = €9,090. Thus the present value (year zero value) of receiving €1,000 each year for infinity is €9,090.
If €1,000 was discounted each year for infinity or say the next 30 years, the annuity table tells us the cumulative discount factor after 15 years is 7.191 and after 30 years is 8.694. After 30

years the present value factors get so small that effectively they account for very little and will only, after a great number of years, bring the cumulative factor up to 9.090. This is effectively calculated as 1 ÷ 11%. Thus the present value of receiving any sum of money for infinity or a lifetime is:

$$\frac{FV}{R}$$

Try the following:

1. Calculate the present value of receiving €2,000 each year in perpetuity using a discount rate of 12 per cent.

(Answer = €16,667)

2. Calculate the present value of receiving €2,000 each year in perpetuity from year four.

(Answer = (2,000 ÷ 0.12) x 0.712 = €11,867)

Note: The value of this annuity at the end of year three is (2,000 ÷ 0.12) = €16,667. To calculate the present value, we multiply €16,667 by the discount factor for year three to get us to year zero.

Thus in summary, DCF is the investment appraisal technique that takes account of the time value of money. The main information points regarding DCF are as follows:

❑ DCF looks at the cash flows of a project, not the accounting profits. Like the payback technique, it is concerned with liquidity not profitability. Cash flows are considered because they show the costs and benefits of a project when they actually occur, unlike the profit and loss account which spreads the capital costs over the life of the project in the form of depreciation.

❑ The timing of cash flows is taken into account by discounting all future cash flows to present value. The effect of discounting is to give a bigger value per euro for cash flows that occur earlier. For example, €1 earned after one year will be worth more than €1 after two years etc.

❑ The discount factor to use is the cost of capital to the business.

Now it is time to look at the two main investment appraisal techniques that involve the use of DCF. These are:

1. Net Present Value method (NPV).
2. The Internal Rate of Return method (IRR).

The Net Present Value (NPV) Method

Present value can be defined as the cash equivalent now of a sum of money to be received or paid at a stated future date, discounted at a specified cost of capital. The net present value is the value obtained by discounting all the cash outflows and inflows of a capital investment project, at a chosen target rate of return or cost of capital. The present value of the cash inflows, minus the present value of the cash outflows, is the net present value.

❑ *If the NPV is positive,* it means that the cash inflows from the investment will yield a return in excess of the cost of capital and thus the project should be undertaken, as long as there are no other projects offering a higher NPV.
❑ *If the NPV is negative,* it means that the cash inflows from the investment yield a return below the cost of capital and so the project should not be undertaken.
❑ *If the NPV is exactly zero,* the cash inflows from the investment will yield a return which is exactly the same as the cost of capital and thus the project may or may not be worth undertaking depending on other investment opportunities available.

Accept or reject criteria for NPV method

Accept the project	Reject the project
NPV is positive.	NPV is negative.
In choosing between mutually exclusive projects, accept the project with the highest NPV.	

We can now return to the Newport Leisure Park scenario to demonstrate the net present value method of investment appraisal.

Example 14.4: *Net present value*

Newport Leisure Park Ltd. is considering investing €135,000 in a new flume ride. The Ride has an estimated life of six years at the end of which it is estimated it will be sold for €10,000. The projected operating net cash flows are as follows:

Year	Net operating cash flow
1	14,000
2	25,000
3	35,000
4	36,000
5	30,000
6	25,000
	165,000

The company's cost of capital is 12 per cent.

Using the net present value method, advise the company on whether or not they should invest in this flume ride.

Approach

The relevant cash flows are discounted to present year (year zero) values and a cumulative net present value is calculated as follows:

Year	Cash flow €	Discount factor 12%	Present value €
0	(135,000)	1.0	(135,000)
1	14,000	0.893	12,502
2	25,000	0.797	19,925
3	35,000	0.712	24,920
4	36,000	0.636	22,898
5	30,000	0.567	17,010
6	35,000	0.507	17,745
Net present value			(20,000)

The NPV is a negative figure of €20,000. Thus the investment does not give a return greater than the company's cost of capital (the ultimate accept criterion) and the project should be rejected based on the projections presented.

Advantages of NPV method
❑ It takes into account the time value of money.
❑ Profit and the difficulties of profit measurement are excluded.
❑ Using cash flows emphasises the importance of liquidity.
❑ It is easy to compare the NPV of different projects.

Disadvantages of NPV method
The main disadvantages associated with the net present value approach are that it is not as easily understood as the payback and accounting rate of return. Also, the net present value approach requires knowledge of the company's cost of capital, which is difficult to calculate.

The Internal Rate of Return

In the NPV method, present values are calculated by discounting all cash flows at the target rate of return or cost of capital. The difference between the PV of the costs and the PV of the benefits is the NPV. A positive NPV tells us that the project based on the projected figures would give a return greater than the cost of capital or the required return. However, what is the rate of return the project is forecast to earn? From our example above, the rate of return should be less than the cost of capital of 12 per cent as the NPV is (€20,000).

The IRR method calculates the exact rate of return which the project is expected to achieve, based on the projected cash flows. It is the discount rate which, when applied to the projected cash flows, ensures they are equal to the initial capital outlay. The IRR is the discount factor which will give a NPV of zero. It is the actual return from the project, taking into account the time value of money.

Accept or reject criteria for IRR method

Accept the project	Reject the project
IRR greater than the cost of capital.	IRR less than the cost of capital.

The calculation of the IRR can be quite complicated and involves a trial and error process. The following is a step-by-step approach.

1. Calculate the NPV based on the cost of capital.
2. If this discount factor results in a negative NPV, then step two involves, through trial and error, finding a discount factor which will give a positive NPV. To be more likely to achieve a positive NPV, one should use a lower discount factor (a lower cost of capital always increases the chances of a project having a positive NPV).
3. Once one has a negative and positive NPV based on two discount factors then, through interpolation, the IRR can be found. This involves the use of the following formula:

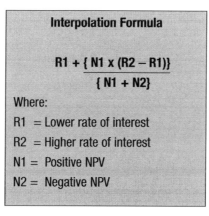

Interpolation Formula

$$R1 + \frac{\{ N1 \times (R2 - R1)\}}{\{ N1 + N2\}}$$

Where:

R1 = Lower rate of interest

R2 = Higher rate of interest

N1 = Positive NPV

N2 = Negative NPV

Example 14.5: *Internal rate of return*

Newport Leisure Park Ltd is considering investing €135,000 in a new flume ride. The ride has an estimated life of six years at the end of which it is estimated it will be sold for €10,000. The projected operating net cash flows are as follows:

Year	Net operating cash flow
1	14,000
2	25,000
3	35,000
4	36,000
5	30,000
6	25,000
	165,000

The company's cost of capital is 12 per cent.

Using the internal rate of return method, advise the company on whether they should invest in this flume ride.

Approach

Step 1: The NPV using the cost of capital of 12% was a negative €20,000. Thus step 2 requires finding a discount factor that will ensure a positive NPV.
Step 2: Using a lower cost of capital enhances the chance of achieving a positive NPV. By using a discount factor of 4 per cent, a positive NPV of €15,798 is calculated.

Year	Cash flow €	Disc 12%	P.V. €	Disc 4%	P.V. €
0	(135,000)	1.0	(135,000)	1.0	(135,000)
1	14,000	0.893	12,502	0.962	13,468
2	25,000	0.797	19,925	0.925	23,125
3	35,000	0.712	24,920	0.889	31,115
4	36,000	0.636	22,898	0.855	30,780
5	30,000	0.567	17,010	0.822	24,660
6	35,000	0.507	17,745	0.790	27,650
			(20,000)		15,798

Step 3: This involves interpolation in calculating the discount rate, which gives a NPV of 0.

$$4 + \frac{\{15,798 \times (12 - 4)\}}{\{15,798 + 20,000\}}$$

$$4 + \{0.4413 \times 8\} = 7.53\%$$

The IRR of this project is 7.53% and is below the cost of capital, thus the project should be rejected.

Advantages of IRR

❑ The main advantage of the IRR is that the information it provides is more easily understood by managers, especially non-financial managers. For example it is easier to understand, 'a project is expected to yield a 25 per cent return which is in excess of the target yield of 15 per cent', than to understand, 'the project is expected to have a NPV of €45,000 when discounted at the cost of capital.'

Disadvantages of IRR

❑ The trial and error process of calculating the IRR can be time consuming, however this disadvantage can easily be overcome with the use of computer software.

❑ It is possible to calculate more than two different IRRs for a project. This occurs where the cash flows over the life of the project are a combination of positive and negative values. Under these circumstances it is not easy to identify the real IRR and the method should be avoided.

❑ In certain circumstances the IRR and the NPV can give conflicting results. This occurs because the IRR ignores the relative size of investments as it is based on a percentage return rather than the cash value of the return. As a result, when considering two projects, one may give an IRR of 10 per cent and the other an IRR of 13 per cent. However the project with the lower IRR may yield a higher NPV in cash terms and thus would be preferable. Suppose project A and project B have both IRRs of 18 per cent. Project A requires an initial investment of €350,000 and has a NPV of €250,000 whereas project B requires an initial investment of €35,000 and has a NPV of €25,000. Clearly project A is ten times bigger and so more profitable, but if the only information on which the projects were judged was their respective IRRs of 18 per cent, project B would be seen to be just as beneficial as project A, which is clearly not the case.

Both the following projects have an IRR of 18%:

	Project A	Project B
	€	€
Cost for year 0	350,000	35,000
Annual saving years 1 - 6	100,000	10,000
NPV	250,000	25,000

Investment Appraisal in Practice

Diagram 14.2: Appraisal methods

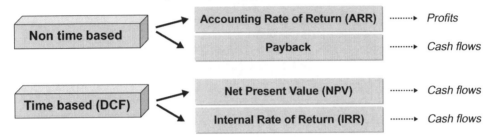

Of the four appraisal methods presented, it is clear that the discounted cash flow methods (NPV and IRR) have a distinct advantage over the payback and accounting rate of return methods. This is because they are cash based and they take the time value of money into account. The NPV approach is considered superior to the IRR because of the disadvantages associated with the IRR method. However it is clear that there is a place for all four methods, which inform judgement, not replace it. If we return to the Newport Leisure Park we can see more detailed information when the results of the four methods are presented together and interpreted.

Newport Leisure Park Ltd investment appraisal summary

Appraisal technique	Result	Evaluation
Payback	4 years and 10 months	The full payback is estimated to occur 80 per cent into the project period. This is a long time to wait for payback.
ARR	9.2%	The ARR is 9.2 per cent and this is below the cost of capital of the business at 12 per cent. The project should be rejected.
NPV	(€20,000)	A NPV of (€20,000) implies the present value of cash outflows exceed the present value of cash inflows over the life of the project by €20,000. The project should be rejected.
IRR	7.53%	In this case the recommendations of both the ARR and the IRR should be the same – to reject the project. The IRR takes into account the extra cost of waiting and thus should give a lower return than the ARR.

A survey by the Chartered Association of Certified Accountants in 1993 showed the following techniques used either often or always by UK manufacturing companies:

Payback	63%
Payback (using DCF)*	42% see below
ARR	41%
IRR	57%
NPV	43%

* Note: the payback method can also be calculated by discounting the cash flows at the cost of capital and then calculating the payback period based on the discounted cash flows. This effectively cancels out the criticism that it does not take into account the time value of money. However it still does not look at the overall profitability or overall cash flows of the project. The discounted payback is dealt with below.

Research on the use of capital appraisal techniques

Hospitality and Tourism

Research by Smullen and O'Donoghue in 2005 in relation to the *use and influence of financial decision support models within the hospitality industry* found the following:

- ❑ 76 per cent of hotels surveyed used capital investment appraisal techniques in their evaluation of investment opportunities.
- ❑ 61 per cent of those hotel companies used the payback method, with 17 per cent using the ARR.
- ❑ Only 22 per cent of companies used the discounted cash flow approach with 13 per cent using NPV and 9 per cent using IRR.
- ❑ Of the companies using the ARR, 75 per cent used the initial capital investment method and 25 per cent used the average investment method.

The research was conducted in early 2005 and was based on hotels with a three star standard or higher with a minimum of thirty bedrooms. The research used a mixture of interviews and questionnaires with a total of seventeen hotels surveyed in Ireland.

UK research on the hotel industry carried out by Collier and Gregory in 1994 was based on a case study of six hotel companies, three of which were UK based and three based overseas, with a spread of small, medium and large companies. This research suggests that a range of methods is used for capital investment appraisal, with the NPV being the least popular, although a number of businesses use the IRR.

Company	Investment appraisal technique	Is IRR used?	Cost of capital
A	Payback	No	N/A
B	ARR / Payback	Partly	Loan rate +
C	IRR	Yes	Loan rate x 1.5
D	Others based on profitability and interest cover	No	N/A
E	ARR / IRR	Yes	Business specification
F	IRR	Yes	Corporate weighted average cost of capital

The Retail Sector

Research conducted by Luby (2006) found that only 50 per cent of respondents used capital investment appraisal techniques. The techniques adopted included:

Payback period	100%
Net present value	60%
Internal rate of return	40%
Accounting rate of return	40%

Comparing Mutually Exclusive Projects with Unequal Lives

When comparing mutually exclusive projects, the appraisal method to use is the net present value approach. However businesses often have to decide on two or more competing projects that have unequal or different life spans. For example, project A has a life of 4 years whereas project B has a life of 6 years. In these situations, to simply compare the net present values of each project without looking at the unequal lifespan would not be comparing like with like. Project B with a longer life would most likely have a higher NPV because it has two extra years to generate positive cash flows. However to simply recommend project B on the basis of the higher net present values could lead to a dysfunctional decision. This is because project A, with a shorter lifespan, offers an opportunity to the business of investing sooner in other projects that offer positive net present values and this needs to be taken into account in any mutually exclusive decision. For example, the cash flows generated from project A could, at the end of its four years, be re-invested elsewhere for two additional years generating additional cash flows which, when discounted, could ensure the NPV of project A exceeds the NPV of project B. What is required is that the net present value of both projects needs to be expressed in equal terms. Thus it is appropriate to use the *'equivalent annual annuity method'* to compare the net present values on an annualised basis.

This is calculated as follows:

1. Calculate the NPV of each project.
2. Divide the NPV of each project by the annuity factor for the period of the project. This calculates what is called the 'equivalent annual annuity' or EAA.
3. Compare the EAA of each project, accepting the project with the highest equivalent annual annuity.

Example 14.6: *Project appraisal with unequal lives*

The management of Express Groceries Ltd are considering upgrading the conveyor belts in the checkout system in the store. Option A has an estimated life based on normal usage of two years, whereas option B has an estimated life of three years. Both options have a zero residual value. Details of relevant cash flows are as follows: The company's cost of capital is 10 per cent.

	Option A	Option B
	€	€
Cash flows		
Year 0	(100,000)	(138,668)
Year 1	50,000	60,000
Year 2	70,000	80,000
Year 3		30,200

Which option should be adopted by Express Groceries Ltd?

Approach

As this investment decision is a mutually exclusive one, the company should use the NPV method. The NPV for both options is as follows:

Option A NPV + €3,303

Option B NPV + €4,679

The next step is to calculate the equivalent annual annuity figures. These are calculated by dividing the NPV of each project by the annuity factor that relates to the period of each project.

Option A is a two year project thus the relevant annuity figure is 1.7355. (See Appendix C annuity table, two years at 10 per cent).
Thus the EAA for option A is €3,303 ÷ 1.735 = €1,904.

Option B is a three year project thus the relevant annuity figure is 2.487. (See Appendix C annuity table, three years at 10 per cent).
Thus the EAA for option B is €4,679 ÷ 2.487 = €1,881.

The company should choose option A as it has the higher EAA value.

The Calculation of Cash Flows – Practical Issues

Operating cash flows represent sales revenues, less variable cost attributed to the project or investment. Fixed costs are also included but only if they relate to the new investment and are incremental. All costs that would occur irrespective of the investment decision should be ignored. The cash flows that are to be considered are those that would not arise without the investment.

The following rules apply regarding relevant costs and revenues for investment decisions:

❑ **Sunk costs:** All past costs that have already been paid (sunk costs) and are associated with the project should be ignored.
❑ **Incremental costs:** Only incremental costs that relate to the decision (the future costs that will change due to the decision) should be taken into account.
❑ **Opportunity gains or costs:** These costs, arising as a result of benefits foregone, should be taken into account. For example, when considering a decision to either continue to use or sell off some old equipment, the opportunity cost (benefit foregone) associated with the decision to hold and use the equipment is the revenue lost by not selling the equipment. This should be taken into account in the decision. No account is taken of the original cost of the equipment as it is already paid for and is considered a sunk cost.
❑ **Replacement costs:** In cases where an asset, for example stock, was originally purchased for some purpose other than the opportunity under consideration, the relevant cost of using that resource or asset is not its original cost (the sunk cost), but is its replacement cost, as the asset will need to be replaced to do the job for which it was originally intended.
❑ **Loan interest and dividend payments:** When using DCF, loan interest and dividend payments should not be taken into account in calculating the operating cash flows as the discount factor already takes into account the cost of financing.

❑ **Incremental working capital:** It will often be the case that capital investment in a project will also require an associated investment in working capital. This is because stocks of materials will need to be made available and debtors may have to increase to allow for the increased volume of sales. These out-goings may be partially offset by an increase in creditors. This outlay should be treated as part of the initial expenditure or capital investment. If there is an extra investment in working capital required during the life of the project, then this extra investment is treated as a cash outflow in the year it occurs. However at the end of the project's life, the total investment in working capital is assumed to be liquidated (turned into cash) at original cost and thus can be treated as a cash inflow in the final year of the life of the project.

❑ **Depreciation:** This is a non-cash item and must be ignored in calculating operating cash flows. Depreciation is a means by which the original cost of an asset is charged to the profit and loss account over the useful life of the asset. However in DCF calculations, the cost of an asset is taken into account at the beginning of the project period and hence there would be double accounting if subsequent depreciation charges were also included.

❑ **Year-end assumption:** In calculating the cash flows of a project, it is assumed that they arise at the end of the relevant year. This assumption is quite unrealistic as wages and many other expenses will be paid weekly or monthly and customers will also make payments throughout the year. The reason for the assumption is to make the calculations of present value easier and because, over the life of a project, this simplifying assumption would make little difference to the final decision. If cash flows occur at the beginning of a year, they are assumed to occur at the end of the previous year.

❑ **Taxation:** Investors are interested in the after tax returns generated from the business and so taxation will usually be an important consideration. The capital investment may attract special tax reliefs (urban renewal, seaside resort renewal) and the profits from the investment will be subject to income tax or corporation tax, (depending on your legal form of organisation). Companies resident in the Republic of Ireland are subject to corporation tax on their worldwide profits. The corporation tax rates in Ireland are 12.5 per cent for trading income and 25 per cent for non-trading income (rental income, income from foreign properties, income from mining and petroleum activities). Corporation tax is payable in two instalments:
  - Preliminary tax, which must equal at least 90 per cent of the ultimate corporation tax liability, is paid one month before the end of the accounting period.
  - The balance, which is payable nine months after the accounting period.
  Capital gains tax (tax on profits from selling capital assets) is charged at 20 per cent and is included in the corporation tax payment.

Example 14.7: *Calculation of cash flows*

Burgerqueen Fast Foods Ltd are considering investing in new equipment costing €100,000. The estimated life of the equipment is four years with an estimated residual value of €20,000 at the end of the four years. The following information relates to the forecast operational performance of the machine for the next four years.

Year	Sales (units)	Contribution per unit €	Fixed costs €
1	6,000	15	60,000
2	6,500	15	60,000
3	5,500	16	60,000
4	5,000	16	60,000

Depreciation of €20,000 per annum is included in fixed costs. Also included in fixed costs is €10,000 per annum of costs apportioned from head-office. An investment in working capital of €10,000 is required at the beginning of year one and €20,000 at the beginning of year two. This working capital will be liquidated at the end of year four. The company's cost of capital is 12 per cent.

Calculate the net present value of the investment.

Approach

This question requires the calculation of relevant cash flows before discounting. This is done by firstly calculating the forecast annual operating cash flows as follows:

	Year 1	Year 2	Year 3	Year 4
Unit sales	6,000	6,500	5,500	5,000
Contribution per unit	€15	€15	€16	€16
	€	€	€	€
Total contribution	90,000	97,500	88,000	80,000
Fixed costs	60,000	60,000	60,000	60,000
	30,000	37,500	28,000	20,000
Add Non-incremental costs	10,000	10,000	10,000	10,000
Operating profit	40,000	47,500	38,000	30,000
Add Depreciation	20,000	20,000	20,000	20,000
Operating cash flow	60,000	67,500	58,000	50,000

The next step is to calculate the net cash flows which includes both capital and working capital transactions, as well as the operating cash flows above. The net cash flows are then discounted at the cost of capital.

Year	Equipment	Working capital	Operating cash flows	Net cash flows	Disc 12%	Present
	€	€	€	€	12%	€
0	(100,000)	(10,000)		(110,000)	1.00	(110,000)
1		(20,000)	60,000	40,000	0.8929	35,716
2			67,500	67,500	0.7972	53,811
3			58,000	58,000	0.7118	41,284
4	20,000	30,000	50,000	100,000	0.6355	63,550
					NPV	84,361

The present value of the cash inflows exceeds the present value of the cash outflows by €84,361 and thus the project is acceptable.

Project Appraisal and Risk

All future projects are subject to some element of uncertainty and risk. For example, all project appraisal methods rely on forecasting of revenues and expenses. These forecasts are not known for certain and hence risk and uncertainty exists. Risk describes the situation where there is more than one possible outcome in the future and it implies a knowledge of the likelihood or probabilities of each possible outcome occurring. Uncertainty occurs where one cannot apply probabilities to the range of possible outcomes.

Risk can be classified into the following categories:

❑ **Operating risk:** This occurs where a business has a high fixed operating cost structure and hence it must ensure it generates sufficient revenues and contribution to cover fixed costs. In general, the hospitality and tourism sectors suffer from a high level of operating risk. Operating risk was discussed in detail in Chapter 6.

❑ **Financial risk:** This arises from the methods chosen to finance an operation. High financial risk implies that a business is highly financed through borrowings and hence must ensure operating profit and cash flows are sufficient to meet the interest costs of these financial instruments. Financial risk was discussed in detail in Chapter 12.

❑ **Business risk:** This occurs as a result of changes to the economic and business environment that can be caused by a range of factors such as hurricanes, terrorism, tsunamis, technological advances, consumer confidence, inflation and fluctuations in national and global economies. All businesses are subject to this type of risk and it is this type of risk that is associated with investment appraisal.

For investment appraisal, it is important to take account of business risk and the following are some of the techniques used to incorporate risk into the various project appraisal models.

Discounted payback

One of the weaknesses of the payback period is that it does not take into account the cost of waiting. The discounted payback method overcomes this by simply discounting the cash flows of a project with the cost of capital for the business and calculating the payback period based on the present value of the cash flows. Returning to the investment decision for Newport Leisure Park Ltd., the discounted payback would be calculated as follows.

Year	Cash flow	Discount	Present value	Cumulative cash flows
	€	12%	€	
0	(135,000)	1.0	(135,000)	(135,000)
1	14,000	0.893	12,502	(122,498)
2	25,000	0.797	19,925	(102,573)
3	35,000	0.712	24,920	(77,653)
4	36,000	0.636	22,896	(54,757)
5	30,000	0.567	17,010	(37,747)
6	35,000	0.507	17,745	(20,002)

When using the discounted payback, it is clear that at the end of the project, the initial sum is not fully repaid. Contrast that with the non-discounted payback period of 4 years 10 months. The discounted payback period introduces an element of caution to the payback model and addresses one of its main criticisms, not taking into account the time value of money.

Sensitivity analysis

Sensitivity analysis was covered in detail in Chapter 7. It assessed how sensitive profit is to changes in the variables that make up profit such as sales volume, sales price, sales mix and costs. The same process and principles apply when dealing with project appraisal. One can get a feel for the sensitivity of the NPV of a project if changes occur to the various inputs to the NPV model. These inputs would include the following:

❑ The value of the initial investment.
❑ The estimated life of the project.

❑   The sales volume forecast.
❑   The forecast price used.
❑   The forecast sales mix used.
❑   The cost forecasts.
❑   The disposal value of the investment assets.
❑   The discount rate used.

Illustration 14.1: *Sensitivity analysis*

Graham's Limos Ltd are considering investing in a new flash limo. The initial cost is €115,000. The estimated life of the vehicle is six years with an estimated residual value of €20,000. The following information shows the relevant cash flows for the project, discounted at a cost of capital of 12 per cent. Based on these projections, the net present value of the project is €10,000 positive.

Year	Cash flow	Discount	Present value
	€	12%	€
0	(115,000)	1.0	(115,000)
1	14,000	0.893	12,502
2	25,000	0.797	19,925
3	35,000	0.712	24,920
4	36,003	0.636	22,898
5	30,000	0.567	17,010
6	54,724	0.507	27,745
		NPV =	10,000

By taking each variable or a combination of variables and changing them, one can assess the changes to the NPV and assess how it may impact on the decision to invest.

For example:

❑   If the initial capital outlay was €20,000 or 17.4 per cent (20,000 ÷ 115,000) greater, then the NPV would be €10,000 negative, a decrease of 200 per cent, giving a sensitivity rating of 11.5 times (200 ÷ 17.4). This implies that if the initial capital outlay increases or decreases by 1 per cent, the NPV will fluctuate by 11.5 per cent. Thus the NPV is quite sensitive to changes in the initial investment and management should focus on the likelihood that this could occur.
❑   Another way to look at this is to assess how much would the initial investment need to increase by for the project to break even or have a NPV of 0. In this case the initial capital outlay would need to increase by €10,000, or 8.7 per cent, to eliminate the positive NPV of €10,000. Management need to assess whether this level of fluctuation in the initial cost is likely.

❑ If the discount rate used was 14 per cent instead of 12 per cent (an increase of 16.7 per cent), then the NPV would amount to €1,975 positive, a reduction of €8,025 or 80 per cent. This gives a sensitivity rating of 4.8 times (80 ÷ 16.7). Thus if the discount factor increases or reduces by 1 per cent, then the NPV of the project would fluctuate by 4.8 per cent.

Year	Cash flow	Discount	Present value
	€	14%	€
0	(115,000)	1.0	(115,000)
1	14,000	0.8772	12,281
2	25,000	0.7695	19,238
3	35,000	0.6750	23,625
4	36,003	0.5921	21,317
5	30,000	0.5194	15,582
6	54,724	0.4556	24,932
		NPV =	1,975

As can be seen above, the NPV of the project is extremely sensitive to changes in the initial investment and less sensitive to changes in the discount factor. Management must assess the likelihood of fluctuation in these key factors. Sensitivity ratings can be calculated for changes in each input variable or a combination of variables within the NPV model. Management can thus get a better feel for their effect on the NPV of the project and ultimately decide on whether to accept or reject a project.

Scenario analysis and the use of probabilities

The use of probabilities in investment appraisal allows a range of outcomes or alternatives to be considered, with probabilities assigned to show how likely it is that these outcomes could actually occur. In its simplest form, these alternatives would include optimistic, most likely and pessimistic scenarios. Once probabilities have been assigned to these scenarios, statistical measures of expected value (return) and standard deviation (risk) can be used to measure the expected NPV and the probability of a negative NPV for a project. This information can be presented graphically in the form of a decision tree showing all the possible outcomes that may result from a particular project and their probabilities of occurrence. Although the use of probabilities gives decision-makers an excellent feel for the likely outcomes and risk inherent in a project, it is difficult to estimate probabilities accurately.

Illustration 14.2 shows the various scenarios with the expected cash flows and probabilities for a project. The project requires an initial investment of €20,000 and the company has a cost of capital of 10 per cent.

Illustration 14.2: *Calculation of expected values*

	Optimistic	Most likely	Pessimistic	Expected value
Probability	0.2	0.5	0.3	
Cash flows	€	€	€	€
Year 1	10,000	8,000	6,000	7,800
Year 2	12,000	10,000	7,000	9,500
Year 3	15,000	12,000	9,000	11,700

The expected values are calculated for each year by multiplying the cash flows by their related probability as follows:

Year 1 (10,000 x 0.2) + (8,000 x 0.5) + (6,000 x 0.3) = €7,800
Year 2 (12,000 x 0.2) + (10,000 x 0.5) + (7,000 x 0.3) = €9,500
Year 3 (15,000 x 0.2) + (12,000 x 0.5) + (9,000 x 0.3) = €11,700

The expected values are discounted at the cost of capital to calculate the NPV of the project as follows:

Year	Cash flow	Discount	Present value
	€	10%	€
0	(20,000)	1.0	(20,000)
1	7,800	0.9091	7,091
2	9,500	0.8264	7,851
3	11,700	0.7512	8,790
		NPV =	3,732

The project shows a positive net present value and unless there are other projects with higher net present values or special non-financial considerations, the project should be accepted.

Non-Financial Considerations

It is important to stress that calculations of costs and returns, however precisely they may be researched and whatever clear cut an indication they seem to give, are no guarantee of investment success. The four techniques inform judgement and do not replace it. Many businesses faced with decisions to accept or reject projects where there are conflicting findings or marginal outcomes, often trust their gut feelings or intuition. In these situations the non-financial objectives of the business can come to the fore and these qualitative factors may outweigh the findings from the appraisal methods.

Examples where non-financial objectives could outweigh the findings from the appraisal methods are:

❑ **Health and safety issues for both employees and customers.** For example a football club investing in an all-seater stadium, or hotels and leisure centres investing in improving their safety systems or companies improving the recreational facilities for its employees. These investments can pay dividends in the long run, but the benefits are difficult to quantify and hence the impact of the qualitative factors can be greater.

❑ **Environmental objectives.** For example hotels and leisure centres investing in environmentally friendly energy efficient systems that may have a very long payback period. In this case the payback may exceed the limit that the company requires for investments, however the fact that this would be an environmentally friendly investment that has long-term benefits could ensure the investment goes ahead.

❑ **Relations with the other stakeholders in the business.** For example the investment in new systems can also require changes in working conditions and practices that may be unacceptable to employee unions or, the redevelopment of a hotel or extension to a hotel may not be acceptable to the local community. The effect on the relationship with other stakeholders can significantly influence any investment decision.

❑ **Ethical values.** For example international hotel and leisure chains refusing to invest in countries that exploit workers and do not have an acceptable human rights record.

❑ **Technological developments.** The development of websites and on-line trading has become a necessary strategy for survival and growth. As the benefits of this type of investment decision are difficult to quantify, the importance of the non-financial factors increase.

Other factors that need to be taken into account before any investment decisions are made:

❑ The effect of an investment on the competitive environment.
❑ The effect of the investment on the risk profile of the business. For example, is the investment appropriate in terms of diversifying the business activities of the company?
❑ The location of the investment. For the hospitality sector, location is an important aspect of the decision to expand and purchase new hotels.
❑ Future trends in the industry.
❑ The effects of the investment on the internal organisation and company stakeholders.

Summary

The four main techniques used in appraising capital investment seek to reduce the risk of investing in projects which yield a poor or negative rate of return. However all are based on assumptions of future economic conditions, revenues, costs and cash flows and if these assumptions are grossly inaccurate then the models will give poor decision-making information.

Investment in any capital project involves a large initial outlay of cash which can have consequences for an organisation's future. Although the various techniques have their uses, they also have their limitations. Organisations should not base their investment decisions solely on one of the techniques. Before a decision is made, a project should be evaluated using all four techniques whilst also taking into account the risk and uncertainty of the projected figures and the non-financial factors.

The main information points covered in this chapter are as follows:

❑ Capital investment involves the sacrifice of current funds in order to obtain the benefit of future wealth. In other words, invest now in the hope of generating future cash flows which will exceed the initial investment.
❑ The main methods used to evaluate investment in capital projects are:
  – Pay back method.
  – Accounting rate of return.
  – Net present value.
  – Internal rate of return.
❑ The payback method of investment appraisal simply asks the question, *'how long before I get my money back?'* In other words, how quickly will the cash flows arising from the project exactly equal the amount of the investment?
❑ This accounting rate of return method calculates the overall profit or loss on the investment or project and relates the level of profit to the amount of capital invested and to the period for which it is required.
❑ The time value of money is the phrase used to describe the fact that monies received in different time periods have different values. Discounted cash flow (DCF) is a capital appraisal technique that accounts for the fact that €1 earned or spent sooner, is worth more than €1 earned or spent later.
❑ To evaluate any project taking into account the time value of money, the cash flows received in the future must be discounted to a present value so that all relevant cash flows are denominated in today's value (present value). This discount factor represents the cost of waiting or the time value of money.

❑ Cash flows received in different time periods will have different values due to:
   – Uncertainty.
   – Interest lost.
   – Inflation.

❑ The cost of capital in a business is the discount factor to use when converting future cash flows to present values, as it represents the minimum required return for investors to compensate them for the interest lost, inflation and risk inherent in any investment.

❑ The net present value is the value obtained by discounting all cash outflows and inflows of a capital investment project at a chosen target rate of return or cost of capital. The present value of the cash inflows minus the present value of the cash outflows is the net present value. If the NPV is positive, the project is likely to be profitable, whereas if the NPV is negative, the project is likely to be unprofitable.

❑ The IRR method calculates the exact rate of return which the project is expected to achieve based on the projected cash flows. The IRR is the discount factor which will have the effect of producing a NPV of 0. It is the return from the project, taking into account the time value of money.

❑ Operating cash flows represent sales revenues less variable costs attributed to the project/investment. Fixed costs are also included, but only if they relate to the new investment and are incremental. All costs that would occur, irrespective of the investment decision should be ignored. The cash flows that are to be considered are those that arise due to the investment decision.

❑ For investment appraisal, it is important to take account of business risk and the following are some of the techniques used to incorporate risk into the various project appraisal models:
   – Calculating a discounted payback.
   – Applying sensitivity analysis to the various inputs within the appraisal methods.
   – Scenario analysis and the use of probabilities.

❑ Many managers faced with decisions to accept or reject projects where there are conflicting findings or marginal outcomes, often trust their gut feelings or intuition. In these situations the non-financial objectives of the business can come to the fore and these qualitative factors may outweigh the findings from the appraisal method.

Review Questions

Question 14.1

a) Compare and contrast the various methods of investment appraisal. To what extent would it be true to say there is a place for each of them?

b) With regard to capital investment appraisal methods, explain why cash flows are preferred to accounting profits.

Question 14.2

a) List the distinctive features of capital investments which make it worthwhile developing and applying a special set of techniques to evaluate them.

b) Briefly describe the term 'cost of capital', explaining its significance in relation to appraising capital projects.

Question 14.3

a) Describe what is meant by the term 'the time value of money' and briefly describe the factors that ensure that monies received in different time periods will have different values.

b) Compare the payback and net present value methods of investment appraisal.

Question 14.4

a) Briefly state what you understand by discounted cash flows and explain why, in appraising capital investments, it is necessary to discount cash flows?

b) Distinguish between the net present value and the internal rate of return methods of capital investment appraisal. You should explain why the net present value method is preferred to the internal rate of return method.

Question 14.5

The Dunne Hotel Group is considering two asset investments. The initial cash outlay for both investments is €70,000 with both projects having an estimated life of five years. The following are the operating cash flows associated with each project:

Year	Project A	Project B
	€	€
1	10,500	8,900
2	15,600	8,560
3	20,567	24,066
4	25,671	30,200
5	18,700	35,631

At the end of the fifth year, the assets will have an estimated residual value of €4,000 for project A and €2,500 for project B. Both investments will be depreciated on a straight-line basis. The company's cost of capital is 10 per cent.

Required
a) Determine which project to recommend according to:
    i.   The payback method.
    ii. The net present value method.
    (Your recommendation should be clearly explained for both methods).
b) Briefly list any other factors that should be taken into account before a decision is made.

Question 14.6

Cantwell Catering Ltd is considering investing in new catering equipment. The equipment will cost €500,000 with an estimated life of five years and an estimated residual value of €50,000. The following are the forecast costs and revenues relevant to the decision:

Year	Sales	Variable costs	Fixed costs
	€	€	€
1	200,000	76,000	120,000
2	220,000	83,600	120,000
3	310,000	117,800	120,000
4	270,000	102,600	120,000
5	210,000	79,800	120,000

The fixed costs for each year include an annual depreciation charge of €90,000. The balance of €30,000 consists of costs that are directly related to the equipment. The company's cost of capital is 10 per cent.

Required

a) Calculate the payback period, the net present value and the internal rate of return for the project.

b) State, with reasons, whether you feel the project is financially viable.

Question 14.7

Landers Leisure plc. invested three years ago in fitness equipment costing €500,000 and with an estimated economic life of five years. The equipment is now expected to last for a further three years. An opportunity has arisen to sell the equipment now for €250,000. This would give rise to a profit on sale as follows:

	€
Sales proceeds	250,000
Less Net book value of equipment	200,000
Profit on sale	50,000

The company accountant has prepared the following projections for the next three years based on not selling the equipment:

	Year 1	Year 2	Year 3
	€	€	€
Revenues earned	187,500	216,250	146,250
Variable costs	63,750	76,250	49,550
Allocated fixed costs	32,500	50,000	
Depreciation	100,000	100,000	
Net profit / (loss)	(8,750)	(10,000)	96,700

Landers Leisure plc. has a cost of capital of 15 per cent

Required

Evaluate the proposals and make recommendations to management on the best course of action.

Question 14.8

Zookeeper plc. is considering the purchase of two male apes to add to their collection of apes at the zoo. The apes are elderly and their remaining useful economic life is estimated at seven years. If the zoo decides to purchase the apes, the capital costs are as follows:

Cost of extra security, cages and living accommodation	€30,000
Purchase and transport costs	€180,000
	€210,000

The company expects the new apes to generate considerable public interest. The company's accountant has projected the following additional revenues and costs associated with this increase in public interest.

	Year 1	Year 2	Year 3	Year 4	Year 5	Year 6	Year 7
	€	€	€	€	€	€	€
Revenues	90,000	85,000	80,000	75,000	70,000	60,000	50,000
Variable costs	27,000	25,500	24,000	22,500	21,000	18,000	15,000
Fixed costs	20,000	20,000	20,000	20,000	20,000	20,000	20,000
Depreciation	30,000	30,000	30,000	30,000	30,000	30,000	30,000
Net profit / loss	13,000	9,500	6,000	2,500	(1,000)	(8,000)	(15,000)

50 per cent of the fixed costs have been allocated from elsewhere in the business and thus are not directly attributable to the project. The company's cost of capital is 12 per cent.

Required
a) Calculate the following, explaining your answer in each case:
   i.   The payback period.
   ii. The accounting rate of return.
   iii. The net present value of the project.
   iv. The internal rate of return for the project.
b) State, with reasons, whether you feel the project is viable.

Question 14.9

Fit and Healthy Leisure Ltd is considering updating its present range of fitness equipment. Management must decided on whether to invest in either top of the range 'new age' fitness equipment or a selection of standard fitness machines which have recently come on the market. The company accountant has prepared the following projected revenues and costs associated with each proposed investment.

New Age Fitness Equipment

	Year 1	Year 2	Year 3	Year 4	Year 5
	€	€	€	€	€
Projected revenues	20,000	22,000	30,000	27,000	20,000
Direct costs	10,000	11,000	12,000	10,800	10,000
Depreciation	9,500	9,500	9,500	9,500	9,500
Total costs	19,500	20,500	21,500	20,300	19,500
Net profit	500	1,500	8,500	6,700	500

Standard Fitness Equipment

	Year 1	Year 2	Year 3	Year 4	Year 5
	€	€	€	€	€
Projected revenues	8,000	15,000	22,000	14,000	8,000
Direct costs	4,000	7,500	8,800	5,600	4,000
Depreciation	6,000	6,000	6,000	6,000	6,000
Total costs	10,000	13,500	14,800	11,600	10,000
Net profit	(2,000)	1,500	7,200	2,400	(2,000)

The accountant has assumed that the estimated useful life of both asset types is five years with an estimated residual value of zero. The company's cost of capital is 10 per cent.

Required
Recommend to management which investment should be made and why, using the following appraisal techniques:

a. The payback method.
b. The net present value method.
c. The internal rate of return method.

Question 14.10

Leisurefields Ltd leases all its property assets. A portion of land with a lease expiring in six years time is not currently being used. Management, in a drive to maximize the return on assets, are considering three possible courses of action.

1. To rent the land to a tenant at a rent of €10,000 per annum.
2. To utilise the land taking crops which would have a net value of €20,000, €18,000, €15,000, €12,000 and €9,000 respectively for the five years starting in the second year. This option would require the land to be cleared during the first year requiring expenditure of €10,000 payable at the end of the year.
3. To sell the remainder of the lease for €39,000.

Cost of capital is 12 per cent.

Required
Advise the company on the course of action it should take.

Question 14.11

Hiteck Retailing Ltd is considering investing in additional checkouts in January. It is expected that the system will be obsolete in five years and will be sold. The following estimates relevant to the investment have been prepared:

	€'000
System cost	1,200
Estimated disposal value at end of year 5.	200
Weighted average cost of capital is 11 per cent.	

Annual forecast	Year 1	Year 2	Year 3	Year 4	Year 5
Additional numbers of customers	14,000	15,500	16,000	17,000	18,000
Average revenue per customer	€70	€73	€75	€77	€80
Average variable costs per customer	€45	€47	€48	€49	€50
Additional fixed costs in '000s	€350	€360	€370	€375	€380
Included in fixed costs are:					
1. Depreciation in '000	€200	€200	€200	€200	€200
2. Apportioned overheads in '000	€70	€70	€75	€75	€75
Opening working capital as percentage of turnover	10%	10%	10%	10%	10%

Required

a) Evaluate the above project using the following methods:
    i.   Net present value.
    ii. Internal rate of return.
b) Compare and contrast the above two approaches to project evaluation.
c) Comment on the proposed project.

Question 14.12

Western Tours is considering purchasing new buses with an estimated useful life of five years. The cost of capital is 13 per cent. A feasibility study has produced the following estimates:

	€
Cost of new buses	750,000
Disposal value of buses at end of fifth year	150,000
Initial investment required for working capital	50,000

This additional working capital will be recovered at the end of the fifth year. The buses will be depreciated using the straight-line method.

Annual forecasts of sales and costs

	Year 1	Year 2	Year 3	Year 4	Year 5
Additional number of tourists	15,000	16,000	17,000	18,000	18,000
	€	€	€	€	€
Price per tour	40	40	40	45	45
Variable cost per tourist	24	24	24	27	27
Fixed costs, including depreciation	210,000	210,000	210,000	210,000	210,000

Required

a) Calculate the net present value of the investment.
b) Calculate the internal rate of return.
c) Calculate the payback period.
d) Comment on the proposed investment.

Question 14.13

The Duke Hotel chain is considering upgrading its fixed assets. It wishes to evaluate this investment over a five year period on the assumption that the assets would be sold and the working capital recovered at the end of the five year period. The accountant has prepared the following estimates of the additional revenue and expenses expected to result from the project.

	€'000
Consultancy study already fully paid	30
Upgrading costs to be incurred in the present year	3,750
Disposal value of assets at end of year 5	500

The weighted average cost of capital is 11 per cent. The assets will be depreciated at 20 per cent per annum, on a straight-line basis.

Annual forecast of sales and costs:

	Year 1	Year 2	Year 3	Year 4	Year 5
	€'000	€'000	€'000	€'000	€'000
Sales revenue	1,800	1,900	2,100	2,250	2,350
Variable costs	720	830	900	930	980
Fixed costs (including depreciation)	790	810	825	835	850
Profits lost in other areas due to the decision to upgrade	35	40	45	45	45
Working capital as percentage of turnover	5%	5%	5%	5%	5%

Required
a) Evaluate and comment on the above project using the following methods:
   i.   Net present value.
   ii. Internal rate of return.
b) How sensitive is the project to the assumptions regarding selling prices and customer numbers?
c) Advise whether or not the company should upgrade its fixed assets.

Hospitality and tourism case example – Jurys Doyle Hotels

This case example focuses on the financial performance of Jurys Doyle Hotel Group plc., providing a view of financial performance appraisal within the hospitality and tourism sectors. The analysis focuses on the period 2003. The financial statements are presented and key performance indicators calculated. Finally an analysis and appraisal of the group's financial performance under the headings of profitability, liquidity, use of assets and capital structure is provided. This appraisal will be achieved through an internal comparative analysis over time, and by an inter-firm comparative analysis with a company in the same sector.

Consolidated Accounts Jurys Doyle Hotel Group Plc.

Profit Statements for year ended 31 December 2003

	€('000)	€('000)
Turnover		253,773
Less Cost of sales		
Opening stock	2,514	
Purchases (including labour costs)	170,705	
Closing stock	(2,317)	(170,902)
Gross profit		**82,871**
Less Expenses		(23,244)
Net profit before interest and tax (PBIT)		**59,627**
Less Interest payable		(13,785)
Net profit before tax		**45,842**
Less Taxation		(7,934)
Profit after interest and tax		**37,908**

Balance Sheet as at 31 December 2003

	€('000)	€('000)	€('000)
Fixed tangible assets			1,087,896
Current assets			
Stock	2,317		
Debtors	17,412		
Bank	10,207	29,936	
Current liabilities			
Trade creditors	14,260		
Bank overdrafts	50,255		
Other current liabilities	78,084	(142,599)	(112,663)
Creditors > 1 year			
Government grants			(278,310)
Deferred tax			(3,347)
			(30,901)
Total net assets			**662,675**
Capital and reserves			
Ordinary shares			20,135
Share premium			182,397
Revaluation reserve			287,435
Other reserves			(22,555)
Retained profit			195,263
			662,675

(Adapted from Jurys Doyle Hotel Group plc. annual report 2003)

Additional operating information for 2002 and 2003

	2003	2002 (12 months)
Daily rooms available (estimate)	6,200	6,000
Daily average rooms occupied (estimate)	4,650	4,560
Annual rooms revenue (estimate)	€152,771,000	€158,118,000
Total sales revenue	€253,773,000	€268,138,000
Average number of employees	3,822	3,898
Payroll costs	€81,656,000	€83,444,000

Source: The additional information that make up the operating ratios for Jurys Doyle above was sourced through the annual accounts and Davy's Stockbroker reports for 2003 and 2002. Where information was not available best estimates were used to enhance the case study in providing an example of relevant management information.

The performance of the company can be analysed under the headings of profitability, efficiency/asset utilisation (including operating performance measures), liquidity and capital structure.

Ratio Calculations

	PROFITABILITY		
Gross profit margin	$\dfrac{\text{Gross profit} \times 100}{\text{Sales}}$	$\dfrac{\text{€}82{,}871 \times 100}{\text{€}253{,}773}$	32.65%
Operating profit margin	$\dfrac{\text{Operating profit (PBIT)} \times 100}{\text{Sales}}$	$\dfrac{\text{€}59{,}627 \times 100}{\text{€}253{,}773}$	23.5%
Expenses to sales	$\dfrac{\text{Expenses} \times 100}{\text{Sales}}$	$\dfrac{\text{€}23{,}244 \times 100}{\text{€}253{,}773}$	9.16%
Return on capital employed (ROCE)	$\dfrac{\text{Operating profit (PBIT)} \times 100}{\text{Capital employed}}$ *(Capital employed = Total assets less current liabilities)*	$\dfrac{\text{€}59{,}627 \times 100}{\text{€}975{,}233}$	6.11%
Return on owners equity (ROOE) before tax	$\dfrac{\text{Net profit before tax} \times 100}{\text{Shareholders' funds}}$ *(Shareholders' funds = share capital plus reserves.)*	$\dfrac{\text{€}45{,}842 \times 100}{\text{€}662{,}675}$	6.9%
Return on owners equity (ROOE) after tax	$\dfrac{\text{Net profit after interest and tax} \times 100}{\text{Shareholders' funds}}$	$\dfrac{\text{€}37{,}908 \times 100}{\text{€}662{,}675}$	5.7%

EFFICIENCY

Fixed asset turnover	$\dfrac{\text{Sales}}{\text{Fixed assets}}$	$\dfrac{\text{€253,773}}{\text{€1,087,896}}$	0.233 : 1
Capital employed turnover (Total asset turnover)	$\dfrac{\text{Sales}}{\text{Net assets}}$	$\dfrac{\text{€253,773}}{\text{€975,233}}$	0.26 : 1

(Net assets = FA + CA – CL)

Stock turnover	$\dfrac{\text{Cost of sales}}{\text{Average stock}}$	$\dfrac{\text{€170,902}}{\text{€2,415.5}}$	71 times
Stock days	$\dfrac{\text{Average stock x 365}}{\text{Cost of sales}}$	$\dfrac{\text{€2,415.5 x 365}}{\text{€170,902}}$	5.2 days
Debtors days	$\dfrac{\text{Trade debtors x 365}}{\text{Credit sales}}$	$\dfrac{\text{€17,412 x 365}}{\text{€253,773}}$	25 days
Creditors days	$\dfrac{\text{Trade creditors x 365}}{\text{Credit purchases}}$	$\dfrac{\text{€14,260 x 365}}{\text{€170,705}}$	30.5 days

OPERATING RATIOS

Occupancy	$\dfrac{\text{Rooms occupied x 100}}{\text{Rooms available}}$	$\dfrac{\text{4,650 x 100}}{\text{6,200}}$	75%
Average room rate	$\dfrac{\text{Rooms revenue x 1,000}}{\text{Rooms occupied x 365}}$	$\dfrac{\text{152,771,000}}{\text{1,697,250}}$	€90
RevPAR	$\dfrac{\text{Rooms revenue x 1,000}}{\text{Rooms available x 365}}$	$\dfrac{\text{152,771,000}}{\text{2,263,000}}$	€67.5
Rooms revenue as a percentage of total sales	$\dfrac{\text{Total rooms revenue x 100}}{\text{Total revenue}}$	$\dfrac{\text{152,771 x 100}}{\text{253,773}}$	60.2%
Operating profit per employee	$\dfrac{\text{Operating profit}}{\text{Number of employees}}$	$\dfrac{\text{59,627,000}}{\text{3,822}}$	€15,601
Payroll cost per employee	$\dfrac{\text{Payroll costs}}{\text{Number of employees}}$	$\dfrac{\text{81,656,000}}{\text{3,822}}$	€21,365
Payroll costs as % of sales	$\dfrac{\text{Payroll costs x 100}}{\text{Sales}}$	$\dfrac{\text{81,656 x 100}}{\text{253,773}}$	32.2%

LIQUIDITY

Current ratio	$\dfrac{\text{Current assets}}{\text{Current liabilities}}$	$\dfrac{\text{€29,936}}{\text{€142,599}}$	0.21 : 1
Quick-acid test ratio	$\dfrac{\text{Current assets - stock}}{\text{Current liabilities}}$	$\dfrac{\text{€27,619}}{\text{€142,599}}$	0.19 : 1

CAPITAL STRUCTURE			
Gearing	Fixed interest debt	€278,310	0.42 : 1
	Shareholders' funds	€662,675	
Interest cover	Net profit (PBIT)	€59,627	4.33 : 1
	Interest	€13,785	

Commentary on the financial performance in 2003

The financial performance of the Jurys Doyle Hotel Group for 2003 will be evaluated under the headings of profitability, asset utilisation, liquidity, and capital structure. This will be achieved through an internal and external appraisal process outlined as follows:

❑ By comparing key financial ratios of the Jurys Doyle Hotel Group over time.
❑ Through an inter-firm comparison with the annual reports of the Gresham Hotel Group plc.
❑ Key ratios of other companies within the wider tourism sector will also be presented to give context.

Profitability

For Jurys Doyle in 2003, turnover fell by 5 per cent with operating profits falling by 23 per cent compared to 2002. The context for all this was that the travel, tourism and hospitality sectors were severely hit by both the 'foot and mouth epidemic' and the aftermath of the terrorist attacks in 2001. 2002 and 2003 were characterised by a depressed global economy and a strengthening euro all of which had the effect of severely curtailing business and tourist travel. With sales and profits falling, the following key financial indicators will provide vital information on the overall evaluation of the profitability performance of Jurys Doyle Hotel Group for 2003. Comparatives with previous years, and with Gresham Hotels is also provided to support the appraisal process.

Table A.1: *Return on capital ratios*

ROCE / ROOE

	2001	2002	2003
Jury's Doyle			
ROCE	9.02%	6.88%	6.11%
ROOE (before tax)	12.6%	7.2%	6.9%
Gresham			
ROCE	6.33%	-	2.4%
ROOE	7.57%	-	1.43%

Overall the return on capital is poor and is decreasing for both companies. Gresham actually made an operating loss in part due to exceptional items in 2002 and thus no return is calculated. To properly evaluate these returns they must be analysed into their two component parts namely operating profit margin and capital employed turnover ratios. Table A.2 compares the ROCE of Jurys Doyle Hotel Group for 2003 and 2002 broken into its two component parts.

Table A.2: *ROCE analysed*

	ROCE		Operating profit margin	X	Capital employed turnover
Jurys Doyle – 2003	6.10	=	23.5%	x	0.26
Jurys Doyle – 2002	6.88	=	27.57%	x	0.25

From the table one can see that ROCE fell in 2003. When analysing the ROCE into its two component parts, the capital employed turnover ratio has improved slightly showing that the group generated slightly more sales per euro invested in the business. However the reason for the fall in ROCE was the reduction in the operating margin of 4 per cent. Table A.3 shows the breakdown of ROCE into its two component parts for both Jurys Doyle and Gresham Hotels for 2003.

Table A.3: *ROCE analysed*

	ROCE		Operating profit margin	X	Total asset turnover
Jurys Doyle	6.11	=	23.5	x	0.26
Gresham	2.4	=	8.7	x	0.275

One can see the main reason for the low ROCE for Gresham is their very poor operating margins. Their asset turnover ratios are however slightly better than Jurys.

Table A.4: *Operating margin ratios*

	2001 (%)	2002 (%)	2003 (%)
Jurys Doyle	29.57	27.57	23.5
Gresham	24.07	-0.17	8.7

The operating margins are decreasing for both companies with Jurys performing significantly better than Gresham. For hotels, the operating profit margin varies but Gresham Hotels and Jurys consistently achieved operating margins in the early 20 per cents. In the booming 'Celtic Tiger' economy, operating margins of greater than 30 per cent were achieved. This is because hotel cost structures have a high proportion of fixed costs, which do not increase proportionate to sales. Thus when sales are booming, profit margins will increase significantly. Obviously as sales decrease so too will profit margins because fixed costs will not fall. This characteristic would also apply to many leisure businesses as well as the travel sector. Table A.4 shows operating profit ratios falling year on year for Jurys and yet still reasonable at 23.5 per cent compared to Gresham which made an operating loss in 2002 (due to exceptional items) and recovered to profit in 2003. Jurys should assess the profitability of each of its hotels to see which hotels are maintaining their profit margins and which are under-performing. Most financial analysts agree that the Jurys Inns have performed very well through this period whereas Jurys four and five star hotels have under-performed. In many respects the operating margins for Jurys would be far worse except for the Jurys Inns low cost model. In evaluating the profitability performance of Jurys Doyle, the causes of the decrease in the operating profit margin need to be assessed. Operating profit margins will decrease if:

1. The gross profit margin decreases.
2. The operating expenses to sales percentage increases.

Table A.5: *Gross profit and hotel operating ratios*

	2001	2002	2003
Jurys Doyle	36.25%	35.7%	32.65%
Gresham	54.04%	49.23%	48.5%

Table A.6: *Hotel operating ratios*

	Jurys Doyle		Gresham	
	2003	2002	2003	2002
Occupancy	75%	76%	76%	76%
ARR	€90	€95	€84	€85
RevPAR	€67.5	€72.2	€63.8	€64.6
Rooms revenue % of total sales	60.2%	59%	58%	60%

The trends for both companies show a falling gross profit percentage. This means that both companies are generating less gross profit per euro of sales. The operating ratios for Jurys Doyle also show that the ARR and RevPAR have both decreased by 5 per cent and 7 per cent respectively. The effect of reducing prices is to boost demand but at the expense of the margin of profit, thus the gross profit margin falls.

It seems both companies have reduced their prices to boost demand and sustain occupancy rates. In Jurys case, room revenue as a percentage of total revenue has in fact increased slightly with occupancy levels falling only 1 per cent. In economic periods where demand for travel and tourism products is depressed, to maintain occupancy levels, hotels reduce prices and take on lower margin business (tour groups) to boost sales/occupancy rates.

The gross profit margins are significantly different for both companies indicating for example that in 2003, Jurys Doyle achieved a significantly lower gross profit per euro sales than Gresham. This however is misleading. The company's 1986 act identifies three categories of expenses namely:

❏ Cost of goods sold.
❏ Sales expenses.
❏ Administration expenses.

The act however does not give definitions of each category and thus we can reasonably conclude that Jurys includes a significant proportion of labour costs in its cost of goods sold computation while Gresham clearly does not. The operating profit margins are however quite similar (see below). It is important to realise that management would have an exact breakdown of each expense item within each category and would apply further analysis in assessing and controlling costs.

Table A.7: *Expenses to sales ratios*

	2001	2002	2003
Jurys Doyle	6.68%	7.83%	9.16%
Gresham	29.97%	50%	40%

The expenses to sales per cent for both companies increased significantly. To give management a greater insight into why this increase occurred they need to identify which items of expense increased significantly and why. Management should assess the reason for the increase and question the value received from the increased expenditure in the area. It is also important to remember that the expenses to sales percentage can increase due to reductions in sales, and this was part of the reason why the ratio increased so significantly for both companies between 2001 and 2003. Overall sales revenue fell by 5 per cent in 2003. A hotel's operating costs would be mainly fixed costs and thus would not fall as sales fall. Hence as sales decrease, the expenses to sales percentage will increase.

Payroll costs are a significant expense for any business in the hospitality industry. As the sector is quite labour intensive with labour costs amounting to between 30 per cent and 40 per cent of total revenue, this expense category requires further analysis for management control purposes.

Table A.8: *Payroll operating ratios*

| | Jurys Doyle | | Gresham | |
	2003	2002	2003	2002
Payroll costs per employee	€21,365	€21,407	€26,163	€26,159
Payroll costs as a percentage of sales	32.2%	31.1%	40.3%	42%

Labour costs as a percentage of sales for Jurys Doyle have increased slightly from 31.1 per cent in 2002 to 32.2 per cent in 2003. This compares favourably to Gresham Hotels where the percentage was over 40 per cent in 2003. The operating ratios for Jurys Doyle show revenue and operating profit per employee falling, with payroll costs as a percentage of sales increasing. These changes reflect the falling sales revenue for the company and the fact that payroll costs are mainly fixed and thus will not fluctuate in line with sales increases or decreases.

Overall Jurys Doyle ROCE decreased from 6.88 per cent to 6.11 per cent. The decrease was due to a fall of 4 per cent in the operating profit margin between 2002 and 2003. This was due in the main to a reduction in the gross profit percentage of 3 per cent and an increase in expenses to sales of over 1 per cent. In the light of the weak global economy that affected businesses over the period, it is not surprising that Jurys Doyle reduced prices to stimulate demand and this adversely affected their operating margins and the overall return on capital.

For Gresham Hotels the news is good as they made an operating loss after exceptional items in 2002 but turned it around in 2003 to achieve an operating profit margin of 9.1 per cent, an increase of 9.3 per cent. This was due to a reduction in the expense to sales percentage of 10 per cent and offset by the gross profit margin falling by 0.7 per cent.

Overall the returns are poor, but in the context of external factors, Jurys Doyle have performed quite well. Although margins are falling they are still respectable and with occupancy levels holding up, and the Inn's model expanding, the company should be well placed for increased profitability in the future.

Asset utilisation and efficiency

Table A.9: *Asset turnover ratios*

	2001	2002	2003
Jurys Doyle			
Fixed asset turnover	0.25	0.24	0.233
Capital employed turnover (Asset turnover)	0.31	0.25	0.26
Gresham			
Fixed asset turnover	0.26	0.26	0.27
Capital employed turnover (Asset turnover)	0.26	0.25	0.275

Overall the capital employed turnover ratios show the amount of sales generated per euro invested in the business. Obviously, the higher the ratio the better. Both companies had very similar asset utilisation ratios between 2001 and 2003. In the 'Celtic Tiger' era these ratios would have been as high as 0.42. However mainly due to external factors, the ratios have fallen significantly but seem to have stabilised in 2003 at 0.26 times. This is also reflected in the occupancy rates for Jurys Doyle which has fallen from 76 per cent in 2002 to 75 per cent in 2003. Gresham's occupancy levels have stabilised at 76 per cent. It would seem that the pricing and yield management strategies have succeeded in maintaining and stabilising occupancy levels but this has come at the expense of lower profit margins.

It is important to point out that there is very little difference between the fixed asset and the capital employed turnover ratios for both companies, confirming the fact that there is very little investment in current assets for hotel companies and that this investment is financed completely through current liabilities.

The key efficiency ratios relating to stock, trade debtors and trade creditors can now be compared for both Jurys Doyle and Gresham Hotels.

Table A.10: *Efficiency ratios 2003*

	Jury's	Gresham
Stock turnover	71 times	23 times
Debtors collections	25 days	26 days
Creditors payment	30 days	44 days

Overall, current assets represent a small portion of the total assets of a hotel company. In Jurys accounts for 2003, current assets amounted to 2.7 per cent of total assets (fixed and current assets).

❏ Stock turnover is 71 times for Jurys compared to 23 times for Gresham. These figures are high due to the fact that the trading stock of a hotel company is food and beverages which is quite small representing only 0.2 per cent of total assets for Jurys, hence the high stock turnover figures. The difference between Jurys Doyle and Gresham Hotels is mainly due to Gresham's lower purchasing requirement.

❏ Debtors collection period is quite low which is not surprising as the hotel sector is a predominately cash business. Debtors tend to represent corporate clients and for this ratio to be more meaningful one should use the credit sales figure rather than the total sales figure (which includes cash sales). The figure tells us that debtors are, on average, paying their accounts every 25/26 days.

❏ Trade creditors represent the credit on purchases of stock. Jurys Doyle pay their account on average every month whereas Gresham Hotels pay every month and a half. The difference is not significant.

Liquidity

Liquidity ratios will vary widely across different sectors and thus industry norms should be borne in mind when looking at the ratios.

Table A.11: *Liquidity ratios*

	Jurys	Gresham	Ryanair	Aer Lingus	ICG
Current ratio	0.21	1.81	2.95	1.77	0.67
Acid test	0.19	1.71	2.89	1.76	0.66

1. The above table shows Jurys ratios slightly lower than the norm for the sector. As the hotel business is predominantly a cash business with low levels of stock and debtors, these ratios would not be too disturbing. However Gresham's ratios are very high in the main due to the fact that the company sold a number of hotels and had paid off a lot of its liabilities. In particular, it reduced its bank overdraft and paid off its short-term leasing liabilities before the year end. Thus the ratio, while accurate, is not the norm for the sector.
2. Ryanair's ratios are also quite high and this is due to having 120.9 million held on deposit to hedge its exposure to adverse movements in currency and interest rates for existing and planned debt. Many airlines operate on much lower current ratios such as Southwest Airlines at 0.67.
3. Ultimately all the above ratios indicate that each company is quite liquid and has no difficulty in paying debts as they fall due.

Capital structure

Table A.12: *Capital gearing*

	2001	2002	2003
Jurys Doyle	81%	50%	42%
Gresham	42%	59%	27%

The above ratios show that both companies would be considered low geared (mainly financed by equity). Also the trend shows that the gearing levels of both companies are falling. In 2003 Gresham Hotels sold a number of its hotels and used the proceeds to reduce its debt. It is important to remember that debt is a cheaper source of finance and, as such, should increase the returns for the business and equity shareholders. However if the gearing ratios are too high then the company increases its financial risk (the risk that it may be unable to meet the commitments of the debt finance). This has repercussions on the company's ability to acquire further debt finance at a reasonable cost. Both companies are low geared and it would seem they could benefit from extra debt finance in the future.

Jurys Hotel: right buy, wrong finance?

When Jurys plc. bought the London Onslow Hotel in October 1993, it was generally felt by most investment analysts to be a good investment, as it was purchased during a period of depressed property prices. However they questioned the form of finance used for the acquisition. Instead of allowing Jurys to gear up its balance sheet and take advantage of exceptionally low interest rates (at the time), the company went the other way and financed the acquisition through an issue of shares to its existing shareholders (a rights issue). The company was considered at the time to be very low geared (mainly financed through equity rather than debt) and thus would have had no problem in raising the finance through a cheap fixed interest loan issue. This would have boosted the EPS figure, but instead this figure has been diluted somewhat by the extra shares issued under the rights issue.

Table A.13: *Gearing and interest cover ratios 2003*

	Jurys	Gresham	Ryanair	ICG
Gearing-Debt : Equity	42%	27%	60%	59%
Interest cover (net)	4.3 times	1.7 times	n/a	3.76 times

Table A.13 shows that all companies are low geared, however the interest cover for Gresham is quite low at 1.7 times. In other words the business can pay its interest out of profits 1.7 times. This is quite low compared to Jurys Doyle at 4.3 times. In 2003 Gresham reduced its gearing and interest costs significantly but profit was recovering from an operating loss in 2002 and was quite low. Thus its interest cover is low but improving. This shows the levels of financial risk attached to a highly geared business in an economic recession, where sales and profits fall to levels that ensure the business finds it hard to comply with its debt obligations. If the gearing ratio was based on the *net debt to equity formula,* then Ryanair would have zero gearing due to the fact that the company's huge cash reserves are greater than its borrowings. This is reflected in the interest cover ratio where interest earned (due to high levels of cash on deposit) is greater than its interest charged and thus interest cover is not applicable here.

Summary

Overall, management at Jurys Doyle should be reasonably content with their financial performance over 2003. Although sales, profits and return on capital have fallen, the company has maintained its occupancy and capital employed/asset turnover rates and controlled expenditure. The company is very liquid and low geared and thus should take advantage of low interest rates to further develop and expand their low cost Jurys Inns model. The Inns are delivering good profit margins and making up for the poorer performance of the groups four and five star hotels. In the light of the weak global economy that affected the hospitality, travel and tourism sectors quite severely, the company has performed well and should be well positioned to take advantage of any upturn in local and global economies.

Retail Case Example: Arnotts

This case example focuses on the financial performance of the Arnotts Group, which trades within the retail sector. The financial performance of the Arnotts Group for 2003 will be evaluated under the headings of profitability, asset utilisation, liquidity, and capital structure. This will be achieved through an internal and external appraisal process outlined as follows:

❑ By comparing key financial ratios and indicators for the Arnotts group over the relevant period.
❑ By comparing with key ratios or benchmarks of other companies within the retail sector.

The published accounts of Arnotts Group

Arnotts
Group Profit and Loss Account Year ended 31 January 2003

	Note	2003 €'000	2002 €'000
Turnover including concession sales		204,192	192,520
Concession sales	2	-56,009	-51,937
Turnover excluding concession sales	2	148,183	140,583
Operating profit	3	21,158	18,020
Share of operating profit of associated undertaking		309	1,294
Profit before interest		21,467	19,314
Net interest payable	4	-1,004	-1,432
Profit before taxation		20,463	17,882
Taxation	5	-3,283	-3,043
Profit for the financial year	6	17,180	14,839
Dividends paid	7	-1,918	-1,678
Dividends proposed	7	-4,671	-4,043
Increase in retained profits		10,591	9,118
Statement of retained profits			
At beginning of year		58,684	51,344
Increase in retained profits		10,591	9,118
Purchase of own shares		-	-1,778
At end of year		69,275	58,684
Earnings per ordinary share	8	96.6c	82.6c
Diluted earnings per ordinary share	8	95.3c	82.0c

Arnotts
Group Balance Sheet 31 January 2003

		Note	2003 €'000	2002 €'000
Fixed assets	Tangible assets	9	240,042	223,367
	Financial assets	10	2,297	2,018
			242,339	225,385
Current assets	Stocks	11	16,470	16,903
	Debtors	12	13,263	13,786
	Cash		8,703	7,665
			38,436	38,354
Creditors (amounts falling due within one year)		13	-42,540	-47,727
Net current liabilities			-4,104	-9,373
Total assets less current liabilities			238,235	216,012
Creditors (amounts falling due after more than one year)		14	-9,729	-14,873
Provisions for liabilities and charges		16	-2,259	-2,011
			226,247	199,128
Capital and reserves				
Called up share capital (equity and non-equity)		17	23,482	23,448
Share premium account		18	953	871
Revaluation reserve		18	132,311	115,899
Other reserve		18	226	226
Profit and loss account		18	69,275	58,684
Shareholders' funds		19	226,247	199,128

Additional information extracted from the notes to the accounts

		2003	2002
		€'000	€'000
Turnover	from note 3	148,183	140,583
Cost of sales	from note 3	-96,813	-92,216
Gross profit	from note 3	51,370	48,367
Expenses	from note 3	45,963	44,422
Other operating income	from note 3	15,478	14,075
Trade debtors	from note 12	12,841	13,469
Trade creditors	from note 13	17,975	17,886
Creditors > 1 year includes bank loans & overdrafts		5,796	12,474
Closing stock in 2001 amounted to €14,107,000			

Ratio analysis of Arnotts Group

	Formula	2003		2002	
Gross profit margin	Gross profit x 100 / Sales	51,370 x 100 / 148,183	34.7%	48,367 x 100 / 140,583	34.4%
Net profit margin	Net profit (PBIT) x 100 / sales	21,158 x 100 / 148,183	14.3%	18,020 x 100 / 140,583	12.8%
Expenses to sales	Expenses x 100 / sales	45,963 x 100 / 148,183	31.0%	44,422 x 100 / 140,583	31.6%
Return on capital employed (ROCE)	Net profit (PBIT) x 100 / Capital employed	21,158 x 100 / 238,235	8.88%	18,020 x 100 / 216,012	8.34%
Return on owners (ROOE) before tax	Net profit before tax x100 / Shareholders funds	20,463 x 100 / 226,247	9.04%	17,882 x 100 / 199,128	8.98%
Fixed asset turnover	Sales / Fixed assets	148,183 / 240,042	0.617 times	140,583 / 225,385	0.623 times
Capital employed turnover	Sales / Capital employed	148,183 / 238,235	0.622 times	140,583 / 216,012	0.65 times
Stock turnover	Cost of sales / Average stock	96,813 / 16,686.5	5.8 times	92,216 / 15,505	5.95 times
Stock days	Average stock x 365 / Cost of sales	16,686.5 x 365 / 96,813	62.9 days	15,505 x 365 / 92,216	61.4 days
Debtors days	Trade debtors x 365 / Credit sales	12,841 x 365 / 148,183	31.6 days	13,469 x 365 / 140,583	35 days

		2003		2002	
Creditors days	$\dfrac{\text{Trade creditors} \times 365}{\text{Credit purchases}}$	$\dfrac{17{,}795 \times 365}{96{,}380}$	67.4 days	$\dfrac{17{,}886 \times 365}{95{,}012}$	68.7 days
Current ratio	$\dfrac{\text{Current assets}}{\text{Current liabilities}}$	$\dfrac{38{,}436}{42{,}540}$	0.9 : 1	$\dfrac{38{,}354}{47{,}727}$	0.8 : 1
Quick-acid test ratio	$\dfrac{\text{Current assets} - \text{stock}}{\text{Current liabilities}}$	$\dfrac{21{,}966}{42{,}540}$	0.52 : 1	$\dfrac{21{,}451}{47{,}727}$	0.45 : 1
Gearing	$\dfrac{\text{Fixed interest debt}}{\text{Shareholders funds}}$	$\dfrac{9{,}729 \times 100}{226{,}247}$	4.3%	$\dfrac{14{,}602 \times 100}{199{,}128}$	7.3%
Interest cover	$\dfrac{\text{Net profit (PBIT)}}{\text{Interest}}$	$\dfrac{21{,}467}{1{,}004}$	21.4 times	$\dfrac{19{,}314}{1{,}432}$	13.5 times

Summary of increases / decreases in key indicators

Turnover excluding concession sales	5.4%
Cost of sales	5.0%
Gross profit	6.2%
Expenses	3.5%
Other operating income	9.97%
Operating profit	17.4%
Net interest payable	-29.9%
Tangible assets	7.5%
Stocks	-2.6%
Debtors	-3.8%
Cash	13.5%
Creditors (amounts falling due within one year)	-10.9%
Creditors (amounts falling due after more than one year)	-34.6%
Capital employed	10.3%

Summary of key ratios

		2003	2002
Profitability	Gross profit margin	34.7%	34.4%
	Net profit margin	14.3%	12.8%
	Expenses to sales	31.0%	31.6%
	ROCE	8.88%	8.34%
	ROOE	9.04%	8.98%
Efficiency	Fixed asset turnover	0.617 times	0.623 times
	Capital employed turnover	0.622 times	0.65 times
	Stock turnover	5.8 times	5.95 times
	Stock days	62.9 days	61.4 days
	Debtors days	31.6 days	35 days
	Creditors days	67.4 days	68.7 days
Liquidity	Current ratio	0.9 : 1	0.8 : 1
	Quick ratio	0.52 : 1	0.45 : 1
Capital structure	Gearing	4.3%	7.3%
	Interest cover	21.4 times	13.5 times

Report on the financial performance of Arnotts
for year ended 31 January 2003

Introduction

Arnotts operates in the retailing sector via a number of department stores with key stores being Arnotts in Henry Street and Boyers in North Earl Street, both in Dublin city centre. The financial statements presented relate to the financial years ending 31 January 2003 and 2002. At that time the economy was experiencing a downturn compared to the economic highs of the 'Celtic Tiger' of 1999 and 2000 and there were many concerns expressed by leading economists of house price bubbles and of a looming recession. Both could have a significant effect on the retail trade.

The chairman's statement however, focused on the positives, commenting: *'the results for the year maintain the group's strong growth record. EPS has increased at a compound rate of 20.3 per cent over the past five years. Over the same period, turnover has grown at a compound rate of 15.4 per cent, net dividend at 17.5 per cent and net asset value per ordinary share at 16.6 per cent.'*

The performance of Arnotts will now be analysed within the above context under the key headings of profitability, use of assets, liquidity and capital structure.

Profitability

In the calculations above, turnover is taken to be 'turnover excluding concession sales' as concession sales relates to outlets such as River Island that rent space within the Arnotts department store.

In 2003 Arnotts achieved a 5.4 per cent increase in turnover and an increase in operating profit of 17.4 per cent. This signals a good improvement in performance from 2002. There was a healthy increase in the ROCE from 8.34 per cent to 8.9 per cent. The ROOE increased slightly from 8.98 per cent to 9.04 per cent.

ROCE is made up of two components, operating profit margin and capital employed turnover (asset turnover). The operating profit margin improved significantly and was responsible for the improvement in the ROCE because the capital employed turnover declined from 0.65 in 2002 to 0.622 in 2003.

Turnover increased over the period by 5.4 per cent and gross profit margin showed a slight improvement moving from 34.4 per cent to 34.7 per cent. The operating profit margin however rose from 12.8 per cent to 14.3 per cent. The expenses to sales ratio decreased slightly from 31.6 per cent to 31 per cent but the main reason for the improved operating margin was other operating income which rose by

5.5 per cent and in addition Arnotts received a royalty income which did not exist in 2002. The operating profit margin of 14.3 per cent compares favourably with international peers such as Marks & Spencer (10.4 per cent) and Debenhams (9.7 per cent). However management will be disappointed with the negative movement in the total asset turnover ratio.

While overall the return on capital ratios are improving, they should get into double figures to compensate equity investors for the risk they are taking. It must be pointed out however that Arnotts revalued their property assets over the period resulting in the revaluation reserve increasing by €16,412,000. The effect of a revaluation is to dilute the ROOE and ROCE ratios. If the revaluation had not occurred then the ROCE and the ROOE for 2003 would be 9.5 per cent and 9.75 per cent respectively.

Efficiency / use of assets

Management use assets to generate sales and profits. The performance indicators under this heading measure how efficient management are in generating turnover and profits from the assets at their disposal.

The fixed asset turnover measures the amount of sales generated per € invested in fixed assets. Although reasonably consistent with 2002, it is somewhat low at 62 cent for every €1 of fixed assets. Property was revalued during the year resulting in increases in property values on the balance sheet of 10 per cent on 2002. This would have a diluting effect on the fixed and total asset turnover ratios. If the revaluation was adjusted for, the capital employed turnover ratio would be 0.67 for 2003, thus recording an increase.

	Arnotts	Marks & Spencer	Debenhams
Fixed asset turnover	0.62	2.33	0.54

The fixed asset turnover of Debenhams is lower at .54 while Marks & Spencer is significantly more efficient. The capital employed turnover decreased from 0.65 to 0.622, a decrease of 9.57 per cent. Management must focus on this performance indicator and ensure it does not develop into a trend.

Stock days, debtors and creditors are broadly similar to 2002 levels. Stock days at 63 days is higher than that of comparable retail outlets but this could be due to the nature of the stock items held by Arnotts. Debenhams holds stock on average 52.5 days while Marks & Spencer holds stock on average 26 days. It should be remembered that Marks & Spencer deal in food items so a lower stock holding period would be required on perishable items, resulting in a lower overall holding period. One should also take into account that the ratios are based upon stock position at the end of year which may not be representative of the entire period. Arnotts' year end is 31 January, when spring/summer ranges have been launched.

The management of debtors and creditors shows slight improvements. Delaying the payment of creditors can be a useful method of financing a business in the short-term but it comes with a cost as early payment discounts are lost as well as the possible loss of goodwill from suppliers if delayed payment is pushed too far.

Liquidity

The group has ample cash available with cash in excess of €8.7 million. There are no major movements in current assets. Current liabilities show a reduction of over 10 per cent on 2002 levels, mainly achieved by reducing unsecured bank loans by over 57 per cent.

Both liquidity ratios show an improvement on 2002 levels, generally brought about by the reduction in current liabilities. The current ratio which examines an organisation's ability to pay short-term debt over a 6–12 month period has improved from 0.8:1 to 0.9:1. The norm for the retail sector is about 0.8:1. The quick ratio which examines an organisations ability to cover debt without the need to liquidate stock also improved from 0.45:1 to 0.52:1. The norm for the retail sector is about 0.6:1.

The retail sector generally survives on lower than normal ratios due to the cash nature of operations. What is important is to look at the sector that the organisation operates in and assess the norms for that sector. The figures below relate to a similar timeframe.

	Arnotts	Marks & Spencer	Debenhams
Current ratio	0.9:1	0.98:1	0.75:1
Quick ratio	0.52:1	0.7:1	0.2:1

Arnotts ratios are in line with the retail sector norms for liquidity. The trend is also improving with the company developing stronger liquidity ratios. The nature of retailing involves high operating cash flows and this should insure there is money available to pay creditors as they fall due.

Capital structure

Capital structure measures how the business is financed. Ultimately the higher a business is financed through debt, the greater its financial risk. However debt is considered a cheaper and more tax efficient form of finance to equity.

Arnotts is low geared with a low level of fixed interest debt. There was significant improvement in reducing debt during the year with a reduction of 34.6 per cent. This has reduced the gearing ratio from 7.3 per cent to 4.3 per cent. Arnotts is mainly funded by equity rather than debt. The reduction in debt has resulted in a significant improvement in interest cover, with cover moving from 13.5 times to 21.4 times. There are no concerns with Arnotts' ability to cover interest payments on debt. Again it must be pointed out that because of the revaluation in property assets, the gearing ratio will be diluted. If the revaluation was adjusted for, gearing for Arnotts in 2003 would be 4.6 per cent.

Conclusion

Taking into account the economic environment and its effect on the retail sector, Arnotts has performed reasonably well for the year ending 31 January 2003. Turnover and profits are up and this is reflected in an improved return on capital. The liquidity indicators have held up strongly and the company has further reduced its debt over the year resulting in significantly higher interest cover ratios. The company would be considered very low geared with minimal financial risk. The asset turnover and returns on capital would have improved even more if the revaluation of property assets had not occurred. However the overall returns on capital are slightly disappointing despite the increased turnover and profit for the period.

Appendix C

Present Value Discount Tables

Present value of €1

Periods interest rates (°/a)

	1%	2%	3%	4%	5%	6%	7%	8%	9%	10%
1	0.9901	0.9804	0.9709	0.9615	0.9524	0.9434	0.9346	0.9259	0.9174	0.9091
2	0.9803	0.9612	0.9426	0.9246	0.9070	0.8900	0.8734	0.8573	0.8417	0.8264
3	0.9706	0.9423	0.9151	0.8890	0.8638	0.8396	0.8163	0.7938	0.7722	0.7513
4	0.9610	0.9238	0.8885	0.8548	0.8227	0.7921	0.7629	0.7350	0.7084	0.6830
5	0.9515	0.9057	0.8626	0.8219	0.7835	0.7473	0.7130	0.6806	0.6499	0.6209
6	0.9420	0.8880	0.8375	0.7903	0.7462	0.7050	0.6663	0.6302	0.5963	0.5645
7	0.9327	0.8706	0.8131	0.7599	0.7107	0.6651	0.6227	0.5835	0.5470	0.5132
8	0.9235	0.8535	0.7894	0.7307	0.6768	0.6274	0.5820	0.5403	0.5019	0.4665
9	0.9143	0.8368	0.7664	0.7026	0.6446	0.5919	0.5439	0.5002	0.4604	0.4241
10	0.9053	0.8203	0.7441	0.6756	0.6139	0.5584	0.5083	0.4632	0.4224	0.3855
11	0.8963	0.8043	0.7224	0.6496	0.5847	0.5268	0.4751	0.4289	0.3875	0.3505
12	0.8874	0.7885	0.7014	0.6246	0.5568	0.4970	0.4440	0.3971	0.3555	0.3186
13	0.8787	0.7730	0.6810	0.6006	0.5303	0.4688	0.4150	0.3677	0.3262	0.2897
14	0.8700	0.7579	0.6611	0.5775	0.5051	0.4423	0.3878	0.3405	0.2992	0.2633
15	0.8613	0.7430	0.6419	0.5553	0.4810	0.4173	0.3624	0.3152	0.2745	0.2394
16	0.8528	0.7284	0.6232	0.5339	0.4581	0.3936	0.3387	0.2919	0.2519	0.2176
17	0.8444	0.7142	0.6050	0.5134	0.4363	0.3714	0.3166	0.2703	0.2311	0.1978
18	0.8360	0.7002	0.5874	0.4936	0.4155	0.3503	0.2959	0.2502	0.2120	0.1799
19	0.8277	0.6864	0.5703	0.4746	0.3957	0.3305	0.2765	0.2317	0.1945	0.1635
20	0.8195	0.6730	0.5537	0.4564	0.3769	0.3118	0.2584	0.2145	0.1784	0.1486

	11%	12%	13%	14%	15%	16%	17%	18%	19%	20%
1	0.9009	0.8929	0.8850	0.8772	0.8696	0.8621	0.8547	0.8475	0.8403	0.8333
2	0.8116	0.7972	0.7831	0.7695	0.7561	0.7432	0.7305	0.7182	0.7062	0.6944
3	0.7312	0.7118	0.6931	0.6750	0.6575	0.6407	0.6244	0.6086	0.5934	0.5787
4	0.6587	0.6355	0.6133	0.5921	0.5718	0.5523	0.5337	0.5158	0.4987	0.4823
5	0.5935	0.5674	0.5428	0.5194	0.4972	0.4761	0.4561	0.4371	0.4190	0.4019
6	0.5346	0.5066	0.4803	0.4556	0.4323	0.4104	0.3898	0.3704	0.3521	0.3349
7	0.4817	0.4523	0.4251	0.3996	0.3759	0.3538	0.3332	0.3139	0.2959	0.2791
8	0.4339	0.4039	0.3762	0.3506	0.3269	0.3050	0.2848	0.2660	0.2487	0.2326
9	0.3909	0.3606	0.3329	0.3075	0.2843	0.2630	0.2434	0.2255	0.2090	0.1938
10	0.3522	0.3220	0.2946	0.2697	0.2472	0.2267	0.2080	0.1911	0.1756	0.1615
11	0.3173	0.2875	0.2607	0.2366	0.2149	0.1954	0.1778	0.1619	0.1476	0.1346
12	0.2858	0.2567	0.2307	0.2076	0.1869	0.1685	0.1520	0.1372	0.1240	0.1122
13	0.2575	0.2292	0.2042	0.1821	0.1625	0.1452	0.1299	0.1163	0.1042	0.0935
14	0.2320	0.2046	0.1807	0.1597	0.1413	0.1252	0.1110	0.0985	0.0876	0.0779
15	0.2090	0.1827	0.1599	0.1401	0.1229	0.1079	0.0949	0.0835	0.0736	0.0649
16	0.1883	0.1631	0.1415	0.1229	0.1069	0.0930	0.0811	0.0708	0.0618	0.0541
17	0.1696	0.1456	0.1252	0.1078	0.0929	0.0802	0.0693	0.0600	0.0520	0.0451
18	0.1528	0.1300	0.1108	0.0946	0.0808	0.0691	0.0592	0.0508	0.0437	0.0376
19	0.1377	0.1161	0.0981	0.0829	0.0703	0.0596	0.0506	0.0431	0.0367	0.0313
20	0.1240	0.1037	0.0868	0.0728	0.0611	0.0514	0.0433	0.0365	0.0308	0.0261

	21%	22%	23%	24%	25%	26%	27%	28%	29%	30%
1	0.8264	0.8197	0.8130	0.8065	0.8000	0.7937	0.7874	0.7813	0.7752	0.7692
2	0.6830	0.6719	0.6610	0.6504	0.6400	0.6299	0.6200	0.6104	0.6009	0.5917
3	0.5645	0.5507	0.5374	0.5245	0.5120	0.4999	0.4882	0.4768	0.4658	0.4552
4	0.4665	0.4514	0.4369	0.4230	0.4096	0.3968	0.3844	0.3725	0.3611	0.3501
5	0.3855	0.3700	0.3552	0.3411	0.3277	0.3149	0.3027	0.2910	0.2799	0.2693
6	0.3186	0.3033	0.2888	0.2751	0.2621	0.2499	0.2383	0.2274	0.2170	0.2072
7	0.2633	0.2486	0.2348	0.2218	0.2097	0.1983	0.1877	0.1776	0.1682	0.1594
8	0.2176	0.2038	0.1909	0.1789	0.1678	0.1574	0.1478	0.1388	0.1304	0.1226
9	0.1799	0.1670	0.1552	0.1443	0.1342	0.1249	0.1164	0.1084	0.1011	0.0943
10	0.1486	0.1369	0.1262	0.1164	0.1074	0.0992	0.0916	0.0847	0.0784	0.0725
11	0.1228	0.1122	0.1026	0.0938	0.0859	0.0787	0.0721	0.0662	0.0607	0.0558
12	0.1015	0.0920	0.0834	0.0757	0.0687	0.0625	0.0568	0.0517	0.0471	0.0429
13	0.0839	0.0754	0.0678	0.0610	0.0550	0.0496	0.0447	0.0404	0.0365	0.0330
14	0.0693	0.0618	0.0551	0.0492	0.0440	0.0393	0.0352	0.0316	0.0283	0.0254
15	0.0573	0.0507	0.0448	0.0397	0.0352	0.0312	0.0277	0.0247	0.0219	0.0195
16	0.0474	0.0415	0.0364	0.0320	0.0281	0.0248	0.0218	0.0193	0.0170	0.0150
17	0.0391	0.0340	0.0296	0.0258	0.0225	0.0197	0.0172	0.0150	0.0132	0.0116
18	0.0323	0.0279	0.0241	0.0208	0.0180	0.0156	0.0135	0.0118	0.0102	0.0089
19	0.0267	0.0229	0.0196	0.0168	0.0144	0.0124	0.0107	0.0092	0.0079	0.0068
20	0.0221	0.0187	0.0159	0.0135	0.0115	0.0098	0.0084	0.0072	0.0061	0.0053

Annuity Tables

Present value of an annuity (€1 received annually for n years)

Periods interest rates (%)

	1%	2%	3%	4%	5%	6%	7%	8%	9%	10%
1	0.9901	0.9804	0.9709	0.9615	0.9524	0.9434	0.9346	0.9259	0.9174	0.9091
2	1.9704	1.9416	1.9135	1.8861	1.8594	1.8334	1.8080	1.7833	1.7591	1.7355
3	2.9410	2.8839	2.8286	2.7751	2.7232	2.6730	2.6243	2.5771	2.5313	2.4869
4	3.9020	3.8077	3.7171	3.6299	3.5460	3.4651	3.3872	3.3121	3.2397	3.1699
5	4.8534	4.7135	4.5797	4.4518	4.3295	4.2124	4.1002	3.9927	3.8897	3.7908
6	5.7955	5.6014	5.4172	5.2421	5.0757	4.9173	4.7665	4.6229	4.4859	4.3553
7	6.7282	6.4720	6.2303	6.0021	5.7864	5.5824	5.3893	5.2064	5.0330	4.8684
8	7.6517	7.3255	7.0197	6.7327	6.4632	6.2098	5.9713	5.7466	5.5348	5.3349
9	8.5660	8.1622	7.7861	7.4353	7.1078	6.8017	6.5152	6.2469	5.9952	5.7590
10	9.4713	8.9826	8.5302	8.1109	7.7217	7.3601	7.0236	6.7101	6.4177	6.1446
11	10.3676	9.7868	9.2526	8.7605	8.3064	7.8869	7.4987	7.1390	6.8052	6.4951
12	11.2551	10.5753	9.9540	9.3851	8.8633	8.3838	7.9427	7.5361	7.1607	6.8137
13	12.1337	11.3484	10.6350	9.9856	9.3936	8.8527	8.3577	7.9038	7.4869	7.1034
14	13.0037	12.1062	11.2961	10.5631	9.8986	9.2950	8.7455	8.2442	7.7862	7.3667
15	13.8651	12.8493	11.9379	11.1184	10.3797	9.7122	9.1079	8.5595	8.0607	7.6061
16	14.7179	13.5777	12.5611	11.6523	10.8378	10.1059	9.4466	8.8514	8.3126	7.8237
17	15.5623	14.2919	13.1661	12.1657	11.2741	10.4773	9.7632	9.1216	8.5436	8.0216
18	16.3983	14.9920	13.7535	12.6593	11.6896	10.8276	10.0591	9.3719	8.7556	8.2014
19	17.2260	15.6785	14.3238	13.1339	12.0853	11.1581	10.3356	9.6036	8.9501	8.3649
20	18.0456	16.3514	14.8775	13.5903	12.4622	11.4699	10.5940	9.8181	9.1285	8.5136

	11%	12%	13%	14%	15%	16%	17%	18%	19%	20%
1	0.9009	0.8929	0.8850	0.8772	0.8696	0.8621	0.8547	0.8475	0.8403	0.8333
2	1.7125	1.6901	1.6681	1.6467	1.6257	1.6052	1.5852	1.5656	1.5465	1.5278
3	2.4437	2.4018	2.3612	2.3216	2.2832	2.2459	2.2096	2.1743	2.1399	2.1065
4	3.1024	3.0373	2.9745	2.9137	2.8550	2.7982	2.7432	2.6901	2.6386	2.5887
5	3.6959	3.6048	3.5172	3.4331	3.3522	3.2743	3.1993	3.1272	3.0576	2.9906
6	4.2305	4.1114	3.9975	3.8887	3.7845	3.6847	3.5892	3.4976	3.4098	3.3255
7	4.7122	4.5638	4.4226	4.2883	4.1604	4.0386	3.9224	3.8115	3.7057	3.6046
8	5.1461	4.9676	4.7988	4.6389	4.4873	4.3436	4.2072	4.0776	3.9544	3.8372
9	5.5370	5.3282	5.1317	4.9464	4.7716	4.6065	4.4506	4.3030	4.1633	4.0310
10	5.8892	5.6502	5.4262	5.2161	5.0188	4.8332	4.6586	4.4941	4.3389	4.1925
11	6.2065	5.9377	5.6869	5.4527	5.2337	5.0286	4.8364	4.6560	4.4865	4.3271
12	6.4924	6.1944	5.9176	5.6603	5.4206	5.1971	4.9884	4.7932	4.6105	4.4392
13	6.7499	6.4235	6.1218	5.8424	5.5831	5.3423	5.1183	4.9095	4.7147	4.5327
14	6.9819	6.6282	6.3025	6.0021	5.7245	5.4675	5.2293	5.0081	4.8023	4.6106
15	7.1909	6.8109	6.4624	6.1422	5.8474	5.5755	5.3242	5.0916	4.8759	4.6755
16	7.3792	6.9740	6.6039	6.2651	5.9542	5.6685	5.4053	5.1624	4.9377	4.7296
17	7.5488	7.1196	6.7291	6.3729	6.0472	5.7487	5.4746	5.2223	4.9897	4.7746
18	7.7016	7.2497	6.8399	6.4674	6.1280	5.8178	5.5339	5.2732	5.0333	4.8122
19	7.8393	7.3658	6.9380	6.5504	6.1982	5.8775	5.5845	5.3162	5.0700	4.8435
20	7.9633	7.4694	7.0248	6.6231	6.2593	5.9288	5.6278	5.3527	5.1009	4.8696

	21%	22%	23%	24%	25%	26%	27%	28%	29%	30%
1	0.8264	0.8197	0.8130	0.8065	0.8000	0.7937	0.7874	0.7813	0.7752	0.7692
2	1.5095	1.4915	1.4740	1.4568	1.4400	1.4235	1.4074	1.3916	1.3761	1.3609
3	2.0739	2.0422	2.0114	1.9813	1.9520	1.9234	1.8956	1.8684	1.8420	1.8161
4	2.5404	2.4936	2.4483	2.4043	2.3616	2.3202	2.2800	2.2410	2.2031	2.1662
5	2.9260	2.8636	2.8035	2.7454	2.6893	2.6351	2.5827	2.5320	2.4830	2.4356
6	3.2446	3.1669	3.0923	3.0205	2.9514	2.8850	2.8210	2.7594	2.7000	2.6427
7	3.5079	3.4155	3.3270	3.2423	3.1611	3.0833	3.0087	2.9370	2.8682	2.8021
8	3.7256	3.6193	3.5179	3.4212	3.3289	3.2407	3.1564	3.0758	2.9986	2.9247
9	3.9054	3.7863	3.6731	3.5655	3.4631	3.3657	3.2728	3.1842	3.0997	3.0190
10	4.0541	3.9232	3.7993	3.6819	3.5705	3.4648	3.3644	3.2689	3.1781	3.0915
11	4.1769	4.0354	3.9018	3.7757	3.6564	3.5435	3.4365	3.3351	3.2388	3.1473
12	4.2784	4.1274	3.9852	3.8514	3.7251	3.6059	3.4933	3.3868	3.2859	3.1903
13	4.3624	4.2028	4.0530	3.9124	3.7801	3.6555	3.5381	3.4272	3.3224	3.2233
14	4.4317	4.2646	4.1082	3.9616	3.8241	3.6949	3.5733	3.4587	3.3507	3.2487
15	4.4890	4.3152	4.1530	4.0013	3.8593	3.7261	3.6010	3.4834	3.3726	3.2682
16	4.5364	4.3567	4.1894	4.0333	3.8874	3.7509	3.6228	3.5026	3.3896	3.2832
17	4.5755	4.3908	4.2190	4.0591	3.9099	3.7705	3.6400	3.5177	3.4028	3.2948
18	4.6079	4.4187	4.2431	4.0799	3.9279	3.7861	3.6536	3.5294	3.4130	3.3037
19	4.6346	4.4415	4.2627	4.0967	3.9424	3.7985	3.6642	3.5386	3.4210	3.3105
20	4.6567	4.4603	4.2786	4.1103	3.9539	3.8083	3.6726	3.5458	3.4271	3.3158

Bibliography

Adams, Debra (2006), *Management Accounting for the Hospitality, Tourism and Leisure Industries*, Thomson Learning.

Arnold, J. and Turley, S. (1996), *Accounting for Management Decisions*, Prentice Hall Europe.

Atkinson, H., Berry, A. and Jarvis, R. (1999), *Business Accounting for Hospitality and Tourism,* International Thompson Business Press.

Atrill, P. (2000), *Financial Management for Non-Specialists*, FT Prentice Hall.

Atrill, P. and McLaney, E. (2004), *Management Accounting for Decision Makers*, FT Prentice Hall.

Atrill, P. and McLaney, E. (2005), *Management Accounting for Managers*, FT Prentice Hall.

Berman, B. and Evans, J. (2004), *Retail Management: A Strategic Approach*, Pearson Prentice Hall.

Blayney, P. and Yokoyama, I (1991), *Comparative Analysis of Japanese and Australian Cost Accounting Practices,* working paper, University of Sydney, Australia.

CIMA (2005), *Management Accounting Official Terminology*, Elsevier.

Clarke, Peter J. (2002), *Accounting Information for Managers*, Oak Tree Press.

Cole, G. A. (2004), *Management Theory and Practice,* Thomson Learning.

Collier, P. and Gregory, A. (1995), *Management Accounting in Hotels,* CIMA.

Cox, R. and Brittain, P. (2004), *Retailing: An Introduction*, FT Prentice Hall.

Creaton, S. (2004), *Ryanair – How a Small Irish Airline Conquered Europe*, Aurum Press.

Drury, C. (2001), *Management Accounting for Business Decisions*, Thomson Learning.

Drury, C. and Tayles, M. (2000), *Cost Systems Design and Profitablity in UK Manufacturing Companies,* CIMA Publishing.

Eccles, R. (1991), 'The Performance Measurement Manifesto', *Harvard Business Review*, 69/1, p. 103.

Ernst and Young (2003), '2003 Survey of Management Accounting,' in P. Atrill and E. McLaney (2005), *Management Accounting for Managers,* FT Prentice Hall, p.103.

Fayol, H. (1949), *General and Industrial Management*, Pitman.

Fitzgerald, L., Johnson, R., Brignall, T., Silvestro, R. and Voss, C., (1991), *Performance Measurement in Service Industries*, CIMA.

Flanagan, C. (2005), *An Investigation into the Performance Measurement Practices of Irish Hotel Groups*, Dissertations for M.Sc. Hospitality Management, Dublin Institute of Technology.

Freathy, P. (2003), *The Retailing Book*, FT Prentice Hall.

Gowthorpe, C. (2005), 'Management Accounting for Non-Specialists', Thomson Learning.

Harris, P. and Hazzard, P. (1992), *Managerial Accounting in the Hospitality Industry*, 5th edition, Stanley Thornes.

Holmes, G. and Sugden, A. (1997), *Interpreting Company Report and Accounts,* Prentice Hall.

Horngren, C. T., Bhimani, A., Foster, G. and Datar, S. M. (1999), '*Management and Cost Accounting*', Prentice Hall Europe.

Kaplan, R. S. and Norton, D. P. (1992), 'The Balanced Scorecard – Measures that Drive Performance', *Harvard Business Review*, 70/1, pp 71-9.

Kotas, Richard and Conlon, M. (1999), *Management Accounting for Hotels and Restaurants,* International Thompson Business Press.

Louvieris, P., Phillips, P., Warr, D. and Bowen, A., (2003), 'Balanced Scorecards for Performance Measurement in SMEs', *The Hospitality Review*, 5/3, pp 49-57.

Luby, A. (1999), *Cost and Management Accounting – Learning through Practice*, Gill & Macmillan.

Mackay, A. (2005), A Practitioner's Guide to the Balanced Scorecard [online], CIMA, available from: <http://www.cimaglobal.com/cps/rde/xbcr/SID-0AAAC564-08E578BD/live/A_practitioners_guide_to_the_balanced_scorecard_rerpt_proj_203_2005.pdf>, accessed 20 July, 2006.

Melia, D. (2003), *A Study of the Use of Qualitative and Quantitative Performance Measures in Irish Hotel Operations,* Dublin Institute of Technology Tourism Research Centre.

O'Donoghue, D. and Luby, A. (2005), *Financial Accounting for the Hospitality Tourism and Retail Sectors,* Blackhall Publishing.

Owen, G. (1998), *Accounting for Hospitality Tourism and Leisure*, Longman.

Power, T., Walsh, S., and O'Meara, P., (2005), *Financial Management – An Irish Text*, Gill & Macmillan.

Youell, R. (1998), *Tourism: An Introduction*, Addison Wesley.

Annual Reports

Annual Reports Tottenham Hotspur plc.
Annual reports Ryanair plc.
Annual reports Jurys Doyle plc.
Annual reports Gresham Hotels plc.
Annual reports Aer Lingus
Annual reports ICG

Arnotts Group plc.
Boots Group plc.
Debenhams plc.
Marks and Spencer Group plc.
Next Group plc.

Other Sources

Sunday Times Business Supplement.
Irish Times Business Supplement
Checkout Magazine
Failte Ireland Tourism Fact File
CIMA, *A Practical Guide to the Balanced Scorecard*

Websites

http://www.forfas.ie
http://www.ireland.com
http://www.checkout.com
http://www.asb.org.uk
http://www.cro.ie
http://www.rai.ie
http://www.revenue.ie

Index